From Naturalism to Expressionism

D0010848

From Naturalism
to Expressionism

German Literature and Society
1880—1918

Roy Pascal

Basic Books, Inc., Publishers

NEW YORK

© 1973 by Roy Pascal
Library of Congress Catalog Card Number: 73-91085
SBN 465-02577-3
Manufactured in the United States of America
74 75 76 77 78   10 9 8 7 6 5 4 3 2 1

Contents

Preface

This study investigates the main areas of contact between literature and society in Germany and Austria from about 1880 to the end of the Wilhelmine Reich. It is based on the hypothesis that all art (this term here includes imaginative literature) is rooted in the artist's life-experience, and that the type of experiences available, the insights and values discoverable, are, if not decided, then profoundly influenced by the structure of society and the character of social life.

'Social life' may seem a reassuringly tangible thing compared with the imagination or aesthetic values and purposes. It turns out to be infinitely complex and elusive, and it is never experienced raw, but always indirectly through the mediation of habits, ideas, purposes that interpret it and give it a prearranged shape. Writers indeed, accustomed to assimilate the world through language and to transform experiences into words, are particularly responsive to other people's verbalizations, often more keenly than to direct experience. For this reason this study concerns itself with contemporary opinion and interpretation of aspects and problems of society in greater detail than with the social facts themselves.

The direct experience of any individual is very limited and varies from person to person. It is supplemented by information and imagination, the capacity for which varies so greatly that while they may tend to reduce the uniqueness of each separate life-experience, they may also intensify differences, for instance in the choice of what is effectively there. We consequently find great variations between writers and groups of writers, variations of ideology, of theme, of style and language. It is the purpose of this study to try to indicate the ground common to these often contradictory variations, though without obliterating the multiplicity of choice it offered.

Art can never be interpreted simply in terms of a particular period, a particular social structure or social class. Every society contains in itself lively elements of past forms and ideologies, and its art too inherits from the past a great wealth of forms, techniques, and themes. With these are transmitted certain psychological functions of art, which have emerged out of the tensions of life itself, the tensions between nature and culture, the individual and society, the imagination and reason, the instinctual drives and moral discipline, the emergent and the obsolescent. What we call art, and in one of its meanings culture, is a progressive response to these tensions, an attempt to recognize them, to conciliate perhaps or declare war, to turn what Hegel calls the 'self-estrangement' of spirit (in *The Phenomenology of Mind*) into the spur to a fuller self-realization of spirit. All these tensions continually upset old equilibria, and through new activities and new social relationships and institutions strain towards a new balance that is very precarious in a rapidly changing period like that under review here. Each period creates its own symbols of the conflicting factors, its images, its rational formulations. Often, especially since Rousseau, the imagination has allotted to a particular social cause the guilt for its 'discomfort in culture', to use Freud's phrase, and has believed that a partial or thorough reform of society would relieve its distress, a belief Freud believes to be illusory. Whether it is so or not, the relationship between social structure and the themes, images, and forms of art is of substantial importance. It must be clear, however, that a study of a short period cannot present a sociology of literature; at most it offers a contribution to its morphology.

Its purpose might seem modest: to indicate relationships between peculiarly modern features of social and intellectual history and certain of the distinctively modern features of literature, its themes, forms, and language. Attention has been directed chiefly upon the best works and authors, and here already large aesthetic assumptions are made. Still less modest is the view (assumption or conclusion?) that it is in the artistically best works that we find the most fruitful engagements with social realities, and that therefore a sociological study is a true contribution to literary criticism. In another respect, the study is extravagantly immodest. All the social and ideological areas indicated by the chapter-headings are vast; pushing into them, the author is fascinated but appalled by the thought of the unsurveyed spaces round his trail. All he could do was to provide rough sketch-maps. Not only problems and trends, but personalities too are fascinating, and it is sad that a study of this type inevitably blurs the living identity of so many gifted individuals.

This study is confined to Germany and Austria, and only the briefest references are made to comparable phenomena in other European societies. Its conclusions, however, if they are of any significance, must apply also to a European development, for the Germany of this period presents an epitome of a general socio-cultural process. Nor is this Germany a piece of a remote and dissociated past. 'Die Moderne' that proclaimed its advent in the 1880s is the beginning of a literary and artistic movement that is still with us and going through further evolution, and in studying it we are observing and trying to understand the sources of our own dilemmas and responses.

There are no footnotes. The text is so condensed and the documentary sources so numerous that reference and explanatory notes would have been overwhelming. Where it seemed helpful the titles and dates of first publication of books referred to are given in the text. Further indications are given in the Bibliography.

Quotations from German texts are usually translated, but where the peculiar flavour of the German seemed required the original has been given. German institutions like 'Reichstag' and 'Reich', 'Kaiser', 'Freie Bühne', are usually not translated, as translation misleads. Some terms like 'Geist' and 'völkisch' also cannot be turned into English and are usually given in German; an explanation of their meanings is given in an appropriate place and the Index should help if there is any uncertainty.

I

Political Germany

With the creation of the Reich in 1871 Germany became a great
power. Unity, the long desired goal of the liberal middle classes,
had been achieved through the defeat of Austria and other
German states by Prussia, and then the defeat of France in a
war organized and led by Prussia. The Reich constitution
assured the hegemony of Prussia and the Prussian aristocracy.
A few but negligible separatist areas or groups remained, the
Prussian 'Kulturkampf' provoked a resentful separatism within
the Catholic Church that however never grew into a real threat,
there was constant criticism of the authoritarian structure of
government from the liberal middle class and of the state as an
instrument of the possessing classes from the socialists. But the
Reich won the joyous allegiance of the great majority of Germans.
When political writers extolled the nation-state as the product
of natural and divine law, they were expressing the general pride
in the Reich as the natural political form of the German people.

Before the Reich came into being, many Germans had fondly
proclaimed that Germany's contribution to the world was of a
spiritual and cultural, not a political, kind. Now, Germany came
to share the presuppositions of the other European powers in this
era of aggressive expansionism. The world appeared to these
nations as their legitimate prey, and their rivalries were the chief
issues of world politics. For some time Bismarck, who as Chancellor directed German policy till 1890, aiming at consolidation
rather than expansion, sought to stabilize the European rivalries,
but even under his governments Germany's foreign expansion
began with the assumption of protectorates in Africa. The 1890s
then brought a frenzy of competition in which the USA and
Japan joined, but primarily between Britain, France, Russia, and

Germany, which resulted in the establishment of German stations and protectorates in Africa, China, and the Pacific, and the project of the Baghdad railway, a means to extend German influence into the Middle East. An intricate network of political alliances was designed to support expansion, while at times bellicose demonstrations against Britain over the South African war or against France over French penetration of Tunis and Morocco betrayed the precariousness of European peace. In 1891 Caprivi, Bismarck's successor as Chancellor, inaugurated an economic policy that favoured expansion into foreign markets, and in close connexion with business interests a shrill agitation emanated from organizations like the Pan-German Union and the Navy League, the German counterparts of Pan-Slavism or the British Navy League, in favour of building up Germany's armed strength. Britain, with her vast empire, industrial power, and navy, was the main standard and rival, and successive German Chancellors refused to enter into agreements that would delay German progress to 'a place in the sun'. The Triple Alliance linked the Reich's destinies with two minor powers, of which Austria-Hungary was unstable and Italy of dubious loyalty. The Reich's aggressiveness, on the other hand, performed the feat of uniting the two most democratic powers, Britain and France, with the most autocratic, Russia.

Germany was by no means responsible for the imperialistic rivalry of the European powers before 1914, the struggle for control over sources of raw materials, for markets, for investment areas. This imperialism assumed might was right, whether embellished or not by the grandiose self-pity of the idea of the white man's burden, the German parallel to which was a Wagnerian brooding on an ultimate twilight of the gods. Expansion, national rivalry, war were generally accepted as a wholesome law of nature. The war-aims of the German government during the First World War – defensive annexations in the West, colonizing extension of German power into Russia and the East, enlargement of the colonial empire – were not significantly different from those of the opposing powers. So engrossed were all in European rivalries that, while governments were in some degree aware of the danger of socialist revolution, few even of the critics of expansionist war-aims were aware that the European powers were destroying the European domination of the world.

Within this world obsessed by power, German policy was more inept and more ostentatiously bellicose than that of its rivals, and its nationalism was more strident. The causes were multiple: the late arrival of Germany on the imperial scene, in which others possessed more, and better positions of vantage; its own geographical location between two great powers and the temptation to foster the creation of a vast central European empire; the inner instability of its chief ally, Austria-Hungary, which promoted a certain recklessness in its statesmen; and the internal structure of the Reich itself, in which parliament (the Reichstag) lacked the responsibility of power. No doubt the lack of a tradition of democratic participation in government also played some part in promoting extremism in German political thinking, for writers on politics extolled more bluntly than their more prudent neighbours the moral right of power and the glories of war as the expression and instrument of the nation.

Germany's power was built on its industrial might, and after 1900 Germany became the greatest European industrial power, second in the world only to the USA. Unification had as important economic as political results. In 1869 the last feudal and guild restrictions on free enterprise were swept away, and the great natural resources of coal, iron, and potash, the rapid growth of the population and the internal market, together with the great reserve of technical skills, made German industrial and commercial development remarkably rapid. The population rose from thirty-five million in 1849 to seventy million in 1914, almost all the increase swelling the great cities, whose population rose from ten to forty million. Berlin exploded from 400,000 to two million, and other industrial cities in like proportions. This rapid transformation of Germany into a predominantly urbanized, industrial nation was facilitated by certain distinctive features. Banks, many of them founded in and since the 1860s, played a much more prominent part in the establishment of industry than in England, and participated more directly in the ownership and direction of the large industries. The average size of businesses was larger than in England. The inescapable competition with the established industries of the older industrial nations led to an early formation of cartels with a common trading policy, and to the creation of great syndicates and trusts, like Krupp or the General Electricity Company (AEG), which embraced many different branches of production. The traditional liberal principles of capitalist business, free trade and free enterprise, were much modified, while management became more technocratic and, in the eyes of workers and the public, more impersonal.

Many smaller, personal businesses also came into being, and there were still many workshops of artisans, maintaining themselves with difficulty under the threat of the competition of large-scale mass-production and particularly vulnerable during the economic slumps that occurred in each decade. The hostility of these small men and small shopkeepers often focused on the larger financial resources available to their great rivals, and during the 1880s and 1890s crystallized into the political anti-semitism that identified the Jews, who were very prominent in banking, with the power of finance. This 'anti-capitalism of the petty bourgeois', as the socialist leader Bebel called it, made the anti-semites a radical and restive ally of conservatism, and it evolved into the radical, anti-democratic authoritarianism from which after defeat in war the National Socialist party arose.

Urbanization and competition led to an increasing demand for cheap food, and a growing conflict between the agricultural classes and those concerned with industry. The great grain-growing estates of the Prussian nobility felt most keenly the competition from Russia and North America, and it was there that the most marked modernization took place, in management as well as in technology. In the interests of efficiency the old patriarchal relationships between squire and men were replaced by the simpler money relationships between employer and labourers, and this led, as was shown in the most important early work of Max Weber, to the employment of cheap Polish labour in place of German, and to a progressive polonization of the eastern Prussian countryside. The smaller German farmers and peasants, unable to command the capital required for modernization, were often forced to leave the land and emigrate into the cities or to America. Politically, the Junkers led a long battle against the free import of foreign grain and for a protective tariff, and thus turned the Conservative party they dominated into the representative of their economic interest, though they always claimed to speak in a special way for the nation as such. Despite some conflict with industrial interests, there was a considerable convergence between the Junkers and the great industrialists during the later decades of the Reich. Politically the Junkers enjoyed a privileged position of power and favourable relations with the higher administration which the leaders of industry could in some part share. Economically many landowners became entrepreneurs, distillers for instance, and in notable cases mine-owners and great industrialists. Landowners and industrialists agreed over certain aspects of defence and fiscal policy, as well as in their general anti-liberal, anti-democratic attitude.

At the other end of the social scale the bourgeoisie and liberalism found their most radical opponents in the industrial proletariat, concentrated in great masses in the large factories and cities, housed in slums and crowded tenements, working for meagre wages and destitute during the slumps that occurred with particular severity from 1874-8, 1885-6 and 1890-3. Though Bismarck's social insurances alleviated distress due to sickness and age, there was no unemployment benefit. There was also no Reich legislation governing child or female labour, hours of work or factory conditions until Caprivi after 1890 secured a statutory day of rest, imposed limitations on the employment of child and female labour, and set a minimum period for notice of dismissal. The efforts of charitable and religious organizations to remedy something of the worst distress – hunger, illness, child neglect, prostitution, crime – made, like the work of the poor-law institutions, only the slightest impact and affected only symptoms.

The rapid growth of the Social Democratic party, which was founded in 1869, reflects the profound alienation of the industrial working class from society. German Social Democracy adopted the revolutionary ideology of Marx in spite of certain tendencies towards the tactical doctrine of Lassalle, i.e. an alliance with the state authorities against unrestrained capitalism. In its general theory Social Democracy rejected all compromise, and attacked not only the capitalist bourgeoisie and the landowning class but also the whole state structure and the churches as the instruments of capitalist exploitation; it organized the industrial and political struggles of the working class in the perspective of a revolutionary internationalism. The rapid growth of the party in the 1870s and the intensification of its agitation during the slump of those years were major causes of Bismarck's repudiation of his alliance with the National Liberals and his reconciliation with Conservatives and Catholics through his new protectionist policy and his abandonment of the Kulturkampf in Prussia. In 1878 the Anti-Socialist laws that Bismarck introduced (with large Liberal support as well as Conservative) did not proscribe the Social Democratic party, which continued to participate in elections to the Reichstag and other representative legislatures, but outlawed its press, its meetings, and its agitation. As a palliative Bismarck introduced his contributory social insurances, for sickness (1883), accident (1884), and old age (1889). This in its way exemplary legislation did not win over the Social Democrats, for the party recognized that it was the price of the political disenfranchisement and social subjection of the working class, which the repeated victimization and imprisonment of socialist leaders made very tangible. While the great majority of the middle class and the National Liberal party acquiesced, out of fear of social disorder, in the political discrimination against the socialists, the unease felt in the 1880s by many young intellectuals and writers over the misery of the proletariat and the oppression of the Social Democrats was a decisive element in the literary revolution of Naturalism.

The structure of society in Germany, the alignment of classes and inter-class conflict, was similar to that in England and France. It was also normal that while material circumstances, social relations and ideologies were changing rapidly, there were many social areas where change was hardly perceptible, for instance in small towns and villages, among master craftsmen, in certain parts of officialdom. Thus, while modern styles of thinking, practical, empirical, scientific, made great inroads into traditional idealistic or religious assumptions, atavistic ideologies were vigorously refurbished in order to resist modern developments. That these ideologies, both the modernist and the atavistic, were more extremist in Germany than among her neighbours may be ascribed to the rapidity and ruthlessness of her industrial and political development. Whatever the cause, while on the one hand a truculent belief in scientism rapidly hollowed out traditional metaphysics and ethics and led to a widespread decline of religious faith (and also to the new theology of modernism, of which Germany is the home), on the other hand racialism and irrational nationalism possessed wide sections of the people. German education in this period was intellectually immensely productive, and a model to the world, while at the same time it was signally hostile to the demands of personal fulfilment. The most modern of the European nations in its technology and science, in many of its practices, ideas and institutions, Germany was also the country in which preoccupation with social rank and prestige was expressed in innumerable graded titles; the country of the Hauptmann von Köpenick. Such conflicts of the old and the new, often expressing conflicts of different groups of interest, were reflected and intensified in a profound misrelationship between the whole political constitution of the Reich and its social dynamic.

Created by wars initiated and led by Prussia, the Reich structure of government reflected its origin in two ways: in the powers vested in the Kaiser and his executive, and in the hegemony of Prussia.

In principle, government was authoritarian, that is, the political executive was separate from and above the representative assembly, the Reichstag. The chief executive, the Kanzler, was appointed by and responsible to the Kaiser; his ministers, called secretaries of state, were appointed by and responsible to the Kanzler. Though the Reichstag was the supreme legislative body, legislation could be initiated only by the ministry, the Reichstag having only the power of discussing and voting. The armed forces owed allegiance directly to the Kaiser and their affairs were outside the competence of the Reichstag. Only in one respect did the Reichstag have substantial power; the annual budget required its consent. Even the military budget required the consent of the Reichstag, though Bismarck minimized its control by submitting the military estimates only every seven years.

In practice, this authoritarian scheme did not work. No Kanzler, not even Bismarck with his immense authority, could govern without a parliamentary majority. Without its approval of the budget, the business of government would come to a standstill, and on very many issues the Kanzler needed popular support. As a result Bismarck and his successors worked by expediency, making alliances at different times with different parties for specific purposes, on the basis of bargaining known derisively as 'Kuhhandel'. Bismarck was often charged with deliberately seducing parties from their principles by the offer of some attractive bargain, and thus of undermining the whole principle of parliamentary responsibility. Himself above the parties, but needing contact with public opinion, Bismarck also made unscrupulous use of the press.

Formally the Kaiser was the source of political power. Wilhelm I prudently recognized that in fact power resided in a nucleus formed of the Chancellor, the Prussian aristocracy that provided most of the ministers, the heads of the armed forces and the higher administration. Wilhelm II, exalted by notions of divine right and the show of sovereignty, at first tried to assert a personal government. His most important political act was the dismissal of Bismarck in 1890 and the initiation of a policy of social reform that included the cancellation of the Anti-Socialist laws. For a year or two he seemed to many to promise to become a 'people's Kaiser', a 'democratic Caesar', and it was in this climate of hope that the great breakthrough of Berlin Naturalism occurred. Though Wilhelm later frequently indulged in sovereign gestures, his personal impact on politics was minimal. In 1908, when an interview he gave the *Daily Telegraph* raised furious indignation in Britain because of his well-meant criticism of British policy, he was sharply informed by the Kanzler to refrain from interference in international politics. Henceforth he frequently complained of his powerlessness and during the war became only a figurehead. The extraordinary powers vested after 1917 in the military leaders Hindenburg and Ludendorff show where lay the true sources of power. The Kaiser's abdication in 1918 was significant only in that it represented the defeat of the Prussian Junkers.

The uncertainty as to where power resided severely handicapped the exercise of government. The Kaiser's power was illusory. Repeatedly Chancellors also complained of the weakness of their constitutional position, since they were forced continually to manoeuvre for a Reichstag majority on the one hand, and on the other depended on the unreliable backing of the Kaiser and his personal advisors. The most harmful fault in the constitution was however the lack of power of the Reichstag. Not only were the parties not trained to exercise or prepare for responsible government, but also there grew a widespread scepticism towards parliamentarianism and parliamentary government altogether.

It is easy to see that the Reich constitution reflected the post-1848 Prussian constitution, but the dominance of Prussia was assured in more tangible ways too. The King of Prussia was *ex officio* Kaiser. The Reich Chancellor was Prime Minister of Prussia, and several of his secretaries of state were also Prussian ministers. If it was sometimes confusing for a Kanzler to reconcile his more liberal Reich persona with the perforce more conservative persona of the Prussian Prime Minister, it was impossible for Reich policy to be opposed to Prussian policy. The army was entirely under Prussian control. The Bundestag, the Upper Chamber of the Reichstag that represented the constituent states, was dominated by Prussia, which controlled a majority of votes and held a right of veto.

Each of the German states had its own legislative assembly (Landtag) and government, which was responsible for such matters as religion, education, police and posts, and whose political complexion ranged from the liberalism of, say, Baden or Hamburg, to the clerical conservatism of Bavaria. But Prussia was unique. It occupied two thirds of the area of the Reich, embracing the greatest industrial regions in the Rhineland, Silesia and Berlin itself, as well as the agricultural Eastern marches, the heartland of the Junkers. Whatever happened in Prussia, therefore – the government's ecclesiastical policy during the 'Kulturkampf' for instance, its educational system, or the administration of the law – was bound profoundly to affect the Reich because of the mere size of Prussia as well as of the intimate links between the Prussian and Reich administration. At the same time the Prussian constitution was unique. While other Landtage were elected on the principle of one man one vote, the Prussian House of Representatives was elected by the so-called Three Class System, which ensured a majority for the conservative-Junker interest, and hence constant parliamentary support for a conservative government (indirectly therefore a firm basis for a conservative Reich government). Hence, throughout the period of the Wilhelmine Reich, reform of the Prussian constitution, i.e. replacement of the Three Class System by an egalitarian franchise, was one of the main interests of the German Liberal middle class, and during the war the most immediate object of socialist policy; it was one of the chief achievements of the 1918 Revolution. Even so enthusiastic a Prussian as Walter Rathenau, the head of the AEG concern, who lived in a carefully restored former Hohenzollern mansion, pointed out firmly that national efficiency and power required the abolition of Junker privilege. A few politicians like Friedrich Naumann and Max Weber, repelled by the growing concentration of power in Berlin and the 'Byzantinism' surrounding Wilhelm II, began to think of a more equal distribution of power between the states such as was achieved in the modern Federal Republic; parallel to this we find a certain nostalgia for small courts and princes in some writers, like Stefan George or Thomas Mann.

Though the Bismarckian framework remained intact till 1918, it could not do more than obstruct the gradual erosion of Junker power. Not only was it difficult to know who actually made the great decisions, but from about 1890 it became clear that bourgeois interests and personalities were deeply involved in all matters of imperial policy. All foreign policy was also a matter of financial resources, of trade and industry. Thus it was that the upper crust of the bourgeoisie, leaders of trade and industry like Krupp, Rathenau or Ballin, became intimately involved in political decisions, less through participation in imperial ministries than as advisors and representatives of pressure groups. During the war these men were given great public responsibilities for the first time, though the emergencies of the home front only brought out what was latent before. The Kaiser's publicized friendliness to such men as Ballin, their admission to court functions and all big social occasions, was an acknowledgement of the importance of a class that till after 1918 could not influence government by parliamentary means.

The structure of government in Germany meant that no political party ever took on the full responsibilities of government. With the exception of the Social Democrats, all – Conservatives, National Liberals, Progressives, the Catholic Centre – at different times participated in Governmental blocs for particular legislative objectives and periods, often abandoning principles for an immediate advantage. The impotence of the Reichstag vis-à-vis the government contributed to the spread of authoritarian, anti-democratic ideas among economically threatened classes, and fostered in the liberal bourgeoisie, especially the professional classes, a feeling of alienation from politics. The great bourgeois party, the National Liberals, after its brief honeymoon with Bismarck in the 1870s, abandoned its liberal identity out of bewildered fear of Social Democracy, while the small parties of radicals seemed condemned to a mere verbal opposition. A sharp observer like Friedrich Naumann recognized in the 1900s that governmental policies were the outcome, not of parliamentary debate and criticism but of discussions between top administrators and private pressure groups. Naumann, a convinced democrat, worked persistently to revitalize the Reichstag, but was only too aware of the political apathy of the educated middle class, who had become used, he writes, since Bismarck had destroyed liberalism, to being a non-factor in politics. The theme of the famous publicist Werner Sombart's articles in the pre-war decade is that the intellectual, faced by a choice between conservative conformism and impotent opposition, can reasonably only decide to have nothing to do with politics. The Catholic Centre, attacked in its heroic period of the Kulturkampf by the Prussian ministry backed by the nationalistic and anti-clerical Liberals, did become thereby in some sort a defender of popular rights, and in spite of later compromises always retained a certain democratic element, so that during the war its opposition to authoritarian militarism and to annexationist war-aims made it one of the forces that created the Weimar Republic. But its clerical and dogmatic basis always limited its popular character; indeed, in Bavaria, where it constituted the ruling party and influence, it was a bulwark of clerical authoritarianism more reactionary in the eyes of the liberal periodical *März*, edited from Munich, than the Reich government.

The only consistently oppositional party was the Social Democratic party. Neither the Anti-Socialist laws nor Bismarck's insurances checked its growth, and great strikes of miners in 1889 and 1905, of dockers in 1895 and 1899, showed the strength of the workers' allegiance. The lapse of the Anti-Socialist laws under the young Kaiser in 1890 and the labour legislation of Caprivi in the following year seemed to promise a reconciliation of proletariat and the nation, and a moderate socialist leader, Vollmar, spoke in 1891 of a positive response of the party to the new line. Hopes of this kind were swiftly dashed by provocative speeches of the Kaiser and severe measures taken against socialist agitators and leaders of industrial action, and the more unrestrained capitalistic policy of the ensuing 'Stumm era' led the Social Democratic party to reaffirm its revolutionary ideology. In the Reichstag elections of 1912 it won more than twice the votes of any other party, and became the largest 'fraction' in the assembly. In fact, however, while the resolutions taken at its congresses still seemed irreconcilably revolutionary, policies indicated something else. Parliamentary and industrial actions were succeeding in achieving limited social reforms, and in the late 1890s Bernstein with other leaders began to advocate a 'revisionist' theory akin to

British Fabianism, based on the hypothesis that socialism could be achieved by non-revolutionary means. The growth of trade unionism, the first recognition of collective bargaining in 1899, strengthened the belief in non-revolutionary gradualism, a symptom of which was the success in 1906 of the trade union leadership in freeing industrial action from political objectives. Revisionism was repeatedly rejected in all official statements of party policy, its adherents were frequently dismissed from key positions, official speakers continued to proclaim the inevitability of revolution, and on innumerable issues, for instance education, child and mother care, and women's emancipation, the party refused to collaborate with bourgeois movements with very similar objectives. Yet the practice of industrial and legislative participation grew steadily. By 1900 T. Ziegler in his *Die geistigen Strömungen des 19 Jahrhunderts* could hold out the hope that Social Democracy was developing into a radical reform party, and soon after the turn of the century Max Weber and Sombart commented on its transformation and ridiculed the bogey terrors common in the bourgeoisie. On the other hand, just as many of the young writers round 1890 had been uplifted by the revolutionary promise of Social Democracy, so from 1911 Franz Pfemfert, the editor of the paper *Aktion* and political leader of a new grouping of radical intellectuals, bitterly attacked the Social Democratic party for having abandoned its revolutionary and internationalist principles.

Thus, long before the war broke out, Pfemfert warned that, if it came, the Social Democratic party would surrender to national interests. In effect, it was the threat from Russia, the arch-reactionary power, that provided the party with its most persuasive argument when war became imminent. The party, like the others, loyally supported the war effort throughout, though holding to a democratic programme that included a peace without annexations and the reform of the Prussian constitution. The civil government, and the military command even more keenly, recognized the vital importance of the home front, insisted, often against the will of employers, on consultations with the trade unions, and placed leading socialists and trade unionists in positions of administrative responsibility. The emergencies of the long and disastrous war led to a progressive embodiment of the Social Democratic party in the political system, and the Soviet Revolution of 1917 made the Majority leaders like Ebert,

Scheidemann and Noske even more determinedly opposed to revolutionary action. Opposition to the war itself came only from the left wing, from such as Karl Liebknecht and Rosa Luxemburg, who denounced it as an imperialist struggle and sought, like Lenin, to turn it into a revolutionary war. While censorship and imprisonment frustrated their efforts, the terrible slaughter, the hunger, the profiteering, the meaningless victories as well as the defeats, led to the formation of the revolutionary Spartacus League in 1916, of the Independent Socialist party in 1917, to mutinies in the fleet and strikes of industrial workers, all carried out in opposition to the policy of the Social Democratic party. The actual breakdown of the Reich was the outcome of military defeats administered to an exhausted nation. General Ludendorff insisted on a request for an armistice, and the new liberal government of Prince Max von Baden accepted defeat and tried to effect an orderly transition from war to peace. But spontaneous mutinies and local risings swept away the old authorities, replacing them with rapidly formed Councils of Workers and Soldiers. The Spartacus League and the newly formed Communist party attempted to turn these Councils into organs of a socialist revolution of the Bolshevik type. But the Majority Socialists were able to assert their authority and, with the aid of the army, to suppress risings in Berlin and other cities. Their objective was a democratic republic, to be decided by a free vote of the people. So in 1919 elections were held for the Constituent Assembly that established the constitution of the Weimar Republic, in which, while democratic government was established and the privileges and dominance of the Prussian oligarchy were overthrown, capitalist property, the great landed estates, the old judiciary and army structure were left more or less intact.

The political development of Austria in this period ran parallel to that of the Reich, though it was framed in a most complex governmental structure and dogged by a critical nationalities problem. Hungary had become independent from Austria in 1867 and had then united with it to form the dual monarchy. Each state had its own administration but shared a common administration for foreign affairs, the armed forces and certain aspects of finance. Both states were composites of many peoples, Austria containing, besides ethnic Germans, Czechs, Slovaks, Poles, Yugoslavs, Croats, Italians and Jews as substantial minorities, while the Magyars of Hungary ruled over Germans,

Romanians, Croats, Slovaks, Jews and many other national groups. The Magyar landowners powerfully reinforced the conservative forces in Austria, but the democratic development of the representative institutions was hampered still more by the colonial position of the nationalities, whose representatives sought to turn the national and provincial parliaments into arenas for national liberation. Their interests dominated all issues, and even the Social Democratic party of Austria-Hungary and the trade unions split on national lines. This unwieldy and precarious empire was held together by a large bureaucracy notorious for its delaying tactics, for a ponderousness which was the safest procedure in a state made up of such manifold and conflicting groups. When the Hungarian government introduced its policy of forcible Magyarization in 1880, it only deepened the national divisions as well as causing many Jews to flee to Vienna or Berlin or Paris.

If the principle of Austrian rule usually seemed to be the 'wise hesitation' that Grillparzer ascribed to an earlier emperor, the inner and outer tensions also provoked violent and reckless acts, like the absorption of Bosnia and Herzegovina in 1908. Industrially not comparable with Germany, Austria's economic and political weakness invited Russian imperialistic projects in the Balkans, and it was her weakness that caused her to throw down the fatal challenge in 1914 and drag the Reich behind her. At the end of the war Austria, like Germany, became a democratic republic, but shorn of her dependencies she was only a fraction of what she had been. The same contradiction between weakness and violence is evident in the temper of Austrian home affairs in this period. For while Austrians were notorious for their easygoing charm, their unpretentiousness, their lightness and perhaps frivolity, there developed among the Austrian Germans after 1867 both a devoted Austrian patriotism and a fanatical Pan-Germanism, a movement calling for union with the Reich and for the enlistment of the Reich in the imperial tasks of Austria. As in Hungary, an anti-semitic movement arose at the same time, whose practical programme of barring the Jews from certain professions was accompanied by vast ambitions of Germanic power. The anti-semitic party led by Karl Lueger governed the municipality of Vienna from 1897 to the war, and though it carried out little of its anti-semitic programme, it spread its ideology none the less vigorously. It was here that Hitler imbibed

what was to be the emotional driving force of the National Socialist party. As with the Reich, the Austria-Hungary of the 1870s
was liberal in temper. But even more rapidly than in Germany
liberalism faded out, with the same result, so marked in intellectual and literary life, of the alienation of the educated bourgeoisie
from political interests, the alienation of culture from politics.

2

The Image of the Bourgeoisie

Though the nobility still enjoyed feudal privileges in the political
and administrative structure of the Reich, and as landed pro-
prietors formed a formidable economic interest-group, the society
and culture of the Wilhelmine period were thoroughly middle-
class. Capitalistic enterprise was the source of Germany's wealth
and power, the driving force in both internal and external
development; even in the great estates of the Prussian nobility,
capitalistic commercial policy, technology and impersonal labour
relations replaced traditional production methods and patriarchal
relationships. The vast physical changes on all sides, the growth of
cities, of shops and consumer goods, of communications, the great
industries, the administrative and educational buildings, so
tangible to daily experience, were evidently due to the combined
productivity of science, technology, capital and business
efficiency, all in the peculiar sphere of the bourgeoisie. Cultural
agencies had mostly the same structure as economic enterprises.
The daily and periodical press, the publishing houses, the theatres
(even the court theatres in part) were run on profit-making lines
(the Deutsches Theater, founded in 1883 as a non-profit-making
cooperative of the working participants, was an exception). The
price of culture largely excluded the poor. If museums and
schools were not profit-making institutions, yet grammar schools
and universities were accessible only to those whose parents could
support them and pay the fees. The theatre and concert
audiences, the buyers of books, the patrons of art were predominantly middle-class. The cultural tastes of the working class, which
created with its class-conscious political organizations also its own
non-profit-making press, remained traditional and epigonal;
indeed, as the potential spending power of these great masses was
discovered, it was bourgeois entrepreneurs who took the main
share through the cheap theatres and crude sensational literature,
music halls and after c. 1910 through the cinema.

In 1872, D. F. Strauss's *Der alte und der neue Glaube,* so shrewdly attacked by Nietzsche as representative of the new age, displays a complacent confidence that forms the pervading atmosphere of the following decades. Religious belief is replaced by a belief in progress, which means trust in the beneficence of the laws of nature in a universe which Strauss can call 'rational and good'. The Darwinian doctrine of evolution defines an 'upward movement' which provides every life with purpose and meaning. Capitalistic competition is the social form of the 'struggle for existence'; private property is the basis of morality, inequality of property the condition of cultural progress. Though Strauss considers a republic to be the logical form of state, he makes his peace with the privileges of monarchy and aristocracy, but he fulminates against Catholic ultramontanes who acknowledge a higher authority than that of the nation-state. 'The most unhealthy stain' on modern society is socialism, whose 'false prophets' preach class war and internationalism and foment strikes for higher wages and shorter hours that will bring ruin to Germany. If on the Catholic issue Strauss anticipates the Kulturkampf, he also anticipates the Anti-Socialist laws of 1878, or rather he demands them, for he calls for sterner measures against the restive workers and accuses acquiescent statesmen of indolence, confusion, or even of malice towards the bourgeoisie.

Strauss, the former radical, is typical of the bourgeois abandonment of liberalism. The stresses of the following years were on the one hand to harden this type of anti-liberalism, but they were to produce also a different reaction, of the greatest cultural importance. The reckless speculative boom of the 1870s, followed by severe economic crises, shook the self-confidence of the bourgeoisie and in many quarters made the distress of the industrial working class the central social problem, always now known as 'the social question'. Humanitarian and religious bodies tried to temper the impact of capitalism, the state came to the defence of the most defenceless workers through legislation. In 1891 the transformation of the great Zeiss business into a cooperative without shareholders, essentially technocratic in structure, was perhaps the most striking and successful effort to overcome the antagonism between owners and workers. From 1872 the 'Verein für Sozialpolitik' had brought many socially-minded economists together with the object of promoting political measures to protect the workers, and of promoting workers' self-help. Such efforts are more important as evidence of a problem and an attitude than for their success; influential economists such as Schmoller, Adolf Wagner and Lujo Brentano, like Max Weber and Sombart, held that it was impossible to do more than impose a few humane checks on the inexorable impetus of capitalism. Schmoller and Wagner were the leading figures of a group of economists known by the misleading name of 'academic socialists', though in fact these men were conservative in politics and were only dubbed socialists by champions of liberal laissez-faire. Their 'socialism' was closely akin to Bismarck's, i.e. it meant a recognition of the necessity of providing legal protection (social welfare, insurances, factory legislation) for the proletariat, and was based partly on humane feeling, partly on the political strategy of winning the workers' allegiance away from Social Democracy and bourgeois liberalism for the paternalistic state that Conservatism claimed to stand for.

Since every technical advance and industrial and commercial innovation caused painful dislocations in living habits, work and work-place, the environment, familiar social relationships, familiar ideas and expectations, a bewildering variety of conflicting attitudes fought for adherents, from the Strauss or Nordau type of glorification of bourgeois enterprise, science and technology, in which culture became progressively more identified with technology, to Jakob Burckhardt's despair of liberal and industrial society, of scientism and the threatening materialistic age of the masses. In his *Deutsche Geistes- und Kulturgeschichte von 1870 bis zur Gegenwart* (1931), a book that reveals the author's own distress and despair, Steinhausen collects a startling number of predictions of doom, extrapolations from this or that tendency considered to be fatal for Germany – it might be socialism or capitalism, the proletariat or the bourgeoisie, the Jews, overpopulation or the relative numerical decline of the Germans, the great cities, the speed of change or decadence, technology or traditionalism, permissiveness or authoritarianism, atheism or spiritualism.

The so-called literary revolution of the 1880s emerged out of these questionings, and many historians, like A. Soergel in his *Dichtung und Dichter der Zeit* (1911), associated the Naturalist movement with socialism. Heinrich Hart, who was intimately involved in the battle for a 'modern' literature, speaks in his reminiscences of the 'social-revolutionary' element in the move-

ment, and Johannes Schlaf calls the early phase of the movement
'socialist'. It is certainly true that the young writers were more
strongly impelled by a social conscience in respect of the proletariat than any generation before them. Many of their works, deeply
influenced by Zola, describe the appalling conditions in the great
cities among the poor, or centre on problems arising directly from
industrial capitalism. In their poems of the 1880s Holz and
Henckell celebrate workers' demonstrations as well as indict their
destitution, and hail the coming revolution. Bruno Wille, the lay
preacher of a Berlin 'free religious' congregation, who was
secretary of the literary club Durch, co-founder of the Freie Bühne
and initiator of the Freie Volksbühne, was a socialist speaker and
Marxist, Paul Ernst also was a zealous Marxist. The great meeting
that founded the Freie Volksbühne in 1890 united the leaders
of the Berlin avant-garde with the leaders of Social Democracy in
a common endeavour that brought a series of meetings where
writers and industrial workers joined in literary discussions. The
Anti-Socialist laws, the new Kaiser, the lapse of the laws in 1890,
all contributed to the growth of socialist sympathies among
intellectuals. But their 'socialism' was not that of the Social
Democratic party. Often it simply meant sympathy with the
sufferings of the destitute and helpless and indignation over social
injustice. The Naturalists themselves use the term in a naive way.
Heinrich Hart, for instance, writes of the 'social-revolutionary
attitude' of Hauptmann's *Vor Sonnenaufgang*, though the
remedies proposed by the 'socialist' Loth are idealistic and not a
little cranky. There is every reason to believe, as J. Osborne
suggests in his balanced discussion of this problem in *The Naturalist Drama in Germany*, that Hauptmann also thought of them
as socialist.

There is some truth in the observation that the displacement of
Zola in the later 1880s by Ibsen as the Naturalistic exemplar
meant both a preference for middle-class over working-class
themes and a decline in revolutionary fervour. The search of
Arno Holz for an aesthetic that excluded ethical (national or
social) constituents was a sign of his withdrawal from socialist
commitment, which he announced to his friend Jerschke in 1885,
even before *Das Buch der Zeit* was published. But there is no
simple and universal change, and the heady years of Berlin
Naturalism (1889-92) form the high-water mark of socialist faith
among the intellectuals and brought the formation of a sort of

intellectuals' faction within the Social Democratic party. As many articles in *Freie Bühne*, the great periodical that grew out of the theatre club of the same name, demonstrate, e.g. those by Wille, Landauer, or Bölsche, this socialism is fused with anarchistic and individualistic (Nietzschean) elements, and during 1891 the Social Democratic leadership fiercely rejected it as anti-Marxist and bourgeois. Several writers were expelled, and one of the consequences was the ousting of Bruno Wille from the Freie Volksbühne that he had founded and his replacement by the orthodox Franz Mehring.

Throughout the pre-war period, and especially in respect of Naturalism, which laid the greatest claim to speak for the proletariat, the criticism of contemporary literature in the socialist press betrays the great distance between culture and the working class. There were differing approaches, as G. Fülberth shows in his *Proletarische Partei und bürgerliche Literatur*. In 1891 Wilhelm Liebknecht caused consternation among the Naturalists by ridiculing the social ineptitude of the new literature (of which he knew very little) and asserting that the times called for politics, not art. The orthodox Marxist viewpoint was taken by Mehring, supported by Karl Kautsky, the editor of *Die neue Zeit*, the party theoretical journal. Mehring rejected all works in which he could detect an implicit or explicit preoccupation with bourgeois values, and in this spirit criticized Naturalist descriptions of working-class misery because of their pessimistic, passive, deterministic character. In 1912 we find Heym criticized in *Vorwärts* for much the same reasons as the Naturalists had been. In addition to these political considerations, there was also in the Social Democratic party a strong distaste for a realism that stressed the sordid aspects of life and a preference for an idealistic and encouraging literature.

Even the more revolutionary wing, however, did not approach the position of Lenin's 1905 article, 'Party Organisation and Party Literature', with its uncompromising demand that literature should become a part of socialist propaganda. On the contrary, occasionally in *Die neue Zeit* and more frequently in *Sozialistische Monatshefte,* which was edited by J. Bloch, articles appeared that held writers like Bölsche, Wille, Hauptmann, and Dehmel to be socialists or socialist allies, and even recommended Stefan George as heralding a new age. Mehring himself excepted from his strictures Hauptmann's *Die Weber*, though his enthusiasm for the play was largely due to his reading into it the revolutionary intentions of one of its chief literary sources. Fülberth overlooks this famous article, but he is right in associating this trend towards a more favourable appreciation of contemporary literature with revisionistic tendencies in the Social Democratic party, and it is certainly found in such leading revisionists as Kurt Eisner and Eduard David. The characteristic view holds that the working class has to appreciate and assimilate the best culture of the time in order to surpass it, that a higher socialist culture will emerge only after the social revolution, and that the best artists of the bourgeoisie anticipate the coming new culture. Working-class writers were particularly affected by these tenets, and as a result tended to imitate the literary forms created by the bourgeoisie, only filling them with a somewhat new social content.

Thus both wings of the socialist movement held that the new literature belonged to the bourgeois class. Even when, with the Naturalists and the Expressionists, indignation over the sufferings and injustices inflicted on the poor is directed against the capitalist, the church, or the state, it always implies a compassion from above, from the level of education and culture, from the artist, from a bourgeois level, in fact. Often, of course, there is no overt expression of indignation nor any sympathy with social reform or revolution, and indeed the claim to personal culture very often meant that social change was rejected as a materialistic seduction hostile or irrelevant to culture and the spirit. But throughout the literature and art of the time there runs an awareness of the fragility of the moral basis of culture. Naturalism opens an era that may be called that of the bourgeoisie with the bad conscience, a bad conscience that haunts all areas of human consciousness. Hence that curious feature of modern European culture, in that it is bourgeois yet anti-bourgeois. Robert Musil commented on this peculiarity in 1913 in an article (on Austria) in *Aktion*. Culture, he writes, now grows in the 'cracks' of society, a product of the bourgeoisie yet not understood by it, so that we have, he suggests, 'probably the beginning of a new function of art'. The causes Musil indicates – the vast growth of population, the breakdown of community, the loneliness and anonymity of the individual – are among the great topics of public discussion.

The Bourgeois with the Bad Conscience

The persistent sense of unease in the cultured middle class takes many different forms, affects literature and art in various ways, and seems to reach in literature two crises, round 1890 and just before and during the 1914-18 war. In a time of such rapid and profound change, it is not surprising that no single interpretation is adequate to the reality, but there is a series of comprehensive sociological analyses that interpret significant stages in this dynamic process and which provided the conceptual framework of the conscious awareness of contemporaries. It is these that form the thread of this section. They are of course not the source of social awareness or social conscience, which were more likely to be awakened by specific issues connected with religion, the family, the state and the concrete conditions of life.

Max Nordau was in many ways a typical liberal bourgeois, with the optimistic faith in science and progress of a D. F. Strauss. His most famous book, *Entartung* (1893), is a provocative and undiscriminating blast against all modern writers, German and foreign, because they do not share his progressive ideas. But his earlier work, *Die conventionellen Lügen der Kulturmenschheit* (1883), written when he was a friend and journalistic colleague of M. G. Conrad, expressed a dilemma in terms congenial to the young writers of the time. The book went through four editions in a few weeks and reached a seventeenth edition by 1899.

Nordau believes in private property and competitive free enterprise, which he justifies on Darwinian grounds. He is opposed like other liberal doctrinaires to the regulation of economic and personal life by the state. He opposes the monarchy and aristocratic privilege, yet believes a hereditary aristocracy is required for social evolution. He hits out not only at the church but also at Christian ethics. All this belongs to the liberal tradition. But Nordau also expresses doubts about the dearest institutions of liberalism. Parliament can, he thought, only be a pseudo-alleviation of authoritarian power, and the press is not the defender of the individual but itself an instrument of capitalistic interests. Nordau usually provides halfhearted suggestions for reforms, and these border on the nonsensical when he comes to discuss the new class created by capitalism: the proletarian who is 'a tragic figure' and 'a fearful criticism of our culture'. He maintains that private ownership is right and communism absurd, but the reality of economic exploitation, crises and poverty wrings prophecies of doom out of him. He even challenges the basic liberal tenet of the growth of production and the ethics of work, recommending the workers to denounce the latter and refuse to work. Nordau revels in prophecies of doom as well as of the glorious future that rationality and science promise, and is as inconsequential as he is opinionated, but his concern over the septic sore within capitalism is genuine and typical and is a sign of that impetus towards the moral 'regeneration' of society that the Harts and M. G. Conrad define as a main source of the literary revolution.

Nordau's spasmodic anxieties over capitalism betray the influence of Marx; Ferdinand Tönnies' *Gemeinschaft und Gesellshaft* of 1887, a systematic academic treatise, acknowledges a debt to Marx's analysis. Tönnies contrasts two sociological models, the close burgher 'community' of an earlier epoch and the competitive bourgeois 'society' of modern capitalism, dominated by the search for profit and the impersonal market. He has a double target: on the one hand the disintegration of moral responsibilities and values through unrestrained capitalism, on the other the disruption of the community and the family, the intensification of antagonism between the social classes and between town and land, the alienation of the educated from the common people that it causes. It enlarges freedom, but creates a depersonalized freedom, and it replaces neighbourly cooperation with a social relationship of 'veiled hostility'. The state itself ceases to represent the people as a whole and becomes the instrument of the bourgeoisie. In spite of the Marxist elements in his analysis, Tönnies is not concerned with the abolition of capitalism; socialism he sees as a problem for the future, not the present. His concern is primarily the moral and spiritual quality of the middle class and its 'culture', now threatened by the rapacious materialism of bourgeois 'civilization'. His patent idealization of the earlier burgher 'community' might suggest a reactionary cast of mind, but Tönnies did not hanker after a return to the past and was actively associated with the 'academic socialists' who pressed for legislation to overcome the worst social features of free enterprise, and also with various reform movements (women's rights, school reform, civil rights for industrial workers etc.).

Tönnies formulates a social attitude close to that of the new writers of the 1880s – indeed very similar to that of the elderly

Raabe, though the novelist became more critical of the older
'community' (e.g. *Stopfkuchen*, 1890). His criticism of the
greedy materialism of the capitalist and dismay over the disruption of communal and family ties, his sympathy with the
exploited and particularly with the old-fashioned artisan, appear
in different contexts in the work of Max Kretzer, Alberti,
Sudermann, Holz and Schlaf, Dehmel, Hauptmann and the
Naturalists generally. Indeed, these themes never disappear from
literature, often deteriorating to the sentimental stereotypes of
magazine novels. In Naturalist works, too, they are often luridly
lit. An article of Conrad Alberti in *Gesellschaft* for 1888 is not
untypical in its sweeping generalizations and its confusion of
bourgeois and philistine. In his view, the bourgeois is only concerned with making money, the only ruling class in history that
does not patronize art, that is hostile both to general ideas and to
great passions; he counts it against the bourgeois that he is deaf
to ambition and fame and opposed to war as much as to
revolution.

Georg Simmel's *Philosophie des Geldes* (1900), the most
widely read and influential work of the Berlin philosopher and
sociologist, enlarges on Tönnies' theses, but mirrors the economic
and social dynamism of the decade since Tönnies published his
treatise. Simmel, again acknowledging a debt to Marx, describes
an advanced money economy, characterized in its technique by
an extreme division of labour and in commercial policy by the
impersonal necessities of the international market. This economic
structure shapes the whole of social life and spiritual existence.
Simmel's chief concern is not the socio-political challenges arising
within modern capitalism, but rather the spiritual problems it
produces in personal and social life, in culture – by which he
means traditional middle-class culture. Less emotively but more
effectively than Tönnies he describes the depersonalization of
capitalist society, seen at its purest in the great cities, where men
are reduced to specialist functions, personal relations replaced by
functional, the things made, like their makers, lose individuality
and become commodities, and cultural values become reified in
obtrusive public institutions. Acknowledging the immense productivity of high capitalism, the increase of wealth and of choice
for the consumer, the freedom it affords in contrast to the
personal but oppressive community of the older society and the
small town, Simmel also recognizes the rootlessness and

abstractness of modern existence, the decline in personal substance and communal ties which matches the disappearance of the craftsman who makes whole objects for a personal customer.

The cultural trends Simmel speaks of are not mechanistically related to the economic process. He sees for instance in the growing mobility, adaptability and rationality of thought both an adaptation of the temperament to the requirements of new social relationships and also a means by which the individual defends his personal identity against social pressures. The most significant cultural expressions of his time are, in his view, those through which the individual, the spirit, what he sometimes calls the soul, defends and asserts itself against the engulfing reality of capitalism. He points to the new religious movements and philosophies of his time, the vagaries of taste in fashion and architecture, the various styles in art and literature, as evidence of a general situation and an answering challenge.

C. Antoni, in his admirable study *From History to Sociology*, refers appreciatively to the productivity of 'the analytical and descriptive psychology and the phenomenological method' of Tönnies and Simmel, but rightly criticizes 'the speculative psychological-philosophical pretensions' of this German sociology. This criticism can be put in another way. Both construct a sociology that reflects the point of view, the values, fears, prejudices, the conception of culture, of the educated middle class to which they belonged; wider validity is in many respects questionable. Perhaps this is a major cause of the sympathy between their observations and conclusions and the art of their times.

Simmel said his main concern as a sociologist was to make the social and cultural environment intelligible to his contemporaries. He was concerned much less with changing this environment than with understanding the results of changes. An obituary essay by Lukács in 1918, not uncritical of Simmel's 'pluralism', is full of admiration for his breadth and intelligence, and states that the sociology of culture associated with Max Weber, Troeltsch and Sombart was founded on Simmel's work. But the later Lukács, the aggressive Marxist of *Die Zerstörung der Vernunft* of 1954, bitterly attacked what he calls Simmel's systematic evasion of concrete social relations and social problems, and in particular his lack of concern for 'concrete historical-social causation', while the young revolutionary Ernst Bloch, in *Geist der Utopie* (1918), angrily denounced his work, with its 'coquettish' love of nuances, as 'empty and aimless'. How bourgeois Simmel's work is can most readily be appreciated if one reads M. T. W. Bromme's *Lebensgeschichte eines modernen Arbeiters* (1905), the auto-biography of a worker who spent his life in small industrial towns in Saxony. There is here a curious justification of Simmel's thesis that the great modern city offers an unparalleled freedom, since Bromme discovers a relative freedom and culture (books, educa-tion etc.) only in the socialist organizations in the great cities. But at the same time the concepts of 'community' or 'concrete personality' attached by Tönnies and Simmel to the small town are shown to be utterly meaningless for the working class, though they may have some meaning for their skat-playing employers, who display plenty of 'Gemüt' when they curse or sack their employees, cut their wages, favour one and persecute another. This book was a sensation when it first appeared, telling the public of a world it normally could forget; it can still shock us by reminding us of the limitations of the sort of cultural categories we find in Simmel.

Simmel had friendly contacts with George and his circle, with Paul Ernst in his idealistic phase, and with Rilke. The general cultural concepts of *Philosophy of Money* correspond with those of various schools, especially symbolists and formalists, who saw in art the expression and defence of the spirit against materialism. In the literature of decadence, in Huysman's *A Rebours*, Wilde's *Dorian Gray*, as in the closely connected symbolist work of painters like Gustave Moreau and Redan, there is a consistent anti-bourgeois theme. It rejects the materialistic laborious bourgeoisie not on behalf of the deprived, but on behalf of the refinement and indulgence of the senses and imagination, of the soul and its mystical intimations, that all presuppose a privileged existence itself bourgeois in essence, though often claiming to be aristocratic. The early George and Hofmannsthal belong to this trend, in that their antagonism to bourgeois culture preserves certain élitist bourgeois attitudes. The same is true of Simmel. Wherever concern is transferred from social problems and social action to the fate of culture, of Geist and soul, it is likely that bourgeois values are asserting themselves, perhaps under cover of a violent condemnation of bourgeois materialism.

In another respect Simmel's work represents a significant trend that links Symbolists to Expressionists. His references to art indicate an assumption that the welfare of the soul is now the especial charge of the artist. Spiritual values are no longer thought to be in the trust of a church, a court, an aristocracy, the universities, all of which now seem to be and have a private interest. Only the artist is without a private interest. This extension of the responsibilities of art, most evident among aesthetes, symbolists, and formalists as various as George, Rilke, Hofmannsthal, the early Thomas Mann and Paul Ernst, and rampant among the Expressionists, is new, so that we find the historian Karl Lamprecht opening his review of contemporary culture in 1901 with the observation that it is a peculiarity of his time that culture, the 'life of the soul', is now entrusted to artists. Rathenau was to say the same.

These various aspects of the self-doubt if not the bad conscience of the bourgeoisie were as much responsible as the Prussian Junkers or the socialists for Max Weber's provocative definition of himself as a 'class-conscious bourgeois'. Weber criticized repressive or bureaucratic features of capitalism, but his criticism was based solely on economic criteria of productivity and growth. Similarly his opposition to socialism was formulated in economic terms, with the object of proving its inevitable tendency towards bureaucracy and consequent stagnation. What annoyed him above all was the importation of ethical values into economic argument, and the attempts to justify or oppose capitalism on moral grounds. In practice Weber was however no more capable of preserving these distinctions in economic policy than he was in politics.

If Weber was not able to be consistent in this, it is not surprising that we hardly find any comparable defence of capitalism in literature. Where capitalism is praised, it is nearly always on those ethical grounds that Weber considered irrelevant and foolish. Max Kretzer, chiefly notable for his descriptions of proletarian misery, actually tries in *Die Betrogenen* (1882) to build the portrait of a generous and humane entrepreneur, but the intention is annulled by the accompanying stories of poverty and vice among his employees; moral sentiments drown everything else. The hero of Schlaf's *Peter Boies Freite* (1902), whose patriotism is kindled and whose will is revived by the sight of the creative energy in the Hamburg docks, is thereby led to give up vacuous idling for marriage and work; that he becomes a small farmer in the United States is an odd outcome. A rugged self-made shipbuilder is admired in H. Popert's *Helmut Harringa* (1911), though chiefly because of his vigorous leadership of the temperance movement. There are occasional poems in praise of industry and technology by Börries von Münchhausen, Ernst von Wolzogen, Dehmel, and some of the worker-poets like Karl Bröger, and a whole volume by J. Winckler, the *Eiserne Sonetten* of 1914; several Expressionists, like Stadler, celebrate the beauty of machines. Some of these poems are close to Weber's spirit in that they extol energy, power, productivity and efficiency for their own sake. But this is very little to set against the main literary tradition with its evil employers, real-estate speculators and unscrupulous money-makers. Approval of capitalism in literature usually betrays the sort of philistinism we find in Max Eyth's popular *Hinter Pflug und Schraubstock* (1898), an account of the author's successful commercial dealings through which the technologist and European brings progress to backward societies.

It is curious that painting is sometimes successful where literature fails. The *Eisenwalzwerk* of Menzel, that the artist-hero of Kretzer's *Die Betrogenen* admires and emulates, captures the energy of a great ironworks that is utterly lacking in Kretzer's novel. When realism began to assert itself against the established painters like Kaulbach, Marées and Böcklin, with their idealized figures and landscapes and heroic and symbolical motifs, the new painters had much less difficulty than their literary counterparts in giving the unpolemical feel of the actual world round them. Thus Max Liebermann's *Altmännerhaus in Amsterdam* and *Waisenhaus in Amsterdam* (1880 and 1881), his *Konservenmacherinnen* (1880) and *Flachsscheuer* (1887), show workers, the poor, whether at leisure or at work, with a still centre in themselves; work is here, what it rarely could be in the modern great factory, still a medium for mental concentration and the controlled and beautiful articulation of the body. Hans Baluschek's *Proletarierinnen* (1900) and *Kohlenfuhren* (1901) show a harsh reality, but women struggling to cope with it. Friedrich Kallmorgen's *Dampferüberfahrt* (1900) and Baluschek's *Bahnhof* (1904) convey the exhilaration of technological achievement and the dynamism of the industrial world. When such topics occur in literature, this 'feel' tends to get lost as the individuals themselves become overwhelmed by daily problems. On the other hand, the calm lucidity of Liebermann, the greatest of the German realist painters, cannot express the energies, struggles and problems of an industrial society, and his later work dwells lovingly on private bourgeois life and relaxations. The pointed polemical illustrations of Th. Heine and other satirists, with their tendency to distort, and the anecdotal, often humorous sketches of Heinrich Zille, are closer to literary methods. The drawings and other graphic work of Käthe Kollwitz, comparable in their militant sympathy with suffering and revolting masses to literary Expressionism, temper the stylization they share with literature by a more individual characterization, which suggests a more personal sympathy and intimacy with the working class than is found among the Expressionists. Some of her single figures, and notably her self-portraits, are supreme expressions of the tragic suffering that forms the explicit theme of many of her compositions.

Perhaps the confusions of taste in architecture most richly illustrate the self-doubt of the bourgeoisie. The post-1870 explosion saw utility and decoration at variance. The churches, railway stations, national and civic buildings, tenements and villas being put up everywhere display a reckless adoption of motifs of opulence and grandeur from Greek temples, Gothic cathedrals, Renaissance and Baroque churches and palaces. Private bourgeois homes were cluttered up with objects, bric-à-brac, cloths and hangings, tassels and massive furniture, like the parental home described by Rudolf Binding in *Erlebtes Leben* (1935). Though from the 1880s efforts were made to restore a sense of functional style, the leaders of reform like Alfred Lichtwark or Ferdinand Avenarius only see the problem as a choice between historical styles and recommend, for instance, Renaissance for public buildings and Sheraton for furniture. *Pan* (1895-9), a lavishly illustrated quarterly founded to raise the level of educated taste, illustrates too the uncertainties of taste. A craving for Renaissance interiors produced the richly carved and furnished Munich showhouses of the painter Lenbach and the publisher Hirth, and that of Thomas Mann's parents-in-law, described in his letters and reflected in *Wälsungenblut*. The *Jugendstil* of the 1890s imposed a certain simplicity on this welter of ornamentation, but itself remained a decoratively somewhat capricious element. In this decade functionalism became a modish word, but it was usually applied to the cultural meanings of styles rather than to materials of construction and interior planning. Thus the Byzantine Berlin cathedral was criticized because this style was unrelated to the Protestant tradition, and the Berlin Siegesallee because its cramped pseudo-heroism had little to do with the modern nation (Isadora Duncan once harangued her fans here and implored them to smash it up). In 1897 Alfred Lichtwark, the director of the Hamburg picture gallery, praised Alfred Messel's famous Wertheim building as functional despite the fact that its basic commercial lay-out was overlaid by a mixture of Gothic and Baroque elements. It is typical of a general change that in 1909 Oskar Bie, the editor of *Die neue Rundschau*, pointed out the contradiction in this departmental store between its mercantile function and the decorative ostentation of its façade, and detected in the confusions of style 'the insecurity of the political compromise' characteristic of the liberal bourgeoisie.

This earlier functionalism, that amounted to little more than a more discriminating use of historic styles, gave birth after 1900 to a more severe and puristic functionalism that expresses, one may say, Max Weber's 'class-conscious bourgeois'. Centred in the great cities of Vienna and Berlin, this movement concerned itself with the total functionalism of material, purpose and design, in interior decoration and fittings as well as in architecture. The work of the Wiener Werkstätte, of Otto Wagner and Adolf Loos, was still not free of a somewhat inorganic, capricious decoration, and the great breakthrough was made by Peter Behrens, who in 1907 was appointed artistic advisor to the AEG concern by Walther Rathenau. Behrens' industrial buildings are the major aesthetic assertion of industrial capitalism, and lead towards the general theory and practice of Gropius at the post-war Bauhaus. Yet this severe functionalism is far less typical of the early part of the century than the confusions and compromises mirrored in the architecture of the great cities, the uncertainties of a new phase of bourgeois selfconsciousness that finds representative formulation in Sombart's *Der Bourgeois* (1913) and Rathenau's *Zur Kritik der Zeit* (1912), *Zur Mechanik des Geistes* (1913), and *Von kommenden Dingen* (1917).

Sombart's analysis of advanced capitalism adds little to that of Simmel or Max Weber, even more bleakly insisting that the profit motive obliterates all moral and spiritual values. He adds a psychology of the entrepreneur, distinguishing the heroic adventurer type and the patriarchal type from the calculating dealer, the 'Händler', who is now replacing the others. His conclusions are deeply despondent. Nothing can hinder this development, which because of the internationalization of the market is inimical to national identity itself; the homeland, he says, means nothing to the bourgeois. On the outbreak of war Sombart discovered this cliché was false, and as his contribution to the war effort he now asserted that German entrepreneurs like Krupp still embodied the heroic, patriotic spirit, and it was the British bourgeois who were the calculating 'dealers'. He was followed in this by other sharp critics of bourgeois capitalism like Max Scheler, who from 1913–15 was the socio-political philosopher of the literary magazine *Die weissen Blätter,* as Sombart had been of *Morgen* in 1907.

Rathenau's work is both more realistic and more visionary. A great industrialist himself, he had long been unhappily aware of the deterioration of patriotism into nationalism, and the involvement of big business in this. He had also shown that economic development was decided by the laws of the market, not by the psychology of the entrepreneur. The main theme of the essays in *Zur Kritik der Zeit* is the growing mechanization of industry in the age of mass-production, the technological rationalization that is leading to the complete scientific mastery of the productive and mercantile process – machines replacing manual labour, synthetic materials replacing natural, market research replacing risk and guesswork, even invention becoming a matter of planning. Society itself becomes technocratic, and the traditional argument over the ownership of capital, over capitalism and socialism, loses its meaning; at the same time non-functional classes, the nobility with the monarchy, become obsolete. The government of states turns into mere management, and ultimately the international nature of the market will create an international political organization that will ensure equality of rights and peace.

But Rathenau's extrapolations are not governed by a utopian optimism. After sketching the perfection of 'mechanized' society, in which he speaks of cities 'as big as countries' and does not forget the conquest of space, he turns away with the question: 'Whom does it make happy?' At the bottom of its consciousness, he writes, 'this world is horrified at itself'. He rapidly reviews some of the symptoms of unease over the mechanization of life and its concomitant, the stifling of intuition, the 'soul', by the all-pervading rational intelligence, but dismisses as futile the hopes set on church reform, occultism, theosophy and so on. Yet he himself can only place his fragile hope on the emergence of new ethical values, a new awakening of the 'soul'.

Von kommenden Dingen, Rathenau's most popular book (sixty-five thousand copies were sold by mid 1918), gives a concrete form to these ethical values. Influenced and emboldened by the experience of the war economy, he now adumbrates a tight control over production and consumption by the state, and a fierce system of taxation of wealth that, with a thorough democratization of the educational system, would in his view prevent the formation of a privileged class. Manual labour will be almost eliminated through the machine, and the proletariat will be 'abolished' through workers' participation in management and more human forms of work. Thus the vast impersonality of gigantic enterprises will be countered by measures that protect and nurture the freedom of the individual, his 'soul', and in the form of a democratic republic the state will cease to be the instrument of privileged classes.

The combination in Rathenau of spell-binding ratiocination, fascination with organization and an ostentatous cult of the soul led to a scathing caricature in Musil's *Der Mann ohne Eigenschaften.* But the dilemma he and, less impressively, Sombart express is highly characteristic of German writers just before and during the war. Sombart's analysis finds its closest literary counterpart, to which he refers with admiration, in Bernhard Kellermann's *Der Tunnel* (1913), a novel set in the contemporary USA, that contrasts the 'heroic' engineer-entrepreneur with the calculating financiers who alone make his project viable, and that at the same time associates technical achievement with spiritual and moral impoverishment. The United States were in these decades the often detested symbol of the perfection of technique. In Kafka's *Amerika,* begun in 1913, the inscrutable world of big business, accepted as a normal, natural ambient by the Americans, exercises a certain fascination over the immigrant Karl Rossmann, but the threatening and grotesque forms it takes for the innocent boy embody its inhumanity. The same dualism occurs in Sternheim's *1913.* Though the ethical pretensions of his great industrialist, Christian Maske, ring hollow, he is a heroic 'adventurer' of the Sombart type (he calls himself one), and as such repudiates, though vainly, the age of impersonal administration and mass-production that he and his like have founded. Grotesque distortion is used here again as a stylistic principle, as it is in Döblin's novel, *Wadzeks Kampf mit der Dampfmaschine* (1918, written 1914), an odd and unsuccessful attempt to come to terms with the ruthlessness of technological progress through extravagant burlesque.

In the work of the young poets round 1910 we often find the fascination of technology, the machine as the embodiment of power, that recalls the enthusiasm of Marinetti and his Futurist manifesto of 1908. However, the lack of response in Germany to Futurism is perhaps explained by the simultaneous and dominant horror at the inhumanity of the machine, a horror that evokes in Heym, Benn, Trakl and others images of castastrophe that anticipate the disasters of the war to come. The castastrophic collapse of cities, churches, factory stacks, and tenements, is a repeated theme of Expressionist painting even before the war (cf. Kandinsky's prose-poem *Fagott* of 1912). In Expressionist plays, particularly in Kaiser's *Gas* trilogy, the vast industrial enterprise, the mass of workers reduced to mere work-functions, become symbolical of the total social situation, and redemption comes only from the spiritual transfiguration of the great industrialist himself. The whole stereotype is remarkedly close to Rathenau.

Though the bourgeoisie as defined by economists and sociologists was the decisive revolutionary force in society, the traditional old-fashioned burgher class and mentality persisted, the master craftsman, shopkeeper, local official, teacher, clergyman etc., forming in the smaller towns a close-knit community somewhat idealized by Tönnies, called unbearably restrictive by Simmel, a drag on economic progress by Weber, a herd by Sombart. Its conformism and conservatism flourished also in the great cities, among high and low officials, cultured and uncultured bourgeoisie. The German language does not distinguish clearly between the term for the entrepreneur and that for the staid middle class, and if writers sometimes reserve 'Bürger' for the latter and 'Bourgeois' for the former, the adjectives 'bürgerlich' and 'bourgeois' usually do service for both. That this undiscriminating usage bothered von Bodenhausen, a great industrialist keen to keep up with modern artistic trends, is evident from a letter from his friend Hofmannsthal recommending an article by Moritz Heimann (*Neue Rundschau* 1916), in which 'bourgeois' is defined as a class label, while 'Bürger' and 'bürgerlich' are said to apply to members of any social class whose values are derivative. This might comfort von Bodenhausen, but it does not cover normal usage in artistic and literary circles. Schnitzler, for instance, in *Der Weg ins Freie* uses 'bürgerlich' typically as indicating the acceptance of social responsibilities – to family, children, a loved person, a job – as opposed to the 'freedom' of the artist (in Schnitzler, as in Thomas Mann, an ironic note is often heard).

There is therefore an unavoidable ambiguity in the term 'bourgeois', that corresponds to the ambiguity in life. There was a good deal of historical justification for the association, in Heinrich Mann's *Im Schlaraffenland*, of Freie Bühne adventurism in art, politics and sexual morality with Berlin financiers and press magnates, but one has to bear in mind that not only were these not representative of the main body of the bourgeoisie, but also they themselves served opposing gods. For instance, while we can say that the great battle in this generation between the new, modern music and the 'classical', between Wagner and Brahms, was a historical clash between the newer and the older bourgeoisie, it is also true that the circles that provided the audiences for Wagner were in the main the same as cherished the chamber music of Brahms, who was writing his clarinet quintet or *Vier ernste Gesänge* in the thick of the modernist revolution. Rigid distinctions are false. One has to think not only of complex and uneven changes of historical periods and in different social classes, but also of the coexistence in every individual of different psychic areas and different levels of experience, that is of different and perhaps contradictory values. The bourgeoisie in its revolutionary aspect was the decisive agent of cultural change; yet it also engendered many retarding elements, and in the minds of contemporaries these might earn the dearest allegiance.

In everyday life the petty bourgeois was much more in evidence than the big, and much of the anti-bourgeois opinion expressed by writers and artists is directed against their old enemy the philistine. He was the butt of the humorous and sometimes sinister grotesques of Wilhelm Busch, and many of the caricatures in the satirical weeklies like *Kladderadatsch*, *Jugend* or *Simplicissimus* pillory with greater or less good humour the brutality as well as idiocy of the petty bourgeois. Criticism, usually more ferocious than good-humoured, and often inclining to the grotesque, runs through the new literature, from Hauptmann and the Naturalists, through Wedekind and

Heinrich Mann, Hesse and even regional novelists like Frenssen and Löns, to Sternheim's comedies *Die Hose* (1908) and *Bürger Schippel* (1911); at the extreme, the hero of Paul Kornfeld's *Die Verführung* (written 1913) finds complacency sufficient grounds to murder the philistine. The older generation, Keller or Raabe for instance, could temper criticism of the philistine with humour, since he embodied, perhaps in distorted form, values they appreciated. The post-1880 generations have almost no sympathy with him, and bohemian circles thrive upon a feeling of superiority to him. Paul Ernst essayed a sort of rehabilitation of him in *Der schmale Weg zum Glück*, but at the expense of truth and precision. Thomas Mann is one of the rare authors to show sympathy with, even nostalgia for, the simple, orderly, conventional 'Bürger', who however usually appears in his tales as a stylized abstraction to serve as a foil to the 'artist', and almost always as a member of the well-off 'Bürgertum', not the artisan shopkeeper or lower official. In *Betrachtungen eines Unpolitischen* Mann defends his sympathy with the bourgeoisie on the grounds that he had not noticed, 'overslept', the evolution of the 'Bürger' into the bourgeois; in fact we can notice in *Buddenbrooks* his strong preference for the traditionalist Buddenbrooks over the 'bourgeois' Hagenströms.

The figure of the artist that appears in so many plays and novels of the period implicitly or explicitly refers to some image of the bourgeois and bears as great a variety of meanings as the latter. It can stand for the opposite of the materialistic values of the bourgeois in the cruder sense of money, security, public opinion etc., the high priest of 'Geist' as with George or Kandinsky. Or he can stand for the opposite of those socio-moral obligations towards family and society that often serve as an evasion of deeper obligations to the self. In this sense the artist symbolizes the freedom and fate of fulfilling the self, a challenge not only to self-interest and advantage but also to order and harmony, and his dedication to art, often tinged with a tragic renunciation of 'ordinary' happiness, represents all spiritual dedication. More vulgarly, many non-artists, as well as the more bohemian writers, thought of the artist as a man gloriously free of 'bourgeois' responsibilities, especially in respect to sex and family. The implied criticism of the bourgeois is often less prominent than the smug narcissism or highfalutin' self-admiration in the self-projection of the artist. Yet there was a real basis for this distinction that artists sometimes claimed on very meagre grounds. Simmel gives the artist a peculiar rank since his relation to work rescues him from the abstractness and fragmentation of the modern worker, in the sense that he dedicates himself to a self-chosen piece of work, and that this work is wholly carried through by himself. Walter Rathenau was to repeat the simplest form of this view when, in *Zur Kritik der Zeit*, he says that only the artist and scientist can escape the 'mechanization' of labour and society in the sense that they do not serve an alien and imposed purpose. The prevalence of the figure of the 'artist' in the more serious writers like Hauptmann, Hofmannsthal, Thomas Mann, indicates at its best a constant search for a symbol of the wholeness of personal existence, vouched for by the identity between personality and work. At the same time, the problematical relationship of artist and bourgeois in Mann's work, no less than the contempt and hatred of the bourgeois common to the most diverse literary circles, illustrate the social alienation of the writer in this period, unable to find in an old burgher tradition any comfort against the pressure and threats of the modern bourgeoisie.

The ambiguities in the usage of the term bourgeois are not due simply to the many varieties of bourgeois. They reveal a deeper social malaise than most writers were aware of. The term served often as a convenient target for resentments which could thus be turned into communicable and even creditable anger or contempt, and the attribution of a social source to one's unease also bore the comforting implication that it might be removed through a social change, the abolition or transformation of the bourgeoisie. It also had much to recommend it since the bourgoisie was identified with ethical and cultural attitudes and social relationships that were repugnant and required to be changed. But for many, perhaps, 'bourgeois' was a term of obloquy for something more general, a symptom rather than a definition of that irrational unease in organized society, that suffering under the necessary restraints of civilization, that some-times spiteful and violent protest against order, beauty and rationality, that Freud considered in *Das Unbehagen in der Kultur* (1929) was the natural condition of civilized man, and that Lionel Trilling (*Sincerity and Authenticity,* 1972) claims to be the essential theme of modern literature.

Aristocracy and 'Volk' as Rivals to the Bourgeoisie

Self-criticism on the part of the bourgeoisie is perhaps the most signal feature of the culture of the post-1880 period. Criticism came also, however, naturally enough, from external sources. The traditional clerical-conservative hostility to the bourgeoisie continued vigorously, for instance in the polemics of Konstantin Frantz, for whom the materialistic and ambitious bourgeoisie was destroying both the political authority of the Reich's 'natural' leadership and the moral authority of the church. Such conservatism finds little direct echo among the writers and intellectuals, but quite a significant number borrow certain elements from this ideology that has its source in the social and ecclesiastical hierarchy. Stefan George could, no less than a Hermann Löns, feel the attraction of a provincial princely court, a haven of culture sheltered from the rude blasts of the imperial court and Berlin. Some, like Hofmannsthal or Rudolf Binding, felt great sympathy for the English gentleman, or for aristocrats like 'der Schwierige'. Rilke found a refuge in unassuming aristocratic homes of this type. None of these would pretend that the aristocracy provided a true alternative to the stresses of bourgeois existence, and Thomas Mann's *Königliche Hoheit* embodies in a masterly fashion both this sort of nostalgia and the awareness that it is only nostalgia, for the fairy-tale element in this story of a happy prince ironizes its happy ending and removes it from any risk of being taken for a tract.

There was too, largely under the influence of Nietzsche and Burckhardt, a more pugnacious partisanship for the aristocracy as a class above the normal restraints of bourgeois moralism. The combination of fastidious refinement and savagery in George's *Algabal* has a sociological as well as a more general symbolical reference, and finds many echoes in later literature. Heinrich Mann's credit with the young radicals round Pfemfert was in part due to the sophisticated Nietzschean immoralism of the admired aristocratic world of *Die Göttinnen* (1902), a novel trilogy he wrote while still contemptuous of democracy and the middle class. The Renaissance cult created even among radicals ideal images of savage, usually aristocratic adventurers, such as we find in Kasimir Edschmid's *Die sechs Mündungen* (1915), a preoccupation, almost obsession, with violence that Thomas Mann found greatly disturbing, and that, particularly among the Expressionists, reveals a puzzling contradiction between the images in the imagination and the rational expression of their thought.

In other writers, particularly some originally closely connected with Naturalism, the aristocratic way of life is presented much more bluntly as the better social alternative. Thus Max Halbe's theme in *Mutter Erde* (1898) is rejection of city life and social reform and return to the ancestral country estate. Similarly in Paul Ernst's *Der schmale Weg zum Glück* (1901), the middle-class hero repudiates the city and wants to become a working landed proprietor, with mental horizons bounded by his property. We even find Thomas Mann, in his rage against the democratic 'Zivilisationsliterat', writing in *Betrachtungen eines Unpolitischen* that the feudal landowner has created 'the most decent and digni-fied of all forms of living' – an opinion unobjectionable in itself and to be deprecated only because it is part of an argument in favour of class privilege and authoritarianism.

In fact, one of the distinguishing features of the popular play and novel, the best-seller, is the admiration of the aristocracy – as one might say that the recommendation of obsolete values is the essence of kitsch. A Prussian officer, especially one in family or money trouble, was a sure tear-jerker; Kretzer uses one in *Der Millionenbauer,* Sudermann one in *Heimat,* and in the latter's *Die Ehre* actions and opinions that might seem morally highly dubious are in fact admirable because the person concerned is a nobleman. Further down the literary scale, in the novels of Ganghofer, Rudolf Stratz, Rudolf Herzog, E. Marlitt or Clara Viebig, the aristocracy claims per se the respect of bourgeois characters and readers, and marriage to an aristocrat is the supreme happy ending for a girl. Even Hartleben's Hanna Jagert, the emancipated independent woman, ends up happily as the wife of an aristocrat (who has nothing to recommend him but his rank). Frenssen's *Die Sandgräfin* (1896), his first and most trivial novel, is the epitome of this type of kitsch. A noble family, whose fortune has been frittered away, is to be rescued; those people from the middle class or peasantry who devote themselves to this purpose are good, the others are wicked; aristocratic faults are to be pardoned, aristocratic happiness is ours. The only touch of the modern world in it is that the family has only female offspring, who marry bourgeois who thereby (though this is not stated so crudely) become the inheritors of the aristocracy. Though Frenssen never reached a high literary level, one can see from this novel what an advance it meant that in his later works he replaced the aristocrat (and his spiritual support, the parson) by the peasant and a home-made religious belief. Bearing in mind the immense popularity of this image of the aristocracy, we can better understand the shock that a play like Hartleben's *Rosenmontag* (1900) would administer to the public as well as the censorship authorities, for in it Prussian officers show themselves weak, rough, heartless.

These regressive imaginings were far less commensurate with the dynamism of the bourgeoisie than a new form of conservatism, the 'revolutionary conservatism' as Thomas Mann later called it, that recognized that 'throne and altar' and the hereditary aristocracy were becoming inadequate to the needs of the times and were betraying their trust through successive concessions to the middle class, liberalism, and constitutionalism. In the 1870s Paul de Lagarde developed a comprehensive and vehement onslaught on liberalism and the bourgeoisie; a headstrong, wilful eccentric, he seizes any stick to flail its greed, materialism, and divisiveness. In his attempt to restore the idea of a united Volk led by a trusted élite and inspired by a 'German faith', Lagarde condemned the bourgeoisie on two main counts: first, that capitalism destroys national unity by splitting the nation into classes with conflicting interests, and second, that bourgeois liberalism, parliamentarianism, weakens the nation's will to power. With Lagarde's racial-national and religious beliefs we shall be concerned in later chapters. Here it must be noted that his doctrine arises in part as a revolt against certain levelling tendencies in democracy and is an eccentric form of the élitist individualism of Carlyle or Renan, an individualism that has its roots in the bourgeois revolution, and yet turns against the bourgeoisie. Not content with older and static forms of authoritarianism, it envisages a more aggressive and dynamic élite of merit, sanctified as embodying the spirit of the Volk. But, while Lagarde attacks liberalism in the name of the Volk, he also does so in defence of the independence of the individual, and much of his credit in the succeeding decades was due to his appearing a champion of individualism. Another example of the unclarity of his thought is the fact that his image of the ideal Volk of the future seems to eliminate the bourgeoisie altogether; more practically, when he speaks of Germany's destiny to expand towards the

East, it is the sturdy German farmer who is in his view to inherit the earth.

In a similar way another but more wayward eccentric, Julius Langbehn, builds in his *Rembrandt als Erzieher* (1890) a blurred ideal image of a Volk united behind an aristocracy (in his case a hereditary one) in which the bourgeoisie, the disruptive social force, hardly figures. The immense popularity of this rambling, vague and often frenzied disquisition on culture, that swiftly went through forty-five editions, was not confined to nationalist and petty bourgeois circles. It elicited a sympathetic response also from moderate periodicals like *Der Kunstwart,* and even from the radical *Freie Bühne* and from such critics as Georg Brandes, Maximilian Harden, Moritz Heimann and Christian Morgenstern, all men of independent and humane minds. We have to ascribe this sympathy in large part to a general distress at the loss of community, to a decline in liberal faith, a dull resentment against the upheavals due to capitalism and the strains of modern existence, for many of these intellectuals would sympathize with Langbehn's continual attacks on the over-intellectualization of education and life, the hegemony of science, the pluralism of society. In spite of the anti-semitism in Langbehn's book and the derision of liberal institutions and representative government, even sophisticated intellectuals admired his much advertised individualism and were attracted by the romantic simplicities of a sturdy independence, embodied for Langbehn in the Low-Saxon peasant, mysteriously combined with a mystic vision of an all-embracing Volk.

In imaginative literature there is some approach to the anti-bourgeois Volk ideology of Lagarde and Langbehn among some of the Naturalists, who took shelter, perhaps temporarily, from city and social themes in rural retreats and even a nature mysticism, a tendency evident in M. G. Conrad, Schlaf and Hauptmann, and more polemically in the former Marxists Bruno Wille and Paul Ernst. But the closest parallel is the work of the so-called Heimatdichter, writers who extolled the virtues of the provincial peasant and the local community as against the city and liberal political institutions, though at the same time making these countryfolk in their local allegiances the respository and exemplars of German nationalism. Some of the most popular of these authors, notably Frenssen and Adolf Bartels, lived in the region singled out by Langbehn, and held up the Low Saxon peasant, past and present, as the ideal German. Bartels joined with an Alsatian, Fritz Lienhard, to create the concept 'Heimatkunst', and carried on a fierce polemical battle against city culture and liberal values in the course of which Bartels became one of the most unbridled and unscrupulous anti-semites, for instance labelling Heinrich and Thomas Mann as Jews in order to denigrate their type of sophisticated urban writing. In fact, Heimatdichtung never was nor became so anti-bourgeois, anti-liberal, or anti-semitic as Bartels would have had it. The novels of Frenssen, e.g. *Jörn Uhl* (1901) or *Hilligenlei* (1905), or Hermann Burte's *Wiltfeber* (1912) – all incidentally massive best-sellers – not only criticize capitalists but also the small-town philistine, and even their peasants, with very few exceptions, have succumbed to the corruptions of the age. In place of the militant simplicities of a Bartels, these novels offer a questioning and anxious longing for a peasant model that eludes discovery. Even so, the clumsy inadequacy of the peasant model in face of the national, religious, and social issues emerging in these books is only too evident, and this fundamental disparity is reflected in faults like sentimentality and imprecision, and in Burte's case turgid and self-admiring philosophizing.

3

Bourgeois Ideologies: Positivism and Lebensphilosophie (Nietzsche)

Scientism and its Critics

Even an outline of German philosophy in this period goes far beyond the bounds of this study. But certain philosophical trends were closely related to the social interests of the bourgeoisie and directly influenced, positively or negatively, the literary culture. If one of the sources of 'die Moderne' was the new gospel of science – H. Hart in his *Literarische Erinnerungen* defines its origin as technology, science and the social movement – the growing criticism of scientism after 1890 illustrates the general self-doubting strain in this bourgeois culture. Lamprecht in his survey of 1901 actually calls modern culture 'a victory over natural science and scholarly historicism'.

The rationalistic positivism embodied in the systems of Comte and Spencer formulated the theoretical justification of bourgeois enterprise. This empirically directed thought claimed that only scientific knowledge was true knowledge, and only a scientific methodology valid, and thus it limited philosophy to questions that could be answered, hence to ascertainable facts and to concrete goals such as the extension of man's power over nature and the enlargement of individual freedom. It entailed a faith in social and technological progress, and believed that the laws governing social progress, like those governing the natural world, could be formulated. It admired specialization as the means of progress, though even a Nordau, who placed his entire trust in science and asserted in *Entartung* that art and literature were bound to be replaced by science, expressed unease at the social and moral indifferentism of specialized scientists. Comte became widely known in Germany only in the 1880s, and it is characteristic that the founders of German sociology, Tönnies and Simmel, were by this time distrustful of 'progress' and anxious to promote resistance to some aspects of it.

Partly because of the hold that idealistic philosophies had enjoyed in Germany, scientism served not only to undermine metaphysical causes and goals but also to destroy the autonomous status that had been attributed to the mind and the will. The very popular *Kraft und Stoff* of Ludwig Büchner (1855) explained that the human organism was a mechanism and that mind, if not merely a function of matter, was at any rate inseparable from brain and body, so that there could be no immortality of the soul, no freedom of the will; temperaments and values were products of physical and social circumstances which allowed only a minimum of choice that did not earn the name of 'freedom'. When through such works as Haeckel's *Natürliche Schöpfungsgeschichte* (1868) Darwin's theory of evolution became widely known, its rapid reception was largely due to the belief that here was proof that man's further evolution, like his past, was an unavoidable natural process that gave a meaning to life and enlisted energies in its realization. Thus writers of conflicting ideologies, like Haeckel, Gustav Landauer, H. S. Chamberlain, even Nietzsche (often a critic of scientism) enlisted Darwin in support of free enterprise, socialism, racism, or élitism, thinking thus to give their philosophies the dignity of a natural law. The term 'social Darwinism' was given to the widespread trend to use evolutionary tenets like the survival of the fittest as a justification of capitalism, power-politics and imperialism.

Naturalism owed its origin and early élan in large part to a faith in science. The most influential of the new aesthetics, those of Bölsche and Holz, start from the statement that the greatest achievement of modern thought is the recognition that everything is ruled by natural law. Just as Zola equated the work of art with a scientific experiment, so these two and other Naturalists work within scientistic assumptions, nature being thought of as the sum of causally connected entities and the artist as nearly as possible as an objective recorder. Innumerable articles in *Die Gesellschaft* and *Freie Bühne* call for a literature that should adopt the principles and procedures of science, and the literary critic O. Pniower claims that criticism too is becoming scientific, since its task is to look for the causality governing the genesis and evolution of a text. In the early Naturalistic texts of Holz and Schlaf and Hauptmann, the emphasis on external realism, physical and social, functions as a demonstration of social and psychological law, in that behaviour and feeling are shown to result from circumstance. Since the psychology is simple and attitudes are closely related to circumstance, a deterministic effect is achieved. This is by no means always the case, for the ethical motivation of Naturalism, the will to reform society, often conflicts with this determinism. There can however be no doubt that a faith in science inspired the Naturalists not only to the empiricism of their realism but also to a rather blind confidence, like that expressed by Nordau, in the capacity of science to solve social problems.

In the field of ethics there were comparable efforts to provide a scientific theory that did not rely on metaphysical assumptions or the dubious concept of free will, but which yet might provide criteria for behaviour. Hence the studies of the Darwinist Paul Rée, Nietzsche's friend, *Der Ursprung der moralischen Empfindungen* (1877) and *Die Entstehung des Gewissens* (1885). *Freie Bühne* has many articles, e.g. by the Hart brothers and Bölsche, on the necessity of building a new ethics without religion, most of which begin with the postulate of a higher evolutionary stage to which human effort should be directed. Bölsches *Das Liebesleben in der Natur* (1898-1902) attempts, through a somewhat rhapsodic account of the sexual life of animals, to remove the moral stigma on sex.

The search for causal processes and natural law led to startling results in psychology. The scientific, experimental, quantifying methods of Fechner and Wundt, while not disproving the concepts of mind, personality, or God, yet directed all attention upon physiological constituents of the psyche; in the same way criminology began to turn away from moralistic conceptions of responsibility to genetic or sociological causes. The work of Freud fitted into this pattern. Its main general impact, dating from his first widely known study *Die Traumdeutung* of 1900, was the realization of the power of unconscious experiences and drives to impose beliefs and behaviour on a human being, and hence of the diminished freedom, responsibility and integrity of the individual. The influence of such attitudes, usually associated with some form of Darwinism, is evident in much literature, yet at the same time with a significant modification. The notion of an inherited taint, such as Zola pursued so implacably in *Les Rougon-Macquart*, or of a cultural 'decadence', appears in many works between Conradi's *Adam Mensch*, Hauptmann's *Vor Sonnenaufgang*,

Thomas Mann's *Buddenbrooks* and Rilke's *Aufzeichnungen des Malte Laurids Brigge*; necessarily the victim is thereby deprived of freedom. But the writers are rarely content with establishing the determinism of a natural causation. What we find accompanying this is some sort of protest against it, an impeachment of the older generation or of society, a lament for the lost energy or freedom, the discovery of some spiritual compensation. While for instance one can find in Schnitzler's work insights comparable to Freud's, in particular the observation of the operation of unconscious or subconscious motives, it is highly characteristic of the artist that Schnitzler – sometimes, it is true, content simply to describe people who lack a feeling of responsibility – is almost always concerned with responsibility and guilt. The tone of his work would be totally different if he was only interested in showing the inevitable process of a natural law. For the same reason he, like other writers and artists, rejected the Freudian aesthetic (of Freud himself, Otto Rank or Ernest Jones) that would reduce the work of art to a pathological origin and a therapeutical purpose and deny freedom to the artist.

Positivism, which had begun so confidently, with clear concepts of matter, nature, law, objectivity or the belief that clear concepts could be reached, itself rapidly discovered the fragility of its own certainties. In 1886 Ernst Mach had published his *Analyse der Empfindungen,* which at that time attracted hardly any notice, presumably because it challenged some of these certainties. But in the more propitious climate of the end of the century it made a great stir and received three new editions between 1900 and 1903. In this work Mach argued that things, material bodies, persons, consciousness, are only concepts we invent, tools ('Notbehelfe') we use; they are not objective entities, but subjective ideas constructed out of bundles of sensations. Mach was aware that this theory threatened man's existential security and ethical responsibility, but he dismissed worries of this kind as being irrelevant to the scientist, whose purpose can only be 'full, pure knowledge' – an argument identical with that of Strauss which Nietzsche had ridiculed in *Unzeitgemässe Betrachtungen,* but not so different from Nietzsche's own attitude in *Menschliches, Allzumenschliches.* Hermann Bahr and Hofmannsthal found in Mach's theory the scientific exposition of their own feeling of the unreality of the external world and a loss of identity, and a justification of their preference for fleeting sense-impressions; one might indeed suggest that Mach's theory is a scientific expression of the decadence of the 1890s. But the grief and despair of Hofmannsthal over this loss of identity and coherence, the awed elation over the irrational meaningfulness that objects might have for him (cf. the *Chandos* letter), are totally different from the scientistic complacency of Mach. The poet applied Mach's conclusions *ad hominem*, as it were, dragging his psychology and epistemology out of the artificial abstractness of science into the living context of life and being. Mach's views echo later in the grotesque dislocations of Carl Einstein's *Bebuquin* (1912), though here again not as a description of human reality but as a denunciation against the distortion of man in the specific world created by the bourgeoisie.

Social Democratic thought vigorously attacked certain aspects of scientism – not those that refuted or ignored the concept of God or the 'Ding-an-sich', the soul or immortality, but the determinism that asserted that men are powerless to exert their will against natural law. This was also, often enough, the burden of the socialist criticism of Naturalist literature in Kautsky's *Die neue Zeit*. In particular, the disintegration of the concepts of matter, identity and consciousness in Mach's theory was to provoke the fierce onslaught of Lenin in his major philosophical work *Materialism and Empirio-Criticism* (1908) where he attacks both the undialectical thinking of Mach and its ethical outcome, namely the denial of the power of the will to change circumstances. But in many ways the popular 'vulgar' Marxism of this period had itself abandoned the dialectical materialism of Marx, and in its crude conception of social law and the inevitability of the victory of socialism itself adopted a sort of positivism. To most bourgeois critics, at least, economic materialism seemed indistinguishable from determinism, and a freedom that was only 'the recognition of necessity' seemed not to be freedom.

The problems raised by scientific determininism were felt particularly acutely in humanistic studies, now typically being called the 'mental sciences' ('Geisteswissenschaften'). The older tradition of historiography was continued by historians like Treitschke and Breysig, for whom history was made by great men who impose their will on the mass of mankind. This view had clear authoritarian implications, and in a period when both positivism and Marxism were claiming that historical evolution was governed by law, this older historiography became polemically

anti-democratic. Nietzsche, for instance, in *Unzeitgemässe Betrachtungen* (1874), asserted that man can be great only by
opposing his 'time', and that, if there is a law governing any
aspect of human history, that aspect is trivial and the law not
worth knowing.

But the trend was set in the opposite direction. Karl
Lamprecht's *Deutsche Geschichte* (nineteen vols, 1892-1913)
impressively illustrated the new concepts, since the course of political events was shown to issue from cooperation and conflict
between social forces, and the 'great man' functioned as the
representative of the latter – 'an evolutionistic, i.e. causal historiography', Lamprecht called it. The emergence of the disciplines
of economic history and sociology, with their inherent concern
with processes and masses, is a characteristic feature of the period,
and the influence of such scholars as Schmoller, Adolf von
Wagner, Tönnies, Max Weber and Sombart spread far beyond
their specializations. If Max Weber's famous study *Die protestantische Ethik und der Geist des Kapitalismus* (1905) was intended
to correct the disrespect for the power of ideas common among
Marxists, ideas nonetheless appear in his book as social forces,
and in this respect it belongs to the positivist tradition. The
importance of Ernst Troeltsch's studies of the social doctrines of
the Christian churches lay precisely in his exposition of the influence of social circumstances and forces on Christian doctrine and
ethics.

Literary studies showed the same trend. Wilhelm Scherer, professor of German at Berlin till 1886, claimed in his *Geschichte der
deutschen Literatur* (1880-2) that the natural sciences now
governed poetic creation as they did religious belief, and he
turned literary criticism into the 'scientific' investigation of the
'laws' governing literature, the most fruitful result of which was
extensive research into the documentary and biographical sources
of literary works and into literary influences and links. Critical
evaluation was timid and eclectic. While the great German
writers Lessing, Goethe and Schiller, were revered as classics, they
were seen in a historical perspective that culminated in 1870.
Scherer's successor Erich Schmidt was more sophisticated and up-
to-date, and a more precise scholar, but he too contributed to
making academic literary studies a refuge from the conflicts
raging in the contemporary literary world; the most prominent
rival to Schmidt's authority, R. M. Meyer, was more daring and

perceptive, but still more arbitrary in his judgements. René Wellek, in his just summary in volume four of *A History of Modern Criticism,* speaks of 'the factualism, source and parallel hunting, biographical obsession, literary insensibility, and philosophical emptiness' of these academic Germanists. With them, their positivistic methodology seems to have been the concomitant of a lack of serious commitment to literature altogether, induced in part, perhaps by the institutionalization of literary studies. Their work is, as Wellek says, much inferior to the great achievements in the previous generation of Hettner and Haym, whose search for the sources of the nation's spiritual identity was guided by the insight that the service of the spirit constituted a profound challenge to political interests and institutional forms.

Positivism did not pass without challenge among scientists themselves. Helmholtz and Du Bois Reymond, for instance, among the most distinguished of scientists, always insisted that Kant had conclusively demonstrated that scientific method and reason were prisoners within the world they could interpret, and that concepts like the soul, or free will, or a transcendental reality, could not scientifically be disproved. Many scientists and philosophers clutched at this plank to save themselves from drowning in a sea of determinism. It was on such grounds that the young Heinrich Mann rejected Naturalism.

Within the mental sciences, the compendious work of Wilhelm Dilthey, from *Einleitung in die Geisteswissenschaften* (1883) onwards, was the most influential attempt to define the limits of scientific method. Dilthey rejected all metaphysical concepts and accepted the validity of a rigidly causal scientific methodology in respect to the study of nature, but claimed that the study of history, thought, literature and art entailed quite different methods. We know man, he wrote, through his expressions in political and social institutions, through his actions and words etc., but we can *understand* his structures and creations only if we recognize the hidden intentions, the psychological operations, that have brought them into being; and this we can only do through our intuitive understanding of what man is – 'we understand more than we know'. Understanding involves the whole personality, not, like natural science, certain faculties only, like intelligence, observation, dexterity etc. It requires that we imaginatively re-experience ('nacherleben') the experience that originated the cultural phenomenon we are investigating. There is nothing mystical in this sort of intuition, for it characterizes our daily intercourse and is a condition of social life. The method of the Geisteswissenschaften is only a systematic development of everyday understanding.

Dilthey thus justified a conception of knowledge that could have little of the objectivity of scientific truth. In place of progressively perfected laws of nature, tested and exploited by technology, Dilthey's 'understanding' penetrated only the individual phenomenon. It was essentially the outcome of a dialogue between the researcher and the spirit embodied in the phenomenon studied, and sometimes Dilthey was alarmed at the absence of practical and verifiable tests of the results and even more of objective criteria of method. Though for instance he could claim that history could restore the experience of a total unique phenomenon (a period, a movement, a statesman, a battle), he could not fail to observe that the interpretations and patterns of historians hugely disagreed, or that historians of a particular age or country shared unconscious prejudices that coloured their results. Because of such inadequacies he sometimes came painfully near to a sceptical relativism, the great compensation for which was the recognition of creativity as the distinctive characteristic of life. It is a central tenet of forms of 'Lebensphilosophie' – of Dilthey and Simmel as of Bergson and Nietzsche, akin in this to Marx – that man is continually creating himself and his world, together with his cultural and moral values; man is, as Nietzsche put it, the animal that is not yet defined, 'das noch nicht festgestellte Tier'. While metaphysical concepts are rejected, metaphysical origins and goals, the essence of life is stated to be transcendence, more accurately self-transcendence; this is embodied for Dilthey or Simmel in human history, in the social evolution of human institutions as well as in an enlargement of mind, while Nietzsche dreams of a more irrational, sometimes a biological leap. In this type of thinking the irrational drives are accepted or celebrated as the sources of change and creation, and the rational mind is justified only as a function of, a servant of 'life'; if science or reason claim hegemony, it is a disastrous usurpation. The result can be an extreme and polemical irrationalism such as we find in Nietzsche or Ludwig Klages, the derisive rejection of the ideal of objective knowledge, truth, logic. With Dilthey or Simmel, however, more in the Hegelian tradition, the rational mind is understood to be an instrument of life, not opposed to it but rather a means to express and communicate it, to express and communicate understanding of it. In contrast to the extreme subjectivism of Nietzsche or Klages, Dilthey's concept of 'experience', Erleben, defines the process of the appropriation of the life of others, and only through this understanding of others does the self itself grow.

Dilthey's theoretical and historical work corresponds indeed to the rich private culture of the German professional classes, remarkably open as it was to the multiple possibilities of thought and imaginative experience, aware of the multiplicity of values, but enjoying them in an area fenced off from the obligations of practical choice and decision. The very breadth of the overriding concept of 'life' in Dilthey's thought, life as energy and creation that transcend any law and rational formulation, reinforces a conservative passivity, since if life and change elude definition, no prognosis of the future can be made and hence the thinker leaves decisions to whatever irrational powers may assert themselves. It is the very contrary in this respect of Marxism, which establishes laws that govern the historical course of culture and serve as guidelines for future action. Thus it was that Dilthey, as Jürgen Habermas points out in *Erkenntnis und Interesse,* lays more emphasis on empathy than on dialogue, i.e. on empathetic contemplation than on active engagement, and Carlo Antoni, in his *From History to Sociology*, rightly criticizes Dilthey's exclusion of 'judgement' from 'understanding'.

Dilthey's distinction between the natural and the mental sciences found much support among those who maintained that neither history, society, thought nor art are subject to causal laws. An important practical instance of this attitude was the widespread academic hostility to sociology, an alleged science that claimed to enunciate laws governing social evolution and that was obnoxious to conservative academics since its chief representatives, Comte, Marx, Herbert Spencer, justified if they did not advocate social change. As a result, sociology was hardly anywhere recognized as an academic discipline till after 1918, and the founders of German sociology, scholars like Tönnies, Simmel, Max Weber, Gothein and Sombart, who joined together to call the first conference of German sociologists in 1910, all held chairs of a different designation. Dilthey himself was an unrelenting opponent of sociology, though in several respects Simmel and

Weber were influenced by his work, and he did once express approval of Simmel's sort of sociology.

Simmel in fact turned away from the study of the laws governing the evolution of a society to that of the forms of sociation to be detected in the most insignificant as well as the most prominent features of private and public life. He has always been praised for the multitude of specific insights he offers, and often criticized for having taken from sociology its critical and reforming energy. His writings remain distinguished for his realization not only that society is extremely complex, and that the relations between circumstances, external and internal motivations, and human thoughts and decisions are most intricate, but also that the character of human individuality and freedom or choice, the peculiarity of consciousness as expressed in thought, culture and art, and also the conditions governing our observation of these phenomena, make sociology necessarily different from a natural science.

Max Weber was a much more strenuous and rigorous thinker than Simmel, and also much more concerned with practical social decisions, with politics. In his search for a sociology that could legitimately guide action he was much more ruthless than Simmel with the ethical or speculative elements that shaped most sociologies, though at the same time he rejected the claim that sociology like a natural science could discover natural laws that would make human decisions and human freedom an illusion. Thus he established themes and epistemological concepts that may properly belong to a science of society – the different forms of authority, the role of bureaucracy, the idea of the type or sociological model. He was not content to refute the determinism of historical materialism by philosophical argument, but carried out the historical researches of *Die protestantische Ethik und der Geist des Kapitalismus* (1905) in order to give a concrete example of the functional role played by belief, ideology, in the evolution of capitalism.

In all this work Weber was treading a knife's edge. On one side, as Paul Honigsheim puts it in *On Max Weber*, he 'suffered under science', in the sense that he detested the doctrine that human decisions and actions are determined by an overriding process or law. He could not abandon his belief in the moral autonomy of the individual personality, and partly for this reason was opposed to socialism. But on the other side he was furthering the encroachment of science into the fields of humane studies. In his extensive studies in the sociology of religion, for instance, his method constantly leads him to distinguish the great religions, Hinduism, Buddhism, Christianity, Islam, in terms of the character of a specific historical class. Perhaps it was a result of the conflict of these two contradictory drives in him that he tended, e.g. in *Wissenschaft als Beruf* (1919), while extolling the calling of the scientist as the unbiased, value-free investigation of reality, at the same time to deny that science could make any contribution to human values and purposes except as a tool. Compared with the scientism of the preceding generation, Weber's is severely self-critical and modest.

By the end of the 1890s, though the natural sciences were constantly extending into new fields and finding startling applications in economic processes, medicine, communications, defence etc., the pugnacious optimism of the earlier period was being shaken. In a similar way Naturalism in art, though never disappearing and always retaining an important area for itself, was also assailed by self-doubt. It is symptomatic that the historian Lamprecht, a leading advocate of scientific historiography, which he hoped might establish a foundation for a scientific politics, could single out for emphatic approval the climax of Sudermann's novel *Der Katzensteg* (1889), in which the hero, deprived of the support of the church, of local allegiances and of common decency, finds in patriotism the only meaning for his life.

About the turn of the century there was a revival in academic philosophy of systems that release the individual from the causal chain of nature. Thus the neo-Kantians, the strongest 'school', defined the will, the moral imperative, as the proof of human autonomy (e.g. Hermann Cohen, *Ethik des reinen Willens*, 1904). A revival of Fichteanism centred in the dogma of a transcendental moral obligation ('Sollen'). The more modern types of philosophy have more marked irrational elements in them, but served the same purpose of rescuing the uniqueness and unique destiny of the self. In their crudest form, these trends produced the extreme irrationalism of Ludwig Klages' *Das Wesen des Bewusstseins* (1921), which rejects science and technology, society, and even intelligence (Geist), as being hostile or irrelevant to the soul, and asserts that the intuitive consciousness of selfhood is the centre of reality and being. The 'intuitive

Wesenschau' of Husserl's phenomenalism is a more penetrating expression of the inadequacy of reason and science. During the first decade of the century the slight but growing influence of Kierkegaard, that can be traced in Rilke, Kafka and Morgenstern, the consciousness of a transcendental loneliness as the central life-experience (to which an essay in the young Lukács' *Die Seele und die Formen*, 1911, bears witness) indicates an alternative form of the rejection of natural science and social action, and with Husserl's phenomenalism leads towards the existentialism of Jaspers and Heidegger. Though philosophy still enjoyed great prestige among university studies, it would be hazardous to claim that these various philosophies 'influenced' literature, but we may say they form part of a general trend evident in the whole culture, summed up in Simmel's statement of 1903: 'The deepest problems of modern life arise from the claim of the individual to maintain the independence and identity of his existence against the super-powers of society, his historical heritage, and the external culture and technique of life' (*Die Groszstädte und das Geistesleben*).

Nietzsche

Throughout this period, the thought of Nietzsche was not only that most acutely responsive to the great cultural dilemmas of European society. It also, bridging the gap between the academies and the artistic culture, between philosophers and publicists, exerted the most direct influence.

Though his great polemic opened with an onslaught on positivism (the Strauss essay, 1873), his work embodies much of positivism as well as a fierce challenge to it; in this respect as in others Nietzsche represents contradictory trends of his times. In the three books immediately preceding *Also sprach Zarathustra* (1883-4) – *Menschliches, Allzumenschliches, Morgenröthe*, and *Die fröhliche Wissenschaft* – Nietzsche rejoices in the success of science, 'Wissenschaft', in destroying all metaphysical certainties and absolute values. Not only religion but all philosophies are asserted to be more ideologies, i.e. pseudo-universalistic projections of the interests of particular groups. The categories of thought do not define reality but only the mind itself, and logic, law, numbers, language itself are called mere 'logical fictions' invented by man in the interests of survival and the conquest of nature, in the same way as he invents ethical values and meta-physical concepts. Nietzsche is Kantian enough to admit there may be a transcendental reality, a 'thing-in-itself', beyond the range of human intelligence, but he dismisses it as 'unthinkable' and totally insignificant, of no relevance whatever to human purposes. In *Zarathustra* itself the concept of the Superman is justified in a twofold scientific sense. On the one hand Nietzsche claims it to be the next stage on the evolutionary ladder, related to man as man is to the ape; on the other he claims that the Superman, in contrast to God, is 'thinkable' in human terms, and therefore is realizable, a typically positivistic argument. The concept of 'life' that embraces everything, energy, change, creation and destruction, will, or more precisely will to power, belongs to a scientific tradition.

Even in his most scientistic works, however, Nietzsche does not sound like a positivist. If he derisively labels all the great religious and metaphysical beliefs of man as delusions, at the same time he insists that delusions are necessary conditions of action and achievement, indeed perhaps more indispensable than truth. The proclamation of the 'death of God' has an impassioned ring about it unlike anything in Büchner or Strauss or Nordau. His great question arises: how is it possible to live without a transcendent purpose and a faith? How, he cries in *Zarathustra*, live in a world in whose rationality and inherent lovableness you cannot believe? His first answer, that remained part of his doctrine throughout, was an individualistic one. It is, that all social, political, historical goals are irrelevant to man's deepest needs, which can be satisfied only by inward self-fulfilment and wholeness and by a new set of personal values to take the place of those altruistic morals that have traditionally secured the dominance of society over the individual. Thus he thinks of the Superman as the product of a biological rather than social development, and fits it on to his individualism by a pseudo-scientific thesis that a new species arises only when the parent species has fulfilled its inherent potenti-alities. In *Zarathustra,* however, the work in which he created the imaginative forms that fascinated the following generation, the anti-scientistic elements outweigh the others. The very concept of the 'Übermensch' is elusive. At times it seems to be a biological-evolutionary goal, to be achieved in time; at others a 'fiction', something to be believed in because of the effectiveness of such a faith in transforming one's life-affirmation, but in itself no more real than the God of earlier generations. This ambiguity pervades the central principle of Nietzsche's ethic, the individualistic 'I will' that replaces the old 'Thou shalt'. Sometimes he seems to suggest that the decision of the will actually transforms reality, sometimes that the assertion of one's own values is the important thing, irrespective of any change in the world.

This sort of ambiguity, perhaps even confusion, so deeply rooted in Nietzsche's thought, accounts for the great difference of response, especially that between those adherents who believed in an imminent birth of the Superman, as a sort of Saviour, and those who rejected such fundamentalism and interpreted his doctrine symbolically. The same problem affects the interpretation of his concept of 'life'. In the early works and in part in the later, 'life' means the creative vital energies and drives that in Nietzsche's view were being sapped by a decadent civilization and an anti-human morality. But in the later works, where life is interpreted more and more as 'will to power', this 'will' is discussed in the concrete terms of physical struggle between individuals and classes. In *Zarathustra* man is called 'a beast of prey' and enjoined to become a 'better' beast of prey, more fierce, more predatory, and in *Jenseits von Gut und Böse* (1886) and till his breakdown in 1890 Nietzsche proceeded to sketch the socio-political embodiment of this idealization of power. The human counterpart to the beast of prey is a self-elected social élite, the 'higher race', disciplining itself to the achievement of power, cynically using the masses, the 'slave race', for its great projects, suppressing all democratic institutions and all humane values, which are alleged to be, like Christianity, the subtle means by which the weak subdue the strong. It is often difficult to know how literally we are meant to understand his political concepts. Some of Nietzsche's most brilliant passages uncover the bewitchment of men by their language and their images, and sometimes he certainly means political terms to be taken only as symbols. In the works from *Zarathustra* onwards, however, he seems himself more and more to have fallen a prey to his own terms, and really to have believed that concepts like master-race or herd were keys to the understanding of the past and guides to future action. In any case, there can be no doubt that the thought of tyranny, barbarism, war, brutal power often intoxicated him, and anti-democratic movements and authoritarian governments have acknowledged their debt to him.

Nietzsche can hardly be called a political theorist. He never wrote with any precision on political structures, and the principles he advocates do not form anything approaching a political structure. His work arises from a criticism of culture, the source of so many of the most potently disturbing ideas of the last two hundred years, in particular a criticism of bourgeois society and values. But, though he is the most impassioned critic of certain ideals of the French Revolution – equality, fraternity, constitutionalism – he still subscribes to other values of the bourgeoisie, struggle and competition, individualism, the élitism of merit. What he does is to intensify these dynamic elements to the point where they come into startling conflict with the regulative democratic ideas with which they were uncomfortably combined in normal liberal-bourgeois doctrine, so that they turn into the idealization of power, of authoritarian government within a society and brutal expansionism in respect of rival societies. In this sense he mirrors the transformation of the German bourgeoisie in the nineteenth century. But he does so in a subtle and alluring way, offering intellectuals the joy both of participating in a spiritual adventure and of shaking free from illusions, the joy both of the release of instinctual drives and of enhanced intellectual consciousness. In *Betrachtungen eines Unpolitischen* Thomas Mann, then at the peak of his veneration for Nietzsche, could not help pointing out a similar contradiction in the very manner of Nietzsche's style. As he says, this fastidious and savage critic of mass-civilization, mass-values, and the trivialization of culture, was himself a supreme journalist. His works are aphoristic not systematic, ever-startling and paradoxical, gay and abusive, full of subtle subliminal argumentation, and always, at whatever cost, witty and enlivening.

Nietzsche's concept of 'life' was adapted by a number of philosophers as a solvent of uncertainties. In Vaihinger's *Die Philosophie des Als Ob* (1911) all philosophical and moral concepts are discussed as logical fictions having a merely subjective validity as instruments of man's practical purposes. Georg Simmel in his philosophy of history considered concepts like nation, country, battle to be artificial constructs that do violence to the fluidity of history but at the same time are essential mental tools in the service of understanding, that is, of life. Fritz Mauthner took Nietzsche's criticism of language further, emphasizing the distortions of reality created by language, and asserting that it is language that creates the errors of metaphysics and that postulates the separation of observer from the observed. But again, like Vaihinger and Simmel, Mauthner justifies this distortion of reality since language in this way serves the life-interests of a community, it is a community's 'think-organ'. In the same way Dilthey's 'life' conception, independently of Nietzsche, yielded a principle common to all value systems and prevented relativism from becoming scepticism. But 'life' is a vague and comprehensive term for all these philosophers, and embraces all aspects of biological and social organization. They do not subscribe to the specifically Nietzschean interpretation of life as will to power, nor, though they may be hostile to liberalism, do they share his worship of the tyrant. It was only during the Great War, in the exaltation of German victories, that Nietzsche's worship of power was adapted to German national interests and systematized in Oswald Spengler's *Der Untergang des Abendlandes* (two vols, 1918, 1923). Spengler defines the successive historical cultures as closed systems in, which all the interrelated cultural expressions – political and social structures, art, science, language – have validity only within each system, so that the dawning age of (Germanic) Caesarism can now dispense with all past moralities; the concepts of truth and objective science are thus relegated to functions of an obsolete democratic-bourgeois society.

There is in the whole period scarcely a cultural area unaffected by Nietzsche's doctrines. M. G. Conrad, a founding father of Naturalism, links Nietzsche with Wagner and Zola as the presiding geniuses of the literary revolution. Nietzsche haunts the pages of *Freie Bühne*, the organ of the Berlin Naturalists, many of whose contributors assert that the main ethical problem is to reconcile socialism with Nietzschean individualism, Tolstoy with Nietzsche. Nietzsche finds adherents among anarchists like J. H. Mackay, drop-outs like Peter Altenberg, Marxists like Bruno Wille or Lily Braun, individualists like Lou Andreas Salome or Hermann Hesse. Frenssen and Burte use him when they build their idea of a 'Germanic' Christ. Richard Strauss and Mahler compose Nietzsche texts, and Busoni's text of *Dr Faustus* is very Nietzschean. Heinrich Mann's cult of the aristocratic immoralist (*Die Göttinnen*) is Nietzschean, and even Rilke, though repelled by Nietzsche's dream of power, assimilated Nietzschean elements in his praise of life. When Stefan George turned from aestheticism to the creation of the positive images of a new 'creative' culture, it was from Nietzsche, whom he addressed as 'leader' and 'redeemer', that he drew the inspiration for the leader-follower relationship and the tone of devotion and command. To balance this anti-democratic aspect, the voluntaristic revolutionism of the Expressionist generation throve on Nietzsche's challenge to bourgeois reality, to social and natural law.

As a broad generalization one might say that before 1918 the implications within personal ethics take precedence over the socio-political. Nietzsche stands above all as the champion of personal liberation and personal fulfilment, as against parental and social authority, mass movements and ideological systems, against the prestige of state, church, race, class; the counter-balancing impetus, the construction of a new and fiercer authority, the worship of grandiose and impersonal power, held a much smaller appeal until after 1918. The common image of Nietzsche was that of a tragic, lonely figure consuming himself in impassioned protest against society, and many readers felt the exhilaration of identifying themselves with this tragic posture, especially writers who only too readily, and despite Nietzsche's scepticism about artists, felt that their profession as artists meant a challenge to society and the bourgeois. Thomas Mann's more subtle distinction between artist and bourgeois, that runs through all his pre-1918 work, is of purer Nietzschean origin, since his irony is directed both against the artist and against the bourgeois. But the antagonism of Nietzsche to 'society', the anti-bourgeois element, is only a part-truth; he also expresses and intensifies a social force that found political expression as imperialism. When Romain Rolland visited Germany in 1898 in the course of his long campaign to bring about a rapprochement between French and German culture, he noted in his diary the impression of vital force combined with nervous and morbid over-excitement that Richard Strauss's music gave him, associated it with the streak of hysteria and brutality in Wagner, with similar features in Nietzsche, and linked all these cultural phenomena with the political manner of the Kaiser: 'Neroism in the air', this friend of Germany called it.

The Major Literary Groups and Positivism

Reference has been made in passing to the contributions of

literature to the changing image of the bourgeois and to the literary responses to the bourgeois and his ideology. These references are mostly confined to direct and tangible evidence. But we can trace also in the various conceptions of art the stimulus of the social environment, and the aim of this section is to outline, with only very general indications, its relationship to what the Germans call the 'form-will' or the 'art-will' of the major groupings.

In his reminiscences, Heinrich Hart defines the source of Naturalism as a combination of technology, science, and the 'social movement'. M. G. Conrad, in his *Von Zola bis Hauptmann*, emphasizes also the part played by the 'ethical' purpose. Johannes Schlaf, in his preface to *Peter Boies Freite,* says the first phase was 'socialist', the second 'artistic-naturalistic'. These retrospective opinions correspond with the early manifestoes of Naturalism, which all combine enthusiasm for science with devotion to the ideal, to ethical and social impulses and it is clear that Naturalism cannot be equated with scientism, but has a more complex origin and function. It was Wilhelm Bölsche who, following Zola, most emphatically aligned the new literature with the natural sciences (*Die naturwissenschaftlichen Grundlagen der Poesie,* 1887). He defined its purpose as the scientific study of man and the discovery of the causal laws governing man, and welcomed the abolition of metaphysics and such concepts as the freedom of the will by science as the condition for a full, unimpeded realism. But even Bölsche will not abandon the ideal. Nature, he writes, demonstrates a general principle of harmony, health, normalcy; and art, to be true to nature, must be devoted to these ideals, in this respect it is and must be tendentious. If the argument is a piece of sleight of hand, it nevertheless is broadly representative of Naturalism in reconciling a scientific with an ethical impulse, and indicates the combination of realistic and idealistic elements in, say, Kretzer's novels, Hauptmann's plays or Holz's *Buch der Zeit.*

No theoretical statement fully represents the variety of trends that make up what is called Naturalism, but Holz's *Die Kunst, ihr Wesen und ihre Gesetze* (1891), which has been traditionally taken as the representative statement of Naturalistic aesthetics, is one of the most exceptional. This was the most determined effort to assimilate art into science, even so far as to reject the saving grace of the artist's temperament with which Zola had tempered his fierce scientism. Holz's conceptions of matter, nature, scientific observation and causation are of the crudest, mechanical, positivistic type. Since his writing is unclear and inconsistent, various interpretations of his views are possible, but it is certain that his intention was to bring art and nature, the artist and the scientist close to one another, and to see the chief purpose of literature in the uncovering of causal laws. His elimination from the artist of all other motivation but the scientific (and craftsman's) impulse indicates a general decline of the earlier zeal for social reform among the Naturalists, to which several poems of *Das Buch der Zeit* had borne witness. Holz's treatise was taken in the following decades as the representative definition of Naturalism, and the numerous Expressionist attacks on the social passivity inherent in the Naturalistic attitude may have been due to this assumption. It stirred up much disagreement, however, among the Naturalists themselves and is by no means the theoretical equivalent of Naturalism, perhaps, rather, a sign of its decline.

Wellek (*A History of Modern Criticism*, IV) rightly says of the various aesthetics of the Naturalists that 'the theoretical level seems deplorably low', and adds that the 'theatrical critics' such as Brahm were 'much subtler observers and analysts'. Naturalism should not be seen in the light of these clumsy aesthetics so much as in the context of the reviews and essays appearing in the newspapers and periodicals. The general tenor of the literary articles and reviews appearing in *Die Gesellschaft* and *Freie Bühne* is not doctrinaire. They are keenly sympathetic to work that discusses the ethical and existential problems of the modern world, and respond more warmly to realistic than to symbolical forms, but do not reveal any commonly held aesthetic dogma, for instance on the vexed question of the scientific 'objectivity' of the artist in respect to a theme or a form.

Impressionism as defined by Hermann Bahr (*Die Überwindung des Naturalismus*, 1891). Schlaf, and the critic Lublinski is the successor to Naturalism, different only in that its 'realism' is turned towards the psyche, feelings, dreams and sensations, in place of the externals of scenes and behaviour so prominent in Holz's theory and writing. But a merely formal, technical distinction of this kind is totally inadequate to the actual great contrast between the two, a contrast of values and concern that is evident even in a single author who may sometimes adopt one, sometimes the other style. Actually, though in painting

Impressionism has a fairly clear meaning, in literature it is of questionable usefulness. 'Impressionists' like Bourget, Huysmans, Wilde (*Dorian Gray*) and the early Hofmannsthal might better be grouped with the symbolists or decadents, like Moreau, Redan, Khnopff, Toorop, with their emphatic antagonism to realism and science. Under whatever aspect one considers them, these writers do not describe social conditions or look for social laws, and are not concerned with social reform. Yet, oddly enough, they pay tribute to deterministic scientism more than do the Naturalists, since their characters lack the ethical impulse, feel they are only playing a role, and are subject to an irresistible process that disintegrates the will and personality and evokes in them only grief, suffering and the longing for death.

Hofmannsthal cannot be identified, of course, with a single or simple attitude, even in this early period of the 1890s. In part he went along also with Stefan George and his friends, who from the beginning deliver a challenge to positivism and do not recognize the relevance of science and natural law to art. The slogan 'An art free from all service', the formula of their aestheticism, repudiates with the claims of bourgeois society social concern and science altogether. After 1900 the change in George's attitude corresponds to the ethical revolt, against both positivism and decadence, that led to the revival of the voluntarism of Kant and Fichte. His art, still hostile to bourgeois society and its technology, was now put to the service of a politico-cultural ideal. The 'spirit' George subscribed to was the antagonist of matter, of materialism and liberal social values, and in his verse, through an elevated language and hieratic rhythm, he created models of ideal relationships and attitudes, not reflections of reality. This poetry of ideal forms is paralleled by a new type of monumental biography that challenged positivistic historiography: Gundolf's *Goethe* (1916), Ernst Bertram's *Nietzsche* (1918), Berthold Vallentin's *Napoleon* (1923), Ernst Kantorowicz's *Kaiser Friedrich II* (1927), and Friedrich Wolters' *Stefen George* (1930). In these works scholarly scrupulousness and analysis were disregarded in favour of the myth of the charismatic leader, the embodiment of an unswerving intuitive will, inaccessible to influences.

The George onslaught on Naturalism, bourgeois society, and positivism was limited by its strong ideological commitment to a heroic ideal and a hierarchical order, and a more fundamental attack on Naturalism and positivism came from elsewhere. E. H.

Gombrich points out, in his 1962 Introduction to *Art and Illusion,* that Helmholtz's recognition that perception is a complex mental act and much more than a mere visual sensation is closely related to the emergence of anti-naturalistic art criticism. The neoclassical sculptor Adolf von Hildebrand challenged the scientistic basis of Naturalism and Impressionism by arguing (*Das Problem der Form in der bildenden Kunst,* 1893) that mental images derive from tactile memories as well as visual sensations, and that classical – i.e. unrealistic – form was required to make up for the inadequacy of the eye as an organ for registering visual reality (this view anticipated the argument of Paul Ernst in his 'neoclassical' period when he criticized Holz's concept of realism). From this insight of Hildebrand's Alois Riegl and Wilhelm Worringer and Heinrich Wölfflin proceeded to investigations into the specific 'Kunstwillen' of different periods and the changing forms of 'seeing' that distinguish different art styles. Wölfflin was less speculative than the others and a more sensitive historian and critic, though at the expense of avoiding questions of historical causation. There was in literary criticism nothing so solid as this thorough dismantling of positivist concepts.

Upon this basis Worringer was to initiate an onslaught on realism that interpreted and guided the feeling of a new generation. His small academic treatise *Abstraktion und Einfühlung,* 1908, was to reach a seventh edition by 1919. Worringer understands realism in the broadest sense as the reproduction in art of organic living forms, the representational art characteristic of classical Greece, the Renaissance, Europe generally (Naturalism being one slight manifestation). Its deepest function, he argues, is the enhancement of life and activity, the celebration of self-fulfilment, and this faith in life, activity and selfhood implies a faith and trust in the cosmos, a pantheistic type of religious feeling, and a trust in the senses, reason and science. It is the art of a civilization that feels 'at home' in the universe, that finds in nature the artistic symbols of this feeling, an art therefore of 'empathy'. Contrasted to it is the art of 'abstraction', the art of ancient Egypt or the Orient and primitive art generally, non-naturalistic, non-representational, geometric, 'crystalline inorganic' as Worringer puts it. This art emerges in cultures for whom the universe is hostile and threatening, whose art arises out of the experience of 'being lost'. They seek in art a refuge from a hostile and meaningless universe and stamp on it conceptual, anti-natural forms, divorced even from space and time (i.e. without perspective and movement), self-enclosed, necessary and immutable. The god that corresponds to this art is transcendent and remote, not immanent. Man therefore does not recognize god or himself in nature, but experiences the world and selfhood as oppressive burdens from which he needs to be redeemed. The abstract forms he creates in art are 'the only expression imaginable of emancipation from fortuitousness and temporality'.

Though Worringer defines empathy and abstraction as alternative principles of art, he leaves no doubt as to their rank. Compared with the monumental grandeur of 'abstract' geometrical art, the 'realistic' art of Greece and modern Europe is, he writes, merely charming, harmless, miniature. Not only this. The peoples whose art is abstract, he asserts, are guided by a true 'instinct' of what the universe is and face it in fear and trembling, while Europe has lost this instinct. Worringer's treatise is a sensitive epitome of the growing suspicion and criticism of traditional European humanism, of the post-Nietzschean longing for the primitive and barbaric. The date of his work almost exactly coincides with that of Picasso's *Demoiselles d'Avignon* and Schönberg's second quartet, perhaps the most decisive breakthroughs to modern art. Worringer was later to be one of the most perceptive interpreters of Expressionism, a term he may indeed have invented, and which he defined in an article of 1919 (in *Genius*) as 'an art in which mind (Geist) declares its autonomy over against the experience of nature' (the latter phrase includes the meaning of laws of nature).

The new art that we can roughly, despite the variants, call Expressionist, has as its starting point the rebellion against materialism and science, by which is meant the prestige of nature and the limitation of man within externally imposed laws, a rebellion in the name of 'Geist'. In this it is related to George's work; but also very different, since while George worshipped a 'Geist' which fused spirit and body, man and nature, 'Geist' for the Expressionists was usually understood as something totally opposed to nature and body. Kandinsky's *Über das Geistige in der Kunst* of 1912 defines the general position. Art must express the inner feeling of the artist, his intuition. All realism limits the spiritual element, and 'emancipation from nature', from matter and nature and everything that is subject to natural law, is the first condition of a true art. While the concept 'Geist' is undefined and very vague, it contains many traditional religious vestiges, as we can see when Kandinsky refers to theosophy and anthroposophy as being manifestations of the re-emergence of 'Geist', presaging the redemption of mankind from matter. Kandinsky does not condemn realism or Impressionism outright, but considers them a very 'low' and still materialistic form of revolt against materialism; in the same way he considers liberals, progressives and socialists, all movements directed towards social reform, as still within the sphere of materialism. The revolution he believes in and foretells, though completely overturning bourgeois attitudes and values, is a spiritual one, and its destinies are in the hands of artists. It is this anti-bourgeois attitude that explains the cooperation of Kandinsky and Klee with Gropius in the post-war Bauhaus; their intuitive mysticism and their opposition to science and materialism, however, seem to be the very opposite of the functionalism of Gropius.

It is evident that Kandinsky's theory drives towards abstract painting rather than to the Expressionism of Franz Marc, with whom he was in 1912 collaborating on *Der blaue Reiter*. Marc's hostility to naturalistic art was directed at direct and surface realism, while he sought what he saw to be the fundamental (cubist) structures in objects and relationships. The dominance of imaginative insight over objective scientific observation is however decisive in his work and relates it to Kandinsky's.

In the literary Expressionists we find a similar standpoint, though the social implications are made much more explicit. There is a standing criticism of Naturalism and Impressionism on the grounds that reproduction of reality implies veneration for social reality, for the bourgeois-capitalist order. Rejecting Sombart's resigned passivity and Rathenau's meagre hope, and finding, as Pfemfert vigorously insisted in *Aktion*, that Social Democracy was becoming a bourgeois institution, the young writers abandoned hopes of social reform but did not abandon hopes of total change, of revolution. This constituted the framework for the formal principles of their writing. Kurt Hiller, the leading spirit of the *Neopathetisches Club*, was from 1911 proclaiming the primacy of 'pathos', of will and energy, as agents of change, and for this reason wrote in the preface to his anthology *Der Kondor* (1912) that the new poetry was not concerned with realistic themes such as 'dynamos' or 'strikes', but with rhetoric, pathos. In 1914 Korrodi repudiated the positivistic (or Marxist) view that art is a product of socio-economic forces and called on the poet to assert his spirit against them, against the whole 'bourgeois-capitalist world'. In 1915 Kurt Pinthus charged realism with having omitted the central force of life, 'the dynamic movement of the soul', and defined the task of contemporary literature, already exemplified in the work of Strindberg, Dostoyevsky and Wedekind among others, as being to 'explode' the inhuman reality of the socio-political nexus; that is, through its anti-realistic forms, its distortions of actuality and normal grammar, to destroy the prestige of reality. In lectures of 1917-18, published in 1919 as *Über den Expressionismus in der Literatur und die neue Dichtung*, Kasimir Edschmid gave the most comprehensive statement of the aims of the new poetry. The Expressionists, he writes, are not concerned with surface reality but inner visions, not with momentary impressions but with 'eternal significance', instead of describing they transmit experience, instead of 'reproducing' they 'create'. It is through these new formal principles that they seek to achieve their great purpose, a new world and a 'new man' to people it, a revolution that is inspired by a religious despair and enthusiasm rather than political and practical, scientific, principles.

It is clear that this type of anti-bourgeois revolutionism meant not only a sharp rupture with socio-political institutions but also with all social agencies of change. A few writers do indeed carry the dislocations of reality, of traditional literary genres, logic and language, to the extreme of absolute negation, like Carl Einstein in his *Bebuquin* or the Dada authors, making art serve a purely destructive function. The main body of the Expressionists, however, held to a positive if vague ideal of a new non-bourgeois society, and the divorce between them and any concrete social agency was patched up as the progress of the war led to the beginnings of an anti-war and revolutionary movement in which many of the Expressionists joined. Even so, the abstractness of the concepts of the 'new man' and the 'new world' in the ethical Expressionism of Hasenclever, Werfel, von Unruh, Kaiser, Toller and such indicates a continuing unease of relationship between the writers and the actual revolutionary social forces, so that in the revolutionary situation of 1918-19 they were reduced to a subsidiary and ambiguous role between the contending classes. With their self-confidence Expressionism itself came to an end. In *Berlin oder Juste Milieu* (1920), Sternheim attributed the disasters of war and the failure of revolution to the materialism of all classes, their failure to devote themselves to 'Geist'. But one can with perhaps more justice suggest a failure on the part of the writers and intellectuals to come to terms with reality. Their protest against empirical reality in the interests of freedom was a justified one, but in their literary work as in their politics they postulated an unreal divorce between man and nature, an unreal freedom, that if tested in practice was bound to be found wanting.

While throughout the period the aesthetic struggle is fought out in terms of realism versus anti-realism, essentially it is, as Kandinsky puts it, a question of the 'what' rather than the 'how'. The same problem, altering somewhat with the passing of time, is the starting-point for each group and for infinite individual variations: the problem of the soul, of the individual, the spirit in a capitalist, bourgeois, materialist society. But the imprecision of nearly all the concepts employed does not hide, and perhaps betrays, the fact that the struggle itself is carried out in the service of values that we can most properly attribute to the bourgeois revolution: realism against reactionary convention and wilful ignorance, science against built-in prejudice; social justice and social freedom, compassion with the oppressed, on one side, on the other rebellion against the limitations imposed by man's social nature, by law, and rationality; self-fulfilment through the liberation of the soul, intuition and insight against calculation and reason. Every form of liberation entails it seems a polar opposite, and is doomed to impermanence.

4

The Jew as Alien and Bourgeois

The importance of anti-semitism as an element in anti-capitalistic and nationalist movements makes it advisable to consider separately the position of Jews in German society in this period.

The anti-semitism that swept through Germany and Austria, as through France, in the latter half of the nineteenth century had distinctive features, although it still fed on a primitive fear and hatred of a people of alien beliefs and manners. From the time when, following the Napoleonic occupation, Jews were granted civil rights in some of the German states, resentment against a community whose liberation symbolized bourgeois liberalism was added to the older hostility, and though a converted Jew, Stahl, formulated the most influential conservative philosophy of 'throne and altar', the best-known Jews were publicists like Börne and Heine, associated in every sense with emancipation. After the new Reich and Austria-Hungary had granted the Jews full civil rights, all these causes continued to promote anti-semitism, but with a new intensity and a change of emphasis – in spite of the fact that, especially in the educated classes, voluntary assimilation involving both conversion to Christianity and intermarriage was rapidly reducing both religious and cultural differences.

In the Reich, as residential and other restrictions on Jews were lifted, a large shift of population occurred, and though the proportion of Jews in the total population did not increase, there was a strikingly larger concentration in the great cities and in certain professions. Jews were still barred, by custom if not by law, from some professions, notably the officer corps and the higher civil service, and entry was made difficult to others, especially to posts in high schools and universities. They were relatively all the more numerous as private practitioners in medicine and law and other 'free professions'. In Vienna a very large influx from Eastern Europe drastically changed the demographic proportions. Its

Jewish population rose from 1.3 per cent in 1857 to roughly twelve per cent in 1890, then dropping to about nine per cent about 100,000 persons, in 1912 (in Berlin the proportion hardly reached four per cent before the war). Among academics the figures were notably higher. In the university of Vienna, nearly half the medical students in 1890 were Jewish, twenty-two per cent in Law, and fifteen per cent in the Philosophical (Arts) Faculty. In 1894 there were two Jewish professors of medicine and fourteen associate professors, and the fact that Freud was never appointed full professor was due to the policy of the authorities. This situation was paralleled in Budapest and Prague, and everywhere professional envy provoked bitter anti-semitism.

Jews became prominent in many areas of public life, particularly those associated specifically with a modern, bourgeois, industrial society. Most of the great banks founded after 1850 in Berlin, Frankfurt and Vienna were Jewish, and were intimately associated with the economic explosion of the 1870s. Walther Rathenau's father founded the great electrical concern AEG, and Ballin, who founded the Hamburg-Amerika line, was also Jewish. These were only the most prominent names. Even in the 1860s it was already a common charge against the Jews that they were responsible for the 'Americanization' of Germany, i.e. for the modernization and rationalization of economic processes and management. In politics too they were prominent in the liberal and the socialist parties. The outstanding leaders of the National Liberals in Germany were Jews – Bamberger and Lasker – and Austrian Jews may almost be said to have created Austrian liberalism and in large part Austrian nationalism. The most influential liberal newspapers – *Berliner Tageblatt, Frankfurter Zeitung* and the Vienna *Neue Freie Presse* – were owned and edited by Jews.

They played, too, a very prominent part in the cultural field. The most representative cultural periodicals of the Reich, *Deutsche Rundschau* and *Die neue Rundschau* (originally *Freie Bühne*), were founded and guided by Jews, as were the popular humorous papers, *Kladderadatsch* and *Ulk*. The most successful and influential literary and cultural critics were Jewish – Brahm, Mauthner, Schlenther, Harden, Bahr, Kraus, Kerr, Jacobsohn, to mention only a few. Several of the most influential philosophers, like Simmel, Husserl and Max Scheler, were Jewish. Many of the publishers most closely associated with the modern movement were Jewish, from S. Fischer, the brothers Cassirer and Bondi at the beginning to Kurt Wolff. The commercial theatre was dominated by Jewish directors, among them Blumenthal, Barnowski, L'Arronge, Brahm and Reinhardt. The efflorescence of music in the concert hall and the home owed inestimably much to Jews as executants, agents, and devoted amateurs. This very active participation in political and cultural life meant, inevitably, an ever-growing assimilation of the Jews into German civil life, the enfeeblement of the religious and communal solidarity, that was a cause of bitter controversy and conflict within the Jewish communities themselves. At the same time, it itself was a chief cause of modern anti-semitism.

An older anti-semitism still continued, an unease at the prominence and success of the Jewish newcomers, a resentment that was expressed in social exclusion and malicious gossip. Lagarde represents a sort of transition from this older form to the more specifically modern anti-semitism. From the 1850s he allowed himself outbursts against the Jews, their penetration of the professions of law and medicine, their prominence in the press and their communal and religious exclusiveness, but he sees these difficulties as arising primarily from their religion, and he urges conversion and assimilation as a cure. But the speculative boom of the Gründerjahre of the early 1870s, and the ensuing slump, brought Lagarde to a more brutal invective, as it did many others. Now he above all identifies the Jews with capitalism, the cause in his view of the political and social disasters of the Reich. Uncritically and hysterically he picks up and spreads the accusation of an international conspiracy of Jews intent on establishing world domination. He calls on the state to expropriate Jewish bankers, 'usurers', and the 'extermination' of liberals and capitalists that he calls for, when he applies the term to the Jews, has a brutally sinister ring. Still, he is unwilling to speak of these matters in racialist terms, and will not identify himself with the modern racialism then being formulated in Germany, whose biological conception of race he considers vulgarly materialistic.

This new anti-semitism was signalled by W. Marr's virulent pamphlet *Der Sieg des Judentums über das Germanentum* of 1873. Like Lagarde or the conservative Konstantin Frantz, Marr attributed to the Jews all the sins of capitalism, the destruction of artisan prosperity, the exploitation of industrial workers, slumps and destitution, and beyond these the spiritual and physical contamination of the German people and a conspiracy to enslave Europe. But while religious conversion and assimilation still seemed to Lagarde, as to Wagner and Treitschke, to be an alternative to the drastic remedies of withdrawal of civil rights and forced emigration, Marr's anti-semitism is racist, not religious, and allows no alternative to segregation and emigration. Eugen Dühring, in his *Die Judenfrage als Rassen-, Sitten-, und Kulturfrage* (1881), makes the elimination of the Jews from economic and public life the central tenet and condition of his socialism and this fusing of anti-capitalism with anti-semitism was to be a characteristic feature of all subsequent anti-semitic parties and movements. The 'socialism' involved was of a type often called 'national', that is, it aimed at an alliance of the anti-bourgeois, anti-capitalist classes, a strong and authoritarian government, and the dismantling of liberal institutions. Thus, in the 1880s, Stoecker the Berlin court chaplain, genuinely distressed by working-class misery, sought to win the sympathy of the Berlin workers for an anti-liberal, Conservative programme by outspoken attacks on capitalism and the bourgeoisie; when his efforts proved unavailing, it was not hard for him to slip into a virulent anti-semitism that found favour with the petty bourgeoisie and even, for a time, with the Conservative party.

There were many variations. In 1879 the historian Treitschke published in the *Preussische Jahrbücher* an article that summed up the various grievances against the Jews and uttered the baneful slogan 'The Jews are our misfortune'. Although he made anti-semitism as it were academically respectable, and in his lectures allowed himself the most reckless abuse, Treitschke remained uncertain what policy to propose, sometimes inclining to a reluctant liberal tolerance, sometimes towards drastic legal prohibitions, sometime despairing of a solution. Even the radical Mommsen, who vigorously chastised his Berlin colleague's capitulation to prejudice and panic, suggested that the Jews should prove their fitness for full citizenship by voluntarily abandoning their religion.

For the various anti-semitic groupings, leagues, and parties, which reached the height of their activity and popularity in the 1880s and 1890s, this was not the problem and no solution. Langbehn, whose *Rembrandt als Erzieher* (1890) expounded opinions reached over many years, expressed in its first version admiration for assimilated Jews and respect for the 'aristocratic' orthodox Jews. But for the thirty-seventh edition of 1891 a malignant section on the Jews was added, contradicting much of what Langbehn had written, calling the Jews 'poison for us' and demanding withdrawal from them of civil rights. In these years, anti-semitic meetings and newspapers were full of the most unscrupulous calumniation of the Jews, alleging a conspiracy on their part to control economic life, enslave Germany and Europe, and pollute German blood through prostitution or marriage. Disreputable demagogues like Ahlwardt, though in frequent trouble for reckless allegations, gained seats in legislatures and much popular admiration. 'Jew' traditionally meant a believer in the Jewish religion and member of a Jewish community, one who observed a number of distinctive ritualistic practices. Conversion to Christianity meant that the convert ceased to be a Jew. Now the religious and ritualistic issue was disregarded, and the term was applied to people of a racial Jewish origin, even if they were converted and married to non-Jews, and often to the children, even grandchildren, of such marriages. It was in respect of this undefined group that the modern anti-semites demanded withdrawal of civil rights, restriction to ghettos, expulsion from the professions and the civil service, forced emigration etc.; even more malignant than the particular demands was the hysterical panic already evident with Marr or Dühring, the blind fear that could conceive of no solutions and made genocide imaginable.

From the middle of the 1890s anti-semitism began to decline as a political force in the Reich, partly perhaps because the Conservative party incorporated some anti-semitic points in its Tivoli programme of 1892, partly because the surge of imperialist fervour offered an outlet for discontent and aggressiveness. Social anti-semitism still remained strong in the army and upper civil service, in the professions and among students, and among shopkeepers and artisans, often as the expression of personal rivalry and resentment, often as a muddled protest against the pressures of big business. In this atmosphere it was not difficult for Sombart to write dispassionately about the Jews in *Die Juden und das Wirtschaftsleben* (1911), but perhaps there was more than a tinge of prejudice in his thesis that capitalism owed its origin in western Europe to the Jews – a thesis Max Weber condemned as historically untenable.

In Austria-Hungary the development was similar, though complicated by the different policies adopted by the constituent states. Thus, while Hungary introduced in 1880 an enforced Magyarization that led many Jews to emigrate to Vienna, Berlin, Paris, the USA, and while in the Polish territories a similar displacement occurred, in Prague the Jews, though split fairly equally into Czech-speaking and German-speaking, became a local bulwark of German culture. In all these lands, as in Russia, there were still outbursts of primitive anti-semitism of the pogrom type, and Jews had reason to fear the celebration of Easter. In Vienna the Jewish population greatly increased, and Jews were very prominent in the medical and legal professions, in all social activities and political parties; they dominated banking, were of great importance in industry and trade, and owned the most influential organs of publicity. Most of the prominent intellectuals and writers were, if rarely Jewish by religious adherence, yet of Jewish or mixed Jewish extraction – one only needs to mention the brilliant names of Schnitzler, Hofmannsthal, Karl Kraus, Freud, Weininger, Mahler, Schoenberg. In Prague there was a comparable constellation round Max Brod, Werfel, and Kafka, though in this historic centre of Jewish learning the ancient religious and communal allegiances were not so easily thrown off.

Anti-semitism here, like that in the Reich, identified the Jew with capitalism, in spite of the fact that most Socialist leaders were Jews. The Oesterreichischer Reformverein was founded in 1882 to protect small traders against liberal free enterprise, and remained for years the chief anti-semitic organization. Its leader, G. von Schönerer, a progressive in such matters as universal suffrage or secular education, constantly abused the Jews as capitalists. As in Germany, this anti-semitism developed a national socialistic programme, including the nationalization of railways and insurance, factory legislation, and a graded income tax. In Austria racist Germanism led to a movement for unity with the Reich in which Jews also were prominent. Karl Lueger, Schönerer's successor, while still, with his movement Vereinigte Christen (founded 1887), calling for the exclusion of Jews from the civil service and many professions, was more successful in amalgamating an anti-semitic, anti-capitalist fervour with traditional clerical anti-liberalism. As leader of the anti-semitic Christian Social party, Lueger was mayor of Vienna from 1897 till his death in 1910, but though he retained his anti-semitic demagogy no significant anti-Jewish legislation was enacted; the anti-capitalistic impetus appeared chiefly in measures protecting the small tradesman and in the exemplary municipalization of the Vienna tramways and the lighting and water supply. Not only a Jewish socialist littérateur like Stefan Grossmann could express admiration and sympathy for Lueger; another and more famous Jewish publicist, Harden, devoted to him what amounts to an unqualified panegyric.

It is roughly the same story as in Germany. As liberalism declined as a political and ideological force, and as aggressive nationalism began to provide an outlet, political anti-semitism declined. But anti-semitism remained as a social-cultural attitude in many classes of the population who could discharge on the Jews their unease and anxieties. If it became possible for a person of Jewish or part-Jewish origin to win a commission in the army or a post in the civil service, he was always likely to meet humiliations, abuse and setbacks, exclusion from clubs, and a host of irritations, though in general he might comfort himself with the thought that all this was much less than formerly. In *Jugend in Wien,* written between 1916-18, Schnitzler includes a note probably of 1912 to the effect that it might be that when, after his death, this autobiographical account was published, the reader would find it difficult to understand the importance of the 'so-called Jewish question' for Schnitzler's generation. The hope was typical and delusory. Adolf Hitler was nurtured on Lueger's anti-semitism, and after the lost war, under the stresses of the 1920s, the image of the Jew as the capitalist exploiter and contaminator of the Germans supplied the chief emotional drive of National Socialism.

Though anti-semitic ideologies usually lump all Jews together, the response of Jews to the opportunities in the Reich and in Austria was of course various. Among the immigrants to the great cities there was constant reinforcement of the orthodox for whom the new freedoms bore the peril of assimilation, the loss of communal identity and religious faith. Clearly, those Jews most intimately connected with European thought, science, and litera-ture were among those most ready for assimilation, and many of these believed that the traditional gateway of Christian baptism still led there. It was a bitter experience for many converts of this type, who would normally also have eagerly embraced German or Austrian nationalism, to find in the 1880s that the new racist anti-semitism spared the converted no more than the orthodox. It was a shock of this type that brought Theodor Herzl, as a student an ardent 'Deutschnational' Austrian, to turn to his own 'nation' and found Zionism. A rival scheme for founding a Jewish settlement in Uganda was supported by influential Jews, and would probably have been no more successful than many other Utopian schemes for escaping the pressures of European society. Zionism, nourished by a profound religious and national feeling, was the only one of such schemes to be permanent. Even then, it needed the constant harassment the Jews received, especially after 1918. Most Jews in Germany adopted typically German attitudes. Several varieties were expressed by Jewish academics in the course of the controversy following Treitschke's denunciation in 1880, the most constant theme being a sincere and passionate devotion to Germany and its culture. One has only to read the autobiographies of Jews born in remote provinces, perhaps in communities surrounded by Hungarians, Czechs, Poles, Ruthenes, Romanians, to recognize that Berlin or Vienna, like Paris, were shining symbols of culture and enlightenment, and that this patriotism for the adopted country was deeply felt. Of course, quite a number of Jews found a new community in the socialist movement in their new countries, following the example of some of the founding fathers of socialism, Moses Hess, Marx and and Lassalle.

The engagement of Jews in German cultural life, as poets, artists, musicians, critics, editors, agents etc., like that of Jewish university teachers and civil servants, involved necessarily a high degree of self-identification with the nation and the culture and a loss of 'Jewishness'. The autobiographies and diaries of men like Mauthner, Grossmann, Holitscher, Wassermann, Toller tell, like Schnitzler's, of humiliations in childhood and youth, but on the whole ascribe them to provincial and obsolescent prejudice. But, though many tried quietly to obliterate their Jewish origins and discard their Jewish connexions, even these efforts betray tension at least. Schnitzler wrote: 'It was not possible for a Jew, especially a Jew in public life, to ignore the fact that he was a Jew; nobody else was doing so, not the Gentiles and even less the Jews'. Anti-semitism, or simply undercurrents of crude prejudice, affected every Jew and could cause unease or worse in people totally unconnected with the Jewish community and religion, and whose Jewishness might mean nothing more than the possession of a single Jewish grandparent. Conversion made little difference to discrimination, even though it might remove legal barriers. Georg Simmel was the son of converted (Protestant) Jews and married to a non-Jew, yet for all his distinction he failed to be appointed to a full chair at Berlin and Heidelberg universities, and one cannot put this down to anything but anti-semitism in the universities. It was impossible, as Schnitzler makes a Jewish intellectual say in *Der Weg ins Freie*, for a Jew to avoid a false note. If he behaved as if there were no Jewish problem or if he insisted there was one; if he identified himself with 'Germanic' attitudes or with Jewish traditions; if he sought assimilation or kept apart: he would be suspected, and perhaps might suspect himself, of falsification, trickery, self-delusion, pretentiousness and so on.

Jews themselves felt uneasy when a Rudolf Borchardt or a Walther Rathenau claimed to speak on behalf of German culture and the German spirit. Even today it is disturbing to read Harden's advocacy of Teutonic virtues – honesty, maleness, energy, nobility, etc. – with which he seems to identify himself quite unselfconsciously. Conrad Alberti, another patriotic Jew, wrote two articles in *Die Gesellschaft* (1889-90) on the 'tragic' situation of the younger generation of Jews, who were longing to lose their Jewish identity yet bound to an obsolete creed and a degenerate community. He appealed to the anti-semites to cease their agitation which, provoking the pride of the Jews, was in his view a chief obstacle to their full and willing assimilation. In 1897 Rathenau published in Harden's *Zukunft* an article, 'Höre Israel', in which he called on Jews to abandon everything that separated them from German life and values, a view in line with Harden's own challenge to the Jews to make a final choice between Germany and Zion. Rathenau, a devoted Prussian and a hugely successful businessman, was still aware in his *Zur Kritik der Zeit* (1912) of the handicaps suffered by Jews, the exclusion from social clubs and the personal intimacy of the cultured German middle class, from university chairs, often from employment in businesses. Conversion he calls a shameful bribe dangled by the Church before the victims. Every Jew, he writes, experiences in childhood a moment of anguish when for the first time he realizes he is a second-class citizen. Yet, from 'Höre Israel' onwards Rathenau identified the Jews with the cold rational intelligence that is the principle and the curse of modern society, and was almost fanatically obsessed by the spiritual superiority he attributed to the blond Aryans.

There were many varieties of what Theodor Lessing unhappily called 'Jewish self-hatred'. There was the hidden self-torment of Nietzsche's friend Paul Rée, a genuine hatred of self that turned into a neurotic withdrawal, and there was the zealous conformism of so many businessmen, lawyers, civil servants, which often committed them to anti-Jewish actions. There was the exalted patriotism of men like Rathenau and Harden. When Harden justified the anti-semitism of Stoecker in view of the evil of Jewish speculators and the unscrupulousness of the Jewish liberal press, it might seem generous on his part, but one suspects, as with his panegyric on Lueger, an attempt to curry favour. There was every good reason for Karl Kraus to attack the Jewish liberal press, yet again the venom in his hostility to Jewish journalists is suspect. The often savage feuds between Harden, Kraus, Kerr and other assimilated Jewish critics may indeed have been provoked by the irritation each felt at seeing his own image in the others. These were commonly shared attitudes. But there were also virulent anti-semites among the Jews. Weininger's frenzied attack on the Jews as a race in *Geschlecht und Charakter* (1903) represents a trend among intellectual Jews, a conviction of their inferiority that demonstrates a self-laceration of the most painful kind. He asserts that the Jew is incapable of veneration, of dignity, morality, true religious feeling and personality – claptrap that he culled from Wagner and other racists and that is of a type not unusual among oppressed minorities. His disgust is oddly qualified by a plea for full Jewish emancipation, on the grounds that, like the emancipation of negroes or of women, it is good for the soul of the emancipators. Weininger put an end to his life in 1903, but his fellow Viennese Arthur Trebitsch lived long enough to write many ferocious attacks on the Jews before he succumbed to persecution mania. From a wealthy assimilated Jewish family, brought up totally out of contact with Jewish traditions, Trebitsch repeated all the most vicious slanders about a Jewish world-conspiracy, the negative destructive Jewish mind etc., and at the same time supported the wildest ambitions of German imperialists. He, like Harden had the bitter experience during the Weimar Republic of being rejected and vilified as a Jew by the German nationalists he wished to serve. The strongly neurotic symptoms in Rathenau's vilification of the (Jewish) intellect in favour of the soul and the intuition, and in his own excessively voluble ratiocination, cannot be understood out of the context of the anti-semitism surrounding him from childhood, and his publications were the subject of constant hostile and envious comment long before he was assassinated as a Minister of the Republic in 1922.

Zionism spread in the first decade of the century, particularly among younger Jews, as a reaction against the self-mutilation that the desire for assimulation brought. For the cultured Jew, Zionism had a variety of meanings, from taking up agricultural labour in Palestine to the proud assertion of the spiritual and intellectual distinction of the Jewish people throughout the centuries. The essays in the volume *Vom Judentum*, issued in 1913 by the university Zionist group in Prague, show a typical diversity of views among German men of letters. Most – like Arnold Zweig, Moritz Goldstein, Moritz Heimann, Gustav Landauer and Max Brod – though proud of their Jewishness are also deeply attached to German culture. More devoted Zionists like Robert Weltsch speak less about the idea of Palestine than the need for Jewish self-affirmation, the restoration of Jewish pride and dignity through the spiritual reform of the Jewish community. The editor Hans Kohn, like Wassermann, sees Zionism in terms strikingly similar to the socio-cultural postulates of Stefan George, as the Jews' battle against 'die mechanisierende, entseelende, entgöttlichende Zweckhaftigkeit des Westens', so that it does not surprise one to find two notable George disciples, Wolfskehl and Erich Kahler, contributing to this volume.

The ambiguous position of the Jews was all the more acutely felt in view of their prominence in the musical, theatrical and literary worlds as producers, conductors, executants, editors, interpreters of German culture. It burst into public discussion in 1912 through an article, 'Deutsch-jüdischer Parnass' in the March issue of *Der Kunstwart* by Moritz Goldstein, the editor of Bong's *Goldene Klassiker Bibliothek,* a Jew devoted to German literature who was continually harassed by German resentment against the participation of Jews in editorial work of this type. It is not hard to see why *Der Kunstwart* published this article, since its tendency was nationalist and its literary critic, Bartels, a notorious anti-semite; more difficult to understand why Goldstein chose it. The article clearly formulates Goldstein's problem: 'We Jews administer the mental property of a people that denies us the right and competence to do so.' He is unable to find a solution, for while he admits that the only thing to do would be to leave Germany, he is too committed to German culture and the German nation to be able to abandon it. Many of the more sensitive Jewish writers felt the same dilemma. Kafka speaks of 'the usurpation of another's property' and characteristically counterposes 'the impossibility of not writing in German' to 'the impossibility of writing in German'. Walter Benjamin suffered from the same conflict. In such Jews there might naturally be a stronger sympathy for Zionism than in the more robust. Goldstein's article attracted indeed the warm approval of Zionists, as it did that of racists and 'Völkische', while it was vehemently attacked by assimilationists like Ernst Lissauer, whose devotion to Germany was such that he was ready to deny that the Jews were a 'people'. In a later review of this great controversy (*Yearbook of the Leo Baeck Institute*, II, 1957), Goldstein notes that though it occurred at a time of relaxed tension the issue was explosive. In the August *Kunstwart* the editor, Avenarius, tried to review all the arguments fairly and dispassionately, but a note of desperation creeps in, and he hints ominously at the unavoidability of undefined violent measures.

Most cultural assimilation took place unconsciously, and some Jewish works allow us to see the process. Wassermann's early stories deal mainly with the problem of the Jew, but in *Der Moloch*, 1903, we find a curious shift of interest, in spite of the fact that Wassermann never lost a Jewish selfconsciousness. The novel begins with the abduction of the daughter of a provincial Jewish pedlar to a Catholic convent, and describes the brutality of peasants and artisans, mainly Polish and Czech, towards the Jewish family. A young Christian landowner intervenes on behalf of the suffering family, only to find that he can make no headway against the evasions of state officials and the entrenched power of the Church. But the central interest of the book turns away from the Jewish family to the young man and his corruption through Viennese society – a typical switch of interest from the social problem of the Jews to the psychological-moral problem of the Christian. A similar adaptation takes place in Gustav Meyrink's mystery thriller *Der Golem* (1915), though we are kept here in the confines of the old Prague ghetto. By romanticizing the Jews of the ghetto, into which he injects a Hoffmannesque mystery and terror, Meyrink is actually adopting the perspective of the non-Jewish outsider. In general, most Jewish writers sought in their imaginative works – like their non-Jewish colleagues – to despecify their experience, to find generalized or symbolic forms that obliterate the specifically Jewish elements; there is very little in this period that approaches the direct concern with Jewish life characteristic of American Jewish writers in the 1960s.

Schnitzler is an outstanding exception. His early plays and stories, that established a myth of Viennese life, bear, it is true, hardly any Jewish stamp or even reference. One may well be surprised, on reading, say, his letters to Hofmannsthal or his autobiography, to find a continuous and painful awareness of the position of the Jew in Vienna (incidentally Hofmannsthal, much further removed from any Jewish community than Schnitzler, shows himself in this correspondence much more sympathetic to the Jewish problem than in his letters to L. von Andrian, though this aristocratic diplomat had a Jewish antecedent in Meyerbeer). But Schnitzler's *Der Weg ins Freie* of 1908 had, as Soergel notes in *Dichtung und Dichter der Zeit* (1911), a new theme. The thread of the novel is a typical temporary affair between a non-Jewish baron and a middle-class girl, but the most complex and weighty of themes submerges its delicate nuances. Since Georg von Wergenthin is a composer he needs cultural friends almost totally different from his diplomat brother's, and these friends are all Jews, writers, music-lovers, doctors, social democratic politicians. Through the medium of Georg's amiability and sympathy, that never deepen into commitment, Schnitzler is able to present a vast variety of Jewish (middle-class) attitudes, largely through the conversation of Jews themselves: the wealthy and the hard-up, the talented and the bogus, those longing to be accepted by Christian society and especially the aristocracy, and those bitterly turning towards Zionism, the compromisers and the challengers, the converted and the orthodox, Austrian patriots and sceptics who can imagine the rekindling of the fires of the Inquisition, liberals rejected by their party and socialists still believing in theirs, writers torn between private and public issues, symbolists and realists. No Jew can escape the general pressure, and in their internecine antagonisms they are still held together by this common fate, which distorts even the most candid simplicity, so that to Georg they may seem too pushing or too reserved, too enthusiastic or too cold, too devoted (to a person or to music and art) or too egoistic, negative or cynical, too well-dressed or too badly dressed, always 'too' something. Schnitzler's novel is the most remarkable exposition in this period of the psychological effects of their social position on the Jews.

Schnitzler's play, *Professor Bernhardi* (1912), places the professional Jew in the centre of the stage. Bernhardi, an able and conscientious doctor, is ousted from his post as director of a clinic by a combination of personal envy and clerical anti-semitism. Refusing to make a cowardly accommodation, he also refuses to align himself with those who wish to turn his case into a representative, political issue. Though Bernhardi is rehabilitated in the end, it is characteristic of Schnitzler that while on the one hand Bernhardi appears as a brave and independent character, on the other he is uneasily aware that he uses his professional devotion and commitment to shield himself from the wider political implications of his 'case'.

It seems strange that the George circle, with its virulent antagonism to liberalism and the bourgeoisie, was not only free of anti-semitism but counted Jews among its most prominent members – Wolfskehl, Gundolf, Berthold Vallentin, Salin, Erich Kahler and the gifted women Sabine Lepsius, Gertrud Kantorowicz and Edith Landmann. It seems that one of the grounds of George's rupture with Klages and Schuler in 1903 was their demand for the exclusion of Jews from the circle. The continuing attraction of George's art for Jews must in part have lain in its élitism, which offered a spiritual community that ignored or looked with contempt on the hindrances and humiliations that practical life imposed on Jews. Membership of the 'circle', of course, did not mean a precise and dogmatic discipleship, and even those closest to George, Wolfskehl and Gundolf differed greatly in their attitude to their own Jewishness. Wolfskehl was always proudly aware of it, in spite of a temporary intimacy with a ferocious anti-semite like Schuler, and he seems to have felt no contradiction between his ardent German patriotism and his Jewish allegiance. Gundolf on the other hand kept any acknowledgement of his Jewishness so scrupulously out of his work that one suspects a profound unease, which may account for the demonstrative Germanism of his *Shakespeare und der deutsche Geist* (1911) and for his obstinate chauvinism during the war. The unbridled and unjust abhorrence of Shylock expressed in his later book on Shakespeare betrays an almost neurotic fear of being identified with the race from which Shylock sprang, so much so that he overlooks the claim Shylock makes to being human.

Though there was a stream of anti-semitic vituperation in 'völkische' journals and from a few critics like Bartels, there is on the whole little direct anti-semitism in the non-Jewish literature – an abominable term, since it falsely suggests that to be non-Jewish had artistic significance. Even the regionalists, with their propensity towards idealization of racial purity and blonde nordics, Frenssen, Lienhart, Löns or Burte, are not distinctively anti-semitic; the artist-hero of Löns' *Das zweite Gesicht* recognizes in his Jewish doctor a homelessness like his own, and makes him his friend. In the lower reaches of literature pamphlets were of course sometimes dressed up as novels. Arthur Dinter's *Die Sünde wider das Blut* (1918), that reached best-seller status, records all the anti-semitic nightmares of the pollution of German blood by the 'vampire' Jew, reinforced by pseudo-scientific notes. What is much more common, as in all European countries, is a type of derogatory comment that betrays insensitivity and thoughtless prejudice, or a fictional Jewish character who, though copied from actual life, yet because of the typifying function of art seems to implicate the whole race (it is the same in Dickens or Trollope). A Jew appears in M. G. Conrad's *Was die Isar rauscht* as the typical modern materialist, the representative of 'Americanization'. In Holz's *Sozialaristokraten* a Jewish journalist of many aliases represents the gutter press, and persuades a literary lion to abandon his liberal affiliations and join the anti-semites (it seems farcical, but alas there were such Jews). In Alberti's *Die Alten und die Jungen* a Jewish financier and his family are corrupt in morals and business (Alberti, himself a Jew, was as savage as any anti-semite against Jewish speculators and jobbers). While Bernhard Kellermann in *Der Tunnel* usually distinguishes sharply between the private and public morality of the entrepreneurs he describes, a Jewish financial wizard shows himself to be both a profligate and a reckless speculator. In all these cases, the nature of imaginative literature makes us ask, are these people corrupt because they are Jews? is that what we are supposed to infer?

The problem can be illustrated in particular works of Heinrich and Thomas Mann. Heinrich, whose early political sympathies went towards an anti-bourgeois élitism, was during 1895-6 literary editor of *Das Zwanzigste Jahrhundert*, a nationalist periodical not without a touch of anti-semitism. His first important novel, *Im Schlaraffenland* (1900), betrays this affiliation though it anticipates his later social criticism too. Its theme is the corruption of newspapers and journalists by the bankers who own them, and the ferocious and lurid satire is directed against a tightly-knit group that worships wealth, revels in luxury and vice, ruthlessly exploits its power, and at the same time flaunts progressive ideas and enjoys the luxury of a bad conscience. A modern reader might not recognize these financiers and editors as Jews; their names and an occasional hint would be sufficient for the contemporary reader, but one can believe that Mann wished to steer clear of vulgar anti-semitism. But the problem was: if the Berlin world of finance and the press, with its misuse of power, its pretences and corruption, was to be satirized, how could an author avoid seeming anti-semitic, since this world was so dominated by Jews? When George and his friends, Wolfskehl, Gundolf and Vallentin among them, issued (for instance in *Jahrbuch für die geistige Bewegung*) their indignant blasts against the modern press and theatre, they could avoid an anti-semitic note only because they kept to very general statements.

Of course, for rabid anti-semites like Bartels, certain attitudes were proof of Jewishness. Thus both the democratic note in Heinrich Mann's works after *Zwischen den Rassen* of 1907, and the refined sophistication of his brother Thomas, perhaps also the fact that Thomas married a Jewish girl, led Bartels to call them both 'Jewish writers'. When Thomas protested, Bartels produced a typically devious acknowledgement. In his *Die deutsche Dichtung der Gegenwart* (1910) he writes: 'The brothers Mann ... are, according to Thomas's statement, no Jews, but their art also seems essentially Jewish' – the perfidy of this 'also'! Stefan George was a victim of the same malice. But before this Thomas Mann had run into difficulties, in part of his own making.

Soon after his marriage to the daughter of the wealthy Professor Pringsheim, an assimilated Jew who with his whole family was profoundly devoted to German culture, Mann wrote his Novelle *Wälsungenblut* and sent it for publication in the January 1906 number of *Die neue Rundschau*. It is a story of a wealthy commercial family, the son and daughter of which, refined Wagnerian sensualists, decadents, find in an incestuous relationship the satisfaction of their narcissism. The Jewish editor of the *Rundschau*, Oscar Bie, drew Mann's attention to what he considered to be the stylistic inappropriateness of two vulgar vindictive Yiddish words in the son's concluding comment, which incidentally gave the only hint that it was a 'Jewish story', as Mann called it in a letter. Mann on consideration decided to eliminate the Yiddish expressions. But then he went further, it seems because of some objection from his father-in-law, and withdrew the emended Novelle altogether – he did not publish it till after the war. In a letter to his brother of 1906 he wrote that he had been disturbed by some gossip that he had written 'a violently anti-semitic Novelle' in which he had compromised the family of his wife, and admitted that on re-reading it, he found that the 'innocent' work was not such as to refute the gossip. For that reason he had withdrawn it. If the incident does not redound to the credit of Mann's sensitivity in the first place, it does illustrate the unhappiness of the whole social position of the Jews. If a writer created in his fiction a Jewish figure or a Jewish setting, thinking of it as symbolic of a general situation, the social atmosphere was such that it would inevitably be taken as specifically and representatively Jewish. In the case of *Wälsungenblut* the reader, if aware that the family is Jewish, inevitably sees the Tristan-and-Isolde sensuality, decadence, luxury, incest as typical of assimilated upstart Jews, rather than as a potentiality of the contemporary bourgeoisie.

The object of anti-semitic movements was to assert the genetic peculiarity of the Jews and thus to shove on to them the responsibility for the pressures, unease, disasters of modern industrial society. Though it is impossible to find a simple definition of the Jewish community in its dispersal in Western society in this period, especially since many of the immigrant Jews were only now emerging from centuries of oppression during which they had survived only through their strong religious and communal solidarity, it is roughly true to say that, far from representing a contrast to non-Jewish culture, the Jews on the whole were becoming markedly assimilated. They themselves, and even in their uneasy situation in the host countries, mirror in a particular way the nature and tensions of modern bourgeois society. We may consider, indeed, that it was their assimilation, social and cultural, more than their separateness, that made anti-semitism a powerful force, for they were thus inevitably involved in those processes that called forth the bewilderments, resentments, and anxieties of modern industrial society.

It is this basic cause that never allowed anti-semitism to die out. That the Jews played so large a part in Austrian and German culture, in literature, the theatre, music, painting and architecture is, for instance, evidence of a remarkable cultural assimilation. Yet, though it was not at all unusual to recognize this fact, the prominence and insidiousness of anti-Jewish feeling and anti-semitic ideology prevented a natural ease of relationship between Jews and non-Jews. The burden of Schnitzler's *Der Weg ins Freie* is the realization of the Baron, reflecting on his relations with his Jewish friends, 'that pure ("reine") relationships between separate pure men (he means simple, spontaneous relationships, without calculation) cannot prosper in an atmosphere of folly, injustice and insincerity'. In spite of this great hindrance and the social pressure towards anti-semitism, however, the world of literature and the arts was much less infected by anti-semitic feeling than almost any other, paralleled in this only perhaps by the socialist movement. The opinion of Christian Morgenstern, a writer of wide and varied sympathies, an admirer of Nietzsche and Lagarde, of Tolstoy and Hauptmann, deeply concerned over the future of Germany, is fair and not untypical. Morgenstern came into touch with many different people in his work as editor and critic, and particularly with many theatre people, which meant many Jews. When his old friend Kayssler, a distinguished actor and producer, allowed his anger with Alfred Kerr, the critic, to burst into anti-semitism, Morgenstern in a letter vigorously reproved him. Kayssler is wrong, he writes: Kerr is 'geistig', and only what is opposed to the higher concerns of the spirit may be attacked. The Germans, Morgenstern continues, fail to come up to the level of the Jews in 'Geistigkeit'; take Reinhardt, the producer, for instance (though we know that Morgenstern on occasions sharply criticized Reinhardt). And he adds that he himself is kept alive (in body as in spirit) almost without exception through Jews.

5
Nation and State

Nationalism and Imperialism

German nationalism had arisen in the face of two challenges, one foreign, particularly French, nationalism, and the other the authority of the German princes. So, though nationalists dreamed of a powerful, self-assertive nation, early nationalism was associated with liberalism and wished to limit the power of government altogether, for which it found a substitute in the idea of a mighty but shapeless force, the popular will. How uneasily such concepts fitted the actualities of politics was sadly revealed during the course of the 1848 Revolution, when the liberal representatives of the popular will turned in their majority against the attempts of the subject peoples of Poland, Hungary, Bohemia and Italy to achieve self-determination, and called on the armies of the feudal states of Prussia and Austria to re-assert German dominion. With the great Prussian victories of 1866 and the German victory of 1870, this dichotomy came, for the great majority, to an end. Patriotism, nationalism, fusing with Prussianism, now had its concrete object, the Reich as established, and lost any subversive implication. It had been a product in a very literal sense of the middle classes, and in general in its new guise it remained so. The aristocracy retained from older separatist allegiances its loyalty to feudal conceptions of authority, as did the Catholic church, though never allowing hostility to the Reich to reach a critical point. At the other end of the scale, Social Democracy denounced the national state as the instrument of the ruling class and was pledged to abolish it, though this attitude necessarily remained abstract as long as all practical politics moved within the framework of the nation. Indeed, theoretically and practically, the nation turned out to be the mightiest instrument the bourgeoisie created in the course of its self-emancipation, though an instrument which developed undreamed of characteristics.

Treitschke, the Berlin professor of history, a former Liberal, was the typical exponent of the new nationalism of the Reich. Throughout his work there breathes the strident self-assertion of a nation long humiliated that has at last caught up with its ancient rivals, a self-assertion that is often bullying and bellicose. It shows the peculiar transformation of liberal nationalism, since for Treitschke the balance of forces achieved in the Reich constitution was a final historic fulfilment of national aspirations, and hence he denounced all the advocates of social or constitutional reform as traitors to the nation. Throughout the period this is the most widespread and common form of nationalism, that in effect identifies the nation with the particular government and social hierarchy; for this reason the censorship prevented, and the law punished, the disparagement of statesmen and other persons and even classes (the law and army) in authority.

The enthusiasm for power, Realpolitik, and for its supreme practitioner Bismarck, often in its virulence betrays among this older generation of historians and publicists like Treitschke and Sybel a consciousness of the failure of the earlier liberal and democratic ideals. Not all disguised their loss under a Treitschkean truculence. Friedrich Meinecke of the younger generation could not hide his regrets, and in his book on Boyen (1896-9) spoke of the grievous problems and uncertainties that the achievements of 1870 had brought. Though in his *Weltbürgertum und Nationalstaat* (1907) Meinecke asserted the legitimacy and necessity of the power-state, of Bismarck's policy and the hegemony of Prussia in the Reich, his regret for the universal cultural humanism of the earlier Germany is apparent. Yet this sort of nostalgia made his realistic acceptance of the status quo even more persuasive, and it certainly lent weight to his support of the war, for he was to claim that with the national unity of 1914 the power state had acquired an ethical purpose and the Prussian oligarchy had merged into a truly national democracy. Only after the war was Meinecke to castigate his generation for seeing in the state only the principle of power and for exulting in the cult of power, both internally and in its international relations.

The Treitschkean type of nationalism was very different from the étatism of Hegel. It emerged out of an impassioned feeling of a national brotherhood and a common destiny, an enthusiastic readiness for self-sacrifice, that unforeseeably flooded Germany in 1870 and again in 1914. Bismarck had managed to canalize these torrential emotions, but for any authority they remained a potential instrument and an incalculable threat. In a political theorist like Treitschke, who shared both the respect for authority and the emotional exaltation, the conflict between the two occasionally appears clearly through the bluster. Normally, for instance, Treitschke expounded the view that the national spirit is supremely embodied in the great men who create the nation's history. But in 1880, in the course of the controversy over the Jews that an anti-semitic article of his inflamed, we find him justifying anti-semitism as the expression of 'the instinct of the masses' and 'the Germanic folk (Volk) feeling', typical symptoms of the demagogic glorification of irrational mass-emotions. In his lectures, till his death in 1896, Treitschke abused liberals and socialists in the most vulgar terms and played up to the most vulgar prejudices of his students, though he sufficiently belonged to an older generation not to abandon his professed devotion to the Prussian ideal of discipline and service.

Beside this nationalism there arose in the 1870s a new and in some ways rival nationalism. The united nation the liberals had dreamed of turned out to be socially riven, class antagonisms were exacerbated by boom and by slump, and Bismarck's change of political partners in 1878, his rejection of the liberals, and the adoption in 1880 of the Anti-Socialist laws asserted in political form the disunity of the nation. A new nationalism, whose leading exponent was Lagarde, saw liberalism as the cause of disunity, and criticized the Bismarckian Reich for the concessions to liberalism embodied in its constitution. Lagarde had in earlier days admired Disraeli's aim of creating a popular basis for Toryism, but his dismay over parliamentarianism in the Reich and the limitations set to the power of the executive and to Prussia led him to extremes. The essays collected in his *Deutsche Schriften* (1878-81) are the first manifestos of a doctrine later to be called 'revolutionary conservatism'. They constitute a rejection of the Reich constitution and all traditional conservative thinking of the 'throne and altar' type, as well as of liberalism and democracy. Recognizing that it was the economic power of the middle class that had undermined authoritarian government, Lagarde seeks a way to control industrial, capitalistic development, and though he

was an impassioned believer in national expansion he saw territorial gain as a means for peasant settlement, not for industrial or
mercantile exploitation. His radical rejection meant that he was
less interested in specific political questions than in creating a new
set of basic political images, summed up in his 'German Faith'.
An authoritarian principle is, he states, inherent in the Germanic
peoples, dedicated to power and the 'heroic' virtues, and he
develops a concept of the nation, the Volk, as an organic entity
with an in-built leadership structure that challenges both the
liberal idea of the political nation and the static conservative-
clerical image. On this basis Lagarde is unremitting in his attacks
on the Christian ethic of love and tolerance because of its levelling
or pacifistic implications; he attacks the Catholic church as an
international organization, and the Protestant church as a time-
serving lackey of established state authority.

All anti-semitic groups and parties in Germany and Austria
shared the main conceptions of Lagarde, that is, all were intensely
nationalistic, expansionist, fascinated by a vague image of a
homogeneous Volk that expressed their hostility to the actual
social order as well as to liberal or Marxist perspectives. Since
such groups were deeply involved in practical issues of daily
politics and concerned to advance the material interests of their
members, and since the 'völkische' ideology is usually couched in
very emotional, inflammatory, and abstract terms, it is not
possible to reduce it to clear notions; indeed its vagueness contributed to its evocative power. In *Rembrandt als Erzieher*
Langbehn supplements his indiscriminate invective against a
society poisoned by liberalism and materialism with a dream of a
'secret Kaiser' who will come to restore a united Volk. Friedrich
Lange's *Reines Deutschtum* outlines a more political 'völkische'
nationalism that is based on Prussian authoritarianism but pro-
poses an alliance of the leadership class, the aristocracy, with the
working class, against capitalism and liberalism, one of many
echoes of a Bismarckian theme. Lange's anti-semitism did not
prevent the Neue Freie Volksbühne from performing his anti-
capitalist, anti-clerical play *Der Nächste* in Berlin in 1893. Many
other variants are to be found in a movement that combined the
most soaring and extravagant national idealism with the crudest
envy and greed.

The conflicts between anti-semitic 'völkische' parties and the
conservative parties abated after the middle of the 1890s, and

both were merged in the new imperialism. This new nationalism, common to the great European nations, was orientated towards foreign expansion. It created for itself an abstract authoritarian ideal of power and service (Carlyle), with an ethical mission to extend civilization and educate the backward races – Kipling's poem *The White Man's Burden* was written in 1899. H. S. Chamberlain's *Die Grundlagen des 19 Jahrhunderts* (1899), adapting the dynamism of racialists to the imperialistic purposes of the Reich leadership, typically formulates German political ambitions within the framework of a grandiose cultural philosophy. All the great civilizations, all the spiritual and cultural values of the past are ascribed to the Aryans, and it is made clear that the modern Germans and the modern Reich are heirs to this great destiny, in respect both to its inherent authoritarian political structure and to its national power. Thus, in this period, the term 'Deutschnational' comes to signify not simply a nationalist or an imperialist, but also one who is pledged to authoritarian government. All civilizations are held to be the result of the dominance of one race, the Aryans, over others, and we find even a Rathenau drawing the conclusion that the disintegration of the 'natural' ruling élite in the bourgeois industrial age threatens civilization itself. These tenets were widespread, and gave rise in the tense pre-war and war years to a vast number of books justifying war as the instrument of the German mission to rescue or renew civilization. They were most comprehensively and ruthlessly formulated by Oswald Spengler in *Untergang des Abendlandes* (volume I, 1918), conceived in the euphoria of German military successes and greeting the new epoch of barbaric Caesarism centred in Germany.

But the new imperialism also satisfied certain liberal cravings, as it did in England, where it was believed by some that national expansion offered an opportunity for broader democratic rights. In his inaugural lecture of 1895 Max Weber discovered in the imperial destiny of Germany, its dynamic expansion abroad, a supreme purpose for his generation, equivalent to what unification had meant to the preceding generation. This liberal imperialism, even though 'it lacked the chauvinistic momentum of the Deutschnationale, is at least as significant a symptom of the times as the propaganda of the flamboyant pressure-groups like the Pan-German Association, founded in 1886 but effective only after 1894, or the Navy League, founded on the British model in

1898. Weber himself, though a man of liberal, democratic leanings, justified the social reforms he pursued explicitly on national rather than moral or humanitarian grounds, that is, with the argument that they would integrate the nation and increase its power. Theoretically in *Politik als Beruf*, and practically, he sought to eliminate ethical values from politics and to view the state (as he did economics or science) as an autonomous organization whose sole criterion was power. Thus for long, though he despised the imperial politics of the Kaiser and had little sympathy with the Prussian aristocracy, he thought no other class was fitted to lead Germany and hence accepted the authoritarian structure of the Reich and the hegemony of Prussia. His democratic theory and activity developed only when he became convinced during the war that the ruling class had failed and that democracy would provide the leadership fitted to restore, consolidate and enlarge German power.

Moderate and genuinely liberal men like Meinecke and Simmel also saw in national ambitions and international conflict a law of nature and an inspiring reality. Clearly such views might easily provoke dilemmas. One such is illustrated by Weber's attitude to the Poles. One of his earliest pieces of research charged the Prussian Junkers with increasing the productivity of their estates at the expense of the German settlers, so that they promoted a steady inflow of cheap Polish labour and a consequent growing polonization of the countryside. At this time Weber was ready to deny Prussian Poles essential rights in order to prevent the emergence of a 'Polish Ireland'. When during the war he found that suppression only intensified Polish nationalism, he inclined to halfhearted schemes for granting the Poles cultural autonomy, in the hope of enlisting their support in the eastward expansion of German power against Russia. It is a story well-known to all imperialist nations: Weber denied to the Poles the national self-determination and the democratic rights to which he as a German was deeply pledged.

The most determined theoretical effort to reconcile nationalism, imperialism, and social reform was made by Friedrich Naumann, who was close to and deeply influenced by Weber. His democratic leanings brought him to sever his early association with Stoecker and the Christian-social party, and in his National-Sozialer Verein (1896-1903) he combined socialistic tendencies with imperialistic objectives, adopting Weber's thesis that a self-confident, expanding nation could provide the working class with the opportunity and inspiration to mature to full political responsibility. Naumann's weekly *Die Hilfe*, founded in 1895, thus joined religious and social concerns with imperialistic projects like colonial expansion and a stronger army and fleet. A most successful publicist, Naumann was not a successful politician. He seemed to express the ineffectual hopes of many. His most popular political work was *Mitteleuropa*, written in 1915 in full confidence in a German victory, and typically presenting the two sides of his policy. On the one hand he envisages Germany's future as the dominant powerhouse of a central European bloc, ruling the destiny of the whole mighty power-base. On the other hand he insists that the Germans must drop their racialist arrogance and accept the lesser nationalities and the Jews on terms of equality, so far as absolute necessity allows. In internal affairs he advocates state participation in economic life, municipal enterprise, trade union participation in social administration, just as he supports industrial expansion, because of the political as well as economic advantages accruing to the working class.

Imperialism was, then, fed from many sources. It might seem surprising that Nietzsche, with his outspoken contempt for German and other nationalisms, was enlisted by so many nationalists, but it was not illogical. His élitism, his praise of war and barbarism, his hatred of the Christian virtues, obviously served their purpose; and also his Europeanism was by no means pacifist or internationalist. He dreamed of a warlike Europe, organized internally for the conquest of the world, and it was easy for Germans to imagine themselves in the role of the founders and leaders of a new Europe.

At the same time, there was a steady stream of criticism of imperialism and war-ideology. A pacifist organization maintained in the periodical *Die Waffen Nieder* internationalist ideals, and liberal papers like *Die neue Rundschau, März, Morgen, Simplicissimus* and *Jugend* kept up a constant criticism of colonial misrule and imperialist pretensions, often bitterly attacking German colonialism in South-West Africa as well as British imperialism. Liberal newspapers like the *Berliner Tageblatt* joined from time to time in disapproval of the more aggressive actions of the government, for instance the warlike demonstration over Agadir in 1911 or the Kaiser's sabre-rattling, so much indeed that, when this newspaper like others swept wholeheartedly

behind the war effort in 1914, it was reviled from the right for
hypocrisy and from the left for treachery. It is impossible to
evaluate the political significance of the anti-imperialist feeling.
Among the Social Democrats, where it was enshrined in doctrine
and repeated resolutions, it showed itself powerless before the
national emotions of 1914, and in bourgeois circles, for instance
in *Die neue Rundschau*, it was accompanied by despairing admissions of its impotence to stem in the least the tide of public feeling
and the trend of national policies in the years before 1914. It is
clear that this ineffectiveness was due in part to the capacity of
human beings to nurse flattering 'convictions' in their minds,
which pay tribute to their conscience without affecting their
behaviour. In the most articulate section of the nation, the
writers, there is much evidence of ambiguity of this type, though
at the same time the relative inconspicuousness of imperialistic
ideas in literature and art may be taken as evidence of attitudes
widespread in the population as a whole.

Art, Literature, and the Nation

D. F. Strauss was expressing a common prejudice when in 1872
he claimed that the German political and military successes
proved the superiority of German culture, and if Nietzsche's
crushing response was known to few, it became a standing cliché
to call for an art and literature that should be equivalent in rank
to Germany's practical achievements. Public authorities understood this in a simple way, commissioning monuments, paintings,
buildings that would enhance the national selfconsciousness and
creating what Franz Servaes called 'a national-patriotic monument industry'. Such projects aroused excited public discussion in
newspapers, the Reichstag and other representative bodies.
Where public money was involved, committees were often
appointed to select designs and recommend an artist, and in a
number of cases the young Kaiser overrode the committees – for
instance in respect both to the site and the artist for the Kaiser
Wilhelm memorial. His interventions repeatedly provoked criticism, and even a loyalist periodical like *Der Kunstwart* deplored
the servile compliance of public authorities and artists to the
Kaiser's wishes. Such discontent became most outspoken in the
extensive arguments over the Kaiser's favourite project, the
Siegesallee in Berlin, with its crowded and theatrical figures of the

historic leaders of Prussia-Germany, on the buttons of whose uniforms, a malicious rumour suggested, the heads of the great scholars and scientists might find their due place. All over Germany national monuments sprouted, giant figures of Bismarck and the old Kaiser and Germania; Romain Rolland visiting Düsseldorf in 1898 notes in his diary with surprise the large number of statues of generals. The general stylelessness of these monuments was a constant theme of criticism, and if any national style did evolve, it was that which reached its height in the Leipzig Völkerschlachtdenkmal of 1913, a massive, almost brutal monumentality, obliterating individuality from the huge figures, and given a mythical elevation through the medieval trappings and the attitudes of prayer and submission to fate that enhance the glorification of power.

A national industry in painting came into being too, led by the virtuoso Anton von Werner and Karl von Piloty, with their great canvases of the outstanding events in the foundation of the Reich, that were hung in public buildings and, in countless copies, in private homes. Even in painters less engrossed by immediate public events, like Feuerbach, Kaulbach, Lenbach or the Swiss Böcklin, there is a predilection for great symbolical figures against a wide background that utter a more subtle consciousness of power. A really profound national symbolism was created only in music, by Wagner in the *Ring des Nibelungen*, a work that was conceived and largely completed (with the exception of *Götterdämmerung*) in the 1850s. Wagner's heroic figures are not triumphant but laden from the beginning with brooding and foreboding. The imagination of the cultured German bourgeoisie was throughout the period engrossed by Wagner's work, in which it found its mythical self-projection, the consciousness of greatness and power, an awed feeling of destiny linking the remote past and the future and enhanced by an anticipation of doom that also gives Kipling's *Recessional* its peculiar solemnity. The depth and power of Wagner's work are the greater because of the absence of specific and contemporary references such as disfigure so much of the nationalist art of the times.

The literary market after 1870 was swamped by patriotic verse, stories, plays celebrating German victories, rejoicing in the superiority of German culture, and excavating from the German past situations that prefigured the coming of the Reich. The great majority of writers contributed to this flood, forgotten names like

Geibel, Wilbrandt, Redwitz, Jordan, Jensen, Graf Schack, Julius Wolff. Most of these writers exalted Prussia as the spiritual as well as military progenitor of the Reich, and Scherer's authoritative *History of German Literature* (1882) made out the Prussian kings to have been consistent patrons of literary culture, provoking Franz Mehring's *Die Lessing Legende* (1892), one of the most devastating attacks on the 'Byzantinism' of Wilhelmine academics. The national cause was often identified with Protestantism, particularly in the Kulturkampf period, and the Luther quatercentenary of 1883 elicited numerous efforts to enroll Luther as a precursor of Bismarck. For these celebrations 'festival' dramas were written and a theatre designed with the object of creating a popular art that would overcome the separation of stage and auditorium, actor and spectator, the cultured and the simple man, and thus mirror the unity of the nation. This feeling of the misrelationship between culture and the community was to find expression in many forms in the ensuing decades, but it was not allayed by these stereotyped pageant plays written in pseudo-popular doggerel.

The new nationalist enthusiasm found its most popular and lasting author in the schoolmaster Felix Dahn, who in the 1870s and 1880s wrote a series of historical novels on the ancient Germans (e.g. *Ein Kampf um Rom* and *Attila*), in which on a large historical background and in the midst of warlike exploits a series of Gothic kings, massively yet not unskilfully characterized, lay the foundations of a German Reich to come. In the 1890s Karl May's stories began to provide an exotic, more thrilling, and coarser counterpart to Dahn's kings, Teutons of one sort or another who make a forceful way through remote countries (then attracting imperialistic attention), asserting order and justice with a heavy hand and a complete confidence in their moral superiority and mission. *Ein Kampf um Rom* and several of May's adventure stories have since that time fed the imaginations of schoolboys, for whom they constitute the harmless fantasies of Leonhard Frank's *Die Räuberbande*, and a perhaps not so harmless substratum of imperialistic assumptions. But Dahn was, and May still is, a best-seller among adults, and we find even Holz and Hauptmann testifying to their admiration for Dahn, an admiration the reformer Loth of *Vor Sonnenaufgang* shares.

Some of the older writers, like Raabe and the Swiss Keller, were appalled by the materialism of the new Reich and the vulgarity of its literature, and their novels become increasingly critical of the values of the new society. Others, like Paul Heyse and the Swiss C. F. Meyer, also repelled by the vulgarity around, retreat from directly contemporary themes and in their narrative work, very much like the better painters, shape the fate of proud isolated individuals. Their preference for Renaissance characters and the compressed and highly stylized form of the Novelle demonstrates an élitist trend, a disregard for the common man, that links them with Nietzsche. The Naturalist revolt was at first largely directed against this élitism, its concern with style, and the social irrelevance of its themes.

The Naturalist recall of literature to social and contemporary themes meant a more critical attitude towards the prevalent nationalism of the 1880s, and was often attacked as unpatriotic and subversive. Yet this literary revolution was borne along on a proud consciousness of the unity and strength of Germany, and nearly all the early Naturalist programmes repeat the stereotyped ambition of creating a literature adequate to the great political and military achievements. Heinrich Hart's reminiscences tell us that it was the victories of 1870 that gave the stimulus for the new literature he vaguely dreamed of, and one of his first editorial successes was the publication of Wildenbruch's as yet unknown patriotic plays. The *Kritische Waffengänge* (1882-4) were vibrantly patriotic. The new realism preached by the Harts was to come from the 'Germanic folk-soul' and would it was believed enhance the national consciousness; they even went so far as to call on Bismarck to take the arts, particularly the theatre, under the wing of the government. M. G. Conrad and his paper *Die Gesellschaft* similarly placed the modernist literary revolution in a nationalist setting, Conrad defending Zola on the grounds that pitiless truthfulness, the destruction of illusions, were a precondition of the restoration of the French nation after the disasters of 1870. In Germany likewise, he thought, realism – Conrad like the Harts constantly uses adjectives like 'erdfrisch', 'quellfrisch', to qualify realism – would consolidate the nation and strengthen its purposes. Hermann Conradi, one of Conrad's ablest contributors, a Naturalist who wrote a remarkably perceptive interpretation of the modern obsession with the satanic, demonic, bestial in man, constantly spoke of the aim of stimulating the feeling of nationhood, and naively enough called for more historical plays on national themes. Karl Bleibtreu had written plays of this kind before his sudden conversion to Naturalism.

The accession of Kaiser Wilhelm II in 1888 gave a new impulse to nationalist feeling, particularly because of the promise of social reform. Thus Conrad, Conradi, and Hauptmann among others were enthusiastic for the young 'social Kaiser' and an era of 'democratic Caesarism'. For the artist-hero of Alberti's *Die Alten und die Jungen* (1889) the new Kaiser embodies his ideals of patriotism, love, honour etc., and inspires him to renew the battle against the materialist and philistine bourgeoisie. The idea of a Reich patronage of literature recurred, to be quelled by Holz's scathing ridicule of 'Prussian mandarins'. The bitter social criticism of Felix Holländer's *Jesus und Judas* (1891) is allayed at the end by the radiant hope born from the lapsing of the Anti-Socialist laws. The patriotic *Der Kunstwart* could find Dahn's *Attila* too chauvinistic, but saluted Sudermann's *Die Ehre* as the masterpiece all patriots had been waiting for (because of a reconciliation of the social classes through an ethos that is in fact dubious and spurious).

The marriage of nationalism and social reform had only a short honeymoon and its failure was all the clearer because of the patronage of the Kaiser, himself so identified with nation and government. He interfered in the award of literary prizes like the Schiller prize, vetoing candidates on political grounds, just as he kept Liebermann, the friend of the Naturalists, out of the presidency of the Academy of Arts. He publicly jeered at *plein air* painting as 'factory work and gutter art'. He was likely to call any writer or artist who described the actual circumstances of the times an 'anarchist', and favoured only the most insipid and trivial conformism. Though the political opinions of writers, even within so-called 'schools' like the Naturalists or the Expressionists, were various and often indefinite, there was almost unanimous anger or shame over the Kaiser's self-confidently proclaimed tastes.

Hauptmann's position is fairly typical of his generation. Brought up a devout Bismarckian, he tells in his reminiscences of the disintegration of the great Germanic figure he built in his studio, that cured him of his ambition to be a sculptor. Social criticism predominates in his Naturalist plays, though Loth, the idealist of *Vor Sonnenaufgang*, is a compendium of nationalist ideals. Yet, because of the satire of the Amtsvorsteher in *Der*

Biberpelz (1893), Harden, himself a critic of Wilhelmine trends, charged Hauptmann with 'anarcho-socialism'. It is significant that Hauptmann's historical play *Florian Geyer* (1895) was a resounding failure. It is set in the Luther period that served nationalist writers so well, and the play embodied Hauptmann's dream of what might constitute a truly united nation. Geyer offers his patriotic devotion to a just society that will overrule the separatist interests of princes and aristocracy, will assure freedom of opinion and equality before the law to Jews as well as Christian sectarians; at the same time he repudiates the class ideology of the have-nots. Perhaps four years earlier this play would have had a resounding success; in 1895 audiences no longer believed in the combination of democratic radicalism and patriotism, and did not feel for Geyer's tragedy. During the later 1890s both these themes more or less disappear from high literature, which turns to private experiences and non-realistic forms.

Of course, many works that lack any explicit nationalistic theme display perhaps incidentally a nationalist prejudice. Wherever Polish characters appear in Naturalist or near-Naturalist literature, the assumption of a racial or national inferiority to the Germans makes itself felt – in Halbe's *Jugend* or *Mutter Erde*, in Holz's *Sozialaristokraten*, in Helene Böhlau's *Der Rangierbahnhof* (1895), where the unreliability of Polish windbags is partly redeemed by the artistic talent of the heroine. In Sudermann's *Frau Sorge* the hero, a young farmer, struggling against a wastrel father, feels a mute affinity with a Polish farmworker who also suffers from the father; but when the Pole threatens revenge for an outrage, the hero dismisses him implacably – a situation familiar to Jews in Germany. *Der Katzensteg* illustrates another general attitude, in that what is admired as patriotism in Germans is abhorred in Poles as treacherous fanaticism. Even where no political meaning is intended, a nationalist prejudice may be detected. In Hofmannsthal's *Reitergeschichte* a Slav woman appears as a symbol of moral anarchy and subversion; in Musil's *Törless* the village whore is a Slav. There may be no conscious nationalist arrogance in such symbols, and all literatures make such identifications; the more unintentional and innocent the choice is, the more securely the nationalist prejudice is lodged in the mind. The sympathy with Czech nationalists shown in Rilke's early short stories is all the more remarkable.

Round the turn of the century nationalism invades literature with the more deliberate intention of challenging democratic or socialist attitudes as subversive of the unity and power of the nation. The repudiation of Naturalism has to be seen in this context, and some of its early champions like M. G. Conrad and Johannes Schlaf now turn to themes on the countryside and the 'homeland'. The critic Moeller van den Bruck illustrates in an exaggerated form the transition from the 'subversive' trends of *c.* 1890 to the post-1900 imperialism. Owing to his defaulting from national service Moeller spent almost all his adult life before the war abroad, and this itself intensified his patriotic attachment. He had started as a literary critic and in his large study *Die moderne Literatur* (1899-1902) had enthusiastically welcomed the experimentation of Naturalists and Decadents as a symptom of a great creative upheaval of culture, of a time of 'transition' in Nietzsche's sense that was bound to issue in a higher and nobler national consciousness. Like Langbehn, whom he admired, Moeller sees art as the expression of a nation's soul, and his political concepts, his idea of the nation, are at this time aesthetic and cultural. Thus he distinguished nations by their spiritual characteristics, and already before 1914 preferred to speak of the conflicts between 'young' and 'old' nations rather than of more specific and political issues. His historical series *Die Deutschen* (1904-10) with its glorification of great Germans was, as F. Stern says in his admirable *The Politics of Cultural Despair*, written in the mood of Carlyle's hero-worship. He edited a many-volumed German translation of Dostoyevsky's works, and used the long introductions to expound a mystic anti-liberal nationalism. His image of Germany throughout this period was ideal and vague; towards the actual Germany of the Reich Moeller was contemptuously antagonistic, ridiculing the flashiness and uncertainties of its culture and its politics. When war broke out, Moeller enthusiastically returned to Germany, and spent most of the war in the Press department of the War Ministry. His political concepts began to lose something of their vagueness, and in *Der preussische Stil* (1916) he found in the Prussian spirit the form of authority and power that the Reich had lacked. Typically, its most significant expression is found in its art, or rather its architecture, and Moeller calls for a return from the bastard styles of Wilhelminism to the simple and aggressive monumentality of a Schinkel or a Gilly. It was this cultural idealism that led him, during the war, to advocate German expansion into the Baltic lands but to oppose imperialistic aims elsewhere. The peculiar combination in Moeller of cultural and political ideals, his radical, anti-bourgeois, anti-liberal nationalism, made him after the war one of the great ideological organizers of the nationalist resurgence against the Weimar Republic, and his *Das dritte Reich* of 1923 channelled many intellectuals towards Hitlerism.

Though in this period we very rarely find in literary men any comparable evolution towards politics, Moeller's progress from relish for the fragmentation of experience, for 'creative chaos', to a search for the consolidation of the self through the consolidation of the nation has something exemplary about it. Paul Ernst's turn from Naturalism is comparable on a modest scale. This former Marxist and disciple of Arno Holz repudiated Naturalism on the grounds that the aesthetic notion of mimetic objectivity and the determinism in the Naturalist portrayal of man are both false. In its place he called for a literature which should point to positive goals and centre in the clash of wills, and these principles he embodied in a series of stilted heroic dramas and in stories and novels often centring in the acknowledgement of allegiance and devotion. Though not stridently patriotic, they were greeted by another former radical, the critic Lublinski, in *Der Ausgang der Moderne* (1909), as a means to fortify the 'national soul', and justifiably linked by him with the more blatant national devotion of Heimatkunst.

Langbehn had summed up the general tenets of this type of nationalism – the idealization of the Volk in the image of the peasant who is both a sturdy individualist and instinctively imbued with veneration for the ancient social hierarchy. Adolf Bartels, who formulated the principles of Heimatdichtung about 1900, intensified the racial ingredient and distinguished this literature about peasant life from the not uncommon bourgeois use of peasant themes by claiming that true Heimatdichtung was not condescending to the peasantry, free of moralizing, but 'utterly devoted to the homeland'. His close associate in the Heimatkunst movement, Lienhard, eager to defend this peasant literature from the charge of romantic sentimentality, claimed its derivation from Naturalism, with which he had earlier been associated. But, like the Harts or Conrad earlier, the realism he now wanted is described as 'fresh', 'with the smell of earth', 'healthy', and the countryside seemed most likely to provide it.

As it turned out, the works of Heimatkunst novelists are much more complex and less optimistic than the theorists wanted. Frenssen it is true never neglects an opportunity to refer to the glorious deeds of 1864, or 1870, or 1813, but even in his most popular work, *Jörn Uhl* (1901), the excellence of his farmer hero is set off against an arrogant, selfish, and incompetent class of peasants, and Jörn himself, spiritually threatened through his unremitting enslavement to family and farm, is rescued only by giving up the farm and becoming an agricultural engineer. In *Hilligenlei* likewise, also set in Lower Saxony, the few 'good' characters are surrounded by grasping, prejudiced, lazy, and hardhearted people, who lack an effective national or communal faith. The young idealistic hero, studying for the church, gets the stimulus for a new faith from his experiences with the Berlin proletariat, and works out a Nietzschean interpretation of Christianity that will inspire the unity and self-confidence of a national community. Frenssen was a friend and disciple of Friedrich Naumann, and we can see in his works the same blend of nationalism and social concern; in *Peter Moors Fahrt nach Südwest* (1907) Frenssen showed his sympathy with the German military campaign in South-West Africa. If Frenssen in his old age lined up gladly with Nazism, it is important to recognize that his earlier attitudes held various possibilities; there was no iron logic in his development, no more than in the political development of Germany.

Other regionalists were more truculent than Frenssen. Hermann Löns became famous through his sketches of the Lüneburg Heath, where close and loving observation is spiced by folklore. An opinionated individualist, he blasts off his detestation of the bourgeoisie, city life, and democracy that shackle the exceptional man and the aristocracy, and often expresses his hatred of 'asiatic' Christianity because its ethics destroy the native German values of energy and power. There is a crude chauvinism in his hatred of the French and English, and his poem 'Wir fahren nach Engelland' became a hit in the Second World War. All the same, his semi-autobiographical *Das zweite Gesicht* hardly attempts to build up an image of a healthy peasant community. It shows a narcissistic obsession and a melancholia that makes the artist-hero feel a spiritual kinship with declining aristocrats and a Jewish doctor – little of that 'joyous and free Germanism' or that 'gospel of a coming people' that was the ideological stock-in-trade of Bartels or of Avenarius's *Kunstwart* and *Dürerbund*.

The gap between the 'völkische' idealist and society seems just as unbridgeable in Hermann Burte's *Wiltfeber, der ewige Deutsche* (1912), another best-seller. The hero, who excels in physical prowess and spiritual hunger, seeks to renew the German spirit with a creed that includes the worship of creativity, racial purity, and a hierarchically ordered community. But he meets opposition and lack of understanding on all sides, in the city, in imperial circles, even among the peasantry, and the crude and naive book drips with self-pity and a sense of doom. It is not uncharacteristic of some völkische circles that Burte's hero is opposed to territorial expansionism, at least until Germany shall have re-discovered its true spiritual mission, lost since Bismarck and the old Kaiser; his theme is rather the 'Heim ins Reich' that was adopted on occasion by the Nazis. Also typical is an extreme irrationalism of thought. Burte uses certain words that he confesses he cannot explain, 'reiner Krist', 'Geist', 'Zeugung' for instance, in the same way as the Hakenkreuz symbol, as a slogan or cliché that releases a mysterious power latent in the Volk. Nietzsche's prophetic tone, often invoked in this work, cracks here into hoarse obscurantism.

In the neo-romanticism of the turn of the century we have a sophisticated version of this Heimatkunst. What is constant in the immense appeal of the Grail symbol, that produced a large and varied literature and is typical of a new idealization of the Middle Ages, is the hostility to bourgeois-urban industrial culture and the ethical claims of society and, in distinction to social obligations, the idea of service, commitment to an undefined and mystical obligation, freely undertaken by the Elect, who thereby acquire a charismatic power of leadership. A few of these authors, like the Wagnerian Hans von Wolzogen, defined the search for the grail in national-'völkische' terms; but the hierarchical, élitist, anti-democratic stereotypes of Ernst Hardt, Karl Vollmoeller or Eduard Stucken were even more profoundly nationalistic when only implicitly so. The Wandervögel, among whom such élitist ideas prospered, naturally slipped into the nationalist mould.

The crudities of Heimatkunst and the mannerisms of neo-romanticism belong only too evidently to a subliterature, full of clichés and evasions, yet we can only fully understand the writing of a Thomas Mann or a Hofmannsthal, when they were opting out of social commitment one way or the other, if we know the alternatives around them. But the distinguished figures also responded positively to the general situation of liberal self-doubt and the reinvigoration of nationalism round the turn of the century, and no one more emphatically than Stefan George. His early aestheticism had expressed his distaste for political realities and his hostility to art forms that seemed to him to pay homage to the realities of contemporary industrial society. His *Algabal* (1892), which was dedicated to Wagner's patron, Ludwig of Bavaria, builds an image of an inhuman tyrant, coldly contemptuous of man, but despite its Nietzschean echoes has only the slightest political bearing. Like his friend Paul Gérardy, who had written a skit on Kaiser Wilhelm that was forbidden in the Reich, George detested the vulgarity of the Kaiser, who offered public slights to Lechter, George's friend and the designer of his books.

With the 'Vorspiel' of *Der Teppich des Lebens* (1900), and decisively with the 'Zeitgedichte' collected in *Der Siebente Ring* of 1907, George's verse begins to acquire a political content and intention. He does not write on specific issues, but constructs the fundamental form and gesture, the models, of ideal political attitudes and relationships. Thus, in a series of poems, 'Gestalten', he creates the model figures of his ideal social order – the charismatic, self-appointed, dedicated leader, the follower and disciple, the hero, the brotherhood sworn to an unswerving purpose. Basic is the dual concept of power and service, the exercise of power that is sanctified by dedication and transmitted through the stages of a hierarchical order; the medieval religious orders of chivalry are a favoured model. These mental images seem to have their antecedents in the spiritualized medievalism of the Pre-Raphaelites, of Puvis de Chavannes or Böcklin, but they are also related to concepts of power and service common among explicit and aggressive imperialists like Carlyle. Their polemical anti-democratic character is sharpened in *Der Stern des Bundes* (1914), where the attack on a disintegrating liberal-individualistic society intensifies to a call for a 'holy war' under a mystic leader and for the consolidation of a new, self-chosen nobility, dedicated to this high purpose. George is far from the arrogance of imperialistic or racial nationalism; his mind is set on a spiritual realm and renewal. Yet the very dissociation of his imagery from modern actualities made it easier in 1914 for his disciples and friends to identify the 'enemy' with Russia, Britain and France, and the 'holy war' with the German effort and the war-aims of the High Command, even to see in the Kaiser and the field-marshals the mystic leadership George had invoked. If this was, as George claimed, a misinterpretation, it remains significant that the types and relationships that George's political poetry invokes – emperor and liege, lord and retainer, knight and page, dedicated power, loyalty etc. – are those in which imperialist authority saw its image. The Kaiser himself liked to think of and describe himself as a shining Lohengrin riding to the succour of the weak. The fastidiousness of George's taste did not prevent him from creating what Schwerte calls 'a Wilhelmine cultic style'.

It may be suggested that Hofmannsthal's rupture with George, when in 1902 the latter invited him to share a joint dictatorship over German literature, was due not simply to Hofmannsthal's attachment to Austria, as he later said, but also to a difference of political principles. Hofmannsthal was, and remained for many years, unpolitical. Occasionally he might join in an international manifesto warning of the danger of war between England and Germany, like that of 1905 sponsored by Lord Kelvin, Meredith and Swinburne among others (George, typically, refused to sign anything so directly political, and told Hofmannsthal it would do the Germans good to come a cropper). Or we find Hofmannsthal lending his support to the Austrian annexation of Herzegovina in 1908. In 1912 an anti-Austrian outburst from D'Annunzio provoked him to a naively idealistic defence of Austrian rule over Northern Italy. Such 'interventions' were only flirtations of a man fundamentally unconcerned with politics. But in 1913 there was a change. His letters show him worried now about the Vienna administration, especially the modernization of the city, worried too that Jews in Vienna are making great profits out of urban development. On top of this, he is beginning to despair about the old nobility which was showing that it lacked what he called an 'Idea' of Austria. Andrian, his diplomat friend, told him that it was time he gave up his delusions about the aristocracy and set about creating an 'Austrian idea', a task Hofmannsthal began during the war.

Germany was during this period swept by what *Die neue Rundschau* or *Morgen* felt to be an irresistible imperialistic enthusiasm, and writers expressed a dissident opinion more through a criticism of authoritarianism than of nationalism. Anti-authoritarianism in literature mainly took the non-political form of disregard for public affairs and concentration on personal life and values, such as we find in Thomas Mann or Hermann Hesse. Heinrich Mann stands out among the older generation for his growing politicization towards the left, and with him too the new sympathy for democratic forms in *Die kleine Stadt* (1909), and the loathing of the petty autocrat and the 'establishment' in *Professor Unrat* (1905), indicate the beginnings of his criticism of nationalism. Then, in *Der Untertan*, publication of which was begun in 1914 though not completed till 1918, Mann shows the aggressive imperialism of his entrepreneur hero to be the concomitant of the greed and lust for power of his class. The same themes are discussed in Mann's essays of these years, for instance in *Geist und Tat* (1910), where he calls upon intellectuals to act upon their convictions and resist authoritarians and obscurantists; or *Der Bauer in der Touraine* (1914), where he criticizes French as well as German chauvinists and says the German militarists threaten war abroad because they believe that only so can they secure their class privileges at home.

Pfemfert, the editor of *Aktion*, saluted *Geist und Tat* as 'the irruption of literature into politics', and tried to fuse the two in his paper. He saw nationalism and imperialism as instruments of the ruling classes and attacked Social Democracy for having betrayed both socialism and internationalism, his chief objective being the consolidation of a left opposition. Boldly proclaiming himself 'vaterlandslos', he campaigned against the rising war-fever and such aggressive actions as the German intervention at Agadir. But, though Pfemfert's *Aktion* was felt by many of the new writers to be their paper, his attitude was shared by few. Hiller's 'Neues Pathos' group, early Expressionists like Heym, Stadler and Benn, forcefully rejected authoritarian as well as bourgeois aspects of German society, and their imaginations dwelt, like those of Kandinsky and other Expressionist painters, already in the pre-war period, on the disintegration and collapse of cities. In the work of Heym, Stadler and Werfel there are poems that seem to anticipate the war, and Carl Hauptmann's play *Krieg* (1914) seems to foreshadow it. Yet in this pre-war period the attitude of these writers was predominantly non-political, even contemptuous of political engagement and organization. In his famous manifesto *Über das Geistige in der Kunst* (1912),

Kandinsky puts political reformers, liberal or socialist, on a low level of his spiritual scale, as still infected with the 'materialism' that is the great enemy to be overcome. Heym indeed, Stadler and Stramm all write of war as a healthy cleansing operation, and Heym and Benn issue a welcome to chaos and destruction. In contrast to Pfemfert, who was also considerably older than this new generation of writers, and perhaps Carl Einstein, whose anarchism was shared by few, the new poets published in *Aktion* do not have a thought-out political attitude, and their imaginative anticipations of war are strangely unrelated to the actual war that came on them, as on most Germans, as an utterly dislocating shock. It was the war that created political Expressionism.

On the whole, the modernist German writers, after a brief period in the 1880s when they felt themselves part of a national movement towards social renewal, remained in different ways aloof from the aggressive nationalism that led up to 1914. Very few however resolutely battled with it. Most withdrew from public issues, perhaps emerging like Dehmel or Hofmannsthal to sign manifestos of cultural or political international friendship or protests against the use of aeroplanes in war etc. Even those like George who worshipped an image of charismatic leadership stood remote from and hostile to the practical objectives and actions of national and imperialistic politicians. The feeling of alienation and dissociation that many of the writers eloquently expressed has one of its sources in this political isolation. Without doubt, too, this alienation explains the fervour of the enthusiasm with which the writers greeted the war that admitted them to the folk-community.

The Writers and the War

The reasons Germans held for going to war were very varied, and if war-aims were formulated they were confused and contrary; Friedrich Naumann asserted that Germany entered the war without war-aims. The patriotic vibration that thrilled through the nation, the readiness for sacrifice, the confidence in a meaningful victory, are not explicable in terms of precise interests, fears or aims, but rather in terms of the universal feeling, so long frustrated, of belonging to a unitary community, the relief at shedding the burden of personal responsibilities and decisions, the self-enhancement that arose from submission to a national destiny that gave meaning to life, to death, to work, to hardship. As time passed, this unity began to crumble. Victory seemed uncertain, the price questionable, and the meaning of victory, even if won, unsure; the prohibition of public discussion of war-aims fostered these uncertainties. The inequality of sacrifice between the rich and poor, the army staff and the front-line soldier, the industrialist and the trade unionist and, after 1916, the dominance of the civil government by the Army Command led to a polarization whose major parliamentary expression was the conflict over war-aims between the socialists and part of the Centre, who sought a peace without annexations, and the imperialists, united in 1917 in the Vaterlandspartei, with their expansionist aims.

German intellectuals succumbed to the war-fever no less enthusiastically than other sections of the nation, and there was a spate of publications by distinguished philosophers and writers justifying the war as a mission of the German people to restore the world to spiritual health (Paul Rohrbach, Rudolf Eucken, Paul Natorp, Friedrich Lienhard). Many of the critics of bourgeois materialism see the war like Leopold Ziegler as a crusade which would replace the capitalistic state by a 'sacrum imperium'; Sombart in his *Händler und Helden* (1915) and Max Scheler in *Der Genius des Kriegs und der Deutsche Krieg* (1915) identify England with the mean spirit of capitalism and glorify the heroic militarism of Germany as transforming and transcending capitalism. In less grandiose terms ninety-three of the most prominent academics, writers and artists signed the famous manifesto of 1914 pledging their support for the war; among the names were Harnack, Max Planck and Röntgen, Hauptmann and Sudermann, Max Reinhardt, Max Liebermann, Felix Weingartner and Siegfried Wagner (Troeltsch, Solf, and Richard Strauss are known to have refused to sign). Even a Käthe Kollwitz believed it was a just war, and only after the death in Flanders of her younger son did she painfully come to realize that he and millions were dying in an evil cause.

The purposes with which German intellectuals associated the war were abstract and intangible, but less the result of a will to deceive than of bewilderment in the face of an unforeseen and unfathomable experience. Max Weber himself, who questioned the necessity for the war and was opposed to the government's annexationist policy, succumbed to the overwhelming experience of national unity and devotion. In Simmel's *Der Krieg und die geistigen Entscheidungen* (1917), a collection of his addresses and essays on the war, we see a typical dedication and vagueness, all the more remarkable in a philosopher celebrated for his questioning of all assumptions. In 1914 Simmel greeted the war as a mighty experience in which individual separateness dissolves in the whole, and material interests are overcome by spiritual. An 'Idea' has been discovered for Germany which, though it cannot at present find a social or political formulation, is felt as a renewal of inward being. In 1916 Simmel recognizes that not all sections of society have been so transformed, but he still celebrates the war as having rescued the spirit from the crushing weight of institutionalized and mechanized functionalism, as the force of 'life', dynamic vitality, that is seeking as yet undefined new national and international forms. Throughout, Simmel argues that Germany in some way embraces the world, and that its war against Europe is a war for Europe. In 1917 Simmel was no nearer clarification of the new world a German victory would found, and he died shortly before the Armistice, deeply dismayed over the prospect of Germany's impending defeat.

Since the censorship forbade the expression of anti-war, pacifist or revolutionary opinion, anything in short considered by the military authorities to be harmful to morale or encouraging to the enemy, there was little opportunity for mutual clarification among Germans, except in half-clandestine private discussions like those in Max Weber's circle at Heidelberg in the latter years of the war. Criticism tended therefore to be framed in abstract terms, and its effect was ambiguous. A typical uncertainty is evident in the periodical *Das Reich*, founded in 1916 at the height of German confidence with the intention of equipping Germany for its new moral responsibilities after a victorious war. Yet it turns out that this new philosophy is Steiner's anthroposophy, and the journal is only halfheartedly nationalistic. It reprinted passages from Kant's *On Perpetual Peace* and René Schickele was among its contributors. In 1916 Kurt Hiller published the first of his *Ziel* annuals, opening with a reprint of Heinrich Mann's essay 'Geist und Tat'. But the pacifism of his own contribution, 'Philosophie des Ziels', was expressed in so general and utopian a fashion as to leave its relevance to present circumstances uncertain. Other contributors, like Kerr or Brod, were not opposed to the war, and Ludwig Rubiner, whose opposition to the war led him to emigrate to Switzerland, speaks in his article 'Die Änderung der Welt' of a decision for 'Geist' as against possessions, for freedom as against organization, not for peace as against war. The next *Ziel* issue in 1918 was a little more outspoken, though the smothered revolutionary sentiments would be more evident to the alert reader.

On the other hand, the great euphoria of the first year of the war remained with many as the essential truth about the war. One of the largest best-sellers was Walter Flex's Novelle *Der Wanderer zwischen beiden Welten* (1916). The hero, Ernst Wurche, a theological student, comes from the Wandervogel movement, rejoices in the community of the army and in the hierarchy of command, accepting without question the responsibilities of leadership. Ardent for danger and self-sacrifice, he never thinks of politics or war-aims, but finds in the comradeship, effort, and risk of the army its own purpose; his chief desire is to be permitted to join in an attack and to kill. Three sacred books accompany him: the New Testament, Goethe's poems, and Nietzsche's *Also sprach Zarathustra,* and this combination of Christianity, Nietzsche, and Goethe is typical. Wurche's Christ bears a sword and preaches 'strength and confidence', not selflessness and love. He takes from Nietzsche the heroic ideal of service, without bothering about Nietzsche's contempt for nationalism; from Nietzsche too, via the Wandervögel, comes a cult of the naked body free of all sexual suggestion. Gothe's belief in personality is grafted on an ideology that interprets self-fulfilment as service to state power. All these pseudo-reconciliations were already common in 'völkische' groups and among the Wandervögel, and in Flex's story, exalted by the labels of 'purity' and 'maturity', smoothed over by the naive self-confidence of the hero and the author, they performed the essential function of kitsch in masking reality.

Jews, too, admitted to the Kaiser's trust in his address 'To my dear Jews', responded ardently to the experience of a community at war. Jewish academics and writers had since 1870 been among the most devoted German patriots, and now extended their cultural allegiance to German imperialist ambitions. Rathenau, one of the rare Jews to enjoy wide esteem in business circles, among intellectuals and writers and at the Kaiser's court, was a signal exception. Even before the war he had sharply criticized the blundering aggressiveness of German foreign policy and the general deterioration of patriotism into nationalism; he had warned that war would be a matter, not just of armaments and soldiers, but essentially of economic organization, and that it would be disastrous. When the war came he was put in charge of the organization of raw materials, and did perhaps more than any other man to make Germany economically capable of waging a long war. But when all around him were exhilarated in August 1914 by the thrill of awe that seemed to transform Germany, he was seized by despair and anxiety. Throughout the war, though working devotedly to ensure a German victory, he steadily opposed the militarists and expansionists, and in his book *Von kommenden Dingen* (1917) he looked forward to a democratization of the social structure and humanization of labour and labour relations that anticipated the ideals of the Republic.

The Austrian Jews, on whom in large part rested the nurture of culture in Vienna, responded much like those in the Reich, and were almost bound to sympathize with Austrian ambitions in Eastern Europe where Jewish communities were often in danger. Only in Prague was there a distinctively Jewish political response. The older generation here had responded much like the Germans, indeed Mauthner became an almost proverbial fanatical German nationalist, typical of those Jews whom German culture had rescued from the cramping distortions of orthodox Jewry and the fanatical hostility in the Polish, Czech, Hungarian and other provinces. But the Kafka generation born in the 1880s had more complex choices to make. In 1900 Prague contained, beside 415,000 Czechs, ten thousand non-Jewish Germans and twenty-five thousand Jews, of whom eleven thousand colloquially spoke German, the rest Czech. Now the dominant standard-bearers of German culture in Prague, many Jewish writers were also sympathetic to the emerging Czech cultural and national aspirations with which some of them identified themselves. At the same time, and perhaps encouraged by this conflict of sympathy, Zionism took strong hold of many of the young. These contrary sympathies, often shared in the same group or even the same person, made militant German-Austrian nationalism rarer in Prague than in Berlin or Vienna. Max Brod it is true, who in 1913 called himself 'a Jewish writer in the German tongue', was reproved in *Die weissen Blätter* in 1915 for his support of Austrian nationalism. Kafka, less mercurial than Brod, remained suspended between German, Czech and Jewish sympathies. Werfel, whose *Die Troerinnen* of 1914 indicated his Christian leanings, from the beginning saw the war as a tragedy and subscribed to the hope of spiritual renewal through suffering and love. In Berlin, the main phalanx of Jewish liberal writers and publicists were converted on the outbreak of war to a militant patriotism, and their new-found ardour gave plenty of opportunity for ridicule (as did that of Hauptmann or Thomas Mann). Patriotic papers like the Austrian *Der Brenner*, that combined artistic avant-gardism with a provincial patriotism not free of racialism, made a point of attacking the *Berliner Tageblatt* and *Die neue Rundschau* and Jewish contributors like Kerr, Harden, Emil Ludwig or Simmel. Even today one can be disconcerted by the patriotic clichés of these Berlin intellectuals – for instance, by Siegfried Jacobsohn's discovery at a 1914 performance of Mozart's *Figaro* that here is the 'Deutschtum' that Germany is fighting for. Harden kept his head better than most, and his repeated criticism of the aggressive expansionism of the militarists led to occasional confiscations of *Die Zukunft*. In Austria Karl Kraus also remained realistic and sober. He did not oppose the war and in fact was hostile to German pacifists and their French counterpart, Romain Rolland. But he savagely mocked the delusions about this 'chlor-reicher' war, and fought furiously against the disastrous lies of popular journalism. Though hampered by the censorship regulations, he tried to make his readers understand what warfare meant and to steer opinion towards rational objectives, hence supporting the movement for peace without annexations in 1917. His bitter attack on warmongers, military leaders, war profiteers and war propagandists in his apocalyptic play, *Die letzten Tage der Menschheit* (1922), combines his wartime experiences with a post-war perspective.

One can hardly overestimate the importance for the Jews of Austria and the Reich of the participation in the national community that the war offered – in this respect their peculiar situation and response illuminates the origins of the war enthusiasm in alienated social groups such as industrial workers and intellectuals. Ludwig Marcuse describes in his autobiography the reactions of a non-political, intellectual Jew. A student at Berlin, he is deeply impressed to hear the ranting chauvinist Roethe invoke God as the German champion, the Prussian aristocrat von Wilamowitz-Moellendorf address his class as 'Dear compatriots', and the theologian Deissmann's call for 'Nibelung loyalty' in this 'religious' war. The surging uplift of the great concourses on the squares and at railway stations seizes him too, and when he reads the Kaiser's address to 'his dear Jews' his heart is filled with guilt and shame and gratefulness for being pardoned his separateness. The Kaiser represents Germanism, Germanism is the embodiment of spirit, 'Geist', and Marcuse pledged himself to the war, like so many Jews, in a spirit of atonement. His devotion persisted, he tells us, until the beginning of the final military and political breakdown, when he organized in Königsberg a revolutionary group of intellectual workers. It was the same with Jacobsohn and Tucholsky, whose change of commitment occurred only after the mutinies in the navy and army and the associated strikes of industrial workers. Ernst Toller went through this transformation from patriot to revolutionary earlier, soon after being invalided out of the army in early 1917. His naive but moving play *Die Wandlung* (1918) centres in the transformation of an alien who, at long last admitted to the national community at war, must, as he sees what brutal interests lie behind patriotism, painfully renounce the loved community for the sake of higher human values.

The response of the imaginative writers generally to the war was no different from that of other intellectuals; most were quite defenceless against the gigantic emotions that swept through the whole people. Many indulged in crude patriotic declarations, no better for being in verse, like Ernst Lissauer's 'Hymn of Hate' or Hauptmann's vulgar derision of the enemy. Worker poets like Bröger and Lersch chimed in, their professions of patriotic faith and their reconciliation of international brotherhood with the will to victory having a peculiar sentimental appeal and political value to the government. There was similar, though less crude, self-delusion in Dehmel's patriotism. This independent man, always anti-chauvinist and anti-racialist, enlisted in 1914 at the age of fifty and took part in the Western campaign. An unqualified patriot, he never descended to xenophobia, always admired French culture, and insisted that the Germans must have reconciliation as the purpose of conquest. There was obtuseness and confusion in his belief that the Germans were fighting a war for peace and international understanding, but he was honest and consistent, just as he was after the war when, like Thomas Mann, he protested bitterly against the injustice of the Treaty of Versailles and refused to sign a public appeal for international cooperation initiated by Romain Rolland, on the grounds that

the French signatories were not ready to oppose their government's policy towards the defeated Germany. Ludwig Thoma's
attitude was similar to Dehmel's, patriotic, bitter after the war,
but never chauvinist. Wedekind, with his characteristic instability, occasionally showed a healthy scepticism towards nationalistic
fervour, even to the point of admiring Heinrich Mann's 'Zola'
essay; but more usually he supported the aggressiveness of the
expansionists.

Most writers were spellbound in the first days of war by the
solemn awe, the 'Ergriffenheit', that had seized the nation
(nationalist ideology claimed that this capacity for 'Ergriffenheit'
distinguished Germans from all other peoples). Amongst those
who later freed themselves from the spell, Rilke had perhaps the
swiftest and most dramatic recovery. The first two odes of his
Fünf Gesänge (August 1914) express the feeling of awe of the first
days and invoke joyously the war-god – 'hörengesagter fernster
unglaublicher Kriegsgott' – and a transformed nation : 'Heil mir,
dass ich Ergriffene sehe.' Yet involuntarily, as it were, the mood of
the later odes changes to lament and questioning, as Rilke awakens
to the suffering and terror that war meant; this 'unworldly', non-
political poet remained from this time freer of illusions about the
war than most of his contemporaries.

It is perhaps stranger that Stefan George shows a similar clarity
of vision. In *Der Stern des Bundes* of 1914 George had reaffirmed
his poetic model of a hierarchical order of knighthood, pledged to a
'holy war' against a corrupt world, and many young men carried
these poems with them into the front line, believing they were
fighting for the new Reich George had prophesied. George's
closest associates Gundolf and Wolfskehl also understood him in
this sense. Both of them published impassioned and inflammatory
pledges in support of the war in the *Frankfurter Zeitung*, an
extraordinary action for writers who for two decades had been
crusading against the press and the prestige of public opinion (as
Jews they would feel a special need to make a public statement).
Gundolf exercises a not uncommon sleight of hand since he
interprets the war as *his* war, a war for 'Geist', even if the
Germans may not know it; all the same he falls into vulgar abuse
of England and France, the 'rabble'. After an enthusiastic spell in
the front line Gundolf worked in the Department of Political
Warfare in Berlin, never faltering in his warlike allegiance. In
1917 he was appalled at the proposals for a negotiated peace and

the talk of a reform of the Prussian constitution, and when the politicians failed him he put his hope in the generals; to George he expressed his horror at the thought of having to live in a post-war world in which France and England remained intact. Wolfskehl was equally unrestrained. In the 1914 article he claimed that the war was 'of God', a divine task imposed on the Chosen People, the Germans, as a means to establish the realm of Spirit. His correspondence with Albert Verwey, the Belgian poet, his friend and George's ally, shows him wooing and bullying Verwey to declare himself for the German cause, and totally unable to understand Verwey's pacifism and democratic convictions. In 1919 he broke off all connexions with his old friend.

George admits in his poem *Der Krieg*, written in 1916-17 and published in *Das neue Reich* of 1920, that 'for a moment' he had been seized by the shudder of awe that passed through Germany in 1914. But very soon, he continues, he had seen that this was not the 'holy war' he had preached. A war against France cannot be a war for 'Geist'; this war belongs to the corrupt world, it is its fevered agony, murder committed against life itself. Hope can come only from an inward change. Though George came to this view quite early in the war, he was reticent even towards his closest intimates, respecting their sacrificial idealism. Also, he could not separate himself altogether from the simpler patriotism; in a poem of 1917 he could admire Hindenburg as the military saviour of Germany, though at the same time he recognizes that the warlord 'cannot save us from the worse enemy'. He was grieved that his poetic symbolism was misunderstood, but the merging of prophecy and direct exhortation in his poetry invited men to act in terms of his images, and his ideal models seemed to find their closest realization in the hierarchical organization of the army and the national dedication to war. It is true, many of the men who took George's poems with them into the front line also took Hölderlin, finding in his purity a model of dedication to an ideal Germany. But Hölderlin also gave the assurance of the soul's self-founded if precarious indestructibility, while the security George projected was the political mission itself. When one remembers that George approved of the German peace initiatives of 1917, it would seem that there was a deep incompatibility between his poetic idiom and the actuality both of the world and of his own views; the political vision and imagery of his poetry seem anachronistic, and invited applications which he himself rejected, not only during the war but also in 1933, when he refused the incense offered by the Nazis.

The remoteness of the poet from political realities is still more striking in Hofmannsthal. At the outbreak of war he identified himself with German rather than Austrian enthusiasm, repeating the clichés about victory and a place in the sun; on Austria his correspondence shows him to have been anxious. This attitude was not unusual. Stefan Grossmann, for instance, became more and more disillusioned with the unsureness and cynicism in Vienna, and left for Berlin, to throw in his lot with the Germans. Hofmannsthal however very soon became more and more distrustful of German ambitions and power, and identified himself completely with the Austrian war-effort. He edited *Die Öster-reichische Bibliothek*, a popular series of historical and literary works intended to make Austrians more conscious of their heritage, and was enlisted by his friend Andrian, now administrator of occupied areas of Poland, to lecture on the deeper national purposes behind the war. In 1916 and 1917 Hofmannsthal lectured in Warsaw, Prague, various German cities, Scandinavia, and Switzerland, working out the 'idea' of Austria as a guarantee of order and civilization, an exemplar of the cooperation within one Reich of different nationalities, the defender of Europe against barbarism, and a model for Europe itself, which he speaks of as a spiritual entity. These fair words were well meant, but the search for ideal purposes hardly hid the brutality of reality. Sometimes Hofmannsthal lends himself to self-deceit, as when he speaks of the Austrian army in Poland as the 'heart' and the best of Austria. Usually he does not know what to make of reality, as when he is shocked to find in Prague a vigorous repudiation of his naive Austrianism. But Hofmannsthal never indulges in chauvinistic belligerency, and his correspondence with Richard Strauss shows his restraint in contrast to the emotional crudities of the German (though Strauss himself would not sign the intellectuals' manifesto in 1914, distrusted general ideological pronouncements, and never broke off relations with Romain Rolland despite his dislike for the latter's political attitude during the war). Hofmannsthal was always unhappy over the hate and propaganda in the newspapers, and he eagerly welcomed the peace initiatives of 1917. With their failure he gave up political activity, though after the war he again joined in international manifestos for peaceful cooperation. He now claimed that he had never supported national aggression, though in fact he had at one time rejoiced over the German expansion eastwards, once even calculating with delight the value of the raw materials in the conquered territories. Such self-betrayals were only too common in all the belligerent nations in these years of stress, and Hofmannsthal was the victim of naivety rather than deceit, for he seems unaware of the realities of power and war, unaware even of the possibility, say, of a Polish or a Czech point of view.

Thomas Mann was another writer torn out of his normal sphere by the war, seized by the great irrational experience, and concerned to find some intellectual justification for it. Notorious among the younger generation for his pre-war 'aestheticism', his 'cold' intellectual irony, he seemed to want to make amends by an even more complete immersion in political writing than Hofmannsthal. Hence his portrait of Frederick the Great as the devotee of duty, already adumbrated in the quite unpolitical *Tod in Venedig*. His first letters and articles on the outbreak of war breathe the awe of a man experiencing something overwhelming, unimaginable and unfathomable, and deeply grateful for being allowed to be present at a historic turning point which marks the transformation of society. This was a normal reaction, not essentially different from the first response of Simmel, Weber, Rilke, Blei and thousands of others; even the pacifist Hermann Hesse allowed his hero Demian, who recognizes patriotism to be a delusion, to feel that there is something holy in the readiness for self-sacrifice and that a deep change is occurring 'in the depths'. But Mann had a special spur. His brother Heinrich was one of the very few German writers to remain critical of the German government and the war enthusiasm, and to hold to international-ist, rationalist and democratic ideals, and it was largely because of his awareness of this that Thomas Mann's thoughts were so pertinaciously directed towards a definition of German culture in contrast to French, and a justification of the German political structure as against democracy. Like so many nationalist publicists, he scattered ugly suggestions that democratic leanings were equivalent to treachery (in the same way Dostoyevsky had called liberalism 'anti-Russian' and André Gide charged Romain Rolland with being 'against France'). But it is curious that Mann remained engrossed with this general problem and hardly modi-fied his views throughout the war, and that he collected and completed his various articles on the war in 1918 in the volume

Betrachtungen eines Unpolitischen, at a time when it could find favour only among die-hards. The book is on several accounts a severe embarrassment to admirers of Mann.

Mann reproduces here all the stock-in-trade of anti-democratic nationalism from Lagarde onwards, relying greatly on Nietzsche and Dostoyevsky (selectively applied) to give his themes subtlety and sophistication. Much of the argument circles round Nietzsche's distinction between culture and civilization, but in a manner nearer to the 'völkische' Löns than Nietzsche, since France and England are equated with civilization and Germany with culture. Civilization applies to a society whose members are dominated by a political consciousness, to democratic societies where decisions are made by majority vote, where values are social and materialistic and thought is rationalistic; culture is something inward, self-centred, irrational, creative, non-political; the deepest artist is not humanitarian, rationalistic, optimistic, he is fascinated by evil, barbarism, risk, death. But though non-political, this culture needs a carapace of power that will shelter it from politics, and this protection is provided by a conservative authoritarianism. Mann recognizes that he is formulating a conservative doctrine, but defends himself by asserting (it is a cliché frequently met in conservative ideology) that 'conservative' is not a political attitude, but a non-political; it is equivalent to 'national', while on the other hand 'democratic' indicates a partisan political attitude. In a similar way Mann tries to take the war out of the arena of politics by exalting it as a fact of 'life', something transcending rational political objectives, beyond morality, a 'Weltwende'. The instinctive participation of the Germans in the war, dissociated from any specific war-aims, proves, he maintains, that the Germans are 'a people of life', inherently nobler and deeper than the French or the English, who have rational, definable war-objectives. Oddly enough, there runs through certain parts of this rambling book a recognition that in spite of all efforts, the march of democracy in the world cannot be stopped, that Nietzsche himself was a brilliant publicist and as a novelist Mann also was engaged in a genre inescapably 'democratic'. Such comments redeem the work somewhat, but may have been induced by the jeers of rightwing papers like *Der Brenner*, or leftwing papers like *Die weissen Blätter*, at the change that had come over the fastidious, ironic, self-centred Thomas Mann.

It took Thomas Mann till 1922 to get reconciled to the

Weimar Republic (still grudgingly) and with his brother, and much longer to recognize the disastrous implications of Nietzschean irrationalism. The *Betrachtungen*, intended to defend the 'non-political' artist, demonstrate what naiveties, immodest ones too, can befall a writer not conversant with or involved in politics, and in what direction political thought is likely to go if the intelligentsia is deprived of opportunities for discussion and participation.

There is no cultural document from the other side, the democratic or anti-war side, comparable in weight or comprehensiveness to Thomas Mann's. This lack is largely due to the censorship; for this reason alone Heinrich Mann was at a serious disadvantage and could never compose a refutation until events made one supererogatory. His most effective reply to Thomas's first war essays was an indirect one, the essay on Zola (1915), in which his discussion of the Dreyfus case and the conflict between men of power and men of intellect bears unmistakable references to Germany and the war. Devotion to inwardness, to the soul, to aestheticism, is for Heinrich Mann the product of 'hopeless times' that itself confirms hopelessness. Zola, concerned not with inwardness but with human relationships, a votary of truthfulness, is by that very fact a republican pledged to explode entrenched privilege. Intellectuals who do not try to find an objective, social form for the ideas of truth, justice, and morality, are traitors to Geist, more guilty than the men of power themselves. Fine words. But it was not only the abstractness of these ideals but also the rather naive and dogmatic identification of them with democracy and France that gave Thomas the occasion for some of his shrewdest counterblows.

Though Heinrich Mann was unable to speak out during the war – the publication of *Der Untertan* was delayed till 1918 and *Die Armen* of 1917 was less politically relevant – he remained a legendary figure of resistance to the war and the war-fever, and much was expected of him in intellectual and literary circles in the revolutionary months 1918-19 when he was the elected chairman of the Munich section of the Political Council of Intellectual Workers. But he showed himself to be a very moderate revolutionary, subscribing to bourgeois-revolutionary principles of freedom, tolerance and democracy, calling for 'radical thought' instead of 'economic radicalism', for the bourgeoisification of the proletariat instead of the dictatorship of the proletariat, in fact a supporter of a constitutional, bourgeois republic.

For many of the younger writers too, opposition to the war took the form of opposition to the power-structure of the Reich on the basis of democratic or socialist ideals. Most writers were at first carried away by enthusiasm, and only slowly won a painful way to critical awareness. Pfemfert and his closer collaborators on *Aktion* were more prepared for and less bewildered by the outbreak of war than most, but the censorship prevented him from creating an anti-war forum. After August 1914 literature and art played a much larger part in the paper than before, and Pfemfert skilfully used poems and descriptive accounts by soldiers to bring home the actual reality of war, in contrast to the heroicizing falsifications of military spokesmen, journalists, politicians and clergymen; he also reprinted material by French and Russians that might indicate common ground with the Germans. He introduced a very effective column, 'Ich schneide die Zeit aus', in which without comment he published extracts from contemporary publications that illuminated the grotesque inhumanity of the war enthusiasts and ideologues. At Christmas Pfemfert in a special number drew pointed contrast between the peaceful message of Christianity and the warfare of Christians; other anti-war writers, like von Unruh, were to make this contradiction the theme of their most powerful criticism of the war. By informed reports of the Russian revolutions of 1917 Pfemfert was able to smuggle in some of his own revolutionary socialist beliefs. Much more prepared than most intellectuals for the issues of the German Revolution of 1918, Pfemfert aligned himself with the revolutionary movement and the Communist party when it was formed. But like so many of the intellectuals, he found he could not go along with the doctrines of implacable class war and dictatorship of the proletariat, and was soon forced into an outsider position. In the same way, Carl Sternheim, who in November 1918 published in *Aktion* (in book form 1920 entitled *Berlin oder Juste Milieu*) a slashing indictment of militarists, bourgeoisie and the 'bourgeoisified' Social Democracy, rejected the political concepts and tactics of the Communists.

The only other critical paper to last, with occasional interruptions, throughout the war was *Die weissen Blätter* (founded 1913), whose editor René Schickele was an Alsatian known for his championship of Franco-German understanding. It was and remained a primarily literary monthly, and in 1914-15 its political position was ambiguous. The chief political articles, written by Max Scheler, support the German war effort on the ground that its purpose can be made to be the renewal of Europe from the corruption of materialistic capitalism, and articles of Wilhelm Hausenstein are still more bellicose. In 1915 Schickele himself acknowledges the 'greatness' of the time. But at the same time Schickele and Annette Kolb vigorously attack the campaign of hatred towards England and France and it was here that Heinrich Mann's Zola essay was published. The most critical articles are directed against writers and intellectuals who have betrayed their humane and liberal past and yielded to jingoism, for instance J. L. Stern's indictment of Dehmel, Holz, Henckell, Wedekind, Julius Hart and Hauptmann, or Schickele's indignant attack on Thomas Mann's war essays. In a review of a periodical publication *Das Zeit-Echo*, which reprinted the views of prominent intellectuals, Schickele allows the humanity of a Werfel or an Annette Kolb to speak for itself alongside the bellicose and self-deluding views of such men as Simmel, Worringer, Paul Ernst, Alfred Kerr or Max Brod. The latter, for instance, a contributor to *Die weissen Blätter*, who had already committed himself to Zionism, proclaims here that the war has taught him that the Austrian government 'loves' him and he it, and that he feels the capture or fall of Lemberg or Czernowitz as a personal gain or loss. Schickele also published poems or tales of Werfel or Albert Ehrenstein to demonstrate the cruel realities of this national war or of the position of the Jews.

In April 1916 *Die weissen Blätter* was transferred to Zürich and was henceforth free of the German censorship. It still remained predominantly literary, and its sharpest political criticism was directed against writers, repeatedly against Thomas Mann for instance, and against the writers of *Die neue Rundschau* and the Fischer-Verlag, which issued a proud catalogue of its publications in 1914-15 (*Das grosse Jahr*) that was savaged by Schickele. The anti-war tone sharpens too, and here were published some of Benn's caustic prose, stories by Leonhard Frank that later made up his famous anti-war book *Der Mensch ist gut*, Hasenclever's *Antigone*, appeals for peace from Georg Brandes and Romain Rolland. Some of Schickele's contributors espouse revolutionary socialist views, most notably J. R. Becher with his emotional visions of human brotherhood or George Gross with his satirical drawings; Barbusse's *Le Feu* was translated here. But Schickele never identified himself with any revolutionary party, and when in November 1918 some of his contributors, like Becher, supported a bolshevik-type revolution, most like Schickele himself pledged themselves to a non-violent revolution that was democratic as well as socialist. The violent conflicts that ensued left Schickele, like so many other intellectuals, without solid footing, since he was against both the use of revolutionary violence and its suppression by violence, both for socialism and against dictatorship, both against the war and against revolution. The outcome was the thesis, that he and Werfel elaborated in his paper at the end of 1918, that the intellectual is guilty of betrayal if he enters the arena of power, that 'Geist' and 'Macht' belong to incompatible worlds: a thesis that sealed the collapse of a faith. All the intellectuals who had believed that revolution was the realization of 'Geist', and that intellectuals were the allies (some thought leaders) of the revolutionary proletariat, were doomed to the same helplessness. Kurt Hiller, the inventor and chief advocate of the concept of the 'activist', who published in 1916 a utopian plan of radical reform (*Philosophie des Ziels*) and on 10 November 1918 became chairman of the Berlin Political Council of Intellectual Workers, was as frustrated as Schickele, or as Pfemfert who aligned himself for some time with the Communist Party.

The emotional repudiation of war for which *Aktion* and *Die weissen Blätter* served as foci was the chief source of the so-called ethical Expressionism, that ecstatically proclaimed that peace and the brotherhood of mankind could be achieved by a decision of the will. The common theme of many of the wartime poems of Werfel, Becher, Rubiner, Iwan Goll and many others, published together in Kurt Pinthus' anthology *Menschheitsdämmerung* (1920), is a vision of a new man inspired by love for humanity, and of a radiant new society. Toller's play *Die Wandlung* (1918) shows the all too typical illusion that the suffering masses will readily respond to this message uttered by an inspired leader. His participation in the Munich Commune of 1919 illustrates the doom of this idealistic activism, crushed from two sides, by authority as being revolutionary, by revolutionaries as being a bourgeois compromise. Its ineffectuality was anticipated by Hugo Ball and the small group who with him founded Dada in Zürich in 1916. These ridiculed the high-flown rhetoric and self-delusion of the ethical Expressionists and admitted only a negative function for art, which in the Cabaret Voltaire became a jeering and hilarious caricature of the moral disorder and absurdity in the world. But in the post-war revolutionary period this attitude seemed to be an evasive irrelevance. Ball, despite his revolutionary sympathies and his associations with Russian revolutionaries in Zürich, was no more able than Schickele or Hiller or Pfemfert to find a positive policy in these years.

The imaginative works in which the agonizing reality of the war was reflected, though too few to present a continuous development or even to be widely representative, illustrate the dilemmas outlined above. Fritz von Unruh's play *Vor der Entscheidung* and his story *Opfergang*, though first published after the war, reflect the situation when they were first drafted – 1914–15 in the case of the play, 1916 of the story. Both form a highly emotional indictment of the destructiveness of war and contrast the message of Christ with the viciousness of bloodlust. But in both works a visionary belief in a spiritual purpose, the hope of progress through horror to a future of light, justify the soldiers in continuing the battle, ready to accept or deal out death as a sacrifice to the future. The Expressionistic form, the incoherence of structure and of language, the prevalence of politically vague images like 'sun', 'love', 'brotherhood', interpret not only a great intensity of feeling but also an emotional and moral confusion, since von Unruh's Uhlan or Vize-Feldwebel can combine their revolt against the war with their acceptance of military discipline, and their high vision in the end justifies their acting as the simplest patriot would. The conflict in *Ein Geschlecht* (written 1915-16) is more irreconcilable but more abstract; birth, sex, biological life are set against order, discipline, power, war, the young against authority.

Reinhold Goering's *Seeschlacht* (1916) is another work in which anti-war conviction cannot find expression in action. Based on the battle of Jutland, the play shows a group of gunners in a gun-turret of a battleship. As they prepare for the battle they reveal differing attitudes to the war and their commanders, one of them saying he will refuse to fight in this war that is 'crime and madness'. But when the battle opens all are carried away by the thrill of danger and comradeship of fighting, and all perish like heroes. It is not surprising that the first production of this play in Dresden in early 1918 caused a scandal, since it shows both that war spares neither side and that it prospers only at the expense of rationality; a later production in that year in Berlin owed its success, one may believe, not only to the skill of its producer, Reinhardt, and to the sophistication of the Berlin audience, but also to the changed attitude to the war in these months.

In Hasenclever's verse we can trace his doubts about the war that he had at first celebrated, for he was deeply affected by the sight of destruction in Belgium. By 1916-1917 his verse shows political repudiation of war and the purposes of war; in his poem *Der politische Dichter* he calls on poets to become political, and himself sketches the pacific, just, fraternal society towards which the poet should 'lead'. Like Schickele, with whose periodical Hasenclever had close connexions, Hasenclever abhorred violence and civil war as much as national war. In 1917 he embodied these ideas in his play *Antigone*, which somewhat surprisingly was passed by the censor and produced in that year; this play is perhaps the most precise presentation of the Expressionist attitude to war and revolution. The conflict between Creon and Antigone appears here as that between an authoritarian warlord (with tones of Kaiser Wilhelm) and a pacifist who appeals to the common man; and though Antigone dies a victim, Creon's power collapses and he himself renounces his old beliefs as 'the new world dawns'. Typically, a last scene expressly repudiates violent revolution, as Antigone's voice calls from the grave for prayer and atonement in place of retribution. The Expressionistic form of the play, the exalted, ecstatic language, the disregard for psychological realism correspond closely to its utopian theme – the superhuman readiness for self-sacrifice arising from a deep, religious love for humanity, the victory of a spiritual force, and the miraculous transformation of mankind. It is typical non-political politics, and anticipates Hasenclever's repudiation of violence during the revolutionary period 1918-19 and indeed his repudiation of the political mission of the poet. Stefan Zweig's pacifist play *Jeremias*, which was performed in Zurich in 1917 but not in Austria or the Reich, is similar in spirit.

There are many variations upon the types of attitude sketched above. A general response can however be defined. It was above all the shock and experience of joining in a communal experience, not enthusiasm for specific war-aims, that enlisted writers and intellectuals, hitherto so markedly deprived of social participation and a public role, for the war. Franz Blei, who remained a stout opponent of imperialistic expansionism and chauvinism, wrote in his *Menschliche Betrachtungen zur Politik* of 1916 that the philosophical efforts of Bergson and Husserl to supplant the individualism of modern society (Gesellschaft) with the collective thinking of a community (Gemeinschaft) are anticipations of the community felt in the war, itself the promise of a 'glory' to come. This communal embrace meant generally, as with Blei, the worship of emotional 'life' values in place of reason, and the cult of primitivistic concepts of Volk and leadership. As intellectuals and poets they were under the obligation to define, in theory or image, the war experience and its purpose, and in so doing they provided various interpretations all divested of the grosser realities of political interests. Out of naivety rather than intention they thus performed a service useful to the men of power and contributed to the mental confusion of their compatriots. Few saw through the seductions of the war experience until the vast destruction began to provoke in the younger generation an impassioned repudiation of war, violence and the classes most responsible for its prosecution. This anti-war, revolutionary spirit is largely to be identified with Expressionism, a further development of an attitude that even before the war was ready to 'explode' the establishment, the bourgeoisie, the prestige of reality itself. Its trust in the effective power of the spirit was its strength and its weakness: its strength, since from it the writers drew the self-confidence to challenge the existing order; its weakness, since it cheated itself about social and psychological realities, so that in the clashes of the revolutionary period the poets were reduced to ineffectuality and indeed in many cases abandoned the dream of political commitment altogether.

Even the idea of fraternity, of service to the community, that begins to loom large in the thought of the intellectuals from 1917 – for instance in the essays of Hiller and Rubiner in the second *Ziel* issue of 1918 – is conceived as abstractly as are the masses themselves in the plays of von Unruh, Hasenclever, and Kaiser, and the common belief that revolution will serve the cause of 'Geist', of an inner self-transcendence, often seems more of an evasion of realities than an expression of them. But if it is easy to perceive the self-deceit and rhetoric of these would-be revolutionaries, it is equally important to recognize the cruelty of the dilemma in which the times placed them, faced by claims from opposing forces which seemed to them inadmissible. Before the war this dilemma was latent and could be evaded; now it became unavoidable, and in one form or another it has remained unavoidable since. In this sense the war closes an era and opens a new one.

6

Culture and the Metropolis

While the German population increased from forty-one million in 1871 to sixty-five million in 1910, the size of the rural population remained stable; the increase was in the cities, above all the large cities. In 1850 there were four towns of over 100,000 inhabitants; in 1871, eight; in 1880, fourteen; in 1913, forty-eight. Berlin grew from 400,000 in 1850 to two million in 1910; Vienna also reached two million by 1914. It was in the great city that the industrial and social forces that were creating a new Germany took the tangible shape of a living area in which they impinged on personal experience in countless ways, as employment, administration, and authority, as factories and offices, workers' tenements and middle-class suburbs, administrative buildings, barracks, schools, churches, police stations, as theatres, concert halls, and cinemas, as trains, trams and automobiles. This new social complex is the dominant point of reference for cultural life in the full sense, ousting the small residential city of the past, Weimar or Salzburg, which might be resuscitated but to a new function, as a festival centre like Bayreuth. In the same way the countryside takes on an intensified meaning as a place of refreshment, perhaps as a challenge to the spiritual dominance of the city, and as such a reluctant tribute to its power. Historians and critics have been puzzled to find a designation for the literary realism of the middle part of the nineteenth century, usually falling back on Otto Ludwig's patently inadequate term 'poetic realism'. It might be most helpful to call it 'small-town realism', as opposed to the 'great-city realism' and its rivals of the period that opens with Naturalism, providing it is understood that such designations do not mean that writers merely reflect a specific social environment. In all cases thought and imagination and often enough experience reach out far beyond the immediate social experience. What they mean is that the social nucleus creates a characteristic group of values and anti-values, of often contradictory and rival choices, which together form the 'tone' of an epoch.

It would however be a mistake to identify the new post-1880 culture or literature with the great industrial city. In fact, the great industrial cities of the Ruhr, Saxony or Silesia hardly have any direct significance in the artistic life of the time. The old cultural centres like Berlin, Vienna, Munich, Dresden, Hamburg or Leipzig, most of them still the residences of princes, retain their preeminence, and it is here that we find the most important theatres and museums, the great publishers and art dealers, the editorial offices of the newspapers and periodicals, most of the pioneering educational institutions, technical and art schools, the whole business apparatus of culture and its keenest consumers. In these cities the culture of the past and of remote places was made accessible, Japanese players and the Russian ballet visited Berlin as well as Paris and London, an Ashanti village camped in the Vienna Prater for some months. From nearby Paris and London German journalists sent reports of colonial exhibitions, of the intoxicating spectacle of dancers from Java. Through the collections of museums and dealers and through frequent public and private exhibitions there was an extraordinary intensification of contact with remote cultures, Oriental, Egyptian, African, sophisticated, archaic and primitive, that facilitated also a sympathetic understanding of neglected phases of the European past and greatly stimulated the European artistic revolution of Picasso's generation, its most prominent German representatives being the groups of Die Brücke and Der blaue Reiter. This great transformation of cultural life had its origin not in the purely industrial cities but in the great metropolitan centres, above all the capitals Paris, London, Berlin and Vienna. Only in the metropolis, where marked features of industrialization and capitalism were breaking in upon a traditional cultural environment, could effective challenge and also assimilation take place. Where such a confrontation was absent, as in the old-fashioned small towns where public opinion and policy were still ruled by the hierarchies of officialdom, the clergy, and the master craftsmen, neither the terrors nor the achievements of industrialization were present, nor the countervailing energies of the metropolis. Here a meagre and blank conventionality prevailed, as we can see from the descriptions of Bavarian small-town society in Ludwig Thoma, of Calw in Hermann Hesse's novels, of the Würzburg of Leonhard Frank, and in innumerable autobiographies.

Berlin

Among the German cities that possessed metropolitan features Berlin was of supreme importance. The capital city of the Reich and of Prussia, Berlin was in many ways unique, yet in its uniqueness comprised all the typical features, economic, social and political, of the new Germany. It was a great industrial and financial centre, directly linked by road and rail with the provinces and abroad, and its population was typical: enterprising industrialists and bankers, speculators of all sorts, a large bureaucracy in which the nobility held positions of influence and power, an extensive educated middle class, a large, politically organized working class and in its slums a slum-proletariat, a high incidence of crime and a vast prostitution, altogether a changing and mobile population that was continually swollen by immigrants from the countryside and the East who included many Poles and Jews. But Berlin was also the residence of the Kaiser, the seat of the Reich and Prussian governments and parliaments, the headquarters of the army, of the political parties, of political and economic pressure groups, of social organizations and reform movements of all sorts, so that all the trends and pressures of the time were most palpable there.

Its university attracted many of the most brilliant academics, and had a peculiar function in public life through the public involvement of professors like Tönnies, Mommsen, Virchow, Wilhelm Foerster, Harnack, Treitschke, Meinecke, Simmel or Sombart. The Berlin daily press came, with the *Frankfurter Zeitung*, nearest to the function of a national press, particularly the *Berliner Tageblatt, Vossische Zeitung, Kreuzzeitung, Nationalzeitung* and *Vorwärts,* while the *Lokalanzeiger* was the modern type of sensational scandal paper. Samuel Fischer was from about 1890 the chief publisher of the modern writers and of the best of the modernist periodicals, *Freie Bühne (Die neue Rundschau).* Here too was Paul Cassirer, who as a publisher nursed modern writers and as a man of influence in the Berliner Sezession and after 1898 an art-dealer made Berlin the great intermediary between Germans and modern, post-Impressionistic art, exhibiting Cézanne, Matisse, Gauguin, Van Gogh, Munch, Hodler, Kandinsky and Kokoschka among others. Herwarth Walden founded *Sturm* there in 1910, and made its rooms an exhibition centre for modern art; in 1911 Die Brücke transferred to Berlin from Dresden. Bondi was here, too, the publisher of the George circle, and here too were the offices of *Aktion*, where literary evenings and exhibitions were held.

In Berlin the new type of commercial theatre established itself most firmly, whether in the form of the variety and revue theatre (Berlin's nightlife was notoriously the fastest in Germany) or on the high cultural level established by Brahm, Reinhardt and others, who were able to reconcile commercial success with artistic achievement. Reinhardt, who was often invited to work in other cities, was the epitome of modernity, the boss of a team of dramaturges and assistants, swift to seize on technical devices like the revolving stage and diaphanous curtains, and using the circus for modern as well as Greek plays, thereby at the same time satisfying the need of a sophisticated metropolitan audience for novelty and change. Berlin was the scene of the historic triumphs of the theatre-society Freie Bühne, which especially between 1889 and 1893 presented the great foreign moderns, Ibsen, Strindberg and Tolstoy and the young Germans Hauptmann, Sudermann and Holz before a socially and artistically important public. The Berlin cabaret was on the other hand of less significance than the Munich, largely because of the lack of intimacy in the capital. Berlin was the abode of the most distinguished realist painter, Max Liebermann, who was in the 1890s the ally of the Naturalists in artistic matters and a member of the Freie Bühne; the older Menzel, like Liebermann a devoted Prussian, composed the first great industrial painting, *Eisenwalzwerk* (1879). Wilhelm Bode, the director of the royal art gallery, was the leading authority among museum directors at a time when they were actively engaged in forming public taste. But here, in Berlin too, the forces resisting change and modernity were active and evident. The Kaiser frequently intervened in social, religious and artistic disputes, and represented not only the philistine vulgarity of the new Germany but also the principle of authoritarianism itself. The Prussian military and officials formed a solid conservative phalanx, their traditions and efficiency imposing, particularly in Berlin and Potsdam, an inescapable respect. But also the new entrepreneurs, the stock exchange and real-estate speculators prospered and asserted themselves in Berlin as nowhere else, ruthlessly transforming the city.

The physical development of the city was likewise a paradigm of the nation's. Its core was Fontane's Berlin. Prussian and aristocratic, with its dignified palaces, museums and university, and its massive, sober, classical monuments, its severe and reserved streets, the village-like suburbs ringed with barracks, and a population of officials, soldiers, servants, shopkeepers and artisans. By 1890 commercialism had struck deep into this core, factories and tenements were destroying the fields and market gardens and the modest old dwellings, trams and railway linking the widening suburbs and the centre. Inner suburbs like Alexanderplatz or Wedding became desolate working-class districts where the victims of society gathered – whores, criminals, the destitute and sick. Kretzer's novels *Die Betrogenen, Meister Timpe,* and *Der Millionenbauer* give a good impression of the changing face of the city, though neither he nor Holz and Schlaf nor Frenssen, however appalled at the misery round them, has the intensity of vision of Heym or Benn and the much later *Berlin Alexanderplatz* of Döblin (1929).

The new monumental buildings of modern Berlin, sharing in the confusions of style of the late nineteenth century, all lost the Prussian note. The domed cathedral, with its mixture of Byzantine, Baroque, and Gothic elements, was widely criticized even then for the lack of any trace of Protestantism; the Kaiser Wilhelm Gedächtniskirche displayed a frigidly correct Romanesque; Wallot's Reichstag flaunted a bastard Renaissance; while the Kaiser's dearest scheme, the Siegesallee, a half-mile of marble figures of the Prussian great in historical costume and theatrical postures, attracted ridicule from Bismarckians like Harden and awoke shame and despair in more sensitive intellectuals like Morgenstern. Even the museums aspired to be temples, and we find a Holz or a Moritz Heimann deploring the mummification of art through museums. Here in Berlin the first modern department store was built, Alfred Messel's Wertheim building, combining modern building techniques and commercial display windows and counters with decorative features that enticed extravagance in the customers. Here too a beginning was made in 1893 with modern town-planning through the city Building Office.

The intellectual climate of Berlin was unmistakably distinct from that of other cities, yet it may be said that it corresponded most closely and fully to the general movement of society and the tension set up by social change. The rural suburb of Friedrichshagen cradled the decisive breakthrough of the modern literary movement, the German counterpart to Zola, Ibsen, Tolstoy and Dostoyevsky, in comparison with which the Munich group round *Die Gesellschaft* seems halfhearted. The leading figures were typically metropolitan : Wilhelm Bölsche, journalist, science popularizer, novelist; Bruno Wille, preacher of a radical 'free religious' congregation, lecturer, journalist, poet; J. H. Mackay, the anarchist, poet, novelist, journalist; the brothers Hart with their impulsive enthusiasms and numerous journalistic ventures; Arno Holz, the most rhetorical of the poets of the city with the highest theoretical pretensions, dramatist and journalist. Many others attached themselves, some like Henckel or Hauptmann really discovering themselves and the 'social question' only when thrown into this atmosphere. Along with them went a great phalanx of publicists, critics, theatrical producers, actors, some filling several roles like Brahm and Schlenther, who were critics and producers, and most, like Harden, concerned with politics, morals and social questions as well as literature. The prominence of theatre critics indicates the importance that the theatre had in the intellectual life of the capital, and if Heinrich Mann complains in *Im Schlaraffenland* of the dominance of Berlin cultural life by the dramatic critics, it indicates that the cultured bourgeoisie did have a real place of meeting. Brahm claimed that the Berlin audiences were the most intelligent in Germany. Visitors to Berlin often mentioned with resentment the control of critics over cultural opinion, and it is true that creative writers had far less direct influence than critics, whose clamorous feuds sometimes drowned the works they were supposed to be discussing. Hauptmann, the most gifted of the Friedrichshagen circle, lived near Berlin for only a short while, and several others of the Berlin writers later moved away; critics and journalists were on the other hand bound to the city, and decided the direction and guaranteed the solidity of metropolitan taste. Alfred Kerr, in his impertinent way, insisted that as a critic he was a better poet than the poets. It was a highly intellectualistic, rational, critical culture, even the cult of 'pathos' in the prewar years was allied with intellectualism; Hiller, Pfemfert, Carl Einstein were all true Berlin intellectuals.

Berlin culture was metropolitan both positively and negatively.

The simplest type of affirmation is that of Bölsche who in his novel *Die Mittagsgöttin* (1891) expressed his choice for the vigour, variety and rationality of the city. In articles like 'Die Poesie der Groszstadt' Bölsche admits the ugliness of Berlin but calls it 'sublime', 'an epic of reality'. In *Das Buch der Zeit* Holz claims the city as the theme for modern poetry, even if he half-unconsciously still tends to identify beauty with the countryside. The new literary movement recognized modern French literature, whether Zola and de Maupassant and Verhaeren or Bourget and Daudet and Huysmans, to be part of a metropolitan culture, and everywhere both adherents and opponents of 'die Moderne' recognize that it belongs to the great city. Many writers speak, like Ellen Key, the Swedish friend of Rilke, of the possibility of beautifying the city; the Harts were advocates of garden suburbs like that of Bournville in Birmingham. The most zealous advocates rise to extolling the metropolis as having a unique beauty; August Endell in his *Die Schönheit der grossen Stadt* (1908) rejoices in the energy, the rhythm ('melody') of work, the 'language' of machines; in the pale anaemic faces of the workers he perceives 'a wonderful severe beauty'. Most poets, however devoted to the Groszstadt, are not able to rise to Endell's enthusiasm. If the editors of the anthology *Im steinernen Meer* (1910) claim that 'nature' can no longer be the main inspiration of poetry, in nearly all these city poems the 'beauty' resides in that remnant of nature that survives around and in the city. The new grouping of Heym, Hiller, Stadler on the one hand is absolutely and polemically metropolitan, on the other describes the city as hell.

But it is also in the metropolis that we find the sharpest critics of the false values of modern society. The criticism of the horrors of industrial poverty and misery, of the snobbery and heartlessness of the well-off, the autocracy of the Court, the sycophancy of the bureaucracy, is nowhere so concrete and pertinent as within the metropolis. Thus the *Freie Bühne* or later *Aktion* were far more acute and unremitting in their criticism of the metropolis than the provincial journals, for instance in their criticism of the pretentious new buildings and monuments. If many provincials, and even some metropolitans, were sick like Bartels of 'the eternal urban atmosphere' of literature, they tended like him to evade the problem by proposing historical or bucolic themes for writers. The refuge writers like Schlaf, Conrad, Ernst, found in the country or small town, in one or other form of 'Heimatkunst', is closely linked to their artistic decline. When one studies the great argument over the city in this period one understands better the significance of the attitude of the young generation of 1911, of Heym, Stadler, Becher, Hermann – Neisse, Benn, Döblin, Sternheim, Einstein, whose horror at the dehumanization and indifference of the city, the commercialization and reification of culture and human relations generally, is not a repudiation of the city but the delineation of the inescapable modern ambience. Here they had to be, just as Hauptmann, as he tells us in his autobiography, had to come to Berlin in order to experience the dominant reality of his time and find himself.

For Rilke too the great city was the decisive reality of his time, and he, like his Malte Laurids Brigge, had to taste in full the desolation and loneliness of the great city. He and Malte chose Paris, and clearly enough because it preserved consoling reminders of an older and more personal and aristocratic culture; Berlin he found, like many Austrians, too crushing, 'too full of reality' as he wrote in a letter. Even the George school knew that they owed much to the metropolis. It is true that there are few more violent attacks on modern city culture than the rampaging of Wolfskehl and B. Vallentin in *Jahrbuch für die geistige Bewegung*, and George's artist friend, Sabine Lepsius, writing on Berlin culture in *März* (1907), calls it nervous and unhealthy, the home of modernistic trends in art that she finds abominable. Vallentin we find actually defending the Wilhelmine architectural muddle of Berlin against the 'stony indifference' of modern functionalism, and concluding that the 'Geistige' should leave the cities and live in small towns. But in fact it was in Berlin that the firmest group of George disciples lived, with Melchior Lechter his illustrator in a nearby suburb, and close to friendly intellectuals like the Simmels and the Lepsius's. George enjoyed regular visits there from 1909 to 1913, and very characteristically refused to seek out the remnants of old-world charm, saying that its ugliness was its beauty. If the early aesthetic George is understandable only in relation to Paris, the later George and his school are as incomprehensible without Berlin as is the Wandervögel movement, which began in the Berlin suburb of Steglitz.

The challenge of the metropolitan culture of Berlin was sharpened of course by the fact that it was the capital and hence enjoyed a peculiar prestige, even power. It was inevitable that the opponents of city culture had to wrestle with the predominance of Berlin. Thus the weekly *Der Kunstwart,* founded in 1887 in Dresden and moving to Munich in 1894, waged under F. Avenarius' long editorship a persistent battle against Berlin's cultural hegemony, against the nervous tension there, the rationality, the immorality, the ugliness; yet though always bolstering up the provinces, it had to have a special section for Berlin culture. The luxury art periodical *Pan,* founded in 1895 to improve bourgeois taste, fought steadily against 'the fatal central-ization of art in Berlin'. It had special numbers devoted to the cultural life of provincial centres like Hamburg, Dresden and Munich, running into trouble with Hofmannsthal's friend Andrian when it seemed to rank Vienna too as a provincial centre. Periodicals like *Nord und Süd, Süddeutsche Monatshefte* or the Catholic *Hochland* had their *raison d'être* in their hostility to Berlin, though it was as much the Prussian, authoritarian or Protestant Berlin as the avant-garde Berlin. The regional litera-ture, 'Heimatkunst', advocated by Bartels and Lienhard from about 1900 and exemplified in the work of Frenssen, Hermann Löns, Hermann Burte and others, differed from the regionalism of the earlier part of the century, that of Reuter, Groth, Anzengruber, Keller etc., in being directed specifically against metropolitan culture, and for this reason always threatening to turn into a reactionary, semi-mystical, irrational 'völkische' ideology. An anonymous pamphlet (by R. Schuster) *Das Berlin-ertum in Literatur, Musik, und Kunst,* reviewed sympathe-tically in *Der Kunstwart* for 1895, struck this note when it attacked the 'hybrid culture' of Berlin, allegedly arising from the swollen and rootless non-German population that lacked 'Bodenwüchsigkeit aus der heimatlichen Scholle gesättigt'. In this ideology the city becomes identified with democracy and impure breeding, with intellect as against soul, mind as against feeling ('Gemüt'). Some of these writers started, like Lienhard, as naturalists, and claimed their countryside themes to be the legiti-mate heirs of Naturalism, that 'earth-fresh' Naturalism that the Harts and Conrad had dreamed of. If one remembers that there were other alternatives to metropolitan themes, other symbol systems like George's or the neo-romantic indulgence in medieval semi-mystical romance, it is more understandable that Jacobowski, with Conrad the founder of *Die Gesellschaft* in 1885, could in 1900, while defining Naturalism as 'Groszstadtliteratur' and believing that Heimatkunst may be a cure for the sickness of city life, hope that Naturalism and Heimatkunst might be reconciled. Jacobowski, like Heinrich Mann in *Im Schlaraffenland*, identifies Naturalism not only with the capital but also with the plutocracy; and perhaps the oddest defence of this not utterly unfounded charge is Otto Flake's, in an article of 1904, where he asserts that literature (culture) and politics must inevitably go hand in hand, and that, since imperialism demands centralization of power, therefore literature too must have its centre in the metropolis and be imperial in spirit and structure.

Few imaginative writers liked the modern Berlin. The description of it and its social life that one finds in the most devoted Berliners like Kretzer or Holz or Heym is usually appalling, even if the vice of the wealthy and the misery of the poor is sometimes sensationally touched up. Many non-Berliners shared the young Hermann Hesse's detestation of the pretensions of the 'Groszstadtmoderne' there, the combination, as he defines it in *Peter Camenzind*, of fastidious aestheticism with the cult of the brothel. Yet nearly all owed a peculiar debt to Berlin. The Bavarian Ludwig Thoma, chilled when he visited Berlin by the coldness in the cultural community, the lack of intimacy and trust and the tense rivalries, the servility towards the Kaiser, put out too by the pervasiveness of the Jews, yet never forgot that the decisive impulses in his own literary life had come from Berlin and that the drawbacks there were less frustrating than the good-humoured clerical obscurantism of Munich. Max Halbe, who migrated from West Prussia to Munich and detested Berlin, like many other authors had his first success there (*Jugend* 1893) while in Munich he gained acknowledgement only years later. It was Berlin that first lifted the censorship ban on Wedekind's *Frühlings Erwachen*, while in Munich he was still condemned to cabaret performances. For all its rationalism, Berlin was most generous in its artistic sympathies. It was the Berlin producer Brahm who really established Schnitzler and Hofmannsthal, who found in Berlin more appreciative audiences than in Vienna. Later Hofmannsthal insisted that Reinhardt, one of the few people he felt truly 'believed in' his work, should produce the *Ariadne* opera (in Stuttgart), and it was in Berlin that Reinhardt gave *Jedermann* its first production (1911). Ernst Barlach, whose religious feeling seems totally out of place in Berlin, found there Paul Cassirer to publish his strange plays and his illustrations and sell his figures, the Cassirer who published Heinrich Mann and Kokoschka's literary oddities, defended 'die Brücke', and sheltered the gentle, mystical Christian Morgenstern.

Munich

Of the other cities of the Reich only Munich could rival Berlin as a creative centre. Hamburg was receptive to new trends but too solidly bourgeois to take any initiative, even after the appointment of Baron von Berger to manage its theatres. Alfred Lichtwark, the director of the Kunsthalle and a most enterprising spirit, tended to look abroad to English reserve or backwards to a purer historicism for an antidote to Wilhelmine vulgarity. The musical life in Dresden was brilliant, and for some years the Intendant Graf Seebach brought a breath of modernism into the theatre, but court control was too near to allow for much experiment. It was here in 1912 that the Strauss-Hofmannsthal *Rosenkavalier* was first produced, but court pressure caused alterations in the Marschallin's bedroom scene and the erasure of some of Ochs' improprieties. The *Ariadne* first night at Stuttgart was ruined by court ceremonial, which lengthened the two intervals to fifty minutes each. All the same, many provincial cities, Leipzig, Nürnberg, Stuttgart and others, welcomed visiting companies from Berlin and Munich with the most advanced modern works, Hauptmann or Wedekind. Such cities provided very appreciative audiences for writers when they went on the literary circuit; Thomas Mann and Hofmannsthal seem to have liked the audiences they faced, Rilke was brought to despair by their obtuseness. If one compares Germany in this respect to Britain or France, one can only admire the vigour of cultural interest and participation in the German provincial centres, the readiness of theatres and literary societies to give a hearing to the most provocative writers. But compared with the metropolis they were not creative. In such cities as Hamburg or Dresden the new industrial society had not shaken the older bourgeois or aristocratic establishment sufficiently to produce a strong pressure for new literary and artistic forms.

Munich was different. Though in 1900 approaching the half-million mark, it had very marked pre-industrial features. Ludwig Thoma calls it an overgrown village. The misfortunes of its kings, the mysterious devotion of Ludwig II to Wagner, gave them a sort of halo, the more radiant because of their remoteness from political and social life. The Catholic-dominated government, if very paternalistic, seemed also a bulwark against the aggressive ruthlessness of capitalism. The urban population was preeminently Catholic and still had a peasant character, robust, uncouth and not a little sly; the state and city officials were very poorly paid and had none of the sophistication or arrogance of Berlin bureaucrats. There was, as a result, a remarkable ease of communication between the various classes and a lack of cultural snobbery. The city had prided itself since the reign of Ludwig I on being the 'Kunststadt' of Germany, and held a large population of artists who created a convivial bohème. The annual exhibitions of paintings were of considerable national importance, as were the visiting exhibitions from Paris. If the older Munich bourgeoisie admired the classicism of Kaulbach or the portraiture of Lenbach, the closest pictorial parallels to the work of the Munich writer Paul Heyse, the Munich exhibitions of the post-Impressionists, Cézanne, Gauguin, Van Gogh, were second in importance only to the Berlin, and it was here that Kandinsky and Marc issued *Der blaue Reiter* and held their first exhibition (1911). Wolfskehl was one of the first critics to appreciate Marc, Kandinsky, and Klee.

The lively and relaxed atmosphere of Munich attracted many writers from elsewhere, Thomas Mann from Lübeck, Halbe from Prussia, the Berliner Karl Wolfskehl, the centre of the George disciples in Munich and George's frequent host, Wedekind from Switzerland where he had spent most of his childhood. The cultural community was peculiarly detached from the city and state, and felt itself to be an independent world; one cannot speak of a 'Munich culture' as one can of a Berlin or Vienna one. The writers and artists created a large bohème in Schwabing, with their private theatricals and cabaret, and found and sought little response among the bourgeoisie. A contributor to *Freie Bühne* derisively called Munich 'an art-city, a beer-city, a city to relax in', and for many it seemed the ideal environment for a bohème that could turn carnival time into a gigantic sexual frolic. Arthur Holitscher writes in his autobiography of the 'parasitic' character of the artistic community there, and perhaps we can see the specific Munich situation reflected in the sharpness of the contrast between artist and burgher made by Thomas Mann in *Tonio Kröger* and other early works. If this were the whole truth, however, it would be difficult to understand how it came about that Munich became the home of the first Naturalist periodical, *Die Gesellschaft,* founded in 1885.

In fact, while Munich was a most charming city, with its noble medieval and Baroque churches, its harmonious modern italianate buildings, its palaces, and the English Garden fanning out from the centre of the city into the far countryside, it did not escape the fate of Wilhelmine cities. Beer was a great industry as well as the source of conviviality. The city was expanding rapidly, with all the attendant land speculation, devastation and cheap building. The villas of the rich showed the same tasteless opulence as elsewhere, the same historical medley. The Gothic Rathaus was a monument to this absurd historicism. The beginnings of a modern architecture were present in such utility buildings as the railway station, that the naive provincials of Frank's *Die Räuberbande* come to Munich to admire. M. G. Conrad settled in Munich to found *Die Gesellschaft* partly because it was less authoritarian than Prussia, but found conditions there such as to encourage him to emulate his admired Zola. Thus the theme of his novel *Was die Isar rauscht* (1887) is the destructive rapacity of land speculators and builders, the corruption of business morality that infects journalism and even the officer class, and is paralleled by sexual licence and family strife. Helene Böhlau describes in *Der Rangierbahnhof* (1895) the stifling narrowness that accompanied Munich 'Gemütlichkeit', and though she is not a great writer her social insight goes deeper than Thomas Mann's typification of the Bavarian in Permaneder. In *Der Marquis von Keith* (1900) Wedekind gives a scarifying picture of the corrupt world of Munich finance and speculation.

Among the immigrants to Munich were the publishers Albert Langen and Georg Hirsch, who came from the North to found respectively *Simplicissimus* and *Jugend* in 1896. These two satirical weeklies, the best in pre-war Germany, attracted contributions from writers and artists all over Germany, and the best writers felt honoured to appear in them. Though the tone of both was sharp, both admitted humorous and serious contributions that had no political or social bearing. They directed their satire at the same sort of things: clericalism, religious and moral hypocrisy particularly in relation to sex, authoritarianism and the arrogance of office, imperialism, militarism, the over-bearing conceit of officers and the stupidity and prejudices of the petty bourgeoisie.

Jugend, with its comforting message of health and happiness and its long series of seductive cover-girls, was far less radical than *Simplicissimus*, led by the brilliant caricaturist Th. Th. Heine and including on its board independent men like Ludwig Thoma and Wedekind, and among its contributors Thomas Mann and the greatest line-artist of them all, Olaf Gulbransson. Reaching before the war a circulation of 100,000, *Simplicissimus* was one of the most important organs of political opposition; the aged Heine's melancholy over its failure to destroy reactionary German nationalism hardly does justice to the real possibilities. The success of these weeklies, like that of *Elf Scharfrichter*, the best of the satirical cabarets of this period, was due to Munich, to the ease of communication, even intimacy, in its cultural community, the lack of cliques and fanaticism, the consequent possibility of gaiety and good humour. In the city itself, as in Bavaria as a whole, the same social changes were taking place as in the rest of the Reich, but not so intensively, not so massively and oppressively, often in a quaint variation that allowed hilarity as well as criticism.

Vienna and Prague

Vienna shows the same characteristics as the other metropolis, Berlin, but with a very different balance of forces. With a glorious past as the head of a great multinational empire, its present was the scene of a long losing battle between the old aristocracy and the forces of disintegration that found political expression in the German-national anti-semites that ruled the city, the Social Democrats, and the separatist nationalities. The old ruling class found delay and postponement the wisest policy, though yielding at times to fits of political violence, and a peculiar atmosphere of indecisive power and cynical conservatism came to characterize Vienna, the capital of an empire, as Kraus put it in 1899, 'on which the sun never rises'. It produced that famous Viennese mixture of consideration, charm, egoism and cynicism that Schnitzler condensed in his plays and stories, that George and Rilke (himself an Austrian) could not bear, that Karl Kraus bitterly attacked. German criticism was often arrogant, and Felix Salten put a reasonable defence of his home city when he wrote (in *Morgen*, 1907, the paper of which Hofmannsthal was a literary editor) that Viennese society was not frivolous and laxly cynical, but humane and tolerant, that authority was not arrogant and aggressive as in Berlin, and that there was no such servility to the military in Vienna as had led in Prussia to the hoax of the Hauptmann of Köpenik.

There were various 'cultures' in both cities, differentiated socially and ideologically, but the culture of the educated in Vienna was much more homogeneous and pervasive than in Berlin, and there was no such sharp antagonism between the intelligentsia and the bourgeoisie. The writers were attached to their city with a peculiar affection, and this affection in men like Schnitzler, Hofmannsthal or Stefan Zweig imposed a certain conservatism and patriotism on their cultural attitudes totally different from the nationalism and radicalism of Germans. The city itself seemed to be contrived to prevent the direct clash of ideologies. In the inner city the Hofburg was surrounded by the mansions of the old aristocracy, the imperial and court offices, the cathedral and Baroque churches and clerical administration, and the commercial services of privilege and wealth; on all sides noble memories and unpretentious grace. The clearance of the Ring separated this core of ancient dignities from the modern and bourgeois world; Burgtheater, Opera and gardens served as links, Rathaus and imperial Parliament belonged to the conflicting classes and nationalities. Further outside were the great factories and working-class districts, while the Prater still offered the simple pleasures in which the whole populace could join. Visible nearby, the Wiener Wald stood for release from urban pressures and for memories of victory over the Turks, and not far off was a vast Alpine world with a population hardly touched by modern developments. Vienna did not oppress like Berlin, its variety offered relaxation, it was a place to saunter through, as opposed to the hurry and tensions of Berlin. Even its most famous bohemian, Peter Altenberg, was relaxed, naive, affectionate, tolerant. Its cultural life was very conservative, tending to live, like the Burgtheater and Opera, on the glories of the past. Not until Gustav Mahler was appointed director of the Opera in 1899 and Paul Schlenther was imported from Berlin to take charge of the Burgtheater in 1904, did a modern spirit begin to erode these buttresses of the establishment. Hofmannsthal complained frequently of the disregard of his plays and the Strauss-Hofmannsthal operas in his own city; he tried and failed to bring Reinhardt there at the end of the war, but was successful in

importing Richard Strauss. Yet his ideal of the English gentleman, his Hans Karl Bühl, like Schnitzler's ideal of 'decency',
are all embedded in actual (upper-class) Viennese society.
Schlenther and Brahm, fairly typical Berlin intellectuals, press-
men, men of the theatre, who were rather contemptuous of
Munich intellectual life, loved and respected Vienna, perhaps
because of the absence of the sharp dichotomy of intellectual and
society.

In the literary and artistic world of Vienna Jews were even
more predominant than in Berlin. Assimilation was also more
thorough, not only in the form of conversion and consequent
admission to public offices or of mixed marriages but in that of
assimilation in Austrian culture. As always, this hardly applied to
the poorest, who remained separate and often orthodox; it was
the wealthier, the more educated, the more gifted who entered
the stream of the higher culture. It has been calculated that in
1912 about nine per cent of the population was Jewish; but what
did 'Jewish' mean? There were very many with Jewish names
whose grandfathers had become Catholic, whose grandfathers
and fathers, like Hofmannsthal's, had married non-Jews and who
had lost all communal or religious attachments to Jewry, not to
speak of those whose Jewish mothers or grandmothers had
married into non-Jewish familes. Very many, like Freud or Karl
Kraus, lost both religious belief and communal ties, without a
formal break; others, like Mahler, entered the Catholic church as
a necessary condition for a career, and there might be an oddity
like Weininger who joined the Protestant church, in his case a
sign of his commitment to the cultural ideology of H. S.
Chamberlain. Schnitzler was a non-believing Jew who maintained his ties with the religious community. The growing anti-
semitism of the period, that led to repeated rebuffs to the social
aspirations of the Jews, also gave rise to Zionism, and Herzl's
movement won adherents in the city in which it was founded. But
in spite of these dissidents, the most marked feature of the Jewish
cultural contributions to literature, music and intellectual life in
general is their Austrian or Viennese character – the degree to
which the work of Jews reflects and interprets the common
culture of the city, to which they, and not only in the most
obvious cases of Schnitzler and Hofmannsthal, became the
accepted spokesmen of cultured Austria.

The modern movement as it took shape in Vienna about 1892,

under the leadership of the versatile Hermann Bahr, was metropolitan in a different sense from that of Berlin. The social movement and the faith in science were hardly in evidence. Bahr had Marxist, scientistic enthusiasms behind him, but brought from Paris the latest phase, the 'nervous romanticism' as he called it, of Bourget and Huysmans, a heightened and sophisticated attentiveness to moods and sensations that was achieved at the cost of energy and social activity. (Bourget's work embodied too a polemically conservative political doctrine that remained implicit in this style.) This elimination of social activity encouraged that questioning of reality, that absorption in dream and play, characteristic of the early Hofmannsthal, Schnitzler, Beer-Hofmann, Andrian. The passive melancholy of this rather lush metropolitan culture is punctuated, especially in the works of Hofmannsthal, by an irruptive and brutal violence (e.g. in *Reitergeschichte, Das gerettete Venedig* or *Elektra*), and both aspects seem to interpret the condition of Austria in this period. In the early 1900s the growing ethical concern of both Schnitzler and Hofmannsthal indicates a wider awareness of the fragility of the society and culture of the metropolis, but it is typically Viennese that Schnitzler's most positive figures, like Professor Bernhardi, are both honest and evasive, or that Hofmannsthal's symbols, with *Jedermann*, turn towards semi-religious simplifications. In fact, however, the decade before the First World War shows such changes in Vienna, such rapid decline in the authority and self-confidence of the ruling class and the cultured milieux, that one can less than ever speak of a single or even a dominant culture. For while Hofmannsthal and Schnitzler represent a conservative though not reactionary line, the younger writers like Stefan Zweig join in the rhetorical exuberance of the Expressionists, and in music Schoenberg is emerging out of his early romanticism and aestheticism to new forms that disrupt tradition more than Expressionism did. And in architecture and design Vienna was the home of the most important revolution against tradition and towards functionalism. Such great changes were highly sophisticated products of the metropolis, and only imaginable in an environment freed of the personal immediacy of traditional culture and social pressures.

A comparison of Vienna with Berlin indicates how much more sharply metropolitan features emerged in the German capital and why cultural initiatives continually emanated from there. Even more clearly, Prague, that made so remarkable a contribution to modernist literature, owes a great debt to Berlin. The older German culture there, even if sympathetic to Slav aspirations, was essentially Austrian. Rilke, though his early stories show sympathy with Czech national feeling, did not long belong to Prague and discovered himself abroad, in Paris and Germany. We are here not concerned with the older generation of emancipated Jews, like Fritz Mauthner who after 1866 opted for Prussia and the Reich. The Prague we are concerned with is that of the generation of Max Brod, born in the 1880s, a younger generation than the German Naturalists.

Prague contained round 1900 about 450,000 Czechs, and a characteristic Czech literature, art, and music was challenging the cultural supremacy of the imperial rulers. There were only about ten thousand non-Jewish Germans living in the city, but twenty-five thousand Jews, eleven thousand of whom used German colloquially. Since the best schools and the university were German (Austrian), the boys of the more assimilated Jewish families were brought up in the atmosphere of German culture, and indeed the generation of Brod and Kafka was the main pillar of German culture in the city. At the same time, many were responsive to the Czech cultural and national movements round them and learned Czech if they did not speak it at home, Brod expending himself generously on behalf of Czech artists and composers (Janaček). At times this dual loyalty might be felt as a divided loyalty, and a third rival arose through the advance of Zionism among the young educated Jews from about 1900. Though Brod in his *Der Prager Kreis* (1966) seems to overestimate its importance, Zionism was certainly exerting by 1910 a powerful emotional pull and contributing to a conflict of commitment.

If in Prague, as in Vienna, the contrast between a glorious imperial past and an unrelated present was striking, the problems of industrialization and modernization were hardly tangible in this romantic, old-fashioned city. Yet its peculiar social composition created something akin to the central cultural problem of Berlin and Vienna. It engendered in an acute form the alienation of the cultured (Jews) from simple social or cultural commitments, a typically metropolitan rootlessness of the intellectuals, much more like their situation in Berlin than in Vienna. The group round Brod, Werfel and Kafka were more closely allied to the Berlin and German writers than the Austrian. Blei published Brod and Kafka in *Hyperion* (1908-10), Hiller put Brod and Werfel into his anthology *Der Kondor* (1912), Brod and Kafka were published in *Die weissen Blätter*, one of the earliest appreciations of Kafka appeared in 1913 in *Aktion*, and in 1918 Rudolf Kayser identified Berlin and Prague as the homes of Expressionism. It belongs to Prague perhaps, and not only to this Expressionist generation, that the socially directed, Naturalist type of response to the metropolis was only slightly represented here, and that the impressionism of Schnitzler and Hofmannsthal was equally rare. The city appears rather in its demonic aspect, like the Berlin of Heym's cycle or his short stories, a source of terror and bewilderment rather than of indignation or indulgence. It thus lent itself to the romantic glamourizing of Meyrink's *Der Golem*. The city as a sordid threat, stretching out glutinous tentacles, changing its shape, alien and unknowable, is the city of Kafka's sketches, of *Amerika* and *Der Prozess*; and if Kafka uses the city chiefly as a symbol, its modern reality was such as to lend itself readily to this symbolical use.

The city and the Literary Forms

The culture or literature of the modern city is by no means the exclusive product of the city. The metropolis is itself only a concentrate of a larger social complex, the elements of which spread over various environments. Any culture, too, has profound historical roots, and both its forms and their mode of functioning are very persistent and change much more slowly than economic practices and social institutions. Urban culture can therefore never be interpreted merely in terms of the city – unless one means by culture simply that typical behaviour that is a fairly direct response to social circumstance and lacks the reflection and generalization of what here is meant by literature and culture. The term 'literature of the city' is, therefore, used here to indicate those modifications in literary expression brought about by the experience of living in the modern city or metropolis.

Some of the urban themes found in German literature have already been indicated in passing, and they could be endlessly multiplied. Urbanization of the psyche may take place where there is no explicit reference to the city, and often is expressed in ostensible revolt against the city. It was naive of Max Brod to believe that by showing (in *Der Prager Kreis*) that he and Kafka and their friends loved the countryside he refutes Peter Demetz's contention (in *Rilkes Prager Jahre*) that Jewish-German Prague writing was predominantly urban; what is decisive is the way they experienced the countryside, what it meant for them. An investigation of the penetration of literature by the modern city would therefore be limitless. All that this section aims at is to indicate some formal changes that may be ascribed to the new living-complex – again with the qualification that urban experience cannot be exclusive, though it may well be decisive. Some of these changes had already occurred abroad, notably in France, and hence often appear in German as adoption or adaptation of foreign models.

All writers on the modern city in the 1880s stress the multiplicity and confusion of scenes and events, the rapidity of change and 'nervousness' of life, as well as the inescapable squalor and misery of the poor. In the new poetry of Holz and Henckell, that Holz claimed created a 'Groszstadtlyrik', we find as its most prominent element the urban landscape of disparate events, sights and noises, that interprets the fortuitous medley of the city without experiential significance for the poet except in the sense that he may share the revolutionary protest of the deprived. Holz introduces also here and there words of a slangy or conversational character that bring with them a whiff of the cheeky Berliner. But the grammar and style of these poems is conventional, tending towards the rhetorical, and the stanza-form and meter is heavy and rigid. Holz himself admitted in *Revolution der Lyrik* (1899) that, while he had broken with the rhythmical formulas of romanticism, he had failed to create a new rhythmical form adequate to his urban themes. The rigid framework he and Henckell adopted remained more or less standard for two decades, for most of the poems in the anthology *Im steinernen Meer* and for the worker poets like Bröger and Lersch. If a looser form in free rhythms occurs, often as an adaptation of Whitman or of Verhaeren, it is accompanied by rhetoric, which no less than regular stanzas and meter conveys the poet's capacity to control this urban world, however confused and terrifying, from some fixed perspective such as the security of his inner life, or the dignity of labour, or human compassion, or the prospect of revolution. In these decades the harrowing disorientation caused by the modern city is found only rarely, notably in such a poem as

Hofmannsthal's *Vorfrühling*, where the light, swaying rhythms and the fleeting suggestivity of the images reinforce the bewilderment and fascination explicit in the urban landscape.

For most poets the city was a negation, and they turned to quite other themes. Rilke confronts more pertinaciously than most the teeming life of the city, where individual life is so devoid of meaningfulness, as in the Third Part of *Das Stundenbuch* or poems like *Morgue*; but his horror and especially the inner illumination countervailing the 'unrelated land' of the city is more successfully conveyed in symbolic poems like *Auszug des Verlorenen Sohnes* than in those where urban circumstances appear in their factuality. With the Expressionist generation the city becomes central, and in a way that deeply influences form. Trakl is not fully representative, for while the horror of the city creates obsessive images of decay and catastrophe, he can still find a refuge in images of faith, home, permanence. Others however respond to the city without the security of other values. Some, like Stadler, may celebrate the exhilaration of machines and technological achievements, and develop a rhapsodic form, at other times mourning the desolation of city life. Others grow intoxicated at the thought of revolution, and like Becher pile factualities one on top of the other in order to build up an impression of chaotic power that one day will be united and irresistible. But the most significant response, that in one way or another underlies the others, is Heym's intense vision of the horror of cities, not untouched by rhetoric but accepted as the inescapable reality. This vision of the demonic city, closer to Rimbaud than to the more rhetorical Verhaeren, introduces new formal elements into German poetry. Heym has not the audacious fantasy and aggressive energy of Rimbaud, and the severe regularity of his metrical form seems almost too rigid and controlled for the apocalyptic landscape he invokes. But his revolt against reality is embodied in the energy of his images, in the violent association of normally disparate fields of meaning through strange conjunctions of image or the use, for instance, of symbolical, non-naturalistic colour images, and a thematic development that does not accord with the logic of normal rational discourse. In these ways Heym accepts the modern city as his reality and speaks in its terms, but at the same time challenges it by re-composing it; the poet's vision becomes embodied within, not in conflict with, the factualities of the city. As the war generation of poets became involved with politics, this new poetic language became overlaid with moral and political purposes that led to a recrudescence of rhetoric, for instance with Becher or Werfel. But the new poetic imagery remained, and it may be maintained that the inter-penetration of hitherto disparate fields of experience, and the consequent unhinging of normal narrative or logical structure, since then so characteristic of the modern lyric, has at least one of its sources in the character of the modern city.

In a *Freie Bühne* article of 1892 Wilhelm Bölsche wrote of the lack of interest in the novel among the avant-garde, a curious fact since perhaps the strongest literary stimulus towards Naturalism had been Zola's work, in which, as in the novels of Daudet, Bourget and Huysmans, Germans recognized the world of the modern city. A reviewer in *Freie Bühne* for 1891, for instance, called Bourget's *Physiologie de l'amour moderne* the analysis of the love specific to the great city. The earliest Naturalist attempts at 'modern' novels were formally very clumsy. Max Kretzer's Berlin series contains some authentic descriptions of the harsh circumstances of the poor, but the narrative structure is as con-ventional (Dickensian) as the moralistic emphases. Novels of failure under the pressure of modern society, on the model of Jacobsen's *Niels Lyhne*, follow usually the traditional biographical form. But we can also observe the emergence of new narrative structures that are a specific response to modern city life.

On the small scale, there is what one may call the sketch, the short piece that is markedly different from the Novelle and the short story for it lacks, or has only a minimum of, story. Its principle is to present a scene from everyday life, with scarcely any event proper, but with an open suggestiveness as regards the lives and characters of the persons who appear. The newspapers offered the opportunity and stimulus for publishing such sketches, and the work of Peter Altenberg, Otto Julius Bierbaum and Kretzer is clearly connected with journalism. What is characteris-tic is the explicit or implicit presupposition that city life is made up of an infinitude of separate incidents and persons, far too disparate to have more than a momentary connection one with another, and far too fortuitous significantly to affect the pattern of life of the people engaged or to have a definable meaning for the author-observer, who can do little more than record the momentary encounter or occurrence. It is noticeable that where Kretzer makes a story out of such slight material, all his faults as a heavy and sentimental moralist are displayed. Where he confines himself to a chance experience, the visits of a Salvation Army lass to a public house or the outpourings of a theatrical agent, without a story and without a 'lesson' that can be formulated, Kretzer writes with surprising ease and naturalness. Altenberg has a more selfconscious impressionistic charm, but unfortunately tends to smuggle in some self-advertisement. The best quality of the sketch is pure recapture, or creation, of a fragment of experience, not fitted into story and hence into interpretation. The short 'stories' of Georg Heym, *Der Irre, Jonathan* and *Der Dieb*, are brilliant examples of this objectivity and reticence.

In the *Papa Hamlet* stories of Holz and Schlaf, that were intended to be the demonstrations of Naturalistic theory, the most obvious element is the attempt at a precise rendering of a changing visual and aural reality, of settings, behaviour, and speech (the so-called 'Sekundenstil'). The tendency towards dramatic form is obtrusive and Holz's theory is in fact most inadequate in respect to the narrative form; the formula 'art = nature − x', where x means 'the technical conditions of artistic reproduction', evades all the problems of narrative structure and perspective, and of course the whole question of language itself. But some of the sketches capture in the inconsequential shape of their events and stylistically too something essential to the modern city. *Der erste Schultag* presents first a scene in a classroom (a hysterical fit of a Jewish boy), then the journey of another boy first to the circus and then to a friend. The centre of concern changes, there are multiple simultaneous occurrences none of which has a conclusion. We notice two consequent features. There is a tendency to excessive, i.e. undiscriminating factual detail, but Holz checks its disintegrating effect by turning incidents into symbols – the struggling bluebottle for instance becomes a symbol of the tortured boy. And because of the expressive limitations of a realism that wishes to be objective recording, Holz starts to discover (and this seems to have been an unconscious process) the need for a complex narrative perspective, or rather for a multiple perspective; so that, for instance, we see the Jewish boy partly as hidden spectators, partly through the minds of his schoolfellows, and partly through the eyes of the schoolmaster. All this is achieved without clumsy grammatical signals. It is a beginning of that 'free indirect speech' so profoundly characteristic of the modern novel, which interprets not simply the multiplicity of facts and events surrounding everyone in the city, but also the multiple points of view that make up this social reality. The *Papa Hamlet* sketch itself embodies a still more differentiated multiple perspective, and more consistently and provocatively replaces the traditional intimacy between author and reader with a harsh objectivity of narration, that interprets the nature of interpersonal relationships in the great city.

In the novel proper, the association of these formal qualities with the great city is quite explicit. In 1887 M. G. Conrad's *Was die Isar rauscht* opened what was intended to be a Munich series comparable to Zola's *Les Rougon-Macquart*. His method is to give a cross-section of the city, so that the reader follows portions of several lives that are simultaneous and separate, occasionally touching one another, but none able to claim a priority of interest over others. Most do not reach any conclusion. At the same time, there is a deliberate attempt to enter into the perspective of different characters. This is sometimes done in a clumsy manner, through letters or long expository conversations, but sometimes there is something close to the modern inner monologue, through which the reader is put inside the head of a character, perhaps disturbed with him by the accidents of city life as he passes through the streets. That Conrad was well aware of the difficulty of binding these disparate elements together is shown by his artificial and sentimental device of linking the various strands to the Isar rolling rapidly.

Many of the best novels of the following decades are quite untouched by this sort of formal innovation – for instance Thomas Mann's *Buddenbrooks* or Hauptmann's *Emanuel Quint*, neither of which belongs to the modern city, and Heinrich Mann's work, which might have profited from greater formal subtlety. But there are some significant thrusts in the new direction. Schnitzler was one of the first authors to adopt systematically the form of the inner monologue (notably in *Fräulein Else*), but the structure of *Der Weg ins Freie* (1908) is more remarkable. A novel teeming with characters, who appear incidentally, some only through remarks of acquaintance or relatives, whose 'story' only in the rarest case is 'completed', whose future remains undetermined, is held together by a framework love affair of a man of only slight intrinsic worth and interest, whose function is above all to link the numerous persons of his acquaintance. The narrative runs tightly alongside the composer Georg von Wergenthin, and we enter the minds of others only through their words, or his understanding of their words. Such a structure would be functional only in a crowded and varied city. It has a further significance since, while the hero and his beloved are non-Jews, nearly all their musical friends are cultured Jews, and the fragmentariness, incompleteness of their personal 'stories' is the structural interpretation of the much discussed precariousness of their social role.

Still more remarkable is the structure of Rilke's *Die Aufzeichnungen des Laurids Malte Brigge* (1910), which has no story. Malte himself is not a person observed, but an observing eye and mind, and the teeming world of Paris round him is not resolved into individual fates, as with Schnitzler, but appears in desolate anonymity. Sections of the novel that describe Paris have therefore the sheer fortuitousness and dissociation of any metropolitan scene, to which Malte succumbs. All he can oppose to it are memories and visions of a different, more personalized world, that of his childhood or of chronicles and legends, and these episodes form a mysteriously articulated counterpoint to the depersonalized city, of a less substantial reality that in the end fails to sustain him. In these and other novels, like Döblin's *Wadzeks Kampf mit der Dampfmaschine* (1918), one can observe a movement, or perhaps a groping, towards the form that Joyce first fully explored in *Ulysses*, and of which Döblin's *Alexanderplatz* is so notable a variant.

In the drama, the Naturalist theme of the destructive power of social circumstances found formal expression in the precise presentation of physical settings, behaviour, and speech; the stage-directions of the early Holz and Schlaf or Hauptmann sometimes go beyond the visual capacities of the stage. In a writer like Sudermann, such novelties are forced into a dramatic structure that is conventionally sensational, and Hauptmann's first play, *Vor Sonnenaufgang*, has a conventionally tragic ending. In the best plays, however, there is a minimum of plot and an openness of ending that indicate not simply a distaste for sensation but a feeling that the predominantly social themes transcend the limits of any personal life and that, while individuals may have different fates, the truly typical situation is one of openness (as in *Die Familie Selicke* or *Die Weber*). The traditional structure of drama is tenacious, but the trend to replace the 'hero' by a group of characters, the dramatic conflict of wills by a more inarticulate struggle of people against circumstances or habitual values, indicates the experiences of city living. Hauptmann's *Die Weber*, the setting of which actually belongs to an earlier stage of industrialization and urbanization, most brilliantly embodies the new trends: a vast number of characters who in turn come to the forefront and then withdraw, no single one of whom typifies the whole; a social struggle the human significance of which transcends the fate of any individual, and the outcome of which remains unresolved at the end. Hauptmann is here very near the Brechtian conclusion: 'Verehrtes Publikum, los, such dir selbst den Schluss!'

Strangely enough, this concern with the dramatic presentation of masses promoted among the Expressionists a formal device the very opposite of the individual differentiation in Hauptmann. We find with Reinhold Sorge, Hasenclever, von Unruh or Kaiser the characteristic use of types instead of persons (the son, the father etc.) as a means to express their awareness of social role and to claim for their figures a representative validity. Wrenching thus the dramatic figure out of the differentiated multiplicity of individuality, their psychology also becomes general, their speech formal, and hence the monumental and rhetorical character of this sort of drama. The masses undergo the same sort of generalization, become in Kaiser or Hasenclever (*Antigone*) or Toller (*Die Wandlung*) a single and almost faceless unit. This general trend to symbolism, so marked among the Expressionists, embodies a social attitude that seems to confine the assertion of will and choice to an élite. While, for Hauptmann's masses, action is an individual choice for each man, the Expressionist masses act as it seems automatically and irrationally; or, to be more exact, while the dramatic leader, the hero, takes a decision to impose his spiritual values on his world, the masses are there only to follow him; they are degraded to mere tools of the inspired leader. This type of dramatic structure is related to the city only in the sense that it reflects the remoteness of the writers from the working masses, except as regimented in the army.

A totally different aspect of city life is incorporated in the dramatic work of Schnitzler. Plays like *Reigen* depict the slightness and fortuitousness of human encounters in the city, where sexual partners are exchanged as easily as those in a dance; the elegant formality, the linking echoes, the delicacy of touch create a new type of dramatic unity of mood, a subdued melancholy that recognizes the perpetual repetition beneath the delusion of uniqueness. Equally sophisticated and metropolitan are the very different plays of Wedekind. His characters have no roots other than money, sex, or pleasure, and thus Wedekind seems deliberately to deprive them of individuality and approximate them to grotesque puppets. The cardboard plots, the disregard for psychology and probability, with the Grand Guignol and farcical effects, all contribute to the cynicism that is the philosophy of this sophisticated world, as do the teeming paradoxes, which nearly all serve to debunk. What is strikingly lacking in almost all Wedekind's plays is a moral perspective that would justify the grotesque caricature; Wedekind seems, like his Marquis Keith, to be a victim of the consuming competition of the great city.

Among the happiest theatrical forms of the great city was the cabaret, which Ernst von Wolzogen, the founder of the Berlin 'Uberbrettl', called the challenge of a hilarious spirit to the screaming contradictions of the city (*Das literarische Echo*, 1901). Its most characteristic products were satirical and parodistic songs, Moritaten, often directed at the sentimentalities of popular taste, and short, ebullient and grotesque sketches feeding on the absurdities of daily life. Such work is very evanescent, since it so depends on the mood of the moment and the artistry of the performer; to eke out the texts of even so brilliant an artist as Karl Valentin one needs memories of gestures and voices to reinforce imagination. Wolzogen claimed that cabaret art is a fusion of high and popular art, of 'style' and vulgarity, and Max Halbe suggested (*Jahrhundertwende*, 1935) that the grotesques of the cabaret, the close relationship between artist and audience, the general mood, were the beginning of the dissolution of traditional theatrical forms. This change however hardly became evident till after 1918, when a profound social upheaval had shaken the fortresses of tradition.

The formal innovations summarized above were almost all steps towards greater formal complexity, and required in the reader or audience a greater sophistication. Popular dramatic forms, like the 'dramas' of the suburban theatres, were looked down on, and though Kafka's delight in the Yiddish players who visited Prague demonstrates an unusual appreciation of naive plays and performances, it must to some extent be put down to his Jewish sympathies. A few writers like Bierbaum and Wedekind were fascinated by popular metropolitan forms like the circus, the variety theatre, farce and melodrama, and Wedekind was one of the few dramatists to incorporate various elements of these into his plays, fitting a naive delight in 'play' and 'theatre' into a sophisticated anti-naturalistic intention. The normal attitude of the avant-garde to the circus was expressed by Max Herrmann in a poem published in *Aktion* (1912) in which he jeers at the crudity of the illusion and the credulity of the 'boorish' spectators. Rilke's interpretation in the *Duineser Elegien* is not only highly sophisticated but more evocative of Picasso's painting than of the smells and thrills of the circus.

In the same way, the usual attitude to the newly invented cinema was one of intellectual and artistic superiority, even in Pfemfert's *Aktion* with its strong socialist sympathies. It is true that there were good artistic grounds for *Aktion*'s hostility to film, for the film was the most crass example of the exploitation and degradation of art by big business. But the critics in *Aktion* also refused to believe that the film could become an art form, and they attacked Hauptmann or Schnitzler for allowing their work to be filmed; Wedekind, though relatively unconcerned about the commercialization of art, refused to allow anything of his to be filmed because filming was bound to mangle it. There were exceptions among the intellectuals and writers, as *Das Kino-Buch* of 1913 shows. Max Brod wrote enthusiastically (*Neue Rundschau* 1909) about films he saw in Paris (*actualités*, trick films, slapstick), H. H. Ewers championed the film as an art form (1913), and Carl Einstein, while fulminating against the brainlessness of films, praised Chaplin as embodying absurdity ('Blödsinn'). Whether literature in this period absorbed any formal influences from films is difficult to decide. It may be that Döblin's early theory and practice shows the influence of film in the immense rush and crowdedness of street scenes and the replacement of psychological exploration by behavioural description. Rudolf Paulsen was of the opinion in 1918 that the speed, violence, and sensationalism of the early films is reflected in Expressionist poetry and prose (*Expressionismus*, ed. Paul Raabe). On the whole these popular forms of city-entertainment did not begin to erode the traditional cultured theatre until after the war, with Piscator and Brecht; whatever the ideology of the writer, and however the established theatre was altered, the intellectual and social status of art and its artistic function till then remained fairly constant.

Simmel's Conception of Metropolitan Culture

So far, the literary works and trends that have been discussed embody direct and usually explicit responses to the urban world, roughly speaking within the orbit of Tönnies' or Nordau's criticism of bourgeois society, variants on which were the commonplaces of journalism. Tönnies indicts the great city as 'the doom and death' of the Volk and of culture, the epitome of the disintegrated 'society' in which each person lives alienated and dissociated, at the mercy of a rootless and capricious freedom. Nordau, in the comprehensive diatribes of *Entartung* (1893), sees the great cities not only as the focuses of all imaginable types of decadence – vice, corruption, drugs, pornography, hysteria, satanism, mysticism, spiritualism, narcissism, symbolism – but suggests too that the nervous overexcitement of city life is due to the polluted atmosphere and food. Georg Simmel's analysis of the city is far fuller and more dispassionate than these, and particularly important since he tries to assess its influence in cultural areas that at first sight seem uncontaminated by it.

The essential elements of Simmel's analysis are contained in *Philosophie des Geldes* (1900), where the 'Groszstadt' is constantly referred to as the typical crystallization of the high capitalism that is his theme. He summed up some of his results in the short essay *Die Groszstädte und das Geistesleben*, written for the Dresden city exhibition of 1903, here accentuating the cultural problems that were his deepest concern. It is clear that as a general rule Simmel means by 'Groszstadt' the metropolis, and preeminently Berlin or Paris; this equivalent is used here.

In Simmel's view, the character of advanced capitalism, and the unremitting adaptations forced on people through the rapid changes in the forms of work and life, result in a growing intellectualization and rationalization of the mind, and a weakening of those temperamental qualities that attach man to habit and the past. The nature of freedom changes too, for while personal life becomes diversified and offers each man more choices, at the same time men become more subject to autonomous economic forces like the market and the work-process, and their own work becomes impersonal and fragmentary. Simmel's investigations are not directed towards the changing of circumstances but towards understanding the mental and cultural attitudes that the urban nexus engenders. This bourgeois bias is evident also in his interpretation of 'the life of the spirit', Geistesleben, for this term means for him the mental activity of the class traditionally concerned with thought and culture, and distant enough from direct economic pressures to be capable of differentiated responses. His arguments are distinguished by a dialectical understanding of the socio-cultural situation, which he sees as both determining attitudes and provoking rebellion, and by his recognition that the individual must both submit and resist if he is 'to preserve the independence and identity of his being against the super-powers of society, his historical heritage, and the external culture and technique of life'.

Thus Simmel sees the prevailing intellectualism of the metropolitan climate to be not simply a mechanical result of social pressures but also a defensive response of the individual, 'a preservative of subjective life against the overwhelming force of the metropolis'. The modern city is therefore not lacking in social coherence, as Tönnies and others had said; its sociality, says Simmel, is of a different character from the muggy closeness of the provincial town. The lack of 'Gemüt', the coldness even aversion in interpersonal relations, is not essentially a sign of 'desocialization' but a positive response to new circumstances and 'one of the elementary forms of sociality' of the great city. This type of observation illuminates Berlin social life and literature, and corrects the criticism of its cold rationality that was so often vented by visitors like Ludwig Thoma; the generation of Pfemfert, Kurt Hiller, Carl Einstein, Carl Sternheim could combine intellectualism with feeling, rationality with pathos, without falling back on provincial Gemüt. With the same dialectic Simmel explains the blasé attitude of some metropolitans as the self-defence of sensitive persons confronted by the cacophony of impressions and values in the modern city, whose denigration of conventional values threatens to devalue the denigrator and leads to that cynical or despairing 'decadence' prominent in the 1890s, from which Schnitzler and Hofmannsthal were not immune. Or Simmel observes that dandyism, eccentricity of dress and speech and literary style, has its origin in the multiplicity and fleetingness of meetings in the great city, so that the individual counters the slightness of personal impact with a conspicuous style. Simmel was no doubt thinking of the stylistic quirks of such contemporaries as Harden, Bahr, Kerr or Bierbaum, and should have included in his psychological explanation a consideration of the commercial and ideological interests behind the modern publicity media. When he comments on the degradation of language into clichés, ready-made formulae handed round like 'sealed jars', he analyses this feature of metropolitan intercourse also too exclusively in psychological terms, and does not examine the social bases and functions of jargon.

Simmel's general theme, that the psychology of the worker is profoundly influenced by the character of his work, and that in particular his consciousness of identity is undermined when he no longer makes a whole object, is developed in an illuminating way in relation to the consumer or observer. Once things are made for the anonymous market, they themselves lose in concrete individuality and, as commodities, are differentiated in terms of price rather than qualitatively; through price all objects become comparable and interchangeable. While this mass-production for the market offers the consumer a remarkable variety of choice, and therefore makes possible many shades of differentiation in habit and personal environment, the choice and differentiation are inessential and fortuitous. Things and people themselves thus become abstract; and this abstractness engenders a cultural resistance. There occurs, Simmel writes in *Philosophie des Geldes*:

a deep longing to bestow on things a new meaningfulness, a deeper significance, a value of their own. . . . The consequences and correlations of money have hollowed them out and made them indifferently interchangeable. But the lively movements in art, the search for new styles, for style as such, symbolism, even theosophy, are symptoms of the demand for a new, more deeply felt meaning of things – whether each thing thereby receives a new, more soulful emphasis, or whether it acquires this through being placed in some new relationship that redeems it from its atomization.

Simmel is here clearly summarizing trends already evident in contemporary art and literature. The symbolism of Böcklin or George, for instance, was one form of this rescue-operation of things, for their procedures meant that things were isolated from their normal contexts and associations and through a new context given a fresh individuality and perhaps too a symbolical meaning. The new symbolism was also deeply impregnated by a mysticism that attributed an irrational significance to things – in 1894 Paul

Gérardy had written in *Blätter für die Kunst* of the re-awakened mysticism that discovers meaning 'in the radiant mystery of things'. The strange, irrational, indefinable meaning that things can take on is the only alleviation of the despair of Hofmannsthal's *Lord Chandos* (1902). In this work there is no sign of acquaintance with Simmel's writings, nor in Hofmannsthal's essay of 1906, *Der Dichter und diese Zeit*, where the term he uses for cities, 'monstrous deserts', is not much more than a cliché. But *Briefe eines Zurückgekehrten*, published in 1907 in *Morgen*, bears signs of the fact that Hofmannsthal acquired and read Simmel's *Philosophie des Geldes* at the end of 1906. A returned German is horrified to find his compatriots absorbed in the chase for money, estranged from things and other persons, and hence themselves lacking in concrete personality. By chance he visits an exhibition of paintings (it seems he is thinking of Van Gogh, exhibited 1903 in Berlin and 1904 in Munich), and suddenly here rediscovers things, things for themselves, 'as destiny, most inward life'. And this discovery of the identity of things, mediated by the artist, helps him to discover a meaning in himself and his world, makes him whole, and overcomes his feeling of alienation. The happy ending is forced, but Hofmannsthal is in this slight work tackling a problem that is more subtle and perhaps intractable than that we find in *Jedermann* or *Das Salzburger Grosse Welttheater*, where repentance seems a convenient way of whitewashing materialism.

This Hofmannsthal discovery is remarkably close to Rilke's experience, as he describes it in his letters of 1907, in relation to the Paris exhibition of Cézanne. He says he was rescued from an aimless existence by these paintings which were for him a 'Dingwerdung'. Since he suggests that his own *Neue Gedichte* are a parallel to Cézanne's paintings, we may infer that beneath the 'Dinggedicht' lies the same psychological-metaphysical motivation. Rilke's prolonged encounter with Paris, like that of his Malte Laurids Brigge, strikingly bears out Simmel's view that the city embodies the reality of the modern world and must be confronted, not evaded. As with Hofmannsthal's more moralistic works, Rilke's poems of city misery with their social indictment (e.g. the 'Stimmen' cycle in *Buch der Bilder* or the social poems in *Stundenbuch III*) are less impressive than the immediate and personal experience reflected in *Malte Laurids Brigge*. Interestingly enough, Simmel told Rilke in a letter of 1908 of his great interest in the *Stundenbuch*, since the pantheism of these poems does not submerge the identity of things but reinforces their unique actuality (*Buch des Dankes an Georg Simmel*).

Simmel himself does not always keep to his dialectical position, and is likely to sympathize most deeply with resistance to the rational intellectualism of the metropolitan climate, with the anti-naturalistic formalism of for instance George, which was closely bound up with the anti-city diatribes of *Jahrbuch für die geistige Bewegung*. An essay of Gundolf's in *Blätter für die Kunst* for 1910 seems directly indebted to Simmel (Gundolf was an intimate of the Simmel household). In this Gundolf accuses the modern world and its money economy of estranging men from things, of thus blinding them to reality and reducing their lives to a mere semblance: 'Men stride through the world as through an avenue of facing mirrors, they possess the semblance of everything and enact it, and themselves eternally remain remote from things.' This consciousness of the metropolitan reality has to be recognized as implicit in the functioning of the whole system of George's imagery, which is not an evasion (like much of the sentimental romanticism of the time) but a direct challenge. There were in George more questionable alternatives that are more akin to evasion – the early aestheticism, the decorative formalism, the Jugendstil affinities, for instance. There is something evasive, similarly, in the occasional enthusiasm of a Hofmannsthal or a Rilke for Kunstgewerbe as a means of rescuing things from the anonymity of mass-production.

Of the many other suggestive thoughts in Simmel's work on the relation of metropolis and culture, those concerning freedom are of the widest importance. He often distinguishes two types of freedom, one socio-political and connected with democratic aspirations, the other more individualistic, the achievement of wholeness or fullness of personality. His own sympathies go towards the latter, the principle of a long German conservative tradition, while the former he calls Anglo-French and sometimes decries as rationalistic and shallow. Hence his anxiety over the march of civilization itself, which surrounds men with an over-powering quantity of institutions and organizations that are the product of man's freedom, 'objectified mind', and yet constitute a threat to his freedom and self-fulfilment. Such concern with self-fulfilment is not necessarily hostile to social reform, but may induce indifference to it, and it has often been labelled by

Marxists as a disguised expression of bourgeois class interest. Simmel on the other hand maintained that freedom in the form of self-fulfilment was a fundamental need of modern man, and meant a profound tension with social organization whether this were capitalist or socialist.

Though at times Simmel points out the advantages of the more personal production and exchange and the closer community of the small town over against the abstract and dissociated world of the great city, he never considers there is a real choice available. Once one has known the emancipation of city-life, he writes, the small town is unbearably narrow. When rooted in his town and guild, making a whole thing for a personal customer, a man may be a whole, but he is also severely restricted. In the great city his work is impersonal, fragmented, fortuitous, unrelated to his personality, while the associations he belongs to are peripheral and can be changed at will. But here he is free, he can join or leave, he is never absorbed by the group. This freedom is precious, and is reflected in the characteristic mobility of urban society, the movement between jobs and up and down the social scale, the free choice of social, religious, political and other affiliations. Simmel does not, however, delude himself about this freedom. It has, he points out, a certain delusory character, since beneath the choices there is a relentless pressure, and the capacity to choose itself is a sign of rootlessness, most in evidence in men who have the least substantiality of personality. Metropolitan life therefore engenders a nervous, superficial culture, an incessant vacillation between a great number of choices: 'men chase in bewilderment backwards and forwards, between socialism and Nietzsche, Böcklin and Impressionism, Hegel and Schopenhauer' – the list of alternatives could be indefinitely extended.

This problem of choice and freedom subtly penetrates much of the literature of the period, always as a dilemma, and often in the form of a contest between the great city and the small town (or village). The small town may be championed by George's friend Vallentin or Paul Ernst, the country by Schlaf or Bruno Wille, but in fact these choices mean a retreat for the individual, not the adoption of an alternative community. The highest tribute to the small town is Heinrich Mann's *Die kleine Stadt*, but this is an Italian town. Hermann Hesse, who consistently detested the great city, shows also the cruel and oppressive philistinism of the small town. Even the 'völkische' authors, with their anti-city programme, find the small town stifling and philistine and admire the peasant because he can be independent of even the village community. On the other hand, almost all writers show the great city as a place of spiritual dearth as well as material deprivation, and the theme of rootlessness and weariness of life, of the burden of choice, occurs constantly, from Conradi's *Adam Mensch* onwards. The absence of obligation makes choice arbitrary and unsatisfying, and this consciousness of an insubstantial freedom in oneself is balanced by the spectacle of an apparent automatism in the masses around one, so harrowingly experienced by Rilke's Malte. Freedom hollows men out to such an extent that Kafka's 'heroes' are almost deprived of other characteristics and use it only to seek admission to the community; necessarily they must be rejected. In Musil's *Der Mann ohne Eigenschaften*, which in its inception goes back to the pre-war world, the compulsive and irrational mechanisms of metropolitan life are balanced by the complete freedom of Ulrich, which is so rootless as to be equivalent to the absence of 'qualities', and in a notable passage Musil relates this dichotomy to the great city, where life grows both fuller of events and experiences and at the same time more 'abstract'. This is one of the great sources of the alienation that is so marked and self-confessed a feature of the culture of the time, the alienation of private values from public, of the artist from society, accompanied by the feeling of an irrevocable commitment to this alien public world, of not having any alternative, as Malte, or K of *Das Schloss*, or Ulrich in their different ways assert.

Ideas related to Simmel's were common throughout the period, both before him and after. There were more flashy variants, like that propounded by Sombart at the first conference of German sociologists in 1910 to the effect that major stylistic innovations in art are due to technological changes. On this occasion Max Weber, in one of his brilliant extempore contributions to discussion, echoes some of Simmel's views. He was ready to admit that a technological change may give rise to a new artistic style (he refers to the then most popular example, the change from the Romanesque to the Gothic arch), but he disputed Sombart's thesis in general on the grounds that technology is only one factor in a total cultural situation. But he went on to suggest that, if one were to take the Groszstadt itself to be a technological product, then one would have to admit that it has greatly influenced 'formal-aesthetic values', partly in that they are adapted to the tumultuous life of the city, partly in that they protest against it. He suggests therefore that the lyricism of Stefan George cannot be understood except as the self-defence of the 'last, inexpugnable fortresses of the soul', alerted by the full experience of the threatening metropolis. Only so, he adds, can modern painting be understood.

The modern city is so complex and changes so rapidly that we should not expect any interpretation of its cultural effects to do justice to all its aspects. Simmel's main writings on the city belong to the years round the turn of the century, and his views might have changed in some respects had he written a decade later. Also, though he is clearly deeply concerned about the spiritual results of metropolitan existence, he retains a certain equanimity in his observations, something in him that George once warned Gundolf against as 'das Geheimrätliche'. Thus his thought does not probe to the depth of feeling of, say, a Käthe Kollwitz, to her intense, purified insight into the suffering of the Berlin proletariat among whom she spent her adult life. Nor does it prepare us for the eruption of horror and hatred often mingled with fascination of a Trakl or Heym, or for the visions of doomed collapsing cities in the Expressionist generation (or the hallucinatory concreteness of the 'unreal city' of T. S. Eliot's *The Waste Land*). It hardly prepares us for the violence of the anti-city bombardment in *Jahrbuch für die geistige Bewegung* by his friends of the George circle, and for the extreme anti-rationalism associated with it (against which he did privately protest). Simmel does speak of certain religious trends as compensations for the rationalism of the urban climate, but he seems not to anticipate the proliferation towards 1912 of groups dedicated to one or other form of mysticism, nor the recrudescence of pagan cults and new community forms among the 'Völkische' and in the youth movement. Nor does he anticipate the emergence of a new primitivism among intellectuals, the cult of 'dark forces', for instance in Herwarth Walden's *Der Sturm* from 1910 onwards and in Futurism, much stimulated by the war experience.

All the same, Simmel's analysis does illuminate cultural phenomena that he himself does not discuss. In particular his appreciation of the growing abstractness of life in the metropolis gives a clue to the new metaphorical speech of the Expressionist poets, the violent conjunction of images that wrenches words out of their normal contexts and grammar out of its normal functions, which we can understand as a protest against the obtrusiveness of things, grown indifferent and banal, and as a means of rescuing words from the 'atomization' into which they threaten to sink and of reviving them to new semantic life. We can more easily recognize that, in Carl Einstein's *Bebuquin* and the products of Dada, the impertinence with which words and things and persons are handled is symptomatic of the chaotic, fortuitous, and lawless relationships of men to their products and to one another, typical of the age of 'money' economy and so obtrusive in the great city. It would seem as if Einstein (in this a precursor of a significant modern trend, as R. H. Thomas shows in his essay *Carl Einstein and Expressionism*) intends by representing existence as inorganic, fragmented, and absurd to reject as an illusion the whole constellation of values that Simmel (and most Expressionists) connected with ideals like the integrated personality, the soul, self-fulfilment. Einstein was indeed to deliver a frontal attack on Goethe's idea of personality as a bourgeois illusion. But, though it is true that in his work and that of Hugo Ball or Huelsenbeck fragmentation of the personality, alienation, the negative is the most prominent feature, it is impossible to understand the hilarity, the indignation, the bitterness or the violence of their works without postulating an implicit model or ideal of wholeness not essentially unlike Simmel's. That the dissociation of things and persons from one another and from any necessary or rational function in Kafka's work can unmask itself at times as an inherent demonic power that threatens human existence, similarly indicates a model against which the present is judged. One might generalize and assert that no significant criticism can be without this dialectical positive element.

7
Religion and the Churches

In 1871 Treitschke commented on the 'immense extent' of disbelief in or indifference to the Christian faith among the educated youth of Germany. The 'crisis of religion' became a common theme in periodicals and newspapers, and D. F. Strauss, in *Der alte und der neue Glaube* (1872), speaks with smug self-confidence of the community of disbelievers like himself. Nothing in the literature of the period is more striking than the frequency of disbelief, even of provocative rejection of Christian tenets and the Christian church; though also there is probably no more over-worked word than 'Erlösung' in some secularized form of its range of meanings from 'salvation' and 'redemption' down to 'release' or 'relief'.

Personal faith is very intangible and diverse, and one can delineate it only very roughly. Alienation from faith and religious community also takes manifold forms and results from different and often multiple causes. Even if we speak of definable groups, the multiplicity is bewildering. There were in Germany various organized churches, the Catholic being the established church, i.e. part of the political structure, in some states, while the Evangelical (Lutheran or Reformed or a fusion of the two as in Prussia) were the established churches in other states. Both Catholic and Protestant churches were divided into numerous orders, sections, or sects, all with their own nuances; in both, even in the ranks of the ordained clergy, faith meant something different for the hierarchies, the university theologians, the religious orders, the parish priests in the country and the city, those engaged like Friedrich Naumann in home missions, those like Hermann Hesse's parents in foreign missions, and the mixed bag of parishioners.

Faith meant something different for the different social classes as well as different individuals. For some, it meant a call to

change of self, for others, a call to change society; for many, one
might say for most, faith confirmed traditional habit and
guaranteed the established order. Where social change was
greatest and most directly felt, in the great industrial cities, the
old belief crumbled with the old social community of parson,
squire and village parish (in 1907 almost one half of the population did not live in the parish in which they had been born).
Where social change was slower – in small towns and villages –
there was more stability of faith. In the Protestant countryside the
lord of the manor still remained the lord of the parson and the
congregation, while in the small towns too the religious status of
people echoed and reinforced their social status. In such areas the
protest evoked by material suffering or social subjection still took
the traditional form of pietism or fundamentalism, and numerous
local messiahs would arise to lead their flocks into the millenium. Such was Max Halbe's father, the source of his *Das
rausendjährige Reich*, and Hauptmann's *Der Narr in Christo,
Emanuel Quint* is the imaginative synthesis of a type of person
and faith that he knew and felt drawn to in his youth, and that he
describes with sympathy in his *Das Abenteuer meiner Jugend*.
The equivalent among the distressed masses in the cities was the
sort of fundamentalism one associates with the Salvation Army,
that is fortified by practical measures of material relief. The
Heilsarmee, introduced from England, was never so successful in
Germany; a caricature of British imperialism in *Jugend*, 1896,
puts the Salvation Army among the imperialists. But Kretzer
wrote a sympathetic sketch of a Heilsarmee lass, and admires the
priggish Wanda of his *Das Gesicht Christi*. Wedekind wrote a
'Moritat' about such a lass, and Kaiser's *Von Morgens bis
Mitternacht* uses one to set off the material and spiritual desola-
tion of the city, though none of these has the weight of the figures
Broch and Brecht later created, nor even of Shaw's *Major
Barbara* (1905).

While pietism and fundamentalism were chiefly features of the
subcultures of the poor and deprived, we must here be more
concerned with the weightier intellectual challenges to belief
itself, which affected the whole of the literary culture.

The Intellectual Attack

The decline in the intellectual authority of Christian dogma and the church was more thorough in the Germany of the nineteenth century than elsewhere in Europe and America. In part this was due to a long Protestant critical tradition. The simple doctrinal and moral tenets of faith had been undermined by writers who were the glory of German literature, Lessing, Goethe and Schiller, as well as by Kant and Hegel, and these, whatever accommodations they made with the faith, remained a thorn in the flesh of the pious. Opposition to the French Revolution, it is true, turned many once-bold Romantic writers into Catholic apologists and some of the 'Biedermeier' writers recreated a religious literature. But the liberal intellectuals called the Romantics apostates, and the liberal onslaught on absolutism and separatism in the 1830s and 1840s included religion and the churches as bastions of reaction. The Young Hegelians Strauss, Ludwig Feuerbach, Arnold Ruge and Bruno Bauer, deepening the historical understanding of Christianity, at the same time stripped it of its claims to universal truth, and Heine's supple and subtle skirmishing demolished the claims of dogma even more effectively. When socialism first began to stir, in the early writings of Wilhelm Weitling or Moses Hess, the established churches were indicted as the instrument of the possessing classes, and the young Marx even wrote that 'the criticism of religion is the precondition of all criticism'. So firmly is Marx's criticism of religion as 'the ideology of the ruling class' embedded in his general revolutionary theory, that its effect was limited for some decades to the working class and those intellectuals who threw in their lot with the revolutionary movement. But criticism of religion came from the right as well as the left. The conservative Schopenhauer was no less bluntly derisive of the Christian faith than Marx, and Bruno Bauer, Marx's old friend, who became a pillar of the state, always remained an implacable critic of the Christian religion.

These currents of criticism were reinforced from the middle of the century by the results of natural science. Vogt, Moleschott and Ludwig Büchner provided plausible explanations of organic life and mental activity on the basis of the laws of nature, sometimes expounding a crude materialism, sometimes more philosophically maintaining that religious and metaphysical concepts, in particular notions like 'soul', 'mind' and 'free will', are logically inadmissible. After the publication of *The Origin of Species* (1859) the evolutionary theory of Darwin was very rapidly employed not only to refute the Christian cosmology but also to justify an anti-Christian ethic of self-assertion and struggle.

Almost all this criticism of Christian beliefs and ethics emerged from the Protestant tradition. The Catholic church maintained its hold over its members, its authoritarianism being supported by the Catholic German states which rigorously suppressed publications and movements that might undermine ancient beliefs and authorities. The last anti-clerical flourish of German liberalism, once the Reich was established, was the Prussian 'Kulturkampf', the five-year campaign initiated by Bismarck with the object of asserting a closer state control over the Catholic church. This, surely one of the most superfluous conflicts in modern German history, had the effect of enhancing the prestige of the Catholic hierarchy and stimulating its resistance to anything smelling of liberal modernism.

As our period opens, we can sum up the position as follows. The churches everywhere enjoy a traditional prestige, Christian doctrine is professed by all public institutions, Christian teaching is obligatory in all elementary and many secondary schools, and the churches are entrusted by the state with important social responsibilities. But, to a surprising degree, and with a surprising aggressiveness, Christian beliefs are being challenged both in intellectual circles, by those who have enjoyed a university education, and in the industrial proletariat where it has become accessible to Marxism. The attack is complex and varied, arises from different causes and serves different purposes. The most intellectual deny on Kantian grounds the validity of theology, more popular being the variant of D. F. Strauss, who claims in 1872 that the whole Christian conceptual system – original sin, justification by faith, salvation, the devil, the Trinity, the personal God – just does not mean anything to modern man. In respect to personal ethics, the Christian concepts of sinfulness and repentance, in particular the identification of sin with the flesh, with man's nature, are rejected as debasing man to himself, torturing him and fettering his natural energies; men of the most contrary ideologies share this view, Marx, Lagarde, Nietzsche, Strauss, Nordau etc. In the sphere of social ethics, attitudes vary greatly. Some, like Schopenhauer and Feuerbach, subscribe to the Christian ethic of love and compassion, even if they fiercely criticize the Christian tenets. On the other hand, Strauss voices the widespread opinion that altruism is fine, but not 'realistic', and that Christian ethics need to be widened to encourage 'healthy egoism', competition, and struggle. A Nordau is more truculent and ridicules the ethical teachings of the Old and New Testaments, calling for a new ethics that will serve social progress and human evolution; indeed there was a common demand for a non-dogmatic natural ethics, evolutionary in character but not necessarily hostile to the moral ideals of Christ, as in the studies of H. Reé or the more comprehensive *Einleitung in die Moralwissenschaft* (1892-3) of Simmel. Lagarde and the 'Völkische' violently attack Christian ethics as subversive of the nation, and create a new 'German Faith' that will weld Germans together in a heroic community intent on extending its power; for them altruism and charity are Jewish wiles to break the spirit of the creative Aryans. Often these racist nationalists direct their fire against the Catholic church, appropriating Protestantism into their myth of a heroic national destiny; there are many variants, and Langbehn, who later became a monk, tried to reconcile 'völkische' and Christian beliefs. If the most absolute criticism of religion on the democratic-socialist side came from Marxism, the influence of which begins in the 1880s to spread among intellectuals, many of the same challenges were made from the élitist anti-democratic side.

Perhaps the sharpest and most persistent criticism of Christianity came from Nietzsche. In his middle phase, e.g. in *Menschliches, Allzumenschliches,* his criticism is directed mainly at the debasement of man through the doctrine of sin and atonement and the condemnation of the body. In the last phase, that opens with *Thus Spake Zarathustra* (1883), while he continues to deride the whole Christian faith as absurd, he now interprets altruism as the ideological weapon of the envious masses, the 'slaves', the 'herd', who in thus seeking to shackle the ruling caste destroy human creativity itself. He thus attacks Christian ethics as the moral principle of the democracy and socialism he hated. That Nietzsche could win over many adherents to this view, at a time when Marx's definition of religion as the ideology of the ruling class seemed to many to indicate the sore spot of Christianity, can be explained only by the ambiguity of Christian doctrine and of the relations between Church and doctrine. Kautsky's Marxist study of early Christianity, *Der Ursprung des Christentums,* has as its theme, indeed, the theory that Christianity originally was the ideology of the despised and rejected, but that its confused character made it a convenient tool for

Constantine and other worldly powers who took it over and gave its doctrine and organization quite other functions.

Apart from the political organizations of the radical right and the radical left through which criticism of Christianity was spread, a number of non-political societies came into being for specific or general anti-religious or anti-clerical purposes. The society advocating cremation, for instance, necessarily directed its propaganda against the established churches, its chief opponents; and various movements opposing the church-tax, which was obligatory in the Protestant states for all those baptized in the established church, were bound to include some anti-religious element – for instance the 'Komitee, Konfessionslos' led by L. Gurlitt and fostered by Pfemfert in *Aktion*, which attacked doctrine as well as doctrinaire authorities, but existed to advocate disestablishment, public withdrawal from the church, and the freeing of teachers from religious duties. The German branch of the League of Freethinkers, founded in 1881 with Ludwig Büchner as its first president, created a centre for the general propagation of anti-religious opinion, and especially for attacks on the political and social privileges of the established churches, on clerical control over education, and on the laws restricting free expression of opinion. For less aggressive temperaments the Ethische Bewegung, the German branch of the Ethical Society, brought together believers for whom the ethical values of Christ were the heart of religion, and agnostics who shared their ethical views; several distinguished academics were prominent in this movement. Haeckel, notoriously connected through his researches and his able journalism with the secularization of ethics, and one of the most prominent advocates of 'social Darwinism', in his *Die Welträtsel* (1899) defined a 'monistic' philosophy which was neither materialistic nor idealistic. This attempted reconciliation of science and religion appealed to many and encouraged the sort of vague nature-mysticism found in the post-1900 works of Bruno Wille and Schlaf, the former Naturalists. In 1906 the Monistenbund was formed, with Haeckel as its president, but like many such societies it soon began to develop its own dogmas. The Keplerbund, formed in 1907 expressly to reconcile science and religion, turned as Haeckel complained in 1909 (*Die Neue Rundschau*), into an organization for denouncing scientists who were non-Christian. Within the Social Democratic party sectarian counterparts to many of the anti-clerical movements were established, for instance a League of Proletarian Freethinkers or a Proletarian Society for Cremation, always more demonstratively materialistic than their bourgeois counterparts, calling themselves atheist where the bourgeois would use the word agnostic.

The variety of attitudes among the critics of doctrine and church was in part due to the great complexity of Christianity, in which the policy of the hierarchy need not represent the opinions of many believers, priests or laymen. Under the impact of this criticism in the new modern environment, both dogma and social policy underwent profound changes, and some understanding of these changes is necessary.

Theological Modernists

For a long time, the chief defence of the churches against the onslaught of modern philosophy and science was to keep mum and try to gag the troublesome. Adolf von Harnack, a modernist theologian who became president of the Prussian Academy and a representative figure of the greatest prestige and authority, complained in 1903 that even the results of theological research were suppressed 'by church and school in alliance'. This research was the outcome of the scrupulous historical methods first developed in the theological faculty of Tübingen university, and there was constant tension between the university theological faculties, subject only to the State, and the churches. This historical research exerted perhaps a profounder influence on theology than the more sensational challenges of Darwinism; in 1907 Harnack could confidently assert that the violent agitation arising from the results of natural science had been only of peripheral significance.

The heart of the Tübingen school was its biblical criticism, and its studies in comparative religion dispersed the solid revelations of Judaism and Christianity into a nebula of pagan sources. The pastoral clergy complained that the effect of such investigations would be disastrous for the normal believer – Hermann Hesse portrays in *Unterm Rad* a parish priest of the Tübingen type, engrossed in his scholarship, utterly lacking in human understanding, and looked on by a fundamentalist shoemaker as an enemy to the faith. The Berlin Faculty was the heir to the Swabians, despite the hostility of the Berlin Oberkirchenrat, which in 1889 unsuccessfully tried to veto the appointment of

Harnack to the university. His *Lehrbuch der Dogmengeschichte* (three volumes, 1886-90) had brilliantly penetrated layers of dogma and legend to destroy much of the supernaturalism that sanctioned many beliefs, and it became the centre of a great battle over the Apostles' Creed waged by the Berlin modernists. From 1886 the periodical *Die Christliche Welt* became the organ of modernism and gave the opportunity for public discussion of the issues, consolidating and emboldening the modernist view. In Albert Schweitzer's early work, *The Quest for the Historic Jesus*, for instance, great areas of Christ's teaching are pronounced to be the product of a specific age and culture, while the influence of Goethe and Nietzsche promotes a concept of holiness far removed from the concrete tenets of traditional Christianity. On such a basis Frenssen could construct in his novel *Hilligenlei* an image of Christ more Nietzschean than evangelical, while A. Drews, like Schweitzer and Frenssen an evangelical parson, could in *Die Christusmythe* (1909) totally deny the historicity of Christ. Ernst Troeltsch, who came to Berlin from Heidelberg in 1915, a theologian of generous liberal sympathies, responded to the challenge of Marxism and historical relativism in his great investigation of the socio-ethical doctrines of early Christianity, *Die Soziallehren der christlichen Kirchen und Gruppen* (1908-12). Troeltsch severely criticized the Marxist Kautsky's materialistic interpretation of early Christianity, and held that religious experience is an *a priori* reality, but his historical and sociological method threatened to undermine the faith and ethical doctrine of Christianity.

The most typical defence against the threat of scepticism and agnosticism in this modernist thought was the neo-Kantianism of Ritschl and the Göttingen school which, while admitting the validity of scientific method and natural law in certain areas of life, claimed that the essential truths of religion belonged to a sphere inaccessible and logically prior to scientific rationalism. These truths could be most clearly experienced and enunciated in the moral sphere, and Ritschl formulated a principle that echoes throughout the literature of the period: 'The function of Christianity is to make morality possible.' As Ritschl and his many adherents understood this, morality means the assertion of man's spiritual freedom; it closely corresponds with the individualism of the liberal era, and is noticeably lacking in any precise socio-moral commitment (as Kantian ethics always is). This is true of most religious philosophy of the time. Rudolf Eucken, for instance, in his influential *Einheit des Geisteslebens* (1888), argues that naturalism, as he calls scientism (literary Naturalism he takes to be the artistic counterpart of scientism), is logically inadequate to the totality of life, since spiritual processes transcend the examinable processes of nature; spirit is an autonomous world with its autonomous values of truth, beauty and goodness. His attack on the mechanistic determinism in contemporary scientific materialism is effective, and his definition of religion as the proof and guarantee of man's free personality, threatened both by natural law and by the majesty of God, chimed in with much secular thought, as did his stress on the ethical imperative of activity. But here again the ethic is very abstract and formalistic, it asserts very few obligations to precise forms of social behaviour. In retrospect it is not surprising that in 1914 the aged Eucken could distress his many English admirers by exalting Germany as the warlike champion of the 'spirit'.

Harnack himself, though always a man of compromise, a mediator, was much more involved with social reform than most theologians and churchmen. He too held that 'religion is the soul of morality, and morality the body of religion', but a more positive sense of obligation is conveyed by his addition: 'Love of one's neighbour is the only practical proof on earth of the love of God.' His *Das Wesen des Christentums* (1900), first given as lectures to Berlin students, and enjoying a vast international popularity, is a remarkably simple-minded avowal of faith in the divinity of Christ, which means for him also a sanguine trust in the world. Its pragmatic direction, its avoidance of the whole topic of sin, its distaste for mysticism, its readiness to discard dogma, are characteristic of the whole of liberal theology and indicate the price theology paid for riding the storm of socialist and scientistic criticism. In *Varieties of Religious Experience* (1902) William James properly numbered Harnack among those moderns for whom religion is 'healthy-mindedness'.

The conclusions of James's investigations into the varied forms of modern religions reflect a strong trend in Germany and contribute to it. He necessarily arrives at a most general definition of religion, concluding that its essence is 'a solemn, serious, tender feeling' that is a response to a 'primal reality' which each religious group interprets differently. Even his own Christian allegiance he calls an 'over-belief' arising from 'personal susceptibilities', and justified not logically but pragmatically, as a necessary life-function. The Jamesian attitude allays intellectual unease but clearly weakens all positive religious commitment; the somewhat easygoing justification of any particular creed as an 'over-belief' turned in Troeltsch to a deep concern over the fact, for instance, that Christianity was so bound up with Europe. The neo-Kantian philosophy comes near to James in establishing a logical justification for religious belief without commitment to any cultic or dogmatic faith. Simmel's essay *Die Religion* (1906) meets more successfully the intellectual and emotional needs of a generation alienated from the positive religions, and was enthusiastically recommended by Wolfskehl. He calls religion a basic psychological disposition ('Verfassung der Seele'), the content of which is infinitely variable. It manifests itself in devotion to any 'cause', to a group, a faith, an idea. It rests upon a recognition that all life is holy, and that the soul finds its 'salvation' in service to life; religion may well exist, therefore, without any concept of God. Simmel in part exploits the traditional religious implications of terms like 'Heil der Seele', in part he secularizes them, and his argumentation recalls Nietzsche's jibes at philosophy as the last refuge of religion. But less complex minds held views similar to Simmel's. Schweitzer found the secret of religion in that 'reverence for life' that he discovered too in Goethe and Nietzsche. The theology of Rudolf Otto's *Das Heilige* (1917), so influential later in theological seminaries, was founded on the feeling of awe, the perception of the holy, that he finds to be common to all cults, from the primitive to the most sophisticated; the Christian conception is claimed to be the purest objectivization of this basic apperception. Though Otto could believe he was thus providing an unassailable foundation for Christian belief, and did indeed stem the disbelief arising from historical and comparative studies and from the natural sciences, he was at the same time eroding the certainties of faith and cult, and with them the authority of the churches.

The theological turmoil outlined above occurred within the framework of Protestantism. In the Catholic church, both the authority of bishops and pope, and theological thinking, remained remarkably intact. A papal encyclical of 1891 aligned the church very firmly against liberalism and socialism, and the revival of Thomism at this time served to ward off the challenge of historical scholarship and modern science. A Catholic parallel to the Modernist movement appeared about 1900, but in 1907 Pius X nipped it in the bud. In 1903 Carl Muth, a Catholic writer earlier associated with anti-semitic, anti-liberal trends, founded the periodical *Hochland* to provide an opportunity for Catholics to face the challenge of modern thought. But, though viewed with great suspicion by the Catholic authorities, the paper always stands for literature with a moral-religious message, and stands by Catholic doctrine. It seems 'modern' only in comparison with the clerical-conservative group round Richard von Kralik in Vienna, with its attempt to restore a spiritual culture through medieval folk plays (Oberammergau to fill the role of the theatre of ancient Athens).

The movement of Protestant theology testifies to a sincere and continuing effort to come to terms with the modern world. It is evident however that its results offer meagre satisfactions for the adventurous intellect or the religious soul. This failure of the Protestant church to provide for intellectual and emotional needs led to an intensified interest in mysticism, and the works of Eckart, Suso, or Silesius were widely read. Nietzsche had written, 'When scepticism mates with longing, mysticism is born,' and this fascinated poring over the curious amalgam of intellectual subtlety and naive faith in these mystics bears witness to a search that could not reach an end; in literature the perhaps most characteristic figure is the 'searcher'. Martin Buber's *Ekstatische Konfessionen* (1909), a collection of Jewish mystical texts, provides evidence of the same unease and search among the Jews, and Buddhism of different varieties also attracted proselytes. On the whole these tendencies implied a direct challenge to modern science and thought. There were other substitutes for conventional religion that claimed to overcome the dichotomy of faith and science and to be more directly related to the problems of modern life.

Substitute and Supplementary Faiths

Under one aspect the post-1880 period in Germany can be called the age of scientific rationalism. Under another, it exhibits a proliferation of irrational faiths and cults that testify to an unquenchable longing to find a faith and practise it in a group. Movements that have their origin in protest against social conditions tend to slip into a religious phraseology and to adopt a cultic form. The Wandervögel for instance, originating in a protest against over-urbanized life and over-rigid conformism, developed a hierarchical structure and a typical myth of the charismatic leader, together with cultic group rituals; even the more sober leaders like Wyneken often expressed a belief that participation brings 'Erlösung' – i.e. not just release from urban restrictions, from the authority of adults and jobs, not just self-help, self-discipline, comradeship, contact with nature and discovery of Germany etc., but a spiritual transformation and redemption that vaguely suggests something like the Christian or Buddhist notion of redemption from the burden of sin and mortality. Germany was full of prophets and saviours.

It is not surprising, in view of the havoc caused by industrial society, that reforming movements advocated total abstinence from alcohol (teetotalism), vegetarianism, naturism and nudism, clothing of natural wool etc., and that these energetic movements radiated somewhat extravagant beliefs in the benefits to mind and body of their cause. But most of these movements also engendered a belief in some coming mystic, joyous consummation, a renewal of man and society. Many writers were attracted at least for a time to one or other of these movements; Hauptmann was brought up wrapped in Jäger wool, Rilke, Morgenstern, Kafka were among the vegetarians, Kafka tried out nudism. Abstinence was associated more with those concerned with the industrial poor, where the ravages of drink were most appalling, and the temperance novel *Helmut Harringa* typically connects it with 'race hygiene' and an ecstatic vision of a purified German stock. Loth, the reformer of Hauptmann's *Vor Sonnenaufgang*, is a compendium of such causes, pledged to eugenics and abstinence, an opponent of such stimulants as tea and tobacco; these fill the gap left by his loss of religion and the waning of his earlier political utopianism.

Apart from such movements, the period threw up a number of messianic leaders who preached redemption and attracted bands of believers, sometimes dressing in robes and sandals in imitation of Christ and wandering from place to place; such were Johannes Guttzeit and his 'Bund für volle Menschlichkeit', or the Bavarian Diefenbach. Both *Die Gesellschaft* and *Freie Bühne* paid sympathetic attention to such figures. In M. G. Conrad's *Was die Isar rauscht* we are told of a hermit who is believed to hold the key to salvation and to whom unfortunates go for help; he dresses in a woollen robe, lives in a quarry near Munich, is a teetotaller and vegetarian. Hauptmann's *Der Apostel* is a sketch, based on Guttzeit, of such a soul-healer, dressed in biblical costume and entranced by his mission. Thomas Mann's *Beim Propheten* (1904) shows a variant that indicates a significant change in the new century. This prophet is an artist, a bohemian, who puts religious symbols to a sophisticated misuse. His message combines the call to poverty and abnegation with exaltation of brutal power and, breathing only hatred and contempt of humanity, is hurled with contempt at his small audience (the kinship is evident with the youthful rebels who hurl their spite at Prince Myshkin and his guests in Dostoyevsky's *The Idiot*). These sketches of Hauptmann's and Mann's are satirical, but a feeling of sympathy with would-be messiahs is often expressed. The frequency with which writers themselves adopt the mantle of the prophet and claim an unmediated, direct, moral or social validity for their imaginative symbols is more understandable when we bear in mind the pervasiveness of the messianic gesture throughout this period.

Another and more powerful religious substitute was racial nationalism in its various forms. This group of ideas has been discussed in the context of political thought, but it must be remembered that for most of its adherents, as for Lagarde, it claimed a religious status. Lagarde himself, a learned orientalist, maintained that he was first and foremost a theologian, and indeed his great linguistic scholarship radiated out from biblical studies. But he was a sort of inverted theologian, determined to demonstrate that the Christian dogmas and institutions were the denial of Christ's true teaching. Like Nietzsche later, Lagarde interprets Christ's doctrine as one of 'life', of energy, strength, self-assertion, which was turned by the Jews (Paul) into a cult of 'death', of suffering, sacrifice, self-abnegation. Life, even the mere survival of an individual as of a nation, depends on a mystic awareness of the Divine, and the most concrete and sustaining form of this awareness is to be found in the consciousness of belonging to a Volk. Lagarde came to hate the Protestant church with contempt, as the lackey of state authority and the sanction of hypocrisy, while he hated the Catholic church with fear. His sturdy insistence on a faith uncontaminated by compromise and institutions elicited Troeltsch's admiration and led him to dedicate the second volume of his *Collected Writings* to Lagarde's memory; it is surprising to us that the liberal Troeltsch does not seem to have perceived the threat to Christian faith and ethics that Lagarde's fanatical nationalism meant.

Some of the implications could perhaps not be grasped at that time, particularly since Lagarde, like his follower Langbehn, often uses a Christian terminology, and for instance speaks of 'redemption' in a way that seems traditional, comparable to the redemption theme in Wagner's *Parsifal,* which may be interpreted in a Christian or a 'völkische' sense. It is true, this new nationalism of the völkische groups did consciously cultivate pagan rituals, the cult of fire or the sun, with their magic symbols that are mysteriously to renew personal and group energy and life. But most, like Wagner himself, amalgamate Christian and pagan ideas and cults. Friedrich Lienhard speaks in his historical novel *Oberlin* of 'Christian renewal through the Germanic spirit', a theme that finds many variations in this type of literature. A. Bonus, a Lutheran parson who left the church in order to become an advocate of the 'Germanic virtues' of power, energy, joy in life (*Deutscher Glaube,* 1901), still enlists Christ as the founder of this pagan gospel and writes with the mannerisms of a Christian parson. The suffering, rejection, and final ecstatic immolation of the hero of Burte's *Wildfeber* are cast in the mould of a völkische Christ. The language of this pagan ideology is full of Christian terms, especially those associated with ceremonies of initiation and dedication and with works of Christian mysticism. Characteristically, the publishing house of Diederichs, that was responsible for many popular editions of the German mystics, was also the chief publisher of the völkische authors of the Dürer League, of the völkische periodical *Die Tat,* and of modern translations of pagan German documents like the elder Edda (cf. the series entitled *Thule*). After 1918 these trends became heavily politicized and amalgamated into the 'Deutsche Glaubensbewegung', which was later incorporated into the Nazi movement.

Nietzsche might well have been pointing to this type of racial nationalism when, in the Fourth Part of *Thus Spake Zarathustra,* Zarathustra warns his 'Free Thinker' against the 'narrow faiths' that promise an illusory refuge from the uncertainties that intellectual freedom inflicts on men. An even clearer testimony to the modern vacuum of belief was the flood of occultist practices and the spiritualist and theosophical doctrines that swept over Germany at the end of the 1880s. Coming from the USA and England, the new occultism, particularly the materializations at spiritualist séances, temporarily or permanently engaged the interest in the main of members of the educated and aristocratic classes. Their appeal was addressed to different intellectual and emotive levels. At the simplest and most widespread, it fortified, with very tangible proofs the Christian doctrine of personal immortality, and allowed participants the solace of believing themselves to be in communication with the dead. At the highest intellectual level, the spiritualist results offered proof that commonsense scientific materialism was insufficient to explain the nature of matter and mind, for, when messages from the dead were transmitted, when ghostly emanations occurred and objects went flying about a room, or when telepathic or telekinetic contacts were made, a spiritual force seemed to be established that promised an escape from the mechanistic, autonomous laws of nature; the reality of spirit and a spirit world seemed to be scientifically proved. Though mediums were repeatedly unmasked as tricksters and charlatans, still a residue of puzzling occult phenomena remained intact, sufficient to lead philosophers, scientists and psychologists in England to found the Psychical Research Society (1882). In Germany a periodical, *Die Sphinx* (1886-96), was the first organ of occultists, and the first eminent advocate was Freiherr Carl du Prel, whose *Das Rätsel des Menschen* appeared in the cheap Reclam edition in 1893, and whose *Entdeckung der Seele durch die Geheimwissenschaften* (1894) claimed to prove the independent and indissoluble existence of the soul. Du Prel was often invited to contribute to the intellectual periodicals of the 1890s, such as *Freie Bühne*, and the 1890 January number of *Die Gesellschaft* was largely devoted to him. Harden got the materialist Ludwig Büchner to review *Das Rätsel des Menschen* in *Zukunft*, and allowed Du Prel two articles (1893) to defend himself against Büchner's crushing arguments. Later another aristocrat, Freiherr A. von Schrenck-Notzing, a medical scientist, became the leading occultist authority; his *Materialisations-Phänomene* (1914) was scientifically and philosophically more sophisticated than Du Prel's work. It was on séances conducted by Schrenck-Notzing in Munich that Thomas Mann's *Okkulte Erlebnisse* of 1924 was based.

Almost all the writers of the time show at least sporadically a lively interest in occultism. Bölsche, the great science-popularizer of the Naturalists, made it the theme of his novel *Die*

Mittagsgöttin (1889), and though the medium is unmasked at the end and the dream of 'redeeming' mankind is shown to be so bogus that the young hero abandons his intellectual and sensual adventurism, his withdrawal almost seems to be a philistine evasion. This uncertainty is characteristic. In *Freie Bühne* we find Heinrich Hart or Paul Ernst pugnaciously asserting a crude materialistic disbelief in occultist phenomena and theory, while Hanns von Gumppenberg, a lively critic and later a great standby of the Munich cabaret *Elf Scharfrichter*, claims (1891-2) that occultist experiments prove the existence of a non-material world. In 1891 Julius Hart expresses the hope that the study of occult phenomena will prove the reality of spirit and perhaps the immortality of the soul. Dehmel, suspicious of occultism yet a fair and liberal man, advocated systematic study along the lines of the Psychical Research Society. Stefan George was impervious to its fascination, but his illustrator and friend Melchior Lechter was devoted to occultism. Perhaps Hofmannsthal's mysterious doctrine of 'Prä-existenz' owes something to spiritualistic (or theosophic) beliefs, stripped of their more vulgar connotations (spiritualistic events occur in the works of the French decadents, and artists like Gauguin, Rodin, and Carrière created 'ectoplasmic' figures). The 'parapsychological' events and figures that often occur in Hofmannsthal's works, however, are essentially symbolical, and no more indicate a belief in a non-material universe than do Rilke's ghosts in *Malte Laurids Brigge*.

Philosophers and scientists continued to demonstrate the philosophical confusions in occultist concepts, the dubiousness of the 'experiments', the banality of the alleged spirit messages, but spiritualism continued to engage the interest of those who found conventional religion unconvincing and scientism insufficient. Christian Morgenstern, a modest and sensitive nature repelled by the credulous sensationalism surrounding occultism, still fixed his hope on inquiries that might prove scientifically the reality of spirit. Such beliefs were strong enough for Freud to tell C. G. Jung, as the latter reports, that they must stick to their sexual theory in order to hold back the 'black ooze' of occultism. The writers who reject it do not do so on philosophical or scientific grounds so much as ethical. Rilke's experiences are extreme yet not untypical. He came into contact with occultism in 1912-3 at séances arranged by Princess Marie von Thurn and Taxis, whose son had mediumistic gifts; his visit to Spain was decided by an occult message and he allowed it to be believed that he was accompanied by a 'spirit'. Rilke even ascribed a cycle of poems to a spirit, a 'Graf C.W.', who he said dictated them to him (1920) – a form of 'automatic' writing of which there are several examples in French and English literature and that is competently discussed by Hans Boventer. But if Rilke acknowledged the possibility of such phenomena, he found the intellectual and moral atmosphere of occultism intolerable. In 1913 he called the Schrenck-Notzing clientèle a 'Gespenstergesindel' and ten years later wrote, 'nothing could be more alien to me than a world in which such powers and interventions had the upper hand'. Thomas Mann's attitude, recorded directly in *Okkulte Erlebnisse* and indirectly in *Der Zauberberg*, is similar. He was disgusted at the claptrap, the intellectual and spiritual meagreness and vulgarity of the phenomena, and alarmed at the threat to moral autonomy that this 'spirit world' presented. Like Hans Castorp, Mann rejects it on ethical grounds, though he has to acknowledge that there are unsolved puzzles here, to which he has no clue. In *Demian* Hermann Hesse seems to justify some occult phenomena, particularly telepathy and telekinesis, but without attributing to them more than a symptomatic importance in Sinclair's spiritual awakening.

The confusions in the beliefs of spiritualists, and particularly the crudely materialistic notions of the spirit world, led Mme Blavatsky and Annie Besant to create a purer doctrine, owing much to Indian religions, in the Theosophic movement. Rudolf Steiner became secretary of the German branch in 1902, in 1913 breaking away to form his Anthroposophic Society, which became centred at Dornach. Steiner was trained as a scientist, but rejecting positivism took from Goethe's scientific work the presupposition of a universal spirit embracing man and nature and the notion of synthetic intuition that transcends empirical understanding. A temporary enthusiasm for Nietzsche's ethical revolutionism strengthened permanently Steiner's opposition to the idea that man is subject to an alien natural law, as also his repugnance to the Christian dualism of soul and body, and thus he came to theosophy with its promise of directly accessible spiritual realities that confirm the freedom of the spirit. His anthroposophy rested on an overriding concept of the spiritual nature of the universe, in which a supernatural destiny rules all life and successive incarnations lead the individual on a ladder of mounting spiritual forms. On these principles Steiner developed, in opposition to the secular and scientific thinking of his time, an educational practice, a therapeutics and an agricultural science which in some respects, notably through his recognition of the psychosomatic character of many human ailments, have proved their effectiveness. Steiner did not found a church, but did create an aesthetic ritual, notably in the 'eurhythmics' he fostered and the ritualistic plays he wrote in 1910, which are reminiscent of the cultic plays of the George circle. He was a leader and speaker of magnetic power, and after 1918 won adherents all over the world, especially through the Waldorf schools. The speculative nature of his thought repelled most intellectuals, who were also alarmed at the authoritarianism that inevitably clings to such a leader. Yet he attracted the devotion of Christian Morgenstern and an inquiring visit from Kafka. When in 1916 Alex von Bernus founded the monthly *Das Reich* to create a spiritual outlook commensurate with the great imperial responsibilities of a triumphant Germany, the core of this new doctrine was Steiner's anthroposophy.

The direct contacts between literature and these spiritualist and theosophic doctrines are only peripheral. It is important, however, to know of their existence if we are better to understand the longing for release from the limitations of secular and social existence, the yearning for 'salvation', that is so often expressed in literature and that also inspired in part the enthusiasm for the war. They also help to explain the formation of innumerable religious-cultic groupings, common to all of which is dissatisfaction with the established churches and religion, rejection of materialism and determinism, and a tendency towards mysticism sometimes of an eccentric and esoteric character. Such groups are the Neue Gemeinschaft of the Hart brothers, the Serakreis round Eugen Diederichs, the St Georgs Bund of Fidus and Gertrud Prellwitz, the Münchener Kartell round Ernst Horneffer (for some years editor of *Die Tat*), the Giordano Bruno Bund, Thule Gesellschaft, Werdandi Bund and the Mittgart circle – several of them connected with 'völkische' religious ideas. Otto zur Linde and his Charon Kreis were perhaps more united in their literary than their religious aims, but in his poetry, like Theodor Däubler and Alfred Mombert, zur Linde claims some semi-mystical, cosmic insight that reconciles the polarities of the empirical world and promises the restoration of the unity of man with the universe. Their symbolism was too private, their systems too arbitrary and pretentious to be transferable to the experience of many others, and all such poets fall into the yawning abyss between poetry and prophecy that after *Zarathustra* engulfed so many.

The Churches and Society

So far we have considered only questions of doctrine and cult. The churches were however great social institutions entrusted with wide responsibilities, and the problems arising from the moral doctrine and social role were as serious as the doctrinal.

Since the French Revolution, the churches had been enlisted by the monarchies in defence of the existing social order; the Catholic church in Austria and Bavaria became as much a pillar of secular authority as the Protestant church elsewhere. The structure of the Lutheran church lent itself readily to this function, since the prince was *ex officio* head of the church, and its affairs were governed by a Consistorial Council made up of high state officials and clergymen appointed by the crown. The finances of the Protestant church were amply supplemented by the church-tax levied by the state on every citizen baptized into the established church. From this one could escape only by publicly withdrawing from the church, a matter of such social and professional consequence that few would do so. In all states the churches exercised considerable powers over school education, usually being directly entrusted with religious instruction.

From the period of liberal militancy in the 1840s, there were numerous efforts to democratize the internal government of the Protestant churches and thus lessen their identification with the political authorities. One of the chief objects of the Protestantenverein (founded 1865) was to win for the laity a stronger participation in church government. This object was achieved to some extent only in Baden and Weimar, and till 1918 the Protestant church, like the Catholic, remained conspicuously undemocratic in structure. In 1907 Harnack, a man of liberal leanings, was to discourage a proposal for an international church congress on the grounds that, while the laity played a significant part in the affairs of the Anglican church, the German Protestant church was 'a church of theologians and priests', in the management of which laymen were not expected to intervene. Harnack pointed out that as a compensation for this exclusion from responsibility the German church tolerated the most divergent and heretical opinions in its laity. As a result of this authoritarian structure, a number of Protestant congregations broke away from the state churches and formed self-supporting 'freireligiöse' communities, that in 1859 combined to create a national association that usually inclined towards radicalism in politics. The Berlin 'free-religious' community broke in two in the 1880s, one liberal radical and the other socialist in its sympathies. The latter appointed as its 'speaker', its substitute for a parish priest, Bruno Wille, formerly a theological student, known as a socialist orator, and a founding father of Berlin Naturalism. From about 1890 the campaign in these congregations for the abolition of church-tax and for demonstrative mass-withdrawals from the state church attracted much sympathy in the Naturalist periodicals *Die Gesellschaft* and *Freie Bühne*. From them emanated a campaign for the outright disestablishment of the church and the withdrawal of its privileges in education, that led in 1909 to the formation of the Weimarer Kartell, in which the free-religious congregations were joined by monists, free-thinkers, and other organizations. Its purposes found considerable support in *Aktion* and liberal papers, which also supported the campaigns initiated against the established church when dissident radical clergymen were defrocked.

Organizationally the Catholic church was more distinct from the state, and indeed since the 1830s had been engaged in Prussia in a struggle with the state authority that had culminated in the bitter Kulturkampf of the 1870s. This struggle gave the Catholic church in Prussia a certain popular, anti-authoritarian character, in striking contrast to its functioning in Bavaria or Austria, where it was the heart of authoritarianism and in effect enjoyed the status of a state church. A Bavarian liberal paper like *März* judged the Catholic church to be infinitely more reactionary than the Protestant, and Ludwig Thoma was of opinion that the predominance of the 'clerical party' made Bavarian politics in this whole period anachronistic. On the other hand, the radical right, the 'völkische', who often claimed the heritage of nordic Protestantism, attacked the Catholic church with particular venom as the instrument of an insidious, anti-national foreign power, Rome. The revival of Catholic thought earlier in the century had been accompanied by a much more thorough centralization of authority in the church, so that the declaration of Papal infallibility in 1870, though it led to the breakaway of Old Catholic congregations, in fact influenced Catholic thinking very little.

Pledged to established authority, hostile to liberal freedoms, clericalism became in the Catholic states the backbone of conservatism, exercising its influence in a thousand indirect ways; Schnitzler's *Professor Bernhardi* or Wassermann's *Der Moloch* show how it might act in matters connected with Jews. Where the church took steps to deal with modern social problems, through its organizations for the relief of the industrial poor or for the protection of working men, these had an emphatically paternalistic character. One of the most amusing contributions to *Aktion*, usually violently anti-clerical, is a mock encyclical devised by Franz Blei (1913), in which the Pope proclaims the disestablishment of the church and the abandonment of religious instruction in schools. Yet, although there was neither in doctrine nor in church organization any such movement of opinion as in the Protestant churches, the Reich Catholic party, Zentrum, preserved something of its oppositional character and occasionally responded to popular anti-government feeling. The disasters of warfare strengthened this anti-nationalist element in the Zentrum, so that it began to work towards that alliance with democrats and right-wing social democrats that founded the Weimar constitution.

Generally, the clergyman of the Wilhelmine era was expected to be, and normally was, a supporter of the social order and authority. Hermann Hesse, drawing on his own experience, describes the Protestant seminary of *Unterm Rad* as a nursery of social conformists, bribed by the promise of clerical status. Bismarck, the young Kaiser and other statesmen repeatedly equate criticism of the social order with godlessness, and Caprivi summed up the social polarities in 1892 as 'either Christian or atheist', to the indignation both of Christian reformers and of a secular 'Social Darwinist' like Haeckel, who was always ready to point out the subversive implications of Christian ethics. Clergymen were similarly expected to be ardent champions of the nation, and regularly appear as such in the literature of the time; the fanatical patriotism of Sudermann's clergyman in his historical novel *Der Katzensteg* (1888) is typical of contemporaries rather than 1813, and akin to that of the parsons in the early

Frenssen novels. Troeltsch had bitterly to acknowledge that religion in his day was an agency of the political authorities: 'The two Confessional parties [Zentrum and Conservatives] are forces of authority, of material power, intimately related to dynastic monarchism and the spirit of military obedience, and to the metaphysical exaltation of the bureaucracy. And they are so precisely in respect to their religious ideas' (*Die Religion im deutschen Staat*, 1912).

However, the situation of the churches and the outlook of the clergy by no means remained static. The distress caused by industrialization allied with the Marxist challenge to Christian beliefs provoked the churches into social action. The foundation of the German equivalents of the YMCA or of homes for prostitutes and unmarried mothers etc. was not sufficient to cope with the immense social and spiritual dislocation, and a fresh impetus came particularly from the priests working in home missions. The most prominent of these was Court Chaplain Stoecker in Berlin, and his charitable Christian work rapidly enlarged into a politico-social programme. In 1878 he founded his Christlich-soziale Arbeiterpartei to defend workers against uncontrolled exploitation, under the leadership of the church and the Conservative party. Though his failure to win over the workers led Stoecker to anti-semitic extremism, he continued to play an important part in so-called 'Christian-social' movements. Largely because of his work, the Prussian Oberkirchenrat became aware that the church must concern itself more actively with the plight of the poor in the great cities, and at its instigation an Evangelisch-soziale Kongress was called in 1890, which thenceforth annually brought together a large number of clergy and academics with a social conscience, whose discussions attracted great attention in the radical and liberal press.

A number of the clergymen and theologians concerned were Modernists, though not all Modernists were liberal. One of the prime movers was Paul Göhre, its first secretary, and symptomatic of a new movement in the church. He had recently spent three months working in a Chemnitz factory, and his account of conditions and attitudes among factory workers sent a thrill of horror through the church. Göhre shocked also in the sense that he maintained that the socialist ideas held by the workers were not evil and materialistic but could be justified on a Christian basis, and this challenge to normal Christian and conservative prejudice explains why his book was so sympathetically discussed in *Freie Bühne*. In later years Göhre, after some years of cooperation with Friedrich Naumann, withdrew from the church and joined the Social Democratic party, amongst other things instigating some notable autobiographies of working men.

In general the Evangelisch-soziale Kongress kept to the middle of the road; in any case it was carefully restricted to discussion and had no executive powers. Under men like the conservative political economist Adolf Wagner or the theologian Harnack (its president 1902-12), the meetings discussed ways of relieving social ills, reproved the attitude of rigid dogmatists, and sought to understand the social and intellectual attitudes of the working class, but without subscribing to a programme, and expressly denying (for instance in Harnack's case) that the Christian ethic implied radical or socialistic conclusions. We find the names of its members regularly appearing among the supporters of many social reforms, for workers' social protection and insurance, the protection of female or child labour, for school reform, girls' education, women's emancipation. Moderate as its proceedings were, they caused anxieties in the Oberkirchenrat, which in 1895 publicly warned the clergy against 'taking sides' on social issues – what the ecclesiastical authority meant was that they should not become too concerned about working-class conditions.

For Stoecker the Kongress was too liberal, and he left it in 1896 to found his more authoritarian, clerical, and anti-semitic Kirchlich-soziale Konferenz. On the other hand Friedrich Naumann, who, also came from the Home Missions and had at first been close to Stoecker, resigned from Holy Orders and through his periodical *Die Hilfe* (from 1895) and his National-soziale Verein (1896) sought a fusion of Christian and socialist ethics within the framework of a vigorous and expansionist nationalism. Naumann has been called the most effective religious tractarian of this period. A man of mobile intelligence and humane sympathies, wide in his interests and very fluent as a writer, he won adherents and admiration in liberal and intellectual circles, even though he never created a mass following; we meet his articles in all the intellectual journals of the time. His lack of success as a politician is symptomatic of the overall failure of radical liberalism, which tried to fuse irreconcilable elements. Harnack, who like Max Weber often worked on particular issues with Naumann, quotes with some relish a comment of a reviewer of Naumann's *Briefe über Religion* of 1903: 'There are not a few readers who in all sympathy will not truly understand how one can be, at one and the same time, a Christian, a Darwinist, and an enthusiastic advocate of naval expansion.' Gustav Frenssen, the novelist who also started as a clergyman and who was a friend and associate of Naumann's, exhibits the same confusions. His first novels show a murky mixture of religious edification, social sympathy with the poor, respect for authority, and national pride, a combination that was possible only in a rural community. As the proletarian urban problem looms up, both the church and the political authority lose credit, to be replaced by a Nietzsche-type concept of Christ and a nationalism that somehow also reinforces individualism. After 1918 he turned towards democracy, and in his old age in the Hitler period fell into a 'völkische' racialism.

There were many other signs of a stirring conscience in the churches. The pacifism of Bertha von Suttner (*Die Waffen nieder*, 1889) had a considerable emotional success and a continuing though small number of adherents. In 1890 a Saxon officer, Moritz von Egidy, issued with his book *Ernste Gedanken* a challenge to the church to return to the ethical principles of Christ's teachings, i.e. to some sort of socialistic sharing, to replace the individualism, materialism, competition, and greed of existing society. The movement Egidy founded, *Einiges Christentum*, brought together members of many dissident movements, free-religious congregations, members of the Ethical Society, vegetarians and many eccentrics; for many bourgeois idealists like Lily Braun it was a stepping stone towards socialism. Egidy, who died in 1898, raised great hopes in the young intellectuals of the Naturalist movement, and appears in a transparent disguise in Adolf Wilbrandt's novel *Franz* and in Felix Holländer's *Der Weg des Thomas Truck*, a novel that presents a compendium of the conflicting Weltanschauungen of the 1890s.

The social conscience was much more under control in the Catholic church than among the Protestants. *Hochland*, founded in 1903 as the Catholic equivalent of Naumann's *Hilfe*, was much more timid in its reminders of social problems just as it was more orthodox and clerical in its theology and ethics. But the church authorities, both Protestant and Catholic, were still passionately engaged on the reactionary side over such issues as evolutionary theory, sexual ethics, women's education, cremation etc. When Georg Heym and Ernst Balcke were drowned in the

Wannsee in 1912, Blacke's body had to be taken to Leipzig for cremation as there was no crematory in Berlin. When one notes that Protestant crematories were built first at Gotha (1878), then Heidelberg and Hamburg (1892), one is filling in the map of liberal opinion in Germany.

All these religious social movements, however much directed towards improvement of the lot of the proletariat, were led by educated bourgeois and envisaged a continuing bourgeois guidance. From the beginnings in the 1870s, however, they encountered a Social Democracy with a leadership tested by adversity and a systematic even fanatical doctrine, that refused not only to yield leadership to the well-meaning bourgeoisie, but even to cooperate – in strong distinction from England, where non-proletarian Social Democrats like Lily Braun found an enviable spirit of cooperation between working-class leaders and organizations and bourgeois radicals or undogmatic socialists, particularly in and through the Fabian Society. In Germany the Social Democrats refused to participate in the Ethical Movement, the Free-Thinkers League or the Women's Emancipation Movement, just as they refused to cooperate with any of the radical religious movements. It is a startling fact that, alongside the bourgeois organizations, there were a Proletarian Free-Thinkers' League with a paper of its own, *Der Atheist*; a socialist Women's Movement, often at loggerheads with the bourgeois one; even a Proletarian Free-Thinkers' League for Cremation. So also the response of the young writers of *c.* 1890 to the new social sympathies stirring in the churches often met with chilly and harsh criticism in the Social Democratic press, when Kautsky's *Die Neue Zeit* pulverized them for their bourgeois vacillations, their decadence, their mystical leanings etc. If the dogmatism and social reactionariness of the churches provoked the young writers to reject orthodox beliefs and social attitudes, the dogmatic rigidity of Franz Mehring and other Social Democrats made it difficult for them to feel confidence in their own humane sympathies. The decline of social themes in the works of the Holz-Hauptmann generation and the dwindling of their reforming energy, like the excessive and often narcissistic utopianism of the Expressionist generation, were at least in part due to this sectarian rigidity of the Marxists.

Literature and Religion

Hostility to all forms of organized and dogmatic religion was almost a trademark of 'die Moderne' in all its forms, not solely of the pugnacious Darwinists, Marxists or Neitzscheans among the Naturalists. The attack takes little account of theological Modernism. In Naturalist works religious belief usually appears as a hypocritical defence of social privilege. Dehmel speaks of the 'mass-humbug' of the churches, Wedekind jeers at their inhumanity, Rilke denies that there is any true worship of God in the modern church and is delighted when he finds in the Samskola in Denmark a school without religious instruction. The Mann brothers are ironical or sardonic about believers, except when they belong to the lowly classes. Hermann Hesse indicts the Lutheran church as a branch of the state bureaucracy. On their first meeting, Stefan George presented to Hofmannsthal, along with volumes of his own and Mallarmé's poetry, a robustly anti-religious tract of Bruno Wille's, and always bluntly condemned the Christian exaltation of the soul at the expense of the body. In 1912 his *Jahrbuch für die geistige Bewegung* delivered a furious attack on the Protestant church on the grounds (no doubt adopted from Max Weber) that it was the instrument of materialistic capitalism and bourgeois liberalism. And so on, in innumerable variations, including that of Trakl who rejected Christian belief while using its symbols, and that of Expressionists like J. R. Becher who borrowed from religion the fervour to attack it to the point of blasphemy. Persistent as were these various sorts of criticism, the hostility is in general directed more against the Christian faith and church than religion itself, and one might even view it as a sign of a longing to rehabilitate faith. Nietzsche would have found in it a confirmation of his charge, in *Menschliches, Allzumenschliches*, that art feeds on and perpetuates religious needs that without its help would die out – 'art saddens the heart of the thinker'.

A few indications have been given, in passing, of religious and anti-religious trends in the literature of the period. Though it is impossible in a short space to give an adequate account, a few salient points must here be mentioned, particularly with a major question in mind: is the imaginative, artistic mode the vehicle of some unique religious insight, or does it simply give a peculiar form to opinions formulated in other ways by philosophers and theologians, by conformists, reformers and revolutionaries?

The most common cause of criticism was the alignment of the churches with the political authorities and the possessing classes, and their indifference to the material distress of the deprived classes. This type of criticism is anti-clerical rather than anti-religious. Even in the scientistic period of Naturalism, when a Holz or a Heinrich Hart jubilantly proclaim 'the end of religion', the writers and their periodicals *Die Gesellschaft* and *Freie Bühne* show great sympathy with religious preachers of social reform like Egidy. An article of Lou Andreas-Salomé in *Freie Bühne* (1891) claims that while no dogma or church can satisfy the moderns, religious feeling is now reawakening out of the 'need of the heart', the feeling of religious obligation to the poor, the workers, mankind; and if the author entitles her article 'Der Realismus in der Religion', she is using the term at least in part as indicative of literary realism. Bölsche's programmatic editorial, ushering in the third year (1892) of *Freie Bühne*, lists the creation of 'an undogmatic religious movement' as among the most urgent issues of the day. Hence a prevailing respect for Tolstoy's religion of the poor and humble, in spite of a general dislike for his sexual asceticism, a respect that took Rilke with Lou to Russia and produced his *Geschichten vom lieben Gott* and *Stundenbuch,* Döblin's *Die drei Sprünge des Wang-Lun,* and most happily of all the sculptured figures of Ernst Barlach, who ascribes his artistic awakening to his visit to Russia 1905-6.

Criticism of the social role of the church appears through innumerable figures of parsons who show themselves indifferent or hostile to the poor, the young, to change and new ideas – the parson in Hauptmann's *Einsame Menschen* is one example of many. Throughout *Buddenbrooks* Thomas Mann's cool irony shows how neatly faith adapts itself to the needs of business, and a sympathetic warmth enters into the writing only when Thomas Buddenbrook discovers Schopenhauer and Hanno surrenders to Wagner. While Pfemfert would have agreed with Heinrich Mann's identification of the church with the socio-political authorities (e.g. *Der Untertan*), his most effective criticism of the war and of the church came when in *Aktion* he contrasted the Christian message of peace with the realities of war. Von Unruh's impassioned protests also, more naively, make this the central accusation. The most extreme of these indictments of the church is Panizza's *Das Liebeskonzil* (1895), which not only revels in the sexual orgies of the Renaissance papacy but also ridicules the Christian divinities, presenting a senile and vindictive God, flanked by a similarly caricatured Jesus and Virgin.

In Halbe's *Jugend* a fanatical chaplain (a Pole) is balanced by an admirable, humane, sympathetic priest, and in many works we find priests with a social conscience, who because of this come into conflict with their superiors. The admirable pastors of Wilhelm von Polenz's *Der Pfarrer von Breitendorf* (1893) and Friedrich Lange's *Der Nächste* (1895) express their solidarity with the socially deprived by resigning from holy orders. A crass extension of such model Christians is found in Kretzer's *Das Gesicht Christi* (1897), in which Christ miraculously appears to the Berlin poor, to succour and comfort them and to remind men of what the church was failing to do. Similarly the painters Uhde and Baluschek placed the idealized figure of the compassionate Christ in realistic settings of destitution and suffering. Both Polenz and Uhde had been regimental comrades of Egidy, and their exemplary clergymen owe a good deal to reforming Christians like him and Göhre. A variant occurs in Felix Holländer's *Jesus und Judas* (1891), in which a theological student devotes himself to the interests of the proletariat but in the stress of political conflict betrays them.

Such imaginative embodiments of religious attitudes, sometimes sentimental, mawkish, one-sided, sensational, at their best vividly show the interweaving of religious conviction with the other, practical and intellectual, strands of a personality. They add however little to what was said in critical discussions and investigations. What is specific to imaginative evocation is most clearly evident in a few works like Hauptmann's *Hanneles Himmelfahrt* and *Der Narr in Christo, Emannual Quint*. Here there is little or no polemical intention, but in the main an attempt to reconstruct what faith means for the socially and culturally deprived, what its function is for them. *Quint*, in spite of faults in the rambling structure and the clumsy narrative, is a remarkable revelation of a distressed, confused, but pure soul, whose 'imitation' of Christ borders on a messianic delusion or even schizophrenia and makes him, like Christ, a victim of his disciples, yet without forfeiting the genuine and profound feeling that leads him to identify himself with his fellows. Döblin's *Die drei Sprünge des Wang-Lun* has something of the same creative insight. Both authors distance themselves from the faiths of their figures, and indeed take these faiths to be illusory, but none the less do something accessible only to the imagination, to art: that is, they show these faiths to be deeply engrained in the persons and times of which they write and to have a creative meaning for the persons who hold them. Troeltsch, so Ludwig Marcuse tells us in *Mein Zwanzigstes Jahrhundert*, found the 'religious poeticizing' of Hauptmann's *Quint* abominable; but perhaps this was the irritation of a theologian over a trespasser on his holy ground.

But there was more than a sympathy with sincere believers among the writers of this period. Particularly after about 1900 we can speak of a wish or will to believe, even if it was difficult to formulate the belief. There is a whole series of imaginative works, mostly novels, that centre in a search, a religious search for an undefined goal, partly a doctrine, partly a semi-mystical feeling, partly a form of self-fulfilment. The most important element is the drive itself, the search, and the concomitant abandonment of the familiar, the tangible, the established. There is something of this in Rilke's *Malte Laurids Brigge*, and still more explicitly in his poem *Der Auszug des Verlorenen Sohnes*, a characteristic variant on the parable. Where a religious content is defined, it tends to be of a mystical, individualistic, heretical type – as in Kolbenheyer's Spinoza novel, *Amor Dei* (1908) and his Paracelsus trilogy (1917, 1921, 1926), or Max Brod's *Tycho Brahes Weg zu Gott* (1916), or the very indeterminate *Christian Wahnschaffe* (1919) of Jakob Wassermann. The great popularity of the Grail theme is largely due to this preference for the search for an indefinable goal, though when a medieval and legendary setting is chosen, e.g. by Ernst Hardt, Karl Gustav Vollmoeller or Eduard Stucken, it usually also serves a romantic élitism. The figure of the 'searcher' becomes one of the topoi of the period. If Barlach's strange mystical plays avoid the normal stereotype they fall into the opposite pitfall, for their symbolism is so private as to seem almost inarticulate. In the best of this type of work the evocation of situation and character gives a reality to the inward compulsion that no analytical exposition could rival.

The Grail theme is only one example of a religious aestheticism that often, in symbolist painting as in literature, borrowed Wagnerian motifs, and that Nordau had already discussed and condemned as 'decadent' in *Entartung*. It found expression also in a revived interest in medieval Passion plays and tales of the golden legend. In 1895 Richard von Kralik put together parts of some mystery plays for a select audience in Vienna, and it is from about this time that the modern popularity of the Oberammergau Passion play begins. In 1895 the composer-conductor Weingartner appealed for financial support for a somewhat fantastic plan of his for an oratorio-opera *Die Erlösung*, a trilogy centring on Cain, Christ and Ahasuerus, for which he required a festival-theatre of his own. In 1912 Rilke was impressed by the *Mystère de la Passion* that he saw in Paris, and his poem-cycle *Das Marienleben* is a tribute to this taste. Sometimes these revivals were intended, like the crop of Luther Festspiele in the 1880s, to found a new national, non-intellectual culture, and the Catholic von Kralik hoped that the spirit of Oberammergau would weld together the educated and the peasant in a popular, Christian culture. More usually, however, this medievalism was esoteric, socially and aesthetically snobbish, an attempt to escape from modern problems, rationalism and the vulgarities of everyday life. This tradition of the revived medieval play embraces Hofmannsthal's *Jedermann* (1911) and *Das Salzburger grosse Welttheater* (1922), the most sophisticated and theatrically skilful of all.

The sophisticated decadence of Bourget and Huysmans, that by 1890 was already claiming to have ousted Naturalism and exercised a deep influence on the young Hofmannsthal, was soaked in an aesthetic religiosity that usually sustained a clerical conservatism. In Hofmannsthal's early work there is an almost complete disregard of church and religion, but at the same time a mystical trend – in the negative sense of grief over the flux of things and the meaninglessness of life, in the positive sense of a longing for and an occasional celebration of an irrational, inexplicable meaning discovered in objects or moods. Typical is *Der Kaiser und die Hexe*, the conjunction of despair over the lack of coherence in life and the longing for redemption. This early Hofmannsthal admired the religious art of the Pre-Raphaelites and Puvis de Chavannes. Later he recognized in Van Gogh's work a mystical revelation of the 'essence' of things. In *Der Dichter und diese Zeit* of 1907 he attributes a religious mission to poets, and calls reading poetry a religious act. Yet throughout, his work shows very scanty contacts with any established religion, and when his friend Andrian was turning back to Catholicism, the best Hofmannsthal could suggest was that they might find common ground in James's *Varieties of Religious Experience*, i.e.

in an attitude which, while it justifies any positive religion, also reduces it to the rank of an 'over-belief'.

This sophisticated and ambiguous attitude hardly prepares us for *Jedermann*, for with the old dramatic conventions the play adopts also the framework of Christian belief: the evil of selfish materialism, the succour of faith and works, the grace of God, repentance and salvation. There is no context of action or reflection here, as contrasted with Goethe's *Faust*, to suggest a symbolical rather than a literal interpretation of the religious theme, and Reinhardt's production in Berlin in 1911, even more the famous post-war productions in the setting of the Salzburg cathedral square, extracted every possible effect out of the religious associations. It was therefore not surprising that the contemporary audience took it as a religious play, lulling the intelligence with its skilful simplicities of form and language, which replaced the vexed social question of wealth and poverty with a rather comforting version of personal sin and redemption. Much the same interpretation could be applied to *Das Salzburger grosse Welttheater*, though the post-war social upheaval made its 'clericalist social doctrine', as K. J. Naef calls it, much more prominent. Hofmannsthal himself was distressed at this literal interpretation. He saw the plays as symbolical of the higher striving in man, of which the inwardness and other-worldliness of Christianity, the whole complex of sin-salvation, are one form, and in 1922 he wrote to Richard Strauss that the religious element in *Jedermann* is 'the celebration of our creative power, our inward freedom'. But it was a risky business to try to put such familiar beliefs to the service of a personal interpretation, and the play has more of its ostensible meaning than Hofmannsthal wished to be aware of: a falling back on simple beliefs, a shedding of intellectual burdens, a concentration on a personal problem and a hope for a happy ending, which in fact makes no impact on any social problem. One has only to compare Hofmannsthal's Festspiele with Tolstoy's *Resurrection* to recognize the aesthetic playfulness, even triviality, lurking within the former, and one can understand that the producer of *Jedermann* could produce also such a piece of monumental kitsch as Karl Vollmoeller's *Das Mirakel* (1912). Some of the most intelligent Berlin critics, like Kerr and Jacobsohn, who both were highly critical of the theatrical religiosity of Wagner's *Parsifal*, could find in Hofmannsthal something far more scrupulous and sincere, yet tainted with the same spuriousness.

In her *Freie Bühne* articles on religion (1891-2), Lou Andreas-Salomé states that religion can be reborn only from grief over the 'deus absconditus', what Nietzsche had called the 'death of God'. From this time the writers are constantly probing the ethical and existential implications of a world without God, and the intensity of their suffering uncovers depths of religious feeling that one hardly meets in the theologians. Thus from about 1908 Rudolf Kassner, Rilke, Morgenstern and Kafka begin to turn towards the religious outsider Kierkegaard. The critic Georg Lukács, not yet a Marxist, makes 'die entgötterte Welt' a basic point of reference in his distinction between the literary genres in *Die Seele und die Formen* of 1911, and this volume contains one of the earliest essays in the Kierkegaard revival. Lukács admires the absoluteness of Kierkegaard, his choice of suffering, his rejection of the ethical compromises of church and society, and what he calls his 'monumentalization' of himself. Lukács was already a political radical, and his sympathy with Kierkegaard and with mysticism, his antagonism to the church and liberal theology, grow out of his fierce contempt for bourgeois rationalism. His hatred of the meanness and hypocrisy of liberal individualism led him, like Wolfskehl, to particularly sharp derision of the 'bourgeois' Protestant church, and Paul Honigsheim reports in his memoir of Max Weber that Lukács and that other revolutionary Ernst Bloch in these years spoke 'with rapture' of the authoritarian and hierarchical Catholic church. It is the mixture of these elements in Lukács that enables us to believe that he was the model for Naphta, the totalitarian Communist Jesuit of Thomas Mann's *Der Zauberberg*.

Most of the religious beliefs that arise from this metaphysical despair conform neither to a Christian creed nor a Christian ethic, but all display dependence on Christian symbolism and ritual. This was so with Nietzsche, for both he and Zarathustra see themselves as re-enacting in their loneliness Christ's passion. Trakl, without any recognizably Christian faith and harshly critical of church and priesthood, is haunted by a desperate religious longing. In his poems the obsessive theme of decay, corruption and suffering is balanced by Christian images of peace, sacrifice and blessing that often recall Christian ritual. In Kafka's novels there is all the formal structure of religion – faith, a 'call', a conviction of sin and longing for redemption – but without any definable content. Dependence on Christian symbolism is still more striking in Stefan George, who resolutely rejected the spiritualism and dualism of Christianity and the concepts of sin and remorse. Even in the political poems of and after *Der siebente Ring*, and in the cultic plays (called 'Weihespiele' perhaps to recall the title of *Parsifal*), there is an abundant use of ritualistic Christian forms like election, initiation, dedication, blessing. And when George raised the dead youth Maximin to the rank of a God, he did so in terms of a ritualistic annunciation, pilgrimage, incarnation, salvation. This import of Christian symbolism into would-be pagan worship is confusing, and it was perhaps fortunate that the Maximin cult was not much more than an episode. Rudolf Steiner's adaptation of the 'Weihespiel' to the purposes of his gatherings seems, on the other hand, quite appropriate.

It is curious that in the neighbourhood of George's formalized ritual a worship of 'chaos' should have arisen that for a year or two round 1900 threatened, so Wolters reports, to engulf the Master himself. The Georgian attack on the barrenness of modern society and liberalism brought into his circle Alfred Schuler and Ludwig Klages who, in the service of creativity, opposed all organization, all fixed social forms, even Geist itself with its intellectual connotations. Wolfskehl introduced them to the writings of Bachofen, whose *Mutterrecht* (1861) had been one of the sources for Friedrich Engels' *Origin of the Family* (1884). They seized on the proofs Bachofen adduced of a pre-patriarchal family, and identified the primeval 'sexual promiscuity' he postulated with the essential creative energy of mankind, the source of the gods, spirits and myths through which men have imposed a meaning on the universe. Schuler, with a strange mixture of learning and idiosyncrasy, sought through magical ceremonies to establish communion with the dead in order to revive this creative energy that civilization, rationalism and science were stifling. It is hardly possible to call these beliefs and practices a religion, at best they constitute a variety of spiritism. George broke off from Klages and Schuler in 1903, repelled by the 'muddiness' and eccentricity of their thinking, the spurious exaltation over some 'great Beyond'. Wolfskehl broke with them too, almost in fear of his life from their violent fanaticism, though his wife, writing on his behalf to their friend Verwey, still com-

plains in 1908 of the 'Wust der Genies, der Spiritisten, Theoso-
phen und Mystiker' surrounding them in Munich. During the
war Rilke was to be profoundly impressed, and also repelled, by a
lecture by Schuler on death.

Beneath these and many other of the more personal faiths, as
well as those widely shared, lies a longing expressed in many
forms, the longing for 'Erlösung'. The word has a wide band of
meaning, from 'relief' to 'redemption' or 'Salvation', and it is
rarely used in a precise way. Its origin is however clearly religious,
and here the translation 'redemption' will normally be used.
Again, Nietzsche is an important source, in particular Zarathustra's message that he comes to 'redeem' man from the
fragmentation and fortuity of being, and that man must perish in
order to transcend (the section 'Von der Erlösung'). Even more
pervasive is the redemption theme in Wagner, in the *Ring,
Tristan und Isolde* and *Parsifal,* redemption from the heavy
burden of life, which is so peculiarly Wagnerian in that the deep
Schopenhauerian pessimism is impregnated with an awed veneration of life, and spiritual transcendence is steeped in sensuality.
No critic or historian can adequately sum up the meaning of
Wagner for the pre-war generations, but this doubly intense
redemption theme must surely be central.

In one form or another it is taken up by many writers. In his
remarkable essay *Wilhelm II und die junge Generation* (1889)
Hermann Conradi ascribes the concern of realists (he is thinking
chiefly of Dostoyevsky) for the sordid, bestial, and satanic in man
to a religious yearning for harmony and self-fulfilment that is
thwarted in writers who, neither bourgeois nor proletarian, are
victims of society and such 'strangers in the world' that they must
seek a religious salvation. Hermann Bahr, while still (in 1887)
half Marxist and half Nietzschean, dreamt of a 'redeemer of the
future', and in his *Überwindung des Naturalismus* of four years
later analysed the disintegration of Naturalism and its replacement by Impressionism in Christian-Nietzschean terms like 'pain',
'passion', 'salvation' (Heil) and in slogans like 'Out of suffering,
salvation; out of despair, grace'. When he writes, 'The cry for a
Saviour is general,' he is transmitting the programme of Bourget
and his friends in Paris, but the statement became true also of
Germany. George addresses Nietzsche in the ode of *Der siebente
Ring* as guide and 'redeemer'. Rilke's Malte Laurids Brigge, who
like Rilke abhors the concepts of sin and atonement as an un-

worthy defamation of man, yet longs for redemption through a mystical 'emptying of self' (Selbstentäusserung). This longing is typical in that it is associated neither with any particular transgression nor with a belief in God; it is the only positive element left over from Christian belief. In Trakl, as in Gottfried Benn, it is the hidden principle behind bitterness and despair; it is the disguised source of the endless and fruitless search of the heroes of Kafka's novels. Perhaps the most comprehensive definition is that in Worringer's *Abstraktion und Einfühlung* (1908). The source of the greatest art, he writes, is 'the need for redemption', and by redemption he means release from the burden of organic life, from individuation itself, a release imaged in the geometric antinatural forms of archaic primitive art. The humanistic implications of the European artistic tradition, the humanization of God and nature, the pantheistic reconciliation of God and nature, make this art in Worringer's view trivial.

It is clear that, however vague its meaning, 'Erlösung' is usually necessarily opposed to 'Lösung'; i.e. it denotes a spiritual self-transcendence, a metaphysical process. This may not mean that more definable, tangible, practical problems with perhaps feasible solutions are not acknowledged – Conradi and Bahr like Stefan George would have recognized their validity – but it does mean that such problems are of a derivative character, second in importance to the subjective spiritual experience, even acquiring importance only as a means to the spiritual experience and change. This remains true of the Expressionist generation, although the intensified pressure of the social problem, due to war and revolution, caused a certain shift of emphases. In some, like Werfel, the specifically Christian theme of salvation through suffering, the message of his essentially pre-war play *Die Troerinnen*, is constantly reiterated, and this notion of a purely spiritual transfiguration is uneasily associated with utopian images of the birth of the 'new man'. But the most typical Expressionistic topos is that of self-sacrifice for the sake of others, in which personal self-transcendence is allied to service to mankind. The self-sacrifice of a burgher for his fellow-citizens in Kaiser's *Die Bürger von Calais* is paralleled in plays of Kokoschka and Barlach, in Hasenclever's *Der Sohn* and Rubiner's *Die Gewaltlosen*. In Kaiser's trilogy *Gas* the birth of a child symbolizes the redemptive renewal of the world, and the use of this Christian topos in the framework of a social reorganization illustrates the typical endeavour to fuse personal redemption with social change. In a simpler sense Sorge's poet in *Der Bettler* and von Unruh's protagonists bring release and help to the poor and suffering.

The prominence in this generation of the theme of suffering as a spiritual purpose, of faith in a God who sends only trials and suffering, has led W. Rothe to associate Expressionist 'theology' with the 'dialectical theology' of Karl Barth and Emil Brunner that was formulated only after the war (*Der Mensch vor Gott: Expressionismus und Theologie*). There are indeed parallels in the essays and the imaginative work of the Expressionists to this modernist movement that stripped religion of the comforting promise that the churches and traditional theology had offered. Yet the confident, rhetorical, often ecstatic prophecies and visions of a new social order and a new moral inspiration, so prominent in Expressionist writing, seem the very reverse of the harsh asceticism of the theologians. At the same time, it is misleading to suggest that social change is the centre of the religious exaltation of the writers. If the socio-moral 'solutions' are isolated, their chief characteristic seems to be their extreme vagueness. Their true centre, even if the theme be poverty, sexual taboos, injustice, war, is a personal religious transformation.

While the concept of death as it appears in modern poetry has been the subject of countless investigations, that of 'Erlösung' has scarcely been examined, though it may be said to record the heartbeat of 'die Moderne'. It illustrates in a poignant way the successes and failures of the artistic imagination. A religious term often used in a secular context, its embeddedness in literature suggests that Nietzsche was right when he stated that art preserves atavistic emotions by inventing new disguises for them. When however he decries them because they have no vital function he is on less sure ground, for emotions of this type repeatedly reveal a peculiar sensitivity to the ethical and existential malfunctioning of society and its dominant creeds and ideologies. The longing for redemption, again, is not the simple outcome of despair, but is sustained by a great hope. Gerhart Hauptmann writes in *Das Abenteuer meiner Jugend* most revealingly about the euphoria in the young writers of his generation, the great expectation that a wonderful era was dawning, that led some to join utopian colonies, some to put their trust in science, some in socialism, some in new religions, some in emancipated sex, nudism, vegetarianism etc. Without this bright hope, where would the energy have come from to criticize the obstacles, social injustice, disintegration of communal spirit, greed and materialism, oppressive and hypocritical morality, trivial and spurious art? If the poets were more sensitive than most people to what Freud later called 'das Unbehagen in der Kultur', it was certainly in part due to this vision they had of a brave new world. It was related to the bright dream of Eden, but not ethereal; it did not look backward like the Romantic dream; it was a projection forward in time, in which the imagination secured the bliss of a meaningful personal existence in new social relationships, a new model of authority and freedom, power and service, nation and individual, and often a new concept of work.

On the other hand, the content of this vision varied from one poet to another, reflecting all the conflicting ideologies of the time, contorted by what must often seem to be exceptional vagueness and exceptional self-admiration. There is a sinister side, too, to this longing for redemption. The metaphysical implications of the word are that there are no practical ways of alleviating the pain of living, and that all hope is placed in a sudden, miraculous, spiritual change. And this is too close for comfort to the hysterical fanaticism of groups that found this or that problem – the predominance of England, the prominence of Jews, the Yellow Peril, the threat of materialism, or of socialism, or of democracy – so terrifying that they lost the tolerance and patience required to find 'Lösungen' and began to imagine violent 'final solutions'. The longing for 'Erlösung' often served this fanaticism, lending a spurious spiritual dignity to the intolerant rejection of the pluralism of values in the modern world and of the democratic institutions required to accommodate them. In this respect, as in many others, the artists seem in their protest against the times to express the contradictions within the times; this is indeed the theme of the deepest imaginative commentary on this period, Thomas Mann's *Doktor Faustus*.

8

The Family; Woman; Youth

The monogamous patriarchal family acquired in the middle classes its highest social and moral credit. Recognized by law and Christian morality as the sole legitimization of sexual union, its stability was reinforced by the laws governing inheritance and by a material affluence usually not so great as to weaken mutual family dependence. The defence of the family and the idealization of family feeling were great themes of the early bourgeois era. Legally and morally, the father was supreme. The law punished incest, murder and violence, it is true, but the wife and children were without property rights and much at the mercy of the will of the father. Literature fostered the belief that marriage was based on love, but wherever property was involved, in the middle class as in the aristocracy and peasantry, it was largely governed by practical considerations. Henry Mayhew, the author of *London Labour and London Poor*, states in his *German Life and Manners in Saxony* (1865) that 'marriages for love are almost utterly unknown', and Max Nordau writes in 1883 that nine out of ten middle-class marriages are essentially money arrangements and no better morally than licensed prostitution. Divorce was effectively impossible for Catholics, and while for Lutherans it was relatively easy, it meant such social obloquy and professional hindrances in the middle classes that only the boldest and better off could undertake it. The moral and practical training of children was chiefly the responsibility of the parents. Only the lowest grade of schooling was compulsory, and children proceeded to the higher grades of education only if the father approved and paid the fees.

Bourgeois sexual ethics, supported by religious teaching, made marriage the only approved framework for sexual intercourse. Social habit was however strong enough to permit the tacit toleration of prostitution and in some places licensed brothels, to meet the unquenchable needs of young unmarried men, and errant husbands were only required to cover extramarital relations in a decent obscurity. Severe standards of chastity were demanded of unmarried and married women, whose fault might lead to social repudiation and ignominy. By the middle of the nineteenth century sexual morality became to a surprising degree synonymous with morality in general. When the Hauptmann in Büchner's *Woyzeck* speaks of 'virtue' and 'morals', he means legitimization of sex by marriage, and Woyzeck gives the classic answer: 'Money, money! If you haven't any money . . . We common folk haven't any virtue, it's just nature with us.'

The later nineteenth century brought an acceleration of two contrary processes in the family and in sexual morality. On the one hand, bourgeois puritanism intensified and spread over other classes, including the aristocracy that had earlier been little affected, and this puritanism was so contrary to nature and to actual behaviour that it necessarily was attended by a prurient hypocrisy. Sex became a taboo subject, the very acknowledgement of sexual functions was suppressed, and authorities either kept works like Goethe's *Faust* from schoolchildren (especially girls) or used bowdlerized versions. On the other hand, the social changes consequent on industrialization began to undermine the old family ethos. Even in the middle class, the role of the family lost in importance as the education, technical training, and employment of children surpassed the competence of the father. The father's authority, still emphatically proclaimed, was no longer commensurate with his social function. The longer education required by middle-class youth imposed a greater strain on the relationship with the father, since the boys depended on the father's financial support; protracted bachelorhood of course exacerbated sexual pressures. The growth of the population, in which girl survivors outnumbered boys, led to an ever-growing surplus of women, doomed if no professional outlet was found to a dependent and defenceless status. The growth of the great cities and the ever-increasing mobility of labour broke down, even for the middle class, that stable familiar environment in which an ethos is securely transmitted.

The changes were still more drastic for the labouring classes. Streaming into the cities, they slipped out of the old village structure of authority, care and belief, and the controls exercised by a solid public opinion. The fathers, often out of work, perplexed, humiliated, and disoriented, lost authority with their children. Divorce of the husband, usually on grounds of neglect or cruelty, was not uncommon. Not only did the sons have to rely on themselves to find jobs, but the girls and women too found employment in growing numbers – by 1907 one third of the registered labour force in Germany was female, most of them working in factories. Wages were pitifully low – waitresses and barmaids usually received none – and in times of unemployment and sickness, poverty became utter destitution. In the working class, premarital sexual relations were customary, and under conditions of social misery turned into the vast prostitution of the modern city with its results: disease, unwanted and neglected children, abandoned and despairing women.

One can speak of an intensifying crisis of the bourgeois family and bourgeois-Christian sexual ethics, to which writers were peculiarly sensitive. Since the eighteenth century writers had attacked marriage as a business bargain or as a class institution, the tyrannical rights of fathers over children, the unnaturalness, cruelty, and hypocrisy of sexual taboos and the viciousness of public opinion in regard to extramarital sex and the unmarried mother. These attacks stemmed almost without exception from a full affirmation of an ideal of the family based on love and mutual care. The post-1870 situation produced new problems with vast new social implications, for which some other standard than the idealized monogamous family seemed often to be required. Marx had foreseen this already in his criticism of Feuerbach and, asserting that the 'secret' of the Heavenly Family was the earthly family, concluded that belief in the former could only be overcome by destroying the latter. Engels was later to write his *The Origin of the Family* (1884) in order to describe different historical forms of family, to relate the form of family to the nature of property, and thus to extend the revolutionary struggle of the proletariat to the bourgeois family itself. Actually the attack on the family, in its various forms, became on the whole a bourgeois theme, and found little response either in the working class or in the leadership of German Social Democracy – perhaps because circumstances themselves had in the working class broken the authority of the father and of conventional sexual morality.

In the modern period the family problem appears in two forms. One is the pressure for professional and legal emancipation of wives and children, and is directed against the authority of the father in the home and the almost complete exclusion of women from the professions. This was essentially a middle-class problem. In the working class, the woman's direst need was to have enough money to feed and clothe and house the family, and though she needed protection from a violent, negligent or drunken husband, her interests were hardly separate from his and the family's; she like them needed factory legislation, improvement of working conditions, adequate social welfare etc. As a result Social Democracy showed very little interest in the aims of the bourgeois Women's Emancipation movement. While the bourgeois women were clamouring for the right to work, the working-class women were suffering from an excessive obligation to work; for the former, prostitution was a moral and personal disaster and a stain on society, for the latter the social outcome of low wages and an unscrupulous bourgeoisie.

On the other hand, the new attitude to sex, powerfully stimulated by such opponents of women's emancipation as Schopenhauer and Nietzsche, was not directly connected with the movement for the social emancipation of women. Schopenhauer was the first philosopher to assert that moral principles are in large part rationalizations of unconscious drives, among which sex is one of the most powerful. Wagner reiterated this acknowledgement of the power of sex in his own way, for some of his works, notably *Tristan*, are an unqualified celebration of sexual love, rich in a sensuality that savours and even longs for doom. Aubrey Beardsley's drawing *The Wagnerites*, the audience at a performance of *Tristan und Isolde*, rows of massive women each sunk in her own dream, brilliantly interprets its orgastic function. Nietzsche, following Schopenhauer's cue but reversing the signs, ridiculed the Christian condemnation of sex as a typically absurd form of anti-life ethics; in *Menschliches, Alluzmenschliches* he makes the very Freudian comment that suppression of so vital a function as sex is bound to be a delusion, since the drive lives on 'in uncanny vampire forms' to torment man 'in repulsive disguises'. While for Schopenhauer art meant 'redemption' from sexuality, Nietzsche asserts in *Götzendämmerung* that Plato was right in ascribing an erotic source to all artistic activity. However, Nietzsche's attitude to the expression of sexuality is ambiguous. While he repeatedly speaks of the absurdity of the Christian condemnation and taboos, he also often praises prohibitions as provoking the creative resistance of men; for instance, in

Götzendämmerung he calls love the spiritual sublimation of sensuality, and hence a 'great triumph over Christianity'. There is no sign that Nietzsche, with his great fastidiousness and his dislike for the 'filth' of authors like Zola, would have welcomed the removal of sexual taboos. Many of his followers, believing with Nietzsche that sex was sinful only because prejudice called it so, drew from this a conclusion he himself did not make, when they believed that the emancipation of sex was the decisive step towards self-liberation and self-fulfilment.

Developments in science also showed a franker investigation and clearer understanding of sexuality, perhaps helped along by a general weakening of the taboo among intellectuals. In the latter part of the century many medical scientists, neurologists and psychologists, in Germany and in France, turned their attention increasingly to sexual pathology, particularly in relation to neuroses and various forms of paranoia. In 1886 the psychiatrist Krafft-Ebing published his investigations into sexual pathology, *Psychopathia sexualis*, a work that won an almost legendary notoriety. Like many other psychiatrists of the time, Krafft-Ebing was particularly interested in homosexualism or inversion, 'contrary sexuality' as it was often called, on which Magnus Hirschfeld also published studies from the 1880s. Hirschfeld's scientific work led him actively to oppose customary sexual morality, and along with a museum of sex he founded the World League for Sexual Reform. It was in such a medical context that Freud during the 1890s formulated his theory of the sexual origin of neuroses; *Die Traumdeutung* of 1900 is a historic landmark not only because it transmitted his work to a wider public than the medical profession but because here he lays the basis for his general theory of the power of sexuality and its pervasive presence in dreams, myths, art, in guilt feelings, sublimations, the superego and other reaction formations. It is difficult to estimate the importance of this psychological work on the public consciousness and on literature in the pre-war period; a few authors like Hofmannsthal clearly show a debt to Freud, but it is only with the surrealists after the war that there is a marked infusion of Freudian motifs, and Dada authors, who might be expected to have responded to his concepts, rejected his psychology and his therapeutic purpose as bourgeois. It is certain that the irrepressible drive in literature against the traditional sexual taboos and hypocrisy manifested itself well before Freud began his work, and continued to draw sustenance much more from Nietzsche than from Freud and his associates. Freud's *Die 'Kulturelle' Sexual-moral und die moderne Nervosität* (1908) fits into an already established pattern of opinion.

Scholars in many other fields testify to an intensified interest in sexual behaviour and a more urgent need to investigate it. Thus anthropologists like the American Morgan, on whose researches into primitive group-marriages Engels relied, or the Swiss Bachofen, with his notions of primitive promiscuity and its successor, matriarchy. Historians also brought much information about sexual practices and ethos in ancient Athens and Sparta or in medieval religious orders like the Templars. These investigations hardly leaked out beyond the academic strata who, for many generations, had enjoyed a privileged familiarity with Greek homosexuality, but they help us to understand the possibility of the rather sudden breakthrough, in books and periodicals, plays, poems and novels, of revolutionary views on family and sex.

The Emancipation of Women

The position of woman in society, that after 1850 became an urgent problem in Europe, America and Australia, became so through the efforts of women themselves. It was preeminently middle-class women who claimed the right to earn a living according to their ability and to have access to professions, especially in grammar school teaching and medicine, and therefore claimed the right to grammar school and university education, the gateway to the professions. With this demand for independence went the claim for legal independence in respect to property, husband and family. The movement was attended by a vast literature of discussion as to the nature and natural intellectual endowment of women, and the bible of the reformer was J. S. Mill's *The Subjection of Women* (1869), which argued that the inaptness of women for intellectual work and public responsibilities was due not to their biological endowment but to socio-cultural traditions and forms. In England many outstanding women proved Mill's thesis by their very existence, Harriet Martineau, Mrs Gaskell, Florence Nightingale, Beatrice Webb among many others. Ultimately what was claimed for women was fulfilment of the independent self, and it was for this reason that Ibsen's *A Doll's*

House was a bone of such violent contention, with Nora's abandonment of her family duties and her choice of independence instead of protection.

Feminism in Germany lagged behind the movement in other advanced countries; for instance, women gained admission to high schools and universities in Australia, the USA, the Scandinavian countries, Switzerland and Britain much earlier. The first challenges, from Louise Büchner (Georg and Ludwig's sister), from Auguste Schmidt and Louise Otto-Peters, the leaders of the Allgemeine deutsche Frauenverein, were met by a strong anti-feminist literature. Schopenhauer's spiteful remarks were often quoted, Lagarde and Nietzsche expressed bluntly, even brutally, their contempt for the intellectual and moral claims of women, and provided the stock arguments for a host of articles and essays that demonstrated the unsuitability of women for higher education, independent careers and posts of responsibility. Otto Weininger summed up these arguments in an extreme and paradoxical form in *Geschlecht und Charakter* (1903), which went through six editions by 1906. He proves (he was twenty-three years old) that the biological function determines the female psyche, they are either mothers or whores; they are not only devoid of genius and unable to understand what truth and freedom mean, but also incapable of love and truly moral feelings. Weininger is modern enough to favour the emancipation of women, but on the odd grounds that it will do men good to raise their intellectual and moral level.

The immediate objects of the Frauenverein, which was formed in 1865 as a federation of a number of associations pledged to this or that cause, were mainly middle-class – the provision of grammar school education and admission to universities for girls, posts in grammar schools and headships of girls' schools for women. In 1890 the Allgemeine deutsche Lehrerinnenverein was created, and things began to change. Liberal Baden led the way. In 1893 the first girls' grammar school was opened in Karlsruhe, women were admitted to medical courses at the Baden universities from 1891 and as full students in 1900. In Prussia, despite the efforts of the capable and energetic Helene Lange, herself a teacher, changes were slower; the first girls gained the Abitur in 1896, but girls' higher schools were not created till 1908. The women's demands met the often vicious jealousy of men teachers, who supported the delaying tactics of the conservative administration, and die-hards like the Berlin Germanist Roethe would never allow women to attend their lectures. Helene Lange was regretfully to acknowledge that the full realization of her educational plans, the opening of education and professions to women, was achieved only through the Revolution of 1918. During this period the women's movement often called on distinguished men to support their demands, and we frequently find among their supporters the names of Harnack, Paulsen, Helmholtz, Delbrück, Simmel, along with Gerhart Hauptmann and Dehmel. Harnack's attitude was not untypical of the liberal academics. He said publicly that he thought it unwise for women to enter the professions as they would swell the numbers of the 'academic proletariat', i.e. he was highly aware of the threat of competition; on the other hand he thought women must find this out for themselves and hence supported their claim for equal rights. Even such halfhearted support was welcome at a time when the movement itself, and its leader Helene Lange, intelligent, able, but a spinster, were the objects of vulgar abuse and innuendo.

But the 1890s brought other problems to the women's movement, above all those of proletarian women – sweated labour, the effects of casual labour and periods of unemployment, malnutrition, overcrowding, prostitution etc. Many of these matters led to the formation of liberal middle-class organizations to promote protective labour legislation for women and children, to provide antenatal and postnatal protection of mothers, and to establish homes for unmarried mothers or repentant prostitutes. But in these matters the women's movement was embarrassed by the Social Democratic party. August Bebel's *Die Frau und der Sozialismus* (1883) described the horrifying situation of the working-class woman with the help of official statistics and concrete experience and, attributing the breakdown of the family, the exploitation of woman and the growth of prostitution to bourgeois capitalism, affirmed that these problems could be solved only by the socialist revolution. Bebel's book could not be ignored, and in fact it forced the women's movement to turn its attention to the problems of the working-class woman. But the women's organizations of the Social Democratic party tried to turn all women's problems into party-political issues. Helene Lange, president of the Frauenbewegung from 1902, was remarkably successful in both guiding the bourgeois movement towards these issues and in keeping it free of party politics. She was helped by the sectarianism of the socialist women, who usually refused to cooperate with the bourgeois organizations, even on such urgent matters as social insurance for pregnant women. Lily Braun, who started as a member of the bourgeois movement but rejected its gentility to join the more political socialist movement, has left in her *Memoiren einer Sozialistin* (1909-11) a lively account of her struggles against the bourgeois lades and then against the sectarian Social Democratic women. It is typical that both the bourgeois and the working-class women looked on Lily's marriage to a divorced man with unconcealed disfavour.

The political enfranchisement of women played a very small part in the affairs of the Frauenbewegung, nothing like that it played in the suffragette movement in Britain. Helene Lange came rather reluctantly to favour it, against the traditions of the movement. It was achieved through the 1918 Revolution, not through a women's campaign.

Sexual problems gave rise to the greatest differences of opinion in the Frauenbewegung. The main body sought to preserve the traditional ethos of the family, including premarital chastity and conjugal fidelity, and found in the disasters of prostitution plenty of confirmation of their attitude. Lange typified this majority opinion when a radical group, the 'League for the protection of mothers', proposed that, in view of the unreliability of alimony payments, the state should take over the financial support of illegitimate children; Lange rejected the proposal on the grounds that the state would thus be subventing immoral liaisons. Only the more advanced would have supported the view of Ellen Key, Rilke's Swedish friend, that marriage is immoral without love, that love is moral without marriage, but sexual intercourse can be condoned only if it is attended by love (*Das Jahrhundert des Kindes*). Round 1900 Ellen Key, a fervent advocate of higher education and careers for women, was a favoured contributor to *Die neue deutsche Rundschau* (from 1904 *Die neue Rundschau*); it is a sign of the enfeeblement of liberalism that in the years immediately preceding the war this monthly's main contributor on women's questions was Lucia Dora Frost, a consistent and niggling denigrator of female intellectual and professional ambitions.

Still, it was a little awkward for Helene Lange and other champions of women's rights that, when they needed examples of able and prominent women, they had to point to such women as Lou Andreas-Salomé or Lily Braun. For both of these women spoke for sexual emancipation and the former was a shining and perhaps notorious example of a 'free' woman in this sense. Lou indeed criticized the ideal of the career woman, considering that the female sexual function necessarily made social equality something unnatural and forced.

Altogether it was more modestly gifted women, novelists like Gabriele Reuter or Helene Böhlau, who were closest to the Frauenbewegung, showing the frustration of girls in protective homes, the distortions of a convention-ridden education and the degradation of marriage into a career. However, any open discussion of sex by women was hindered by the feeling of its extreme impropriety, and while very brave women might speak about prostitution as a working-class phenomenon and problem, they could hardly speak openly about sexual problems in the middle class. If any woman did emulate the men, like Laura Marholm in *Karla Bühring* (1895), the story of a woman who uses men for her lust and despises her lovers, she would raise whoops of indignation from even fairly advanced critics like Leo Berg, the author of *Das sexuelle Problem in Kunst und Leben* (1891) and *Der Übermensch in der modernen Literatur* (1897). Maria Janitschek's *Vom Weibe* (1896) was called 'obscene', yet the only reason for this was the fact that the short stories of this collection do speak about the sexuality of women and admit that women commit 'faults'. Actually, the author's attitude throughout is one of condemnation of sexual licence and regret for women's frailty (the most interesting sketch is a study of a peasant girl turned by rape into a hysteric). The book, published by S. Fischer, has a most disarming Jugendstil cover design, a chain of ladies in flowing robes decorously dancing round an altar of flame and fire.

If one were to judge the attitude of the new Naturalist writers to women's emancipation by their chief periodicals, *Die Gesellschaft* and *Freie Bühne*, one would conclude that support for it was a distinguishing feature. While Paul Lindau, a lion of the earlier generation, the influential critic of the *Berliner Tageblatt*, wrote in 1890 of the 'questionable morals' of *A Doll's House,* Ibsen's play was felt by the young writers to express their own revolt. A leading champion of women's rights, Irma von Troll-Borostyáni, who wrote for both periodicals, bravely

demanded political as well as economic enfranchisement; not by
accident she was also a champion of the new realism in literature.
The leading theoreticians among the Naturalists, the Hart
brothers, Wille, Bölsche, all supported the opening of educational
and professional opportunities for women, and refuted the widespread opinion that woman was biologically inferior to man.

Curiously enough, however, the imaginative literature of the
Naturalists and their associates tells a different tale. Wedekind,
notorious for his provocative attacks on conventional sexual
morality in respect to women and men, wrote his first published
play, *Kinder und Narren* (1891), as a satire on would-be
emancipated girls, and all the emancipated women who appear
in his later works are comic or grotesque. He quite consistently
takes learning and career as unnatural for women, usually as
substitutes for frustrated sexuality. But Wedekind always
distanced himself from Naturalism. Hauptmann was at its heart,
and *Das Friedensfest* (prompted incidentally by an anecdote
from Wedekind's life) and *Einsame Menschen* were both published in *Freie Bühne*. The former is one of the most powerful
evocations of the close, suffocating, tense atmosphere of the
bourgeois family, in which the patriarchal myth creates, like the
east wind on the Pennines, a perpetual cloud of hatred, remorse,
conflict and devotion. Ida, the one ray of light in the gloom of the
father-son conflict, is by no means an emancipated woman; she
wants only to be a loving helpmeet to Wilhelm: 'Ich bin alles
durch dich' (Hauptmann does not notice that she will thus
perpetuate the conflict in the coming generation).

Einsame Menschen is perhaps the outstanding attempt to
present the theme of the emancipated woman, embodied here in
Anna Mahr, a Zürich student, in whom Johannes Vockerat finds
an intellectual and spiritual companion. Vockerat, though a
philosophical Darwinian, cannot overcome his piety to his
religious parents and his wife, and when Anna leaves him commits suicide. The whole failure seems to be symptomatic of the
German middle class. The centre is not the emancipated woman
(as in Ibsen) but the man who longs for a wife who can also be
an intellectual companion, and whose irresolution leads him to
delude himself about his feelings for Anna. Though theoretically
progressive, Vockerat is not only unable to revolt against family
piety, as he knows, but is also, and this he does not know, an
egoistic, spoilt and tyrannical husband, very largely the cause of

the timidity and ineffectiveness of his devoted wife. He is so feeble that some critics see Hauptmann's purpose as ironical, but both Anna's attitude and the views held by Hauptmann's associates suggest that he did not mean to question the genuineness of Vockerat's progressive ideals but to show the external and internal obstacles to their realization. In this play the emancipated woman only passes, a visitor, over the stage. Later, Hauptmann succeeds in creating strong and independent female characters only when they belong to the working class and derive their strength precisely from their family feeling, not from revolt against the family – thus the women heroes of *Der Biberpelz* (1893) and *Die Ratten* (1911).

In general, the progressive writers tend to run down the 'progressive' woman. Bölsche makes his scientist-hero (a hardly disguised self-portrait) of *Die Mittagsgöttin* (1891) abandon the lure of spiritualistic and sexual adventure and marry a devoted, unobtrusive home-maker. Otto Erich Hartleben's *Hanna Jagert* (1892), that caused an enormous scandal, has a heroine who, of working-class origin, has by her own labour built a business that makes her independent enough to have successive liaisons with a socialist workman, an ambitious manufacturer and a nobleman. But when a child is to be born she readily abandons her independence and marries the aristocrat. More usually the emancipated woman is cruelly satirized. In Sudermann's *Sodoms Ende* (1891) the intellectual Adah, a converted Jewess, is a frigid, ambitious, nymphomaniac monster, not unlike the Jewish distiller's wife, Frau Pimbusch, of Heinrich Mann's *Im Schlaraffenland*, also a bluestocking. The emancipated wife in Max Halbe's *Mutter Erde* (1898), the daughter of a reforming professor, is devoid of all natural feeling and simply out for power over men. To get a more sympathetic view one has to turn to unassuming novels like Gabriele Reuter's *Aus guter Familie* (1895), that describes the vain attempt of a bourgeois girl to gain emancipation from parents, or Helene Böhlau's *Der Rangierbahnhof* (1895) and *Halbtier* (1899), that arraign the enslavement and economic dependence of wives, or the popular stories of Clara Viebig, whose heroines (e.g. *Rheinlandstöchter*, 1897) miraculously combine rebellious sentiments with all the womanly virtues, the chief of which is devotion.

The negative attitude to the emancipated woman characterizes nearly all male writers throughout the period. Even Hauptmann or Dehmel, though always ready to sign manifestoes in favour of women's rights, were always rather quizzical about them. Most writers held the view expressed in Leo Berg's *Das sexuelle Problem in Kunst und Leben* that woman could not be the intellectual or spiritual equal of man, that true friendship is impossible between man and woman, and so forth. As might be expected, the George circle, with its hostility to liberalism and its worship of the male, was absolutely hostile to what *Jahrbuch für die geistige Bewegung* called in 1912 'die gottlose progressive Frau'. As one would expect too, the völkische authors with their ideals of Germanic heroism were equally hostile. Hermann Löns's hero in *Das zweite Gesicht* first runs down his wife because she has emancipated notions of the marriage bond, and then becomes bitter when she abandons her advanced views and frustrates his hopes of a *ménage à trois* (very typically he wants freedom for the 'creative' man but not for the woman). One comes across admiration for the emancipated aristocrat, like Heinrich Mann's Herzogin von Assy, who is above bourgeois morality, and an exception is always made for the woman artist or the actress, though her emancipation is of a moral kind, and usually sexual rather than intellectual; in both cases they are looked on as exceptions to the normal rule, not as representatives.

What is perhaps surprising is that this negative attitude continues in the revolutionary generation of the Expressionists. *Aktion* picks up again the progressive tradition of *Freie Bühne*, staunchly supporting the radical aspects of the women's emancipation movement and even publishing articles in favour of birth control and legalized abortion, but there is again a disparity between theoretical opinions and the workings of the imagination. For the poets, even those whose political views were fairly close to Pfemfert's, almost without exception present the ideal of woman as the devoted servant of the man and her highest gift as self-sacrifice: such are Das Mädchen in Sorge's *Der Bettler*, Das Fräulein in Hasenclever's *Der Sohn* or his Antigone, the women in Kaiser's *Gas* trilogy, or the women, suffering angels of peace, in the plays of von Unruh. That is, where women are allowed a significant role at all, then it is the traditional ideal image of the self-sacrificing, devoted helpmeet of the creative man that emerges from the depths of the writers' imaginations, in spite of whatever advanced notions they may hold on the plane of rational consciousness. One can criticize Thomas Mann for rejoicing over this masculinity in his anti-democratic *Betrachtungen eines Unpolitischen* of 1918, and one can question his assertion that the anti-feminism of Nietzsche is truly German, but there is no doubt that the traditional bourgeois conception of the place of woman was very deep-seated even in the most radical bourgeois circles.

Youth Problems and Youth Movement

There is nothing new in the claims of literary and artistic movements to represent 'youth'. The Sturm und Drang, the Young Germany of the 1830s, asserted this. But the Naturalists and Expressionists and their contemporaries meant something more than these other rebels against ossified middle age, and were claiming more than independence and the right to sow their wild oats. Altogether, in this period a more substantial challenge was delivered to paternal and social authority. It centred on school and family, the great training-grounds of youth.

The schools and universities of Germany remained after 1870 the responsibility of the various states, and their organization therefore presents an extremely complex pattern in which, in different areas, a different proportion of responsibility was allotted to ministries of education, the church, local authorities, and in the case of independent schools the boards of governors (a helpful and judicious account is given in *Education and Society in Modern Germany*, by Samuel and Thomas). Common to all systems was the rigid separation between the elementary and the grammar and secondary schools. The former were compulsory for all children, nearly always single-denominational, and if not outright church schools then always subject to inspection by church authorities. The secondary and grammar schools were fee-paying, hence mainly middle-class, and not in Prussia subject to church inspection, though in Catholic lands they were often church schools. The elementary school, 'Volksschule', had been one of the great hopes of earlier liberalism, but after 1870 it receives surprisingly little attention in the radical journals and in literature. Here the chief issue that is raised by critics is essentially a political one, the compulsory religious teaching required of the teachers and the powers of the church in the school administration, and we always find *Freie Bühne* or *Aktion* supporting radical teachers like Gurlitt. In educational circles criticism of the social and religious segregation policy of the system was often voiced and the idea of a comprehensive school, the 'Einheitsschule', linking elementary and secondary education under one authority, won favour not only in radical-liberal circles but also among the more fervent nationalists like Friedrich Lange, who saw it as embodying the same spirit of national unity as Lagarde's 'German faith'.

That the Volksschule figures rather rarely, compared with the grammar school, in literary works is an indication of the bourgeois bias of literature as a whole; in the cultured classes the problems of secondary education caused the greatest stir and passions in this period. The foundation of the Reich brought in this field not only a continuing great expansion of numbers but also a number of new types of schools, the Realgymnasium and Realschule, and technical schools like art schools and trade schools. These owed their origin to the new industrial society and the demand for 'modern' subjects – history, modern languages, German, as well as science – as opposed to the established grammar school, the Gymnasium, with its almost exclusive emphasis on Greek, Latin and mathematics. The bitter battle between the adherents of the new and old type of school was exacerbated by the continuous immense growth of scholarly and scientific knowledge. Neither side would relinquish its claims, and as a result the syllabus became more and more overloaded and pupils more and more heavily burdened; the ministries refused to lower standards and hence were in part to blame for the ferocious pressures imposed by the masters in secondary schools.

In these circumstances Wilhelm II instigated the calling of a Reich school conference in 1890, and his address to the conference was one of those utterances that filled the young generation of writers with such hopes of a 'Volkskaiser'. He called on the assembly to consider the whole purpose of education, castigated the overemphasis on information and learning, and called for more attention to physical education, personal development and modern subjects, especially German, to fit boys for the modern needs of Germany. *Freie Bühne*, like *Aktion* later on, found itself in agreement with the Kaiser, and enlarged on his attack on the overemphasis of learning and in particular on the excessive respect for remote subjects like classical antiquity.

Things did not greatly change in the state system of schools. The education ministries and their officials remained pledged to the social privileges of the Gymnasium as to its classical curriculum, and influential academics like Harnack maintained its superiority as a training for the university and the higher civil service. The grammar school masters were a powerful body, closely linked personally with ministries, and were successful in maintaining their prestige, just as they were the strongest force in resisting the claims of girls to secondary education and university admission. There were some reforms. The leaving examinations at the Realschule and Realgymnasium were recognized as equivalent for purposes of university admission to that of the Gymnasium, and in some Gymnasien, like that at Neuruppin where Georg Heym was a pupil, work-demands and discipline were relaxed and sporting and other outdoor recreations introduced that brought masters and boys together. However, the great expansion of numbers in secondary education increased rather than lessened the dominance of the Gymnasium over other types of school. From time to time news of the suicide of grammar school boys would shock public opinion and set off discussion in the press, but official inquiries would usually attribute the misfortune to evil habits or the influence of Schopenhauer or Nietzsche, not to the pressures of work and the ferocity of masters. A general complacent awareness of the great efficiency of the intellectual training given in these schools, which was justifiably felt to be a proud achievement, stifled criticism of the psychological and social effects.

The most effective protest against the ruling educational principles came from the pupils themselves, in the form of the Wandervögel movement, initiated in 1897 by grammar school boys in the Berlin suburb of Steglitz and spreading with remarkable speed throughout Germany and Austria. It was different from other youth organizations like the YMCA since it was not charitable, not religious, not political, and above all not organized and controlled by adults. The motivation was multiple. Its simplest aspect was the longing to get away from the city, to discover the countryside and the farms and indulge a romantic nature feeling. There was a longing for the simple life, for long tramps across country, for camping in barns and cooking one's own meals, for singsongs to the guitar round the campfire. There was the thrill of discovering one's native land and its varied and often remote landscapes and people, which made the longer holiday jaunts of the Wandervögel so memorable. But the decisive attraction was the freedom from the authority of parents and schoolmasters, the freedom of the young to organize and decide for themselves, to set up groups, form a federation, organize district and national congresses, and edit their own papers. Actually, wellwishers among the adults, schoolmasters and others, were quite closely associated with the movement, fostering it, giving help of practical and theoretical kinds and writing about it; a number of its members remained associated with it when they were no longer schoolboys or students. Yet one can properly speak of a youth movement and a youth ideology, for what was created grew out of the groups and their activities.

This ideology was not systematic, of course, and most members would join for simple reasons, to get out with other boys into the country at a weekend or a holiday period, and to be free of adults just for these times. But the temporary rejection of adult authority encouraged a rejection of the ethos of the normal bourgeois parent and schoolmaster, in particular of the 'material-ism' that placed security, a good income, and social position as the first objectives. This anti-bourgeois orientation corresponded of course to much social criticism in the adult Germany of these years, the trend among the Wandervögel however was markedly towards the radical right rather than the left. Their criticism of the big city, industrialization, the mechanization of life, the destruction of individualism, the disintegration of the national community chimed in with 'völkische' ideas, and anti-democratic, anti-liberal ideas and attitudes were common among the Wandervögel. Anti-semitism was rife too, and Jews were not admitted to most groups, usually on the grounds of 'race hygiene', a concern that led some groups to abjure alcohol and tobacco.

It would be hard, as Harry Pross states (*Jugend, Eros, Politik*, 1964), to discover any new idea in the Wandervögel ideology; the true novelty was the social structure of the groups, par-ticularly when on tour, and this incorporated a political idea in the powerful form of a heightened experience. For the 'horde', as it has been called, was led by a leader whose initiative and ability gave him an authority that could be called autocratic were it not that the groups were very small, relationships highly personal, and authority dependent on free consent. But it was on such a model that political inclinations towards 'völkische' ideas of the 'natural' Germanic leader, as opposed to democratic or socialistic ideas, were strengthened. In the same way the cult of the camp-fire, so natural in groups of camping boys, encouraged playful semi-pagan folk rituals that linked up with the serious pagan Germanism of the 'Völkische'. That the 'Heil' greeting, the swastika sun-symbol, terms like 'Gau' and 'Gauleiter' were taken over after 1918 by National Socialism from the Wandervögel does not mean they meant the same; these young people managed simultaneously to hold many contradictory religious, political and social opinions. Among the group leaders there were fanatical radicals of the right and racialists, but not all of them inclined to the right. One of the most influential supporters, the progressive schoolmaster Gustav Wyneken, whose *Was ist Jugendkultur* (1914) was the most persuasive defence of the idea of an autonomous youth culture, was an opponent of chauvinism and racialism, and so convinced a democrat that Stefan George, so Edgar Salin tells us, called him 'an arid rationalist without faith and without veneration'. At the great rally on the Hoher Meissner in 1913, however, Wyneken's eloquent humanism was drowned in the tide of chauvinism and racialism that was sweeping over the youth movement.

There were variants on the Wandervögel, and its own groups were by no means uniform. A few working-class youth groups were formed but, like the socialist women's movement in relation to the Frauenbewegung, remained separate with specific social interests, such as the protection of the young factory worker, which made them more a youth branch of the Social Democratic party than a youth movement proper. There were attempts to create a youth movement linked to the army and state, a German form of the Scouts movement, which also had its organization in Germany (Pfadfinder, founded 1909). But it was its autonomy that was the cause of the great popularity of the Wandervögel, and if political principles were imbibed, they were those 'natural' to middle-class boys and left them free from burdensome obligations. Their freedom in fact reflected most of the prejudices of the older generation that they believed they were challenging. On women they shared the conservative view, and most groups did not admit girls; where they were admitted they were given menial 'feminine' tasks like cooking and cleaning. Clearly the intimate association of girls and boys on expeditions would have met the strenuous opposition of parents, school and church, but it was opposed too by the patrons and leaders of the Wandervögel. The

most persuasive arguments of the supporters of the groups stressed
the value of male companionship and friendship, the development of initiative and the 'male' virtues, and the consequent relief
it brought from the sexual pressures of puberty. This somewhat
idealistic enthusiasm needs modifying, perhaps, in the light of
Hans Blüher's thesis (*Die deutsche Wandervögelbeweguung als
erotisches Phänomen*) that homosexual relationships sustained
the permanent structure of the movement. For conventional and
unconventional reasons, therefore, girls were not welcome, and
those who were permitted to take part formed a recognizable
type, the devoted servants of the men, their hair in long plaits,
dressed chastely in 'reform' garments or in folksy dirndl
costume – the opposite in social and sexual attitudes of the
emancipated woman.

The direct effects of this youth movement and its songs and
dances on literature and art are very small. Very few writers of
note were connected with it, and even if a Löns shows some
ideological and sartorial sympathies, there is little reflection of
group life in his work. Clearly there are connexions between the
occasional dance festivals of the George group and the more
ethereal Wandervögel activities, but although George could
approve of some of the Wandervögel ideals, he was altogether too
sophisticated for it. We find before the war considerable
sympathy for the youth movement, as well as criticism, in the
pages of *Aktion*, that illustrate the ambiguity in this revolt of
youth. In 1913 Kornfeld owes his notion of the 'battle of the
generations' partly to Freud, but partly to the Wandervögel.
Pfemfert himself wrote enthusiastically about the great rally on
the Hoher Meissner, but warns the young to steer clear of party
politics. Another contributor, on the other hand, sharply indicts
the chauvinism and anti-semitism prominent at this rally. In the
following year, when Wyneken was forbidden to lecture on the
'mission of youth' in Vienna, and when a democratic youth group
formed under his auspices was banned as a danger to the family,
the teachers and the state, *Aktion* stoutly defended him and the
revolt of youth. Even Pfemfert does not seem to have realized that
the ideology and structure of the youth movement were such that,
when the war broke out, its members found in the unity of
national feeling, the expansionist war-aims, and the leadership
structure of the army, the realization of their dearest values. The
outstanding literary product of the Wandervögel movement was

a war book, Walter Flex's *Der Wanderer zwischen zwei Welten*, that embodies in sublime naivety the confusions of the youth movement (see p. 108). The youth movement tried to create a free area outside the confines of school and home, and did not promote any precise educational reforms. But through adult circles associated with the Wandervögel, perhaps influenced by them, reforms were initiated, directed particularly against the three great grievances: the overloading of the curriculum and the insistence on the acquisition of knowledge; the rigid discipline and the remoteness of teachers from boys; and the lack of an inspiring purpose. There was a revival of Fichte's educational theory with its emphasis on the self-activity of the pupil as the means to the strengthening of the ethical will. The importance of art, sport, and handicrafts was recognized. For many, the British public schools seemed to offer a model of a community and a study programme; Harry Graf Kessler was to describe in his autobiography the English preparatory school he attended, with its unpedantic and stimulating lessons, its games, and the friendly relations between the masters and the boarders, and to contrast it to the heavy and stifling pedantry of the Hamburg Gymnasium to which he afterwards went. In 1898 Hermann Lietz founded the first of what became a new type of boarding school, the 'Landeserziehungsheim', on the model of an English public school at which he had taught. It is typical that though Lietz created a school that, as a friendly community concerned to develop the creative activity of the boys in work and play, greatly appealed to radicals like Lily Braun, the chief inspiration of Lietz's reform was the enhancing of nationalist consciousness through the inculcation of an anti-liberal, anti-democratic conservative authoritarianism. On the other hand, the 'Freie Schulgemeinde' founded by Wyneken in 1906 at Wickersdorf embodied the democratic principles of his youth groups; its overriding principle was democratic service to the community, and this was embodied in his school in, for instance, the participation of pupils in administration. All these boarding schools were outside the state system, and being expensive were accessible only to the wealthier classes. Yet, though the liberal papers like *Aktion* might express their awareness of this élitism, they still admired the freer and more humane type of education there. We find Hofmannsthal keenly supporting a plan for a new school on British public school lines just because it would be an élite school.

The great expansion of the universities did not lead to any such reforms. In 1911 the proportion of students to the total population of the Reich was almost three times that in 1875, and this meant not only a great increase of numbers but also the presence of many students lacking the traditional academic background of the home. The excellent seminar system, so fruitful for small classes, began to fail as classes grew, unless the professor, like Mommsen or Simmel, excluded all but the best. The rapid expansion of knowledge required more and more specialized work, and made a student's success in his studies more and more dependent on his utter devotion. The same narrow specialization governed the professors too and submerged them in their job. Since the universities were state institutions and all appointments were made (on the recommendation of the faculties) by the Ministers of Education, the professors were all civil servants, and most acquired the conservative and authoritarian attitudes of the typical civil servant. Since, too, the senates were entrusted with considerable autonomy and the professors in their turn enjoyed absolute power within their department, the rank of professor enjoyed great prestige and engendered great professional pride. The scientific and scholarly achievements that this system made possible made it an example to the world.

However, after 1900 there were protests against the conservative and authoritarian character of the professorial body, which allowed no participation in administration to the categories of unsalaried 'extraordinary' professors and 'Privatdozenten', and which made lecturers directly dependent on the goodwill of their professor. These matters did not appear largely in public discussion, and one of the few admissions of trouble is an article in *Die neue Rundschau* for 1909 by the Germanist Friedrich von der Leyen. The author claims that the specialization and authoritarianism of professors were weakening their concern for the university as a whole and reducing the lecturers to servility. He suggests that lecturers should be given a salary, administrative responsibilities and more independence; he also points out that students now came from very diverse backgrounds, often without an academic tradition, and calls for greater attention to their intellectual and personal needs. Such criticism bore hardly any fruit in this period.

The changing character of academic work and its relation to

contemporary culture can perhaps be assessed from the example of German literary studies. The creation of the academic study of 'German philology' belonged to the liberal and patriotic movement of the first part of the nineteenth century, to the Grimm brothers, Gervinus, Hettner, Haym and such great scholars, through whom German studies came to be looked on as the key to the self-awareness of the German nation. After 1870, with Scherer and others, a complacent nationalism replaces the old search for a national identity, and an often trivial and routine academicism replaces the scholarly syntheses of the earlier generation. Up to about 1900 it was still usual for the liveliest students of any faculty to attend a course in German literature. But about this time, as Paul Fechter states (*Menschen und Zeiten*, 1948), the brightest began to prefer philosophy. The new generation of writers had already expressed their dissatisfaction with the academics. We find for instance Conradi attacking the philistinism of the Germanists Scherer and Kluge, or Brahm in *Freie Bühne* hitting out at the pedantic triviality of the *Goethe-Jahrbuch*. The George circle always denounces the smugness of the literature professors, their bureaucratic remoteness from vital questions and urgent evaluations, while from the other end of the political spectrum *Aktion* attacks the Berlin professors also for reactionary political and social attitudes (Roethe) or conformity to fashion and convention (Erich Schmidt).

The modern writers were discovering a new literary tradition – Lenz, Kleist, Grabbe, Büchner – in place of the accepted classics, and it infuriated them to hear the academics still deploring the lack of moral discipline, harmony, feeling for form, in these tragic innovators. A sensitive and independent mind like Simmel could break through the academic clichés and write to Paul Ernst (1910) that the 'formal perfection' of the classical verse-drama had repeatedly seduced German writers, Schiller as well as Hauptmann and Ernst himself, to deny their own genius, though Simmel did not know perhaps that he was returning to a theme of Hettner. A few unconventional academics like Gundolf, Arthur Kutscher and the young Fritz Strich responded to the new valuations of their time, but in general a great gulf opened in this period between the creators of literature and the whole apparatus of publishing, theatre, and criticism on the one side, and academic literary studies on the other.

German students shared in the freedoms of the university in

that the curricula were generally very free and much was left to the student's initiative, the period of study was not limited, and a student might study at various universities. They had a far more adult status than British students, for the universities accepted none but the most elementary responsibilities for student life outside the classroom. On the other hand, the university provided almost no facilities for the social and intellectual recreation of students. Almost the only permanent form of student association was the 'Verbindung' or 'Corps', retaining from its earlier traditions a strong nationalist character, now more and more aping the habits of the officer class, and often meeting only to drink or to duel. Apart from its sociable value, it was an extremely useful employment agency, since here students met the old boys, the 'alte Herren', who made it a point of honour to help their young associates to jobs if they showed they conformed to the traditions. In some universities Catholic associations and other forms of Verbindungen gave an opportunity for more humane and intellectual meetings, and here and there, as notably at Marburg, Wandervögel groups were established. On the whole, intellectual and spiritual education was left to the seminar and to private relationships. The public side of student life was dominated, especially in public opinion and in literature, by the rowdy, bellicose, arrogant drinking-clubs, the Verbindungen, hotbeds of anti-liberalism and anti-semitism, where young men were initiated into freedom by drinking to excess and whoring, and under cover of this freedom were channelled into jobs.

Youth in Literature

The theme of youth and its problems is common in German literature since the Sturm and Drang, and the conflict of young people with old, children with fathers, often under the rubric of nature versus convention, feeling versus practical calculation etc., is familiar. What distinguishes the period after 1880 is the immense frequency of this group of themes in literature, the sharpness of the criticism of the adult world, the prominence of the sexual problem and the extreme self-assertion of youth. If the social emancipation of woman gets a poor showing in literature, the emancipation of youth is always under the spotlight, the source of the most grotesque satire as of the most rhapsodic idealism. Every writer has experience of home and school, and few fail to insert some critical comment somewhere in their work. In *Betrachtungen eines Unpolitischen* Thomas Mann writes that the only piece of social satire in his writing up till then was the account of Hanno's schooling in *Buddenbrooks*, and this certainly has an autobiographical basis. The material is so immense that here only a schematic summary can be attempted.

The figure of the modern Prussian teacher, the reserve officer and fanatical disciplinarian, bringing order into the more easy-going old-fashioned school, appears in Raabe's *Horacker* (1876) and reappears very often (e.g. in *Buddenbrooks*, or Heinrich Mann's *Professor Unrat*). Admitted by grace to a regimental officers' mess, the reserve officer earned this distinction and exploited his privilege by becoming the champion of Prussian militarism in the school. But the truly characteristic modern note is struck by Holz in his sketch *Der erste Schultag* (in *Papa Hamlet*, 1889), with a ferocious schoolmaster who rules by terror over his natural enemies, the boys. Mann's Unrat is similar, always setting traps for the boys, and brought into direct sexual rivalry with them in the Blue Angel.

Even if masters are not presented as monsters like these, the school as a whole, the educational purposes of the masters, are repeatedly shown to be hostile and crippling to at least the more sensitive boys. Emil Strauss' *Freund Hein* (1902) shows the failure of an artistically gifted boy to keep up with the academic requirements. While his friend, a poet (an echo of Kai in *Buddenbrooks*), is rebel enough to hold his own against the bullying of teachers, Heiner can escape only by suicide. A schoolboy suicide occurs in Stilgebauer's *Bildner der Jugend* (1908), again due to anxiety about the leaving examination (Abitur). In this book a liberal and humane headmaster tries to reduce the boys' workload and to prevent the Baden school from becoming a Prussian training establishment; his failure is due to an alliance of church dignitaries, conservatives, and envious colleagues. Stilgebauer throws in the fashionable sexual theme, and seems to wish to make the headmaster a champion of a more liberal attitude towards sex; he is however so confused a writer that he does not notice that the headmaster's opinions are quite conventional. In Hesse's *Unterm Rad* the theological seminary that is the poor boy's channel to position and security is shown to be the means by which he is bribed to become a pillar of the state. The constant pressure of work is calculated to stifle all independence of behaviour and thought, and all the masters, however helpful they would wish to be, are slaves to the concept of work and success. Hans, the sensitive boy, suffers a nervous collapse, but finds a precarious contentment in work as a manual labourer; his death, by suicide or accident, follows on the shock of his first sexual awakening. There are innumerable other works in which school is savagely indicted as the agency of a hostile and materialistic bourgeois world and the enemy of the individual child, and we begin to recognize certain clichés – for instance, in Hanns Johst's novel, *Der Anfang* (1917) and his play, *Der junge Mensch* (1919) – the schoolboy suicide, the grotesque figures of hateful and hated schoolmasters, and the attack on Christian sexual morality.

It is a relief to come across Leonhard Frank's *Die Räuberbande* (1914), refreshingly nearer to more normal situations though free of sentimentalization; 'normal' in the sense that the group of schoolboys here lives in a secret imaginative world (from Karl May) without serious conflict or confusion with the actual real world of home, school and work, so that the fantasy world for most of them drops away as they grow out of childhood. In the more fashionable modernist literature, attention is only too often focused on the vulnerable, sensitive boy, and the powers of self-defence that lie not only in obtuseness and vulgarity but also in the imaginative powers are almost polemically ignored. There is in the great majority of these books about schools no reference to successful educational experiments. Even though the system of education was harsh and often ignoble enough to justify a fierce indictment, something wider than the school was involved in this criticism, a polemic against the state, the principle of subordination, the ethics of bourgeois society etc., and this makes the works as a whole unreliable as social documents.

The two most searching studies of school life in imaginative literature in this period – Wedekind's *Frühlings Erwachen* (1891) and Musil's *Die Verwirrungen des Zöglings Törless* (1906) – are both centred on the sexual problems of puberty, and yet both radiate outwards towards more general problems. Wedekind's play, though banned from the stage for fifteen years and too bold even for a *Freie Bühne* production, is his most tender and least provocative work and the great seminal source of so many works on children and parents, children and school. Masters and parents are intimately associated with the fate of these fifteen-year-olds. The masters, it is true, are grotesques in the style we recognize as Wedekind's, only concerned with examination success and the moral (sexual) conventions. But the parents are not caricatures. In their different ways they are kind and loving, genuinely concerned for the welfare of the children, and only because of their acceptance of conventional values do they contribute to disasters, driving Moritz to suicide because of guilt-feelings toward his parents, Wendla to death at the hands of the backstreet abortionist, and Melchior to the Borstal. But just as there is sharp differentiation between the parents, so there is between the children, and the play ends not with the tragedy of the vulnerable and innocent but the challenge of the strong and intelligent Melchior. The scenic structure of this play, owing much to Lenz and Büchner, allows Wedekind to introduce without provocative emphasis many behavioural characteristics due to puberty and the guilty consciousness it arouses in the children – masochism and sadism, masturbation, homosexual love; Siegfried Jacobsohn, reviewing this play when at last, with a few cuts, it received public performance in 1906 (by Reinhardt in Berlin), was astonished at its delicacy and truth. We can still admire its truth, in spite of the sometimes stilted and rhetorical language, and especially because we are not misled to believe that all the unhappiness and disasters are simply the result of the wilful abuse of power, and can feel they come from deep down in the human psyche and from the complexity of human relations. Though authority and a false sexual ethos are indicted in the play, it is not implied that a changed ethos would remove all the strains and dangers of youth.

Robert Musil's short novel, *Die Verwirrungen des Zöglings Törless*, owes its sophistication in part to the fact that two decades of battles with public opinion and the law had succeeded in making possible an unembarrassed and unemotional discussion of sexual problems in imaginative works. All the same, it is a most remarkable book that hardly fits into the pattern of books dealing with the complex of boys-school-parents, since there is no criticism of the parents, no rebellion against parental authority, and no true criticism of school and teachers. True, the parents, who only faintly intrude on the scene of this boarding school, are ineffectual and ignorant about the boys' under-surface life, however kindly their good will; this however we take not as something that might be corrected, but an inevitable feature of the relations

of parents with sons of eighteen to nineteen. The teachers are
rather narrow-minded and the school work is all pretty meaningless (when Törless gets interested in irrational numbers the
mathematics teacher tries to steer him away from such awkward
and useless interests). But here again, neither teachers nor curriculum are accused of being the cause of the troubles, and the
school is accepted as a natural necessity, useful in several ways
and a means towards a career and adult freedom. The teachers
are not felt to be the enemies of the boys, the rules are broken
with no rebellious intent, and at the end the assertion of
authority is beneficent. It would be wrong to see in this the
reflection of a milder system of education, the Austrian upper-
class boarding school, as opposed to the schools in German books;
Schnitzler's autobiographical account of the Akademisches
Gymnasium tells us that there were ferocious and incompetent
teachers in Austria as well as Germany.

Thus, the theme of the novel is not the power of institutions to
make boys bestial, but the character of a community of boys – it is
a direct ancestor of *High Wind in Jamaica* and *Lord of the Flies.*
In this community, and using the rules and conventions of the
school for their own purposes, powerful boys find the opportunity
to bully a weaker one, Basini, whose wish to be admired delivers
him into their hands. They use him for homosexual practices that
include vicious beatings, and degrade him to the point where his
death by lynch-law is only just prevented as the authorities step
in. At one level, the book is concerned with the stresses of puberty
in boys living in a regulated community. Some find relief with the
local prostitute, Basini trying to acquire prestige by boasting of his
association with her, while Törless, the fastidious intellectual, is
aware of the spuriousness of this sort of adulthood. When Reitling
and Beineberg use their power over Basini to force him to their
sexual purposes, it is characteristic that the homosexual relationship, like the heterosexual, causes no anxiety or guilt-feeling in the
boys; what worries Törless about it is the misrelationship between
physical and spiritual intimacy – his own brief intimacy with
Basini tortures him because he is consorting with a boy he
despises, whom he still despises when he helps him with the advice
to confess to the headmaster. But, remarkable as the book is as a
study of the sexual ethos and behaviour of boys, of a school as a
citadel of boyhood, its main concern does not stay at this level.
For Törless, the school is a microcosm of the world itself and,

dominated by intellectual curiosity and craving 'an intensification of intellectuality', he observes his fellows for the insight he gains regarding human society. In particular he observes the way in which the craving for power operates in the boys round him, how the enjoyment of power becomes an irrational self-purpose, how submission can turn into a desire for self-abasement and humiliation. The questions the book raises are not questions of sexuality but questions of power, the psychological sources of power, its capacity to dehumanize.

There is another question that the author perhaps did not intend. Törless tries to act throughout the novel as an observer, a dispassionate intelligence, an attitude we are told that characterizes the 'artist' he is to become. He is not completely successful, for he is occasionally disgusted at the abuse of Basini by his two friends, is himself seduced by Basini, and then, much against the grain, remembering the 'loving advice' his parents offered him, takes pity on Basini and helps him. But this participation is reluctant and for the most part involuntary, and when Törless comes before the Commission of Inquiry he explains his non-intervention on the grounds that his chief concern was to look behind the masks of conventional appearance and see how people really are. The reader, however – and the viewer of the recent excellent film of this story – cannot help suspecting either a pathological inhibition or an ideological stance in Törless' unwillingness for so long to carry out a simple human action to help a victim. This comment is made here because Törless' behaviour represents something widespread in this period, a theory of the artist as investigator and recorder, the representative of 'Geist' as opposed to life and social involvement, such as we often find expounded by Thomas Mann. In the case of Musil's *Die Verwirrungen*, while this attitude preserves his story from the superficialities and false conclusions of many studies of youth, it does so at the risk of a certain cold dehumanization, that was a charge often made against Thomas Mann in this period and that he himself incorporates in the pact Leverkühn makes with the devil in *Doktor Faustus*.

The double theme of the distortion of the personality by school discipline and of the torment inflicted by sexual taboos is repeated in imaginative evocations of student life. The modernity of Max Halbe's *Jugend* (1893), on the surface a conventional seduction-tragedy lies in the fact that the student's sexual behaviour is part of his general intellectual revolt against the religion and ethics of the older generation, and that it is not love that brings the two young people together but rather the eruption of long-suppressed sex (one suspects the influence of Strindberg's *Miss Julie*). In contrast to popular sentimental idealization of the free life of the student, most serious literary works show the emptiness of the freedoms of drinking (in the Verbindung) and whoring. In Heinrich Mann's *Der Untertan* these freedoms are simply the delusory compensations of Dietrich Hessling's 'subjection'. In Hesse's *Demian*, the drinking and whoring of the student Sinclair, described with evident authorial distaste, are associated with the meaninglessness of his academic studies, and he abandons this senseless revolt when he adopts a Nietzschean élitism that despises both the conventional sexual ethic and the vulgar rebellion against it. Hanns Johst's *Der Anfang* has a stupendous ritualistic drinking bout at a students' 'Komment', associated with a ferocious attack on the 'Alte Herren' and the conforming students, but the visit to the brothel is presented as a positive step to freedom. In this novel the hero's mother, on the day he gains his Abitur, gives him money to get sexual experience from a whore. The drunken orgy of the Komment is described also in *Helmut Harringa* by the teetotaller Popert, and the moral is driven home when a student, on the ensuing brothel visit, contracts venereal disease, ultimately to commit suicide in order to avoid contaminating the race.

The social criticism of these works is accompanied by criticism of parents and parental authority. It is they, and chiefly the father, who force the children to submit to the materialistic values of school, university, and job, and who hypocritically cover over material and social interests with spurious religious and ethical ideals. This criticism of parents may be intended to be directed against the mere misuse of their authority, but in an imaginative work it naturally acquires a symbolical rank and becomes a criticism of parental authority altogether, even of the older generation altogether. In this connexion Ibsen's *Ghosts* was the most inspiring pioneer, with its burning accusation against both parents, against the older generation, for the legacy of evil and the conventional loyalty that perpetuates it. Though no German work in the earlier part of our period has the power and scope of Ibsen's play, there is a comparable implied accusation in the many works on the theme of family conflict, in Hauptmann's *Das*

Friedensfest, Halbe's *Jugend*, Wedekind's *Frühlings Erwachen*, for instance. What they implied comes into sharper profile when one compares the sentimental cult of family love and obedience to parents in the popular play and novel, in Clara Viebig or Suder-mann for instance, both of whom offer also a pretence of independence, or in Georg Hirschfeld's morally even worse con-fused plays *Die Mütter* (1896) and *Agnes Jordan* (1898).

The confrontation of youth and parent-guardian reached its climax in the Expressionist generation. In *Aktion* there are, before 1914, several contributions on the theme of 'the conflict of the generations'. Sometimes we find the researches of Freud being invoked, the Oedipus theory being eagerly offered as scientific proof of the inevitability of father-son hostility. We can assume influence from the youth movement, which is also favourably discussed in this paper. The ethical vitalism of Nietzsche con-tributes, as it had done since 1890, since the young could feel themselves to be the bearers of energy and the old to be the representatives of suppression and stagnation. The symbolic murder of a parent by the son begins to obsess writers (D. H. Lawrence's *Sons and Lovers*, 1913, is an English parallel). Thus in Reinhold Sorge's *Der Bettler* (1912) the son tends his sick father devotedly as long as he believes him to be a creative genius; when he discovers the father's projects are bogus, he puts him out of his misery by poisoning him. Hasenclever's *Der Sohn* (1914) is still more abstractly based on the principle of the conflict of the generations and the law of life that requires the supplanting of the old by the young; the process is completed when the father dies as the son threatens him with a revolver. Here the main accusation levelled at the father is the suppression of his son's sexual needs, and the first thing the liberated son does is to visit a whore. What is not so rationally accountable in this play, and to a less degree in Sorge's, is the wider claims made for this revolt of youth. For the son transforms a revolutionary gathering by his impassioned but simple slogan of war on fathers; round this slogan there collects a number of images of very conventional enjoyments, the luxuries of wealth and sex, and very oddly these all combine in the son's mind into an exalted religious mission, the progress of man 'upwards' towards 'highest energy' and 'highest freedom'. Only too often the Expressionists confuse freedom from conventional restraints with some ecstatic self-fulfilment of mankind; thus the only concrete basis for the exalted consciousness of a mission in the hero of Johst's *Der junge Mensch* (1919) is his worship of sex. The 'son' of Kaiser's plays, *Die Koralle* and *Gas,* however, has been purified of all but his social functions, and is a more credible symbol of an ethical revolt against capitalism and class society. In Kafka's *Verwandlung* and *Das Urteil* the father-son relationship is stripped down to its most elemental psychological features of power and the feeling of guilt. Some critics see Kafka's whole work as a series of metaphors for his struggle with his father, as he defines it in the letter to his father written in 1919.

It is easy to find historical evidence for oppressive fathers that bears out their incrimination in imaginative literature. Hasenclever's father was as powerful a would-be tyrant as Kafka's, though not so naive; Morgenstern had a self-willed father who tried to stop his consumptive son from marrying when he was well over thirty. But of course there were many other sorts of fathers, Hauptmann's, for instance, of whom he was, and had reason to be, fond, or Wedekind's, who with his mother, in spite of their both having rather quick tempers, made a remarkably liberal home to which all the children were attached. The conflicts of father and son that we find in literature, though in some cases based on social fact, are actually rarely confined simply to the character of the family and of family law, and very rarely culminate in a mere plea for a change in family law or ethics. We see that most of the works broaden out, sometimes clumsily, into an attack on the older generation in general, on the ethics of social success and conformity, on conventional sexual ethics particularly; that is, the son-father conflict assumes importance in relation to much bigger and more general issues, so that as a result it acquires the status of a symbol rather than remaining a socio-psychological fact. This is so much the case in Kafka's work that, even if one were to accept the psychoanalytical interpretation and understand the 'authorities' in *Amerika, Der Prozess,* and *Das Schloss* as father-symbols, then one would have to conclude that the most important feature of Kafka's artistic self-projection is precisely the obscuring of the psychological source, the discovery of more general situations of which the father-son conflict in the end turns out to be just one example. In the same way, in literature generally, the 'conflict of the generations' turns out to be, not the true principle and source of social revolution, but one specific and typical form of the social tension and dynamism of the period.

9
Literature and Sex

The social emancipation of women and youth both involved sexual emancipation in one form or another, and both gave rise to much argument over conventional sexual ethics. In the preceding chapter some indications have been given of the criticism of the normal taboos that came from philosophers, cultural anthropologists and social reformers. To a surprising extent, however, the vast, unorganized, and one must say irresistible campaign for what we may roughly define as sexual emancipation was a matter of the imaginative writers, the literary critics, artists generally. Leo Berg observed in *Das sexuelle Problem in Kunst und Leben* (1891), a work mainly devoted to recent French literature, that Naturalism was most deeply concerned with human sexuality – he refers to Zola and Ibsen, but writes also of the sexual themes in Flaubert, Daudet, and the Viennese Sacher-Masoch – and he goes on to claim that 'sexual life is the most significant thermometer of an epoch, a nation, a society'. Ten years later S. Lublinski's *Bilanz der Moderne* claims that the modern writers had renewed the Romantic view of sex as a symbol of 'cosmic life' and the essential world mystery, though describing it more truthfully in its sensual-physiological reality.

It is clear, from these and the many other essays on sex in the literary periodicals, that the authors are contending with a new phenomenon. It is no longer a question of love versus social prejudice or material advantage, the problem of *Werther* or *Kabale und Liebe*. This tried theme does of course frequently crop up, but almost always is a sign of kitsch, as with Ganghofer or Marlitt. What was new was the acknowledgement of sexuality without love, i.e. without profound attachment to a person, and the contention that sexual intimacy blessed by neither marriage nor love is not necessarily a sin or a crime, even for a woman. In this respect the moderns link up with some writers of the older generation, like Anzengruber and Fontane, who like Thomas Hardy also challenge conventional moral judgements on erring women in *Der Schandfleck* and *Effi Briest*. But what constitutes the peculiarity of the younger moderns is the simultaneous cele- bration of sex as a profound spiritual experience, while Fontane's or Anzengruber's tolerance is in part based on their somewhat sceptical attitude towards eroticism. By no means all the moderns are so enlightened. Sudermann's *Die Ehre* seemed very advanced to most contemporaries, yet the 'hero' Robert, while forgiving his sister her illicit association, fortifies the conventional ethic by con- signing her to never-ending remorse and work. On the other hand Frenssen, so conventional in many respects, in *Hilligenlei* allows a girl to emerge from an illicit affair and build a married life without any stain or guilty remorse.

A further typical feature of the modern attitude was the re- cognition that sexual attraction, whether attended by love or not, was a mixed and contradictory drive, in which a longing for devotion or submission might be allied to a desire to dominate, an instinct to protect might reveal itself as an instinct to destroy. Particularly Ibsen's *Rosmersholm* and *Hedda Gabler* and Strindberg's *The Father, Miss Julie, The Dream Play* and *The Dance of Death* offered these bitter truths, which were absorbed by a generation that at the same time pressed for the emancipa- tion of sexuality from Christian and bourgeois condemnation. Hence comes that most curious feature of this period, that, while emancipated sex is celebrated and with Nietzsche or Nordau the taint of sinfulness is contemptuously rejected, on the other hand sexuality appears repeatedly as the bearer of another curse and a more unmanageable guilt that destroys its votaries. In Leopold von Sacher-Masoch's novel, *Die Venus im Pelz* (1870), a patho- logical variant, classified by Krafft-Ebing as masochism, was for the first time openly described, in which sexuality found its fulfil- ment in self-abasement.

It is true, the repeated discussion of sex in the literary periodi- cals, for instance *Die Gesellschaft, Freie Bühne (Neue Rundschau), Sturm* and *Aktion*, is rather innocent on these problematical implications. In the bold first years of *Freie Bühne* we find articles by Johannes Schlaf and others attacking prudery, the laws directed against obscenity, the whole attribution of sinfulness to sex, often associated with a Nietzschean defence of sex as a creative drive. There is a skilful defence of the preoccupation of the French Naturalists (Zola, the Goncourts, Daudet) with the sordid aspects of sex, the degradation of the whore for instance, which is claimed to be, not a sign of the writers' immorality, the customary charge, but of their profound concern with morality, their indignation over the affront to human dignity offered by modern society. Julius Hart and Bruno Wille write with high moral fervour on behalf of free love, condemning the normal type of arranged marriage as 'Ehe-Prostitution', though both are worried by the problem of how to reconcile free love with the settled family that children require. Bölsche hammers away at the need for sexual education in schools. In *Das Liebesleben in der Natur* (1898-1902) he provided detailed information on sexual behaviour in the animal kingdom as a basis for a rational and scientific discussion of human sexuality, a worthy but somewhat pedantic and idealistic approach that Sternheim makes gentle fun of in *Tabula Rasa* (1916). Most of these writers, while emphasizing the biological function of sex, acknowledge a specific character in human sexuality that is the foundation of personal attachment, love, and a more or less stable marriage. Sharp critics of conventional sexual ethics like Ellen Key and Simmel, for instance, at the same time held sexual promiscuity to be psychologically, morally and culturally harmful.

The attitude of Schnitzler or Karl Kraus is rarer. Kraus's sardonic realism contrasts strongly with the moral idealization of the Harts and the reservations of Simmel. Consistently, and with great force, in *Die Fackel* and other journals like *Der Sturm*, Kraus made bitter fun of the immense muddle of the conventional opinion and language on sex, the hypocrisy and absurdity of the moral and legal condemnation of a natural drive in itself morally neutral. Indeed, he brilliantly demonstrated (in *Sittlichkeit und Kriminalität*) how this false morality perpetually engenders crime. Closer to Wedekind than to the more moralistic Naturalists, Kraus sought to emancipate sex itself from its psychological and emotive as well as moralistic accretions. The imaginative counterpart of Kraus's view was provided in the early tales and plays of Schnitzler, where satire is directed not at the fact of sexual promiscuity but at the illusions that people need to justify or spice light and transient affairs (*Reigen*, 1900, is an elegant and sophisticated example of this aspect of his work). On the other hand, Schnitzler also created the legend of the Viennese 'süsses Mädel', whose charm and affection lends the warmth of a wished-for permanence to her liaison with a gentleman-officer. Sometimes, as in *Liebelei* (1896), the emotive accompaniment of sexual relationship cannot be denied and leads to disaster. In some works there seems to be a criticism of the heartlessness of the young men. But in general Schnitzler seems to be asserting the possibility, perhaps the advantages, of a sexuality that provides a passing pleasure without making further claims (his autobiography suggests this too). There is no doubt that this legend of light, easy sexual relationships refers to an actual freer and more light-hearted sexual ethos in Vienna than in Germany, Protestant or Catholic, and sometimes it has been taken as true of Vienna generally. This is a profound mistake. It was true of the small class of young officers, noblemen, and the sons of the upper bourgeoisie, in respect to their relationships with working-class girls. But not at all with bourgeois girls; and the general sexual ethics of Viennese society, sternly upheld by the church as by law and custom, observed and paid tribute to the same taboos as elsewhere. In Hofmannsthal's work sexuality is always burdened with a guilty threat, and like the strange fantasies of a Klimt point to severe ethical inhibitions and prohibitions. Only these can account for the hilarious and riotous pornography of *Josephine Mutzenbacher*, the fictitious life-story of a whore that appeared anonymously in 1906 for the secret delectation of generations of Viennese readers.

In general, the first generation of 'die Moderne' freed literature for the discussion of sex and marriage, though it was still some time before homosexuality, incest, and other variants became subjects for public consideration. What is strikingly absent from most theoretical argument is something that is perhaps the most prominent feature of imaginative literature, the recognition of the terror, the malign power of sex.

That the prominence of sexual themes in literature and serious discussion was not due simply to a deeper humanism or a more refined ethical sensibility is evident from the simultaneous growth of pornography. This, like obscenity, cannot be precisely defined, as the actions of the police show only too clearly. What is meant here is the means for the enjoyment of a furtive sexual titillation as a type of masturbation, the enjoyment of the most blatant crudity as of the suggestive, veiled allusion, that win popularity because they refer to something forbidden without seriously attacking or even questioning the right of the powers – the customary values and authorities – that issue the ban. Through the ages literature and the theatre have provided an outlet for enjoyments of this kind, that can have an aesthetic quality if such releases from suppressions are publicly and frankly shared. In the modern period, however, there was a further factor, the skilful commercial exploitation of pornography which, in the great cities with the vastly increased public for theatrical shows, publications, picture postcards etc. catering for this need, and with its profitability, outstripped the capacity of the authorities to control it. Most advocates of sexual emancipation deplored this development almost as strongly as the advocates of conventional ethics. In 1892 we find Harden inveighing in *Zukunft* against the growing exploitation of nudity in Berlin theatres. Otto Julius Bierbaum, very much an opponent of the straitlaced and author of the suggestive erotic lyrics of *Irrgarten der Liebe* (1906), wrote an indignant article in *Morgen*, 1907, against 'Die pornographische Hochflut'. Przybyszewsky, the author of *Vigilien* and other works notorious for the exaltation of sexuality, wrote angrily in *Aktion* (1913) on 'Erotomanie'. The variety theatres, suburban theatres and cabarets owed much of their appeal to what the law called obscenity, and were usually looked down on even by the avant-garde as vulgar. But the illustrations in papers like *Jugend* and *Simplicissimus*, the former expressly devoted to youth and health, and both appealing to sophisticated tastes, also constantly exploit the hidden and forbidden pleasures. The great series of *Jugend* cover-girls, ostensibly brimming with healthy nature and usually framed in flowers, are among the early successful efforts in an erotic genre well established since then. A considerable under-the-counter trade developed in pornographic art, pictures and photographs of nudes etc. which caused the police many problems, not least when the postcards were copies of Old Masters. On the whole the police took a lenient view of the coarseness and obscenity common on the variety stage and in cabarets, the sort that appears in Heinrich Mann's *Professor Unrat*, recognizing that it was a safety-valve with no harmful implications. They were far more severe with plays and publications in which a serious challenge was delivered to conventional sexual morality; that is, the police were most determined where a pornographical intention was least operative.

Free Discussion and Sexual Freedom

In serious literature one can distinguish two intentions. One was the exploration of sexual behaviour in the modern world, an aspect of the contention that art is concerned with truth; the other was a new ethical valuation of sex, usually a defence or celebration of sex as natural and creative, and an attack on morals and institutions that condemn sex to hide and adopt various disguises, though often enough the theme can be the terrors of undisguised sex too. The two attitudes, the aesthetic-realistic and the ethical, are rarely if ever entirely separated, a confusion typical of Naturalism or Realism, which has normally been defined in terms of truthfulness or objectivity but actually drew its vigour from moral values. In both aspects the franker treatment of sexual themes evoked indignation and horror in the average readership and suppression from the police and law. A quite reticent review of Edmond de Goncourt's *La fille Elisa* led to the confiscation of No. 3 of *Freie Bühne* for 1891 because it mentioned that the prostitute kills her lover. Public authorities and the law wanted the facts of sexual relations and especially their social aspects to be kept secret, and took action against authors whatever their opinions about sexual behaviour. We find indeed that many of the most notorious writers actually held quite conventional opinions. Kretzer, who horrified the bourgeois with his scenes of depraved city life, always shows a naive bourgeois moralism in respect to extramarital sex, prostitution and the 'orgies' of the rich. M. G. Conrad's *Was die Isar rauscht*, whose robust frankness was also considered very daring, shares the conventional condemnation of adultery and illicit sex. Sudermann and Halbe both became notorious for plays that actually demonstrated the disasters attending free love and unrestrained sex. Even the sexual orgies in Oscar Panizza's *Das Liebeskonzil* could be defended as intended to indict a decadent pope. The confiscations and suppressions carried out by the police exemplify the same confusions as we find in the French authorities in their actions against Flaubert or Zola, or in many countries in respect to Ibsen's *Ghosts*. Of course, the writers were not always single-minded in their frankness, and their protestations of an 'innocent' intention are often not persuasive. When Dehmel for instance defended himself in the police court against charges of obscenity, on the grounds that the poems in question (from *Aber die Liebe* and *Weib und Welt*) were statements of fact and showed the evil of sexual lust, few people would believe him. In general, the writers over two decades fought a successful battle for public acknowledgement of the reality and presence of sex, and bit by bit the public became used to reading and seeing things that would have horrified and thrilled them earlier. In 1886 Kretzer had to be very daring to advocate (in his novel *Drei Weiber*) that mothers should tell their daughters the facts of procreation, and proudly claimed that in this he had anticipated Wedekind's *Frühlings Erwachen* (1891). In 1906 this play was even allowed on the stage (still with a few cuts), and by 1914 people were getting used to the description even of homosexual and incestuous relationships in literature. In particular one might single out the exploration of the eroticism of the great modern city. This feature of the work of French authors like Bourget, Daudet, and Huysmans had been enthusiastically saluted by the young Naturalists and Hofmannsthal and was embodied in numerous ways in German literature, moralistically in Kretzer, satirically in Heinrich Mann, with sophisticated grace in Schnitzler. It would be difficult to overestimate the contribution of imaginative literature in the liberation of this whole area of experience for free investigation and discussion.

However, almost always something more is involved and intended. The theme, love in the modern metropolis, for instance, could hardly be undertaken without a concept of some other sort of love, and the awareness of the fleetingness, impersonality, nervous sensuality of urban eroticism so often evident in novels and plays could not come into existence without an implicit criticism, based perhaps on a longing for the older ideal of permanent and personal love, perhaps on allegiance to a contrasting ideal of creative energy. The continuous concern for the figure of the prostitute illustrates the alternatives. When this figure begins to loom large, with the Naturalists, she is a figure of material and spiritual desolation, with no place in society, no honour or security, a tragic figure in herself and an indictment of society and the church. We see her thus in the *Buch der Zeit* of Holz, in Kretzer, M. G. Conrad, Sudermann, Hauptmann, and indeed throughout the period. But she is also given another role, as the woman who refuses to accept the drudgery of job and family, who challenges convention, who seeks gaiety and pleasure, or serves the primordial sexual needs. Such are the prostitutes with whom Altenberg boasts familiarity in his Viennese sketches, symbols of bohemian life, or those celebrated in Dehmel's poems as 'Venus pandemos', or the kept women of Wedekind's plays. Karl Kraus's savage derision of the hypocrisy of the upholders of conventional sexual morality is never more devastating than when he ridicules the language of judges, lawyers and newspaper editors in cases involving 'fallen' women. But his enthusiastic apologia for the moral right of the prostitute leads him himself to misuse language and betray his dearest cause. In 'Die Chinesische Mauer' (Werke, X) he succumbs to the cliché 'Freudenmädchen' (fille de joie), calling the profession a 'service to joy' and making the astonishing claim: 'The joy-market is the only institution of bourgeois society which is not rotten from the roots'. There is a good deal of masculine self-interest in this sort of approval of prostitution, for it secures for the male the opportunity of sexual gratifications without the risk of personal responsibility or even emotional involvement. This personal immunity is safeguarded both by those who worship the whore as the devotee of a vital urge that has a deeper than personal function, and by those who value her because she provides pleasure without commitment. The latter view is common in Wedekind's plays. In Tod und Teufel, Casti-Piani puts the view that the right of a woman to sell her body is one of her few privileges, particularly since she can do this without personal, emotional involvement. More frivolously, the Freudenmädchen Simba of Marquis Keith replies, when someone suggests she is a victim of society, that she doesn't call champagne parties a martyrdom. The most determined apologists of sexual liberation tend, like Wedekind and Kraus, to be opponents of the social emancipation of women.

The most extreme literary idealization of the whore is found in the Expressionist generation, especially in the poems of Stadler and Becher, several of which were published in Aktion. Here the prostitute is given a religious status as the votary of the life-force. The sexual act of the male is taken to be the symbol of self-fulfilment and creativity, bringing a mystical renewal from the primeval sources of life, all the purer for being divested of the accidentals of individuation. The impersonal service of the prostitute is thus exalted. This attitude is not surprisingly found also among the 'Völkische' with their semi-mystical paganism; in Burte's Wiltfeber and Löns' Das zweite Gesicht sexual promiscuity is justified as a sign and renewal of male creativity. We often meet exalted notions of the transcendent effect that sexual liberation will have upon mankind, and it was perhaps thoughts of this kind even more than ideas of social reform that made the Writers' Council in 1918 put sexual emancipation as the second point of their revolutionary programme. When one considers the ecstatic faith expressed over two generations before 1918 that the liberation of sexual relationships from religious and moral taboo, from personal and social pledge, would inaugurate a new era and a new man, one cannot help remembering Nietzsche's remark on the 'narrow faiths' that will arise from the 'vacuum of belief'. But this sort of ecstatic hope, that since then has not stopped welling up, is due to more than a single cause, the decline of religious faith, and perhaps more certainly arises from the continuing dislocations of social habits and morals and spiritual values.

Of all the lyrical celebrants of sex from Dehmel to the poets of Kurt Pinthus' anthology *Menschheitsdämmerung* (1920), Rilke, perhaps in some respects the boldest, goes the deepest. In some moods he fits into a conventional pattern, and the recurrent image of tending maiden hands is familiar male-centred romanticism. He is more 'modern' in such poems as *Pietà*, in which the sexual element in Mary Magdalen's love for the dead Christ is emphatic, though the mingling of spiritual and sexual love is not untypical of the Catholic tradition and here less provocative than in, say, Becher. *Hetärengräber* is akin to many other apotheoses of the whore, the 'river-beds' into which the 'body' of young men has been poured, except that her status in Greek custom and religion gives the poem a dignity lacking in comparable poems of Dehmel, Stadler, Becher and others. But in several poems, from the *Stundenbuch* onwards, Rilke finds a theme and tone peculiarly his, beyond both the guilty shame attending sex and the rhetorical provocation and self-admiration of so many of the poetic rebels. The prayer for sexual fulfilment in *Mach einen herrlich* (*Stundenbuch* 3) has a remarkably unideological simplicity, while *Geburt der Venus* (*Neue Gedichte*) evokes the sexual forms of the female nude with the grace and naturalness one normally could expect only in visual art. The negative side, the degradation of sex in the great city, is most frankly discussed in *Die Aufzeichnungen des Malte Laurids Brigge* as a desecration of spirit and personality. In the unfinished *Sieben Gedichte* of 1915 Rilke celebrates the sexual act itself, the physical ecstasy of the sexual organs, disregarding any personal, individualized content of the mating. That is, it is not love, nor is it a biological function, but a physical ecstasy which is experienced also as psychic renewal. These remarkable poems enable one to understand what Rilke might have meant when he wrote, in a letter, that a phallic god was needed.

The language of these poems betrays something further. Rilke had to avoid both the scientific and the vulgar vocabulary for the sex-act and the sex-organs, as both would have negated the experience he was to convey. The language he uses manages to evoke physical actualities and their psychic resonance, without reducing them to the level of animal copulation or disfiguring them through spiritualization. Yet, though he is very direct, his language is also highly metaphorical, and the metaphors assert precisely that the sex-act acquires its heightened human value through the associations expressed in the metaphors. That is, it is of so great an importance because it relates to and stimulates other areas of existential experience. Through the religious terms of death and rebirth, the images of water, seed, forest and others, the sexual experience links up with these other central realities of physical and psychical life, feeds on them and nurtures them.

The *Sieben Gedichte* were not Rilke's last word. The ecstasy of sex had been, in an occasional earlier poem such as *Östliches Taglied* (*Neue Gedichte*), qualified by anguish over the depersonalized element in sexual union, a feeling of 'strangeness' or 'betrayal'. This becomes the central theme of the third *Duineser Elegie*, which is devoted to sex as opposed to love. Rilke addresses sex as 'the hidden, guilty river-god of the blood' – hidden and guilty not because of a moral or religious taboo but in its very nature, because sex is that dark primeval forest within man where the lover and the beloved both lose their identity, surrender to 'das zahllos Brauende' in man, and merge into the ancestral line of fathers and mothers. Rilke cannot, like Goethe in *Selige Sehnsucht*, confidently reconcile self-loss in sexual union with self-recapture at a higher level; nor like D. H. Lawrence does he put his hope in spiritual growth through the mutuality of sexual fusion. The annihilation of the separate individuality in the ecstasy of union, celebrated in *Sieben Gedichte*, remains to haunt him and create terror.

Neither this sort of terror, nor the wider terrors associated with sexuality, are much referred to in the articles on sex in the literary journals. Here one finds of course descriptions of the social disasters and the suffering caused by an oppressive sexual ethic, but rational argument (and often works of imagination) tend to suggest that the horrors and terrors of sex will disappear if suppression and taboos are removed. It is therefore surprising to find that, whether social institutions and ethics are in part blamed or not at all, the destructive power of sex is throughout a dominant theme of literature. It is clearly so in Flaubert and Zola, polemically so in Strindberg, and these writers instead of being abhorred by the pious and conventional should have won their cheers for demonstrating the fatality within sex when social or psychological controls are released. So, in Hauptmann's works it is a recurrent theme, for many of his male characters are victims of their sexual desires and some of the women use their sex as a weapon to dominate – in *Gabriel Schillings Flucht* for instance, or *Fuhrmann Henschel*. Heinrich Mann's Professor Unrat, inhuman in his authority, is still further dehumanized through his sexual infatuation. In many forms we find the Strindbergian theme of a mortal battle between the sexes, sexual attraction as the disguised form of a will to dominate and perhaps destroy the partner (it is under this rubric that Sacher-Masoch's *Venus im Pelz* and *Unsere Sklaven* are discussed in Berg's *Das sexuelle Problem in Kunst und Leben*). Hanna Henschel is an instinct-led fury of this type, ruthless to others and at the mercy of her sexual appetites, without love, an implacable enemy of her child and her husband. Laura Marholm shows in *Karla Bühring* (1895) a woman who uses for her sexual gratification a man she despises. Kokoschka's *Hoffnung Mörder der Frauen* (1907), an opaque, inarticulate work, has as its centre the deathly struggle between man and woman. In Hermann Löns' *Das zweite Gesicht* love masks the wife's will to shackle her husband. The battle of mother and father in Barlach's *Der tote Tag* (1906) is a battle over the son, whom the mother wins and destroys. Sexuality is repeatedly related to violence, and the theme of Lustmord, sexual murder, occurs for instance in Wedekind's *Die Büchse der Pandora* and the brilliant short stories of George Heym. The anti-naturalist 'decadent' painters of the 1890s harp on the same theme, with images of the Sphinx, Chimera, Delilah, Salome and so on.

Jugendstil often cheats by presenting sex under the guise of flowers, buds, tendrils etc. that enhance the innocent appeal of the cover-girls of *Jugend*. Franz Stuck designed the cover for Wedekind's *Frühlings Erwachen* and made it a sweet Spring scene, with birds, burgeoning shrubs and meadows. In literature, however, the vindication of sex by no means meant that it was represented to be innocent and harmless. Even Schnitzler, who created a legend of easygoing sexual relationships, shows in *Liebelei* and elsewhere that there is always a threat of disaster present. Sex in the works of Hofmannsthal, who was never bothered about conventional prejudice and once playfully addressed a letter to Schnitzler 'My dear pornographer', usually is ominous. True, within the convention of comedy and in the world of the aristocracy, as in *Der Rosenkavalier*, it can seem to be manageable. But in his early work Eros is always associated with hypersensitivity, paralysis of the will, and often with a death wish. Most commonly the eruption of sexuality appears as a symbol of terror, inward anarchy, and self-betrayal, as in *Märchen von der verschleierten Frau* or *Der Kaiser und die Hexe*. In *Reitergeschichte* the fascination the woman exerts over the Wachtmeister symbolizes and brings to a head the social disorder and moral disintegration that is only stemmed by stern discipline. In a somewhat similar way, sexual licence appears in Alfred Kubin's *Die andere Seite* (1908) as a sign of social and moral disintegration. In *Elektra* (1903) Hofmannsthal, always interested in abnormal psychology, makes the bloodthirsty revenge taken by Electra a hysterical outcome of the sexual outrages committed on her. In general, the association of sexuality and violence in Hofmannsthal shows less the fascination with evil of Wilde's *Salome* then a characteristic moral concern.

One may include Kafka here, elusive as his meanings are. The absence of love from his novels has often been commented on; there is also a complete absence of moralistic criticism of sexuality. Sexuality has a place in *Der Prozess* and *Das Schloss* chiefly as a means to acquire power over another person; in the heroes sexual approaches are a desperate expedient towards the achievement, as they hope, of their goal. Yet the spiritual barrenness of these merely physical unions, the sordidness of the circumstances, the distress and feeling of emptiness accompanying them, the despairing frenzy of lust, indicate the waste and shame of sex when it is only a means to personal advantage, and divorced from personal love. Perhaps the only real gain of K in *Das Schloss* is indeed something he understands too late – his affection for Frieda, the personal relationship, the only breach in the tower of his egoism.

The general problem arising in the great campaign for the

liberation of sex from taboo, namely that sex freed from sin and guilt still is full of disaster and threat, is well illustrated in the work of Wedekind. From his very earliest beginnings Wedekind was dedicated to the cause of sexual liberation, embarrassing the Naturalist champions of free expression with the boldness of his themes. Almost all the issues are raised in his plays. He ridicules the religious and moral taboos on sex, the hypocrisy attending them, the sexual licence luxuriating behind respectable façades, and shows the torments deriving from suppression and from the guilt feelings of the naive; he introduces the themes of sexual murder, homosexualism and masturbation, uses brothels for some of his settings, has a whole gallery of self-confessed and unrepentant whores, brothel-keepers, pimps, and libertines. In his late essay *Die Erotik* he ridicules the 'modesty' attached to sexual matters, behaviour and organs, and if he supports the idea of the monogamous family, he does not believe in sexual faithfulness. He himself was notorious for his bohemian life among adventurers and artistes like the extraordinary Rudinoff, and prostitutes. No wonder he enjoyed in his own time, and later, the reputation of a reckless libertine.

But, though Wedekind could never resist the temptation to shock and like Bernard Shaw loved to screw up his views into a paradoxical form, a closer scrutiny of his work shows a more conventional, even moralistic, streak than the legend would admit. For instance, in the playlet *Tod und Teufel* (1905), which is set in a brothel, the first part shows the discomfiture of a champion of women's emancipation, who is persuaded by the sophisticated arguments of the brothel-entrepreneur Casti-Piani to devote herself henceforth to the pleasures of sensuality. 'Typically' Wedekind. But in the second act, the philosophical rake confesses that the unrestrained indulgence of the senses, of sexuality, leads to disgust and weariness of life, and he commits suicide. The play becomes a moral tract; or seems to do so, since Wedekind seems more to enjoy the paradox than to want to draw conclusions. In a more complex situation, the hero of *Der Marquis von Keith* seems to win all the points in the arguments over sexual morality, as against the representatives of convention. Yet, as the play proceeds, he turns out to be a vulgar swindler and speculator, only concerned to make easy money and unfortunate only in that he is outwitted by more expert operators, so that all his sexual ideas, like the rest, begin to appear merely as a cynical ideology masking his crude greed. Equally, Anna the courtesan, far from being the votary of sexual joys, shows that she has the shrewdest idea of where her material interests lie, and leaves Keith to marry a successful businessman. Again, the moral implications seem to reinforce conventional attitudes towards money and sex; one has to say 'seem', for one is unsure how conscious of the implications Wedekind was and what this capricious man wanted the audience to think. Likewise in *Schloss Wetterstein*, where those who try to preserve conventional family ethics are tormented and the 'Edelhure' Effie also comes to a bad end.

In spite of the reputation of the Lulu plays, *Erdgeist* and *Die Büchse der Pandora*, one is forced to a similar conclusion in regard to them. In the prologue the Tamer promises the audience that they will see not the domesticated animal of the usual theatre, but the 'true beast', 'the wild and lovely beast', above all Lulu the snake, created 'to foment disaster, to lure, seduce, poison, murder', woman in herself, the 'Urgestalt des Weibes'. In the plays (which were originally conceived as one) Lulu partly fulfils this prescription. She fascinates all men of all ages and classes. She gives herself without feeling, without scruple, without any sense of responsibility or guilt; sex in her is divorced from love and from personal attachment. She is not even a calculator, but slides into one liaison after another, responding to any sex-urge she may arouse. This is the innocence, the 'Kindereinfalt' the Tamer speaks of, and it leads her ultimately onto the streets of London, where she falls victim to Jack the Ripper. Her lovers believe variously in the reality of love, of permanent relationship, even of soul-communion, but all these are shown to be the tragi-comic delusions of sex, unmasked by Lulu's naturalness (the only man to outwit her is Casti-Piani, and this because he is a total cynic). Throughout, all the lovers appear consequently as carica-tures, and the situations are repeatedly farcical – Wedekind skilfully finds a serious function, the ridicule of conventional delusions, for the situations of conventional farce.

It is therefore understandable that readers at the time (*Pandora* was not allowed on the public stage during Wedekind's lifetime) and even some English critics of English performances in 1970, could believe that in *Lulu* sex is presented without frills or prurience, without the aura of guilt or shame, as 'the thing itself'. But is this so? Sex here produces a terrible degradation and

mutilation of the personality to the point of caricature, its gratification justifies ruthless yet self-destructive self-interest and
ultimately, in the horrific ending, causes the degradation of Lulu
herself. Earlier she was the innocent servant of sex, who had
indignantly rejected the proposal that she should 'sell the only
thing that belongs to me', but she finishes up as the most
desperate and defenceless of street-walkers. Can we say this is the
'moral' of the play? Does it demonstrate that the Tamer of the
Prologue was wrong, and that Lulu is not essential woman, that
when men are stripped down to their sexuality, when 'pure'
sexuality reigns, without love, permanence, motherly and fatherly
instincts, then we do not discover 'essential' man but only a
caricature, a horror, a creature deprived of humanity? It seems
that Wedekind was not fully aware of what he intended, that he
was too fond of shocking people, of paradox, that his works lack
the deep concern over the human predicament that we find, say,
in Strindberg or Hauptmann, and that the caricature and farce in
his works betray the cynicism in his character as an artist, which
perhaps only *Frühlings Erwachen* is free of. Perhaps too, in
Lulu's case, he was caught by the snare of using her primarily as a
symbol of woman, of sex, and then finding that she also has a
destiny as a person that hardly fits on to her role as a symbol.

But Wedekind's confusions have a positive value too, and are
characteristic of the explorative initiative of artists in this field of
experience.

Variants: Incest and Homosexuality

This exploration extended also to sexual variants, in particular to
incest and homosexuality. To what degree the emergence of these
as topics for public discussion indicates a change in social habits is
very unsure; all we can reliably infer is a greater will to consider
them openly and enquire into their ethical status. It is of course
most likely that such an enquiry influenced habits.

We know very little about the incidence of incest. Its
appearance and non-appearance in literature seem to indicate
that the ancient taboo still in this period retained its power over
intellectuals. Nowhere do we find such naive rebellion as sometimes in medieval romance, or in Ford's *'Tis Pity She's a Whore*.
Trakl's incestuous relations with his sister intensified his feelings of
guilt and suffering. Often such relationships are presented in so

veiled a form that one can only guess whether incest is implied. In Kretzer's *Drei Weiber* a mother arranges the marriage of her daughter with her own lover, and in *Sodoms Ende* Sudermann makes an aunt propose a similar arrangement for a niece. Whether these are to be taken as analogues of incest or not, in both cases the appalled condemnation of the authors is clear, and the elder women are shown to be abominable in every other way too. This is the normal attitude. The fact that father and daughter in Herbert Eulenberg's *Anna Walewska* (1899) are Poles adds a further suggestion of depravity. A more frank presentation of the problem, and an attempt to take a more tolerant view, is found in Arno Holz's *Sonnenfinsternis* (1908). As long as the cabaret artiste with the tell-tale stage-name of Beatrice Cenci is believed to have been a victim of her father's lust, her lover, the painter Hollriedel, is humane enough to refuse to share the common horror at a stain of this type. But when he finds that it was Beatrice who was the guilty party, and as she describes in lurid detail and horrified self-condemnation how she seduced her father in an attempt to enhance her own standing, Hollriedel cannot suppress his horror. She commits suicide, and at the end Hollriedel does, somewhat ambiguously, take back his condemnation. The uncertainty in his (and Holz's) attitude is less of a fault than is the reduction of the incestuous desire from an irrational drive to a calculated instrument of the ambition of a social climber; this trivializes the issue, in spite of the bravura of the confession.

At the other end of the scale, Hofmannsthal's treatment of incest in *Ödipus und die Sphinx* (1905), with its evident debt to Freudian psychology, investigates its irrational and symbolical meaning. Oedipus enacts the curse in a dream at Delphi in which he kills his father and marries his mother. Burdened by the consciousness of guilt he seeks release in death. But his guilt is also a sign of divine election, and a chorus of dead kings greets him as their proper successor. Even the envious Kreon, like the Sphinx, acknowledges his peculiar and divine destiny which in the end the 'deep dreamer', guilty yet doomed to live, accepts. Incest here is a symbol of the enhanced guilt that attends enhanced life, and, as often in Hofmannsthal, its features are blurred by the symbolic meaning it bears. The incestuous union of brother and sister in Thomas Mann's *Wälsungerblut* of 1906 is a different type of psychological case. The title recalls the incest of Siegmund and

Sieglinde in Wagner's *Ring*, but only to set off the decadence of Wagnerites against their cult of primitivism. The opulence of the bourgeois home, the luxurious sensuousness of the brother and sister, their lack of contact with the world outside, their Wagnerian aestheticism and the substitution of the 'cold ecstasies' of art for natural life and feeling, their cynical decision to acquiesce in and exploit the sister's society marriage, all this shows incest as a relationship that belongs to social and psychological degeneration, a joint narcissism. Though Mann eliminated from the final version traces that suggested satire of a wealthy Jewish family, the story is told with a fastidious aversion very different from the sensuous fascination of the same theme in *Le Crépuscule des Dieux* (1884) by Elémir Bourges, who had introduced the same Wagnerian references as Mann was to do.

The incestuous relationship of Ulrich and his sister in Musil's *Der Mann ohne Eigenschaften* belongs to a later period; its treatment is free of moralism, and if it fails the cause can only be assessed in the light of Ulrich's mystical search. In the Expressionist generation incest begins to loom largely as a symbol of revolt. It is so also in Hauptmann's *Der Ketzer von Soana* (1918). Prudently left uncertain, the suspicion of incest enhances the status of the outlaws and hence of the priest's rebellion against the sexual ethics of the church. In Hesse's *Demian* there is at the beginning a fleeting mention of a rumour of an incestuous relationship between Demian and his mother Eva, given substance by the later love of Sinclair for the elder woman; here again one is aware of a symbolical relationship, intended to convey the idea of the rebellion of an élite against the values and taboos of a philistine generation. Perhaps von Unruh's *Ein Geschlecht* (1917) best expresses the function of the incest motif for the Expressionists. The sexual desire of the Eldest Son for his sister is a condensation of his longing for life and his antagonism to order, law, control. She and their mother are won over to the vital spirit he worships, but he violently repudiates family ties along with all other authority, and the theme jerkily widens out into a frenzied attack on politicians and armies. Inchoate like so much of von Unruh's work, here, as often, the symbolical meaning of incest drowns its actuality, and it would be misleading even to look for any conclusion concerning the ethical or religious status of incest.

It is quite a different matter with homosexuality. The attention

246 From Naturalism to Expressionism

paid it by medical scientists like Krafft-Ebing and A. Moll indicates that it was of more common occurrence than public opinion wished to recognize, and in the nineties Magnus Hirschfeld linked it up with the general socio-ethical problems of marriage and woman. Weininger's *Geschlecht und Charakter* built on this research to assert that homosexuality was not a perversion but just as natural as heterosexuality, and to demand the legalization of homosexual practices. The great scandals involving prominent men, first the Wilde case in England, then the Eulenburg-Moltke affair in Germany, led to widespread discussion in the press. When Harden was sued for libel over his allegations of homosexual practices in the aristocratic Eulenburg circle, which he maintained made the men involved dangerous influences at court, intellectuals and writers rallied in his support. But while they defended his right to criticize favourites of the Kaiser, most tended to agree with Karl Kraus that a statesman's sexual habits were irrelevant to his political fitness. *Morgen*, the paper of which Hofmannsthal was poetry editor, organized pro-Harden statements along these lines from Wedekind, Thomas Mann, Dehmel and Liebermann, among others. *März* was not quite so confident, for though it echoed Kraus's view it was at the same time appalled at the 'effrontery' of homosexuals and the publicity they were getting, and it resolutely opposed proposals to legalize homosexual practices.

Such scandals, like that in 1913 of Colonel Redl, the Austrian spy, did not necessarily indicate a growing incidence of homosexuality. Since the time of Frederick the Great it had been rife in the Prussian army and almost a part of the professional officer ethos. There are grounds, however, for believing that it was growing in the middle class, both through the social dislocations and the weakening of religious taboos. Male segregation was extended through the expansion of boarding schools, through compulsory military service, and the continuing connexion of reserve officers with the army. Still more tangibly, from the 1890s the middle-class youth movement, an almost exclusively male movement with a male ideology, inevitably fostered sexual intimacies. Hans Blüher was to extend his investigations of the positive role of homosexuals in the Wandervögel movement to the whole of history, and in his *Die Rolle der Erotik in der männlichen Gesellschaft* (1917–19) was to attribute to male organizations and homosexual ties the chief creative energy in Western society.

Blüher's position is extreme, and represents a current more powerful after the war than before, for his book is a general onslaught
on liberalism, on the equality of man and the liberation of woman
('Liberalism destroys all great and far-ranging values'). Though
not an anti-semite (he acknowledged a debt to Freud), and enough
of an intellectual to be aware of the obsolete absurdity of the
student corps, Blüher can approve their anti-semitism and that
of the Wandervögel as a sign of a healthy anti-rational and
anti-democratic national instinct. His book anticipates, in its
sexual as well as political radicalism, the epoch of National
Socialism.

The exclusive idealization of male love, friendship and
intimacy may of course not imply homosexuality except in the
most generalized sense. It belongs to a social pattern in which
males possessed power and the privileges of culture, and where
the major institutions – the government, the army, the churches,
the economy, the schools and universities, publicity, literature and
art – belonged to the sphere of the males. The traditional belief
that true friendship was possible only between males was not at all
opposed to heterosexuality; its effect was, rather, to debase
sexuality altogether. This is the sort of masculinity that admiration of the Greek example was meant to produce in schoolboys,
attended by a skilful or embarrassed obscuring of its sexual ethos.
It is the type we find in the anti-feminists Schopenhauer and
Nietzsche, neither of whom was homosexual. If such ideals, allied
to the segregation of youths in schools and universities, cadet
corps and army, promoted actual pederasty, then this was understood, like masturbation, to be a temporary aberration that would
disappear upon maturity, under the influence of lively feelings of
sin and shame.

In imaginative literature the most remarkable signs of a new
attitude towards homosexuality occur in the context of works
about puberty, such as those already discussed by Wedekind and
Musil. In this context, however, the full implications are not
examined, since it might be taken as a mere transient phenomenon of youth. The most notorious case of adult homosexuality in
literature was the lesbian Gräfin Gschwitz in Wedekind's *Lulu*
plays, whose hopeless love for Lulu leads her to sacrifice herself
for the heartless beloved and to perish with her. She is the most
selfless, truest and least deluded of Lulu's lovers, and Wedekind
wrote in the Preface of *Die Büchse der Pandora* that she, not

Lulu, was the 'tragic protagonist'. Actually, one is tempted to laugh at her, especially in the earlier scenes, when she is dressed in a flamboyantly masculine fashion and shows herself so gullible; and even at the desolate end, the passion she expresses is couched in a stilted and rhetorical language that, against Wedekind's will, hinders sympathy. The ambiguity of this lesbian figure is probably not due simply to an artistic failing in Wedekind, but reminds us that the great defence of homosexuality in this period is almost always associated with male homosexuality and its alleged service to intelligence, to political or artistic creativity, courage and initiative etc.

In the German literature of this period, male friendships are usually innocent of sexual implications, despite the well-known reverberations of the Wilde case and the homosexual themes for instance in the novels of André Gide. Thomas Mann's *Der Tod in Venedig* stands out not only for its literary quality but also for the explicitness of the homosexual theme (Philippe Jullian calls it, in his *Oscar Wilde*, 'the first overt pederastic novel' since Dorian Gray). The homosexuality is not artificially isolated but is embedded in the larger theme of the strain of artistic discipline, so that discussion of the sexual aspect alone is bound to be a distortion. If it is isolated, the work appears profoundly ambiguous. The critic Kerr voiced a widely shared opinion when he attacked it (*Berliner Tageblatt*, 1913) for immoralism cloaked in aestheticism, while a critic who did not consider homosexuality to be immoral accused Mann in *Aktion* (1914) of having veiled and dressed up pederasty so as to make it palatable to the public (he mentions that another novel describing a homosexual relationship openly had had to be published abroad, to escape confiscation). Both criticisms fail to recognize that Mann's Novelle is concerned with the discipline of art, and beyond this the discipline of the artistic personality, the struggle between passion and control, chaos and order, reality and form, of which there are many symbols in the rich pattern of the work. Thus homosexuality is a symbol, not *the* issue, and Mann made his intentions clear when, in a letter to C. M. Weber of 4 July 1920, he wrote that he had first conceived the story in relation to the aged Goethe's passion for the girl Ulrike von Levetzow, i.e. a heterosexual passion. This comment cannot be overlooked, though when Mann continues and says the work was intended to show 'passion as confusion and degradation' we may well demur at the puritanical tone and see more in Aschenbach's passion than this. Certainly however Mann did not intend the homosexuality of Aschenbach to bear a stigma, for he goes on in the letter to refute the common notion that male homosexuals are effeminate. On the contrary, the 'severity' and 'dignity' of Stefan George are extolled, and Mann can express the view that Blüher's *Die Rolle der Erotik* is 'great and profoundly Germanic'. We are not so far from the Thomas Mann of the *Betrachtungen eines Unpolitischen!*

In referring to Stefan George Mann is acknowledging a cult of male eroticism that scandalized many people; yet it is curious that he should have done so in the context of *Der Tod in Venedig*, since homosexuality here is a symptom of artistic and personal disintegration. For George it is the very opposite. It is also not easy to define what relationship it actually meant. All the George circle were strongly anti-feminist and insisted on the distinctive creativity of male friendship, though most were in no sense homo-sexuals. George's many personal poems are all addressed to male friends, but it is far-fetched to suggest there was a truly erotic element in these friendships, except perhaps in his profound and jealous affection for Gundolf. George's apotheosis of Maximin, the lovely and intelligent youth whom he transfigured into the symbolic leader of a new age, has on the other hand an undis-guised erotic element, and it is not surprising that his poems of adoration in *Der siebente Ring* (1907), together with other poems celebrating male love and the attraction young men felt for George himself and his work, should have brought on him the suspicion of pederasty.

The Maximin affair occurred however at a time of crisis for George, involving sexual ethics as part of greater issues. Towards the end of the 1890s Wolfskehl had discovered Bachofen's works, and had communicated his enthusiasm to his fellow Georgians in Munich, Schuler and Klages. Bachofen's anthropological theory of a matriarchal society preceding the patriarchal, and beyond that of a horde in which sexuality was not regulated, was eagerly linked by these men to their hostility to regulated, bourgeois society and their worship of creativity. In the years 1900-3, when Munich saw, especially at Carnival time, an extraordinary eruption of sexual licence in the artistic community, Schuler and Klages developed their 'cosmic' ideology, seeking to restore the creative psychic energy that is sapped in their view by authority and organization, that lies all round us in the universe and

nature, and is expressed most directly in sexual generation.
George himself was half won over to these mystical fantasies, with
the ritual magical cults that Schuler tried to reinstate, and to the
general dionysiac revelry of these years the George group contributed allegorical masques of a Renaissance type in which classical
stylization balanced the dionysiac theme. But he began to take
alarm as Schuler and Klages urged him to abandon poetry and
lead the world to a renewal of its original vitality, when their
worship of the earth-mother and the womb revealed itself as the
triumph of chaos over form, and when Klages began to replace
the more structured principle of Geist with the chaotic ecstasy of
'soul'. Wolfskehl too was scared by the fanatical and irrational
sectarianism of his friends, which included anti-semitism, and on
his appeal George made a clean rupture with them.

George's Maximin experience covered precisely these years,
and Maximin died shortly before the rupture. The cult that
ensued has therefore to be seen in the light of the total challenge
of the 'Kosmiker'; that is, George's celebration of the male Eros
was not merely an answer to a riot of heterosexuality, but meant
authority and organization as opposed to chaos, the structures of
poetry as opposed to the superstitious and arcane practices of a
sect, Geist as opposed to Seele. Though one can only guess at
relationships which are not explicit, it seems that George's homosexuality was very different from the pederasty of his contemporaries Wilde, Gide, Maynard Keynes or Lytton Strachey. The
idealization in his love is evident in his preface to *Maximin* and
suggests sublimation. He exalts the 'purity' of the 'divine' youth,
the 'something strange' in him that eludes possession, the 'virginal
paradisal radiance' of his personality. In the poems he applies the
terms of Christian adoration to the youth. We have to conclude
that it seems likely that George's homosexuality was of a subli-
mated, spiritual type; is this what Philippe Jullian means when,
in *Dreamers of Decadence*, he wittily calls George's works 'the
basilica of Sodom'?

But there is a more important and more indubitable difference
between George and the Gide-Strachey type. With the latter,
homosexuality is an element in and symbol of the disruption of an
obsolete social and moral order, the self-assertion of a vital force
against established authority; with Proust it is the sign of the
decay of a ruling class; but for George (as for Blüher, who quotes
George in his *Die Rolle der Erotik in der männlichen Gesellschaft*)

the celebration of male eroticism, though directed against liberal and democratic trends, claims to represent a heightening of moral and social energy, of order, hierarchy, and authority, the complete reverse of the anarchical and chaotic features so prominent in the whole movement for sexual emancipation. When in *Jahrbuch für die geistige Bewegung* (1912) Wolfskehl felt constrained to defend the George school against the charge of homosexuality, he contrasted to the detested individualistic notions of sexual emancipation the male ideal of 'heroisierte Liebe', i.e. a love that has thrust above the merely personal level and has enlisted in the service and leadership of the nation. One may suggest too that the stylized formalism of George's verse, like that of August von Platen, the homosexual poet whose artistic reputation he rehabilitated, is a form of resistance to the insidious threat of sexuality.

The Insight of Art

In the literature of this period there is an unprecedented pre-occupation with sex, associated usually with a direct or indirect plea for the liberation of sexuality from the religious and ethical stigma. All or nearly all of the themes found in imaginative literature are to be found in the newspapers and periodicals, the scientific and scholarly books of the time. Can a specific contribution of imaginative literature be identified in respect to the evaluation of sex in personal and social life?

A reference to the visual arts may help to focus the question, although the material is too vast to be properly discussed here; for sex became even more obtrusive in the visual arts than in literature. The influence of Wagner and the Pre-Raphaelites combined to produce in the painting of the pre-Naturalist period idealized figures whose spirituality often seems the disguise of thwarted sensuality. Makart and others found in historical paintings the opportunity for luxurious nudes, somewhat like Paul Heyse or even C. F. Meyer in literature. Böcklin, whose powerful symbolism is often not explicit or explicable, created in the Pre-Raphaelite tradition a stereotype of a fully armoured knight embracing the naked Andromeda he is rescuing. With Max Klinger the sexual motifs breed a more haunting symbolism, though often still encased in a rather stiff classical framework. In the 1890s, under the joint influence of Naturalism and Decadence, sexual motifs begin to run riot. The female form begins in the Naturalist school to lose the bashful idealism it had had, and figures like Franz Stuck's *Sünde* or *Eva* offer a coarse sexual invitation comparable to Wedekind's figures at their simplest and most boisterous. On the other hand, in the wake of French and Belgian 'decadents' the lure and terrors of sex promote a strange, chimerical, symbolical art such as that of the Austrian Gustav Klimt. The closest parallel in literature is perhaps some of the work of Hofmannsthal, but the painter's images are more disturbing and potent since they come more directly from his unconscious, supplant reality, and provide no standpoint for judgement, whereas lure, dream, neurosis in Hofmannsthal are placed both in a framework of normal reality and morality and in a time sequence that provides for some sort of clarification and resolution. In the work of the brilliant draughtsman Th. Heine, the famous caricaturist of *Simplicissimus,* there is sometimes a Beardsley-like combination of lasciviousness, terror and wit, but neither he nor any German artist can express the ubiquity of sexuality, its fascination, terror, and absurdity, with such sophisticated ambiguity and mockery as Beardsley. Jugendstil ornamentation was sometimes used for the suggestive and subtle purposes that Beardsley invented, but only too often it covered up sexual realities under ostentatiously innocent symbols and thus turned into the kitsch of popular illustration.

After the turn of the century there is evident a certain rejection of the lure of sex, its mystery and terror, for instance in the sculptures of Kolbe and Lehmbrück, that recapture the innocent naturalness of the female and male nude and recall Rilke's *Geburt der Venus.* A polemical assertion of masculinity appears in some rather mannered figures of Kolbe, and the masculinity of a work like Artur Lange's *Die Quelle der Kraft* (1908), a group of male nudes engaged in a strenuous wrestling match, is Wilhelmine in its suppression of erotic suggestions. Hodler's later paintings are closer to the male eroticism of the youth movement or the George school; in *Jüngling vom Weibe bewundert* (1903) four women, chastely attired in 'Reformkleidung', stiffly turn their heads to admire a naked youth. With the Brücke group, however, whose first exhibition was held in 1906, these sorts of idealization and stylization were abandoned. Their onslaught on bourgeois conventions was not less impetuous in sexual matters than in formal, and the nudes in the interiors and bathing scenes of Ernst Kirchner and Otto Mueller show a frank and unabashed delight in sexuality, heightened and made more direct by the simplification of forms. In Expressionist painting sexuality is usually loaded with symbolic meanings, but the most distinctive work was the satire of the 'activist' George Gross. His sardonic caricatures of the sexual behaviour of the upper classes and the petty bourgeoisie, comparable in their grotesque distortion and polemic to Sternheim's comedies, are more effective than any literary satire. They belong however to the post-1918 period.

Through the visual arts and literature (and the musical drama) sex became, more insistently than through any other media, a publicly recognized fact, demanding public acknowledgement and discussion, hauled out of the conspiracy of secrecy. This is the first and most obvious achievement, and this alone was enough to cause widespread resentment. There can be no doubt that the disregard or provocation of established opinion and authority was made more possible because of the relative economic independence of writers and artists from any particular patron or authority. The second point is more peculiar to literature. Sexual problems which were discussed theoretically elsewhere are presented in literature through personalized characters and specific situations, and thereby are experienced more vividly and in their true complexity. Personalization, particularly in the form of story or drama, introduces too the category of time, sex as part of a psycho-physical process, and in this respect the imaginative literary mode surpasses not only theoretical exposition but also pictorial presentation. This property of literature was always praised in naive traditional aesthetics, and is not to be despised; on this score alone one might admire Rilke's poems, Hauptmann's *Fuhrmann Henschel* or *Rose Bernd*, Hofmannsthal's *Reitergeschichte* or *Oedipus und die Sphinx*, Wedekind's and Schnitzler's plays, Heinrich Mann's *Professor Unrat*, Thomas Mann's *Der Tod in Venedig*, Musil's *Törless* and many other works.

But there is something more, specific to literature, and arising from the process of imaginative embodiment. Sex in literature is always an element in the larger context of a person's family, career, private and public relationships, of his dreams and ideas, his conscious and unconscious aspirations and values, his search for self-realization. No literary work of value can treat of sex in isolation, and equally the physiological functions cannot be isolated from the reverberations through the whole personality. That is, where sexuality does dominate all else, or where sexuality appears as merely physiological (or as mere 'pleasure'), for instance in Przybyszewski's *Vigilien* or Wedekind's *Tod und Teufel*, in fact it is presented, with or without the conscious connivance of the author, as so great a human deprivation or distortion as to undermine the whole will to life. The general vital functioning of sex is also considered in philosophical and scientific works; but it is only in imaginative literature, I believe, that without the support of ethical presuppositions the theme powerfully emerges that sex cannot be isolated, that its suppression, thwarting, and its liberation reverberate throughout the psyche – and not merely, as Freud demonstrated, in the form of pathological perversions and neuroses, but in the whole area of spiritual, existential valuations that formulate the worth or worthlessness of living altogether. Thus the imaginative writers, however deeply they delve into the bestial and sordid side of sex, do not thereby prove that sex is bestial, but demonstrate rather that if sex becomes bestial, man ceases to be man. Conradi said in 1889 that the bestiality of human life as portrayed by Zola, Dostoyevsky, Strindberg and such arose from their moral indignation over the dehumanizing of man in modern society, and this can be applied to the dehumanizing of sex, whether this is caused by the suppressions of a faulty morality, or by its commercialization, or by an excessive imbalance between the impersonal biological function and the personal psychical function. Simmel expressed a fairly usual view when he insisted that sex in man is not equivalent to sex in animals, and that it is 'bestial' when unattended by love that implies a personal and lasting union. Theoretical statements like these have no more force than truisims, and it was the imaginative writers who, sometimes against their conscious intention as in Wedekind's *Lulu*, demonstrate them to be truths, even if only negatively. Maupassant called the sex-act, when considered as an isolated, impersonal event, something '*ordurier et ridicule*', and it was this that evoked the disgust and horror of Baudelaire. So in Germany too, even if much of the literature shows the failure of humans to achieve through sexual union an enriching inter-relationship and integration, its function seems always to be the preservation of this ideal image, vague as it may be, as the implicit criterion of any relationship and the ticket to happiness.

10

Literature and the Law

The relationship of literature and society finds expression in more ways than through the explicit statements or the social themes of literary works, and these themselves cannot usually be equated with similar views found in normal, non-imaginative writing. The choice of the imaginative mode at least means that a peculiar way of urging a view is chosen, and sometimes that a polemical view is being deliberately avoided. The artistic form imposes a number of obligations that restrict or bend an argument. When in the writer the language of poetry, narrative, or drama begins to take shape, when he selects a particular form (lyric, dramatic, epic and their subdivisions), he adopts a set of presupppositions that decide that certain aspects of reality shall be allowed to appear while others shall be excluded. Such presuppositions are usually unconscious, but in times of change some of them are felt to be irksome conventions and are changed, not with the result of abolishing conventions but with that of creating new. Literary criticism must necessarily concern itself most directly with the obligations, the tyranny, imposed by such linguistic and formal conventions which, though some reflect a specific social situation, in general reach back to ancient and more permanent human situations. This study cannot undertake such anthropological inquiries, and must limit itself in this chapter to obligations external to the artistic forms, pressures imposed on literature by society through the law.

There are stretches of history when external obligations of this kind are hardly noticed by writers, so closely are they in tune with the law and the morality it upholds. In our period, however, there was a constant and irritated awareness of legal penalties that punished or prevented the expression in literature of facts or opinions that demanded expression. Some cases have already been mentioned when authors and publishers suffered, when books were confiscated by the police and plays forbidden performance, not the least important result of which was a self-censorship that authors and publishers exercised, often as an unconscious habit. When the censorship was abolished in November 1918 Herbert Ihering wrote that hitherto police regulations had to be considered to be 'an aesthetic principle', i.e. that the language and themes of literature, and especially of the theatre, had been deeply affected by the nature of the law. A brief account of the law and its application will indicate what grounds Ihering had for his assertion.

Publications and the Law

During the first part of the nineteenth century the censorship governing publications had been a chief object of liberal attack, and one of the positive results of the 1848 Revolution had been the abolition in Prussia and other states of the censorship of printed publications. Subsequently the Reich guaranteed this freedom for publications. They were of course still subject to the laws that protected private persons from injury and defamation of character and public institutions from subversion. With laws of libel we are not concerned here, though a slighting reference to Thomas Mann in a libel case brought against a certain Bilse gave rise to 'Bilse und ich', Mann's interesting essay on the fictional use of real persons. The laws against defamation were never codi-fied in the Reich, and varied from state to state in formulation and in application. Criminal proceedings could be brought on charges ranging from promoting, or potentially promoting, civil unrest and strife, to offence to the religious or moral feelings ('Schamgefühl') of people. Three great sanctuaries could not be desecrated with impunity: the state authorities, the church and the family. Defamation of the monarchy, the law and its admin-istrators, the army – particularly the officers – the Christian church and its clergy, anything which might bring them into disrepute, was punishable; so also writing that contravened Christian sexual morals and the ideal of the family. The impreci-sion of the law, the undefined and subjective character of moral and religious feelings, the great variation from place to place in legal interpretation, unavoidably made police action seem capricious and malicious, and often roused widespread indigna-tion against it.

Since the institution of the Anti-Socialist laws in 1878 the police had had the power to stop meetings where socialist agitation was suspected and to arrest those responsible, and to confiscate agitational literature. Though these powers were in principle limited to socialist subversion, in fact they spilled over, as always, into neighbouring spheres, and gave the police the courage to act against any sort of challenge to authority. The lapse of the Anti-Socialist laws in 1890 did not reduce the pugnacity of the police. They had the power to confiscate any publication, book, pamphlet, periodical, that was suspected of contravening the law. They might also bring an action against the author, the publisher and the bookseller, who were all legally responsible and liable to fines and/or imprisonment. These might appeal against confiscation to a court of law, and if they were successful the confiscation would be annulled, but of course an issue of a periodical confiscated some months before was as good as lost. On the other hand, a confiscation might give a periodical notoriety and publicity, and wily editors might therefore provoke police action – with some reason Wedekind considered Langen, the editor of *Simplicissmus,* to have deliberately provoked the famous confiscation and lawsuits of 1898. Since the police was not a Reich organization but a state and indeed a local body, it behaved very differently in different places, so that a book might be confiscated or an author charged in one place while no objections were raised in another. M. G. Conrad was very angry with the Prussian authorities because two of his early (pre-Naturalist) books had been confiscated there, and he tells us that it was largely the 'brutal authoritarianism' in Prussia that persuaded him to settle in the more tolerant Munich, where in 1885 he founded the first periodical championing Naturalism, *Die Gesellschaft.*

Many of the police-court cases promoted sales or had other results unwelcome to the authorities. The action brought against Hermann Conradi and his novel *Adam Mensch* in 1890, that was prematurely closed because of the death of Conradi, implicated other Naturalist works and engaged other Naturalists like Gerhart Hauptmann as witnesses. It was known as the 'Realist case', attracted widespread attention, and without doubt consolidated the young Naturalist movement. The charge here was immorality, and Conradi was deliberately challenging conventional morality and hypocrisy in the spirit of his essay on Dostoyevsky. Oskar Panizza was imprisoned for a year for the blasphemy of his play *Das Liebeskonzil* (1895). At the trial M. G. Conrad bore witness to its artistic merits, and though Panizza suffered very greatly from confinement, his new notoriety led to the success of a new Swiss edition of the play. Hans Leybold's periodical *Revolution* was shut down in 1914 because of a blasphemous poem by Hugo Ball. One of the most famous incidents was the confiscation of *Simplicissimus* No. 31 of 1898 because of a witty persiflage of the Kaiser's oriental journeyings by Wedekind, illustrated by Th. Heine. Heine was fined and imprisoned for nine months, the printers were fined, the editor Langen escaped punishment by fleeing to Switzerland, from where he directed the paper for the next five years. Since the poem was unsigned, Wedekind escaped at first, but when his manuscript was discovered he too went abroad, soon however to return to receive the same sentence as Heine. But *lèse-majesté* (and Wedekind's poem was in any case very mild) was not necessary to earn confiscation and punishment. Satirical comments on or drawings of lieutenants of the Reserve might get *Simplicissimus* into trouble, and its editors were often in court. An issue of *März*, the moderate liberal periodical, was confiscated in 1914 (before the war) because of an article that denounced the German educational system as a 'training for the barracks'. Ludwig Thoma, who was on the editorial board of *Simplicissimus* and *März*, writing in his *Erinnerungen* of his fairly frequent appearances in court, contrasts what he considers to be the viciousness of the Reich Court of Law at Leipzig with the fairness of the Stuttgart courts.

In some cases the police authorities were combating works that deliberately challenged conventional morality and the established order. Typical were the charges of sexual licence and blasphemy brought against Richard Dehmel because of certain poems in *Aber die Liebe* and *Weib und Welt*. Although Dehmel argued before the court that his descriptions of sexual passion were animated by the intention to demonstrate the evil of lust, the most skilful lawyer could not put that one across. But the police, though their officials show some skill as literary critics, were not over-refined in their interpretations. Often they swooped on works because they contained facts or opinions that the authorities wished to keep dark, even though the authors might in no way condone these facts or opinions. This was especially the case where sexual morality was the issue; it has to be remembered

that at this time not only could a Stoecker, the anti-semite parson,
call the Naturalist theatre a 'brothel', but also Franz Mehring
condemned it likewise, in the socialist *Neue Zeit*, as a 'Bordell-
und Schnapskneipe'. *Freie Bühne* No. 3 of 1891 was confiscated
simply because a review of E. Goncourt's *La Fille Elisa* informed
the reader that it was the story of a prostitute who killed her lover
(the courts later cancelled the confiscation). The case of Heinz
Tovote's Novelle *Der Erbe* illustrates the irritating futility of
police action. This was first published in a periodical, *Der
Zeitgenosse*, in 1891, and then in August of that year as a book.
In February 1892 the police suddenly confiscated all that
remained unsold of the edition. Tovote appealed, and the action
was heard in December, when the court cancelled the confiscation. In this story, an extravagant woman of fashion hears from
her doomed husband that most of his property is entailed and
that therefore, since they have no child, she will be left after his
death with a meagre pension. She then, with many misgivings,
undertakes sexual adventures in order to get a child, and succeeds
both in this and in persuading her husband that the child is his.
But his death is shortly followed by that of the child, all her
scheming is negated, and the widow disappears into a desperate
life of degradation. We do not need Tovote's preface to a later
edition to see that the story, which is not without psychological
finesse, is highly 'moral'. The woman herself is aware that she
degrades herself and her sad end appears as a proper punishment.
The only difference from the average *Gartenlaube* story is that
the fact of sexuality is not hidden (sexual intercourse is indicated
by asterisks and a break in the narrative, a 'fade-out' technique).

   In the exceptional circumstances of the war a strict censorship
was introduced for all publications. Nothing that might help the
enemy or weaken the fighting spirit of the Germans was to be
permitted, and since responsibility for the censorship was vested
in the military authorities, the interpretation of these vague
instructions meant the throttling of information as well as
criticism. Thus it was that wartime publications in Germany
cannot be taken as reflecting all sections of opinion, and in any
case opinion was starved of information. It was not easy to
publish critical views even on matters only indirectly or remotely
connected with the war. Heinrich Mann's *Der Untertan*, which
had begun to appear in a periodical before the war, could be
published only after its close. Rilke expressed an unfounded fear

that the Third Part of his *Stundenbuch* (1915) would get him into trouble with the censor. It may be that considerations of this kind led some of the Expressionists to adopt symbolical settings for their themes, like Hasenclever with his *Antigone* and Toller with his *Die Wandlung*. The application of censorship to the production of plays continued a peacetime practice and is therefore discussed in the following section.

For newspapers and periodicals a censorship department was established on the outbreak of war in the Kriegspresseamt of the Ministry of War, and hence was subject to the close supervision of the military authorities. Stefan Grossmann, who had left Vienna for Berlin out of enthusiasm for the warlike determination of the Reich, and was throughout a most patriotic journalist, was still tingling with indignation in 1931, when he published his memoirs, over the rulings of this censorship office. No observations concerning possible future military operations were permitted, no discussion of war-aims or of Alsace-Lorraine, no articles advocating peace, no discussion of food problems that might cause alarm; journalists were not permitted to add up the official casualty figures issued from time to time. It is true that skilful editors and journalists could at times outwit these regulations, but they did so at considerable risk. Harden's *Zukunft* was several times confiscated because this ardent patriot criticized the expansionist programme of militarists and extreme nationalists. Oppositional periodicals like *Aktion* had to adopt all sorts of subterfuge, while *Die weissen Blätter* was published in Switzerland from April 1916, losing of course many of its German readers. The less politic monthly *Neue Jugend* was forbidden after five numbers in March 1917.

Even if we disregard the exceptional situation during the war, and even though police action against books, authors and publishers was quite frequently cancelled by the courts, it must be inferred that the law exerted a restraining influence on writers. Since the law, e.g. that on blasphemy and obscenity, represented an old-fashioned or minority view, a hotchpotch of traditional prejudice, custom, authoritarian presuppositions and confused moral concerns, its assertion did not contribute to the clarification of opinion but rather to the widespread confusion of minds. It is true that the repeated battles with the law, vigorously publicized by the liberal press, did lead to a progressively more liberal interpretation of the law, so that writings banned at one time became accepted later, and public opinion accepted later what had shocked it earlier. The courts themselves contributed to this liberalization of opinion, for they often cancelled police actions. The clumsiness of the repressive actions, the evident unfitness of the police for decisions of this kind, the malice often evident in them, further confused a complicated matter, for while writers and publishers were morally and financially outraged, there seemed no likelihood of any change in the law or the powers of the police, nor did any of those who suffered know how a more equitable relationship might be established. The peacetime censorship presented a simpler problem.

Censorship

The greatest excitements and scandals arose not so much over the confiscation of publications as the banning of performances of plays, often indeed of plays that were already published.

The right of publication applied as much to plays as to any other form of literature. But the theatres, cafés chantants and other places of public entertainment, including the cinemas, came under special regulations. A complex and unsystematic body of theatre law had grown up in the various states and cities over many generations, largely provoked by the uncertainty of the entertainment business, the consequent financial insecurity of employees and creditors, and the prostitution always rife in the acting profession and fostered by the wretched and irregular wages and the always imminent unemployment. So, in this period of free enterprise, the theatres were exceptional in that all except the Court and Municipal theatres required to be licensed and came under police supervision on financial as well as moral grounds. This peculiarity extended to censorship of the material presented on the stage.

As a place of public assembly, where an emotive experience shared by a large audience may trigger off violent reactions, theatrical performances have always attracted the attention of authorities. In Germany, under the impact of the 1848 Revolution, the Prussian government abandoned for a time the censorship of plays, but adopted in 1851 a new set of regulations drawn up by the Berlin Chief of Police von Hinckeldey. These became the basis for the censorship exercised in the Reich, though there remained some differences between the constituent states. Court theatres and civic theatres were not subject to the censorship authorities, since the Intendant appointed by the prince or the city authority was entrusted with this responsibility. For this reason the court and civic theatres played very little part in the dramatic or theatrical history of the period, for this self-censorship was more severe or more timid than the censorship of the law, as Hofmannsthal learned at the Dresden production of *Rosenkavalier*. This did not mean the court theatres were always behind the times. It was the Duke of Meiningen who instigated the first big (though not public) performance in Germany of Ibsen's *Ghosts*, in 1886, even though, owing to the boycott by decent citizens, he only filled the theatre by issuing tickets to his officials. The Berlin Intendant, Graf Bolko von Hochberg, incurred the Kaiser's wrath for allowing Hauptmann's *Hanneles Himmelfahrt* to be put on at the Royal Theatre, and Dresden and Munich and Hamburg had as Intendanten men of artistic initiative who did what they could to keep up to date. One occasionally finds the argument that precisely the Hoftheater should risk experiments, since they were not so dependent on box office receipts as the commercial theatres; but the argument was either naive or malicious.

The regulations for other theatres and places of entertainment put censorship in the hands of the police. A special department of the police was responsible – the Theatersicherheitspolizei, a branch of the Sittenpolizei – and this included officials of some education more or less acquainted with artistic problems. Theatre directors were required to present to the local police two copies of every play they intended to produce, to guarantee that the play as produced would correspond exactly to the text submitted, and to provide the opportunity for police officials to attend rehearsals. The police, i.e. the local Polizeipräsident, had the power to forbid a production altogether, or to require the suppression of scenes, bits, or words if permission was to be granted. The permit was valid only for a particular production at a particular theatre, so that the same play or even the same production at another theatre or of course another city had to be put again through the same procedure.

In Prussia the theatre director had the right of appeal against a prohibition to the administrative head of the region (the Oberpräsident) and, more important since the permanent official was likely to support the police, to a court of law, the Oberverwaltungsgericht. In Bavaria any appeal had to be made direct to the Bavarian Minister of the Interior, a less satisfactory procedure, since the complaint against the police was thus heard by the minister responsible for the police, not by an independent authority. The principles guiding the decisions of the censorship officials were the same as the regulations governing publications, and their vagueness inevitably led to actions that seemed capricious or malicious. Often the mere mention of unpleasant facts led to a prohibition, for instance in the case of Sudermann's plays, which though risqué were morally conventional. In many cases the law courts reversed police prohibitions, for instance over Sudermann's *Sodoms Ende*, Hartleben's *Hanna Jagert* and Hauptmann's *Die Weber*. But one court decision did not settle the matter. The police of a different city could ignore such decisions, perhaps on the plea that the court ruling applied only to a certain production at a certain theatre. After *Die Weber* had been released for production at the Berlin Deutsches Theater, it was subsequently banned in seventeen cities and had repeatedly to fight its way through the courts. Wedekind's *Frühlings Erwachen*, published in 1891, was banned till 1906, when a Reinhardt production, with cuts, was permitted; but it and other plays of his were subsequently repeatedly banned. On occasion a local Prussian police chief might impose a ban that the Prussian Minister of the Interior had expressly lifted, as happened in Kassel in 1891 over Sudermann's *Die Ehre*. Plays incurring a ban in Prussia, especially because of some alleged impiety towards the Hohenzollerns, like Dreyer's farce *Das Tal des Lebens* (1902), would not be found objectionable in Dresden, Bremen or Vienna. Performance of Karl Schönherr's historical play *Glaube und Heimat* (1910), an indictment of Catholic brutal intolerance in seventeenth-century Austria, which was actually permitted in the Austrian capital, was banned in Munich and other Reich cities, while it received the warm approval of the Kaiser.

The story of the censorship, fascinatingly told in H. H. Houben's *Verbotene Literatur*, if it reveals much stupidity and malice on the part of police officials and great wiliness among the lawyers on both sides, also is a credit to the German courts of law, even if the laws they were administering were technically defective and morally questionable. The judgements often went against public opinion and the views of governments, especially in Prussia, where the government was less representative of

popular opinion than elsewhere and where conservative prejudices were expressly encouraged by the Kaiser. The most
notable fracas broke out over *Die Weber*, and was exacerbated by
the Kaiser's cancellation of his box at the Deutsches Theater
where Brahm had put on the first public performance after the
Oberverwaltungsgericht had cancelled the police ban. On 21
February 1895, the Prussian House of Representatives was the
scene of a debate on this play, in the course of which the Minister
of the Interior pointedly expressed the hope that the Oberverwaltungsgericht would come to different decisions in future
– as close to a political intervention into the administration of
law as he dared – and encouraged the police to disregard its
rulings when fresh applications were made. The reasoned judgements of the courts, extracts from which are given in Houben, are
interesting not only from a legal point of view. They constitute a
peculiar and not at all inconsiderable type of literary and
dramatic criticism.

Much of the credit for the victories over the censors must go to
the directors of theatres, on whom the initiative for any appeal
rested, and to a lesser degree to their clever lawyers. Brahm, who
is properly admired as the creator of the realistic stage and
ensemble acting and the champion of Naturalism, and deserves to
be remembered as a perceptive critic, ought also to be honoured
for the skill and persistence with which he fought the censorship.
His protests and appeals were certainly those most dreaded by the
Berlin police authorities in the 1890s. The theatre critics of liberal
papers like *Berliner Tageblatt*, *Vossische Zeitung* and *Frankfurter
Zeitung* backed up these protests, and when, towards the end of
this decade, a reactionary ministry proposed to introduce sharper
censorship regulations, the so-called Lex Heinze, the public
outcry was such that the bill was dropped. The banning of
Sternheim's *Die Hose* in 1911 provoked a resounding newspaper
battle, as a result of which the ban was withdrawn (though
Sternheim's more cutting satires, directed more at the big
bourgeoisie than the petty, *Die Kassette* and *1913*, were not
released for public performance till after the war, as also *Tabula
Rasa*, his satire of socialist functionaries).

The censorship authorities often acted on the most trivial
grounds and took little account of the literary context in which
some alleged impropriety occurred. Yet really trivial plays, and
the trivial theatre, the variety theatre etc. suffered much less than

the serious. And this on principle. When *Hanna Jagert* was banned in 1892, the director Blumenthal contested that the treatment of free love in Hartleben's play was serious and decent. The police argued however that the play should not be permitted on the stage precisely because it seriously questioned the normal opinion of what was moral and decent. The same attitude was reported nearly twenty years later by a minor dramatist Lothar Schmidt, when a play of his had been banned in Berlin. He tells in *Aktion* (1911) that he went to police headquarters on Alexanderplatz and asked the censorship official there why his play had been banned (sexual indecency was alleged) while the most crude and suggestive obscenities were allowed in variety shows and farces. The official, as he reports, showed himself to be an intelligent and sophisticated man. He explained that the vulgarities of the entertainment stage were quite harmless, indeed a safety valve, while it was the serious plays, that made people think about morals, that had to be controlled.

If the law courts often corrected the overzealous actions of the police in matters of personal morality, they were much less likely to be tolerant when political matters like *lèse-majesté*, defamation of statesmen, of public institutions, especially the army and the law, were concerned. Heinrich Mann's account of the case of *lèse-majesté* in *Der Untertan* is not very far from the truth. A ruling of the Berlin Oberverwaltungsgericht, reproduced by Houben, shows the authoritarian principles of a court that actually often outraged the Conservatives by its fairness:

The police is empowered to forbid the performance of a play if the effect of the performance is considered to be likely to create a danger to public peace, security and order. This does not merely apply to disturbance of order on the part of the spectators through rowdyism or other excesses, but applies also to the consideration that the audience may be inwardly misled to views that endanger public wellbeing and order. This includes for instance the disturbance caused by the thought that the existing political order does not grant the individual citizen his rights. In particular, the undermining of confidence in the administration of law is a reason to ban a dramatic work.

Such a ruling in effect bans from the stage any serious discussion of the social order and the ideology that supports it. And if the lawyers thought like this about the sanctity of law, it is understandable that the political authorities would have the same feelings about the political order, and the military authorities about the officer class.

During the war, the censorship of plays came under the control of the regional military governors, and naturally became very severe, though one can suspect that the severity was in part due to their dependence on civilian advisors and police, who might be anxious to pay off old scores. Thus a renewed ban was placed on Wedekind's *Frühlings Erwachen*, a completely unpolitical play by an author now an unqualified patriot. Hartleben's *Rosenmontag* (1900), that had arduously won the right to public performance, came once more under the ban, since it dared to suggest that German officers were not exclusively governed by *esprit de corps*. Very occasionally a 'dangerous' play might slip through, like Hasenclever's *Antigone* in 1917, perhaps because of its Greek disguise. If the military governor was lax or liberal, the highest army authority might intervene. René Schickele's *Hans im Schnakenloch*, published in 1915, is a play set in Alsace and concerned with the conflict between French and German allegiances in the border province. Schickele, an Alsatian himself, comes down on the German side, but shows sympathy and generosity towards the pro-French Alsatians. The play with some cuts was publicly performed in 1917 at the Kleines Theater in Berlin, and received favourable notices even in the rightwing press, *Germania* and the *Kreuzzeitung*. But Ludendorff at High Command had received some protests, and he instructed the Oberkommando of the Mark to investigate the affair. They found it inexpedient to pronounce a ban, but the play was quietly dropped from the Berlin repertoire. Meanwhile the play was being performed elsewhere, and when Ludendorff persisted in his inquiries, the censorship officials stuck to their guns, admitting only a little more blue pencilling. In the end Ludendorff got his way by requiring that all proposals about performances had to be submitted centrally to the Oberkommando in den Marken.

Ludendorff's insistence was based on the principle that no play might be performed that might damage the war-effort and the military resolution of the people. His language contains a curious yet typical example of semantic ingenuity. What he wrote was, that performance would unfavourably affect 'die Volksstimmung zum Krieg'. Now, 'Stimmung' means mood, and 'Volksstimmung' means the mood of the people. 'Stimmung zu . . .' is grammatically very odd, and seems to be an arbitrary variant of 'Zustimmung

(zu . . .)', which means agreement, approval, support. The grammatical oddity thus insinuates that the 'mood of the people' is
identical with approval and support of the war, a useful and
perhaps unconscious confusion on Ludendorff's part. Perhaps
there is in his phrase also a trace of another meaning of the
verb 'stimmen' = to vote, and a subliminal reference to 'Volks-
abstimmung', plebiscite, with its insinuation that approval of the
war implies in some way a conscious vote in its favour. The
language of the police, the lawyers, the courts, even the plaintiffs
and witnesses engaged in cases over censorship is throughout a
goldmine for the linguist.

The frequent absurdities, contradictions and public uproar
caused by the censorship procedures led the authorities to try
some changes. In Munich, where in fact the censorship was more
severe than in Berlin, in the 1900s a council was set up to advise the
Chief of Police on censorship matters, consisting of representative
citizens, mostly 'reliable' schoolmasters and academics, but
including also from time to time the writers M. G. Conrad and
Max Halbe. Thomas Mann accepted an invitation to join this
body, believing that a writer could help the police to avoid the
more absurd and unwarranted bans. To his pain and surprise he
found the council and himself bitterly attacked by the writers'
association, the Schutzverband der deutschen Schriftsteller, who
pointed out forcibly that the council's advice could be utterly
ignored by the police, and that his membership of it merely
strengthened the prestige of police actions. Mann resigned in
great discouragement. In Austria the general procedure and
results were very similar to those in the Reich, and if the Vienna
censorship was more timid than the Berlin, there was also less
challenge to it. Max Halbe's *Jugend* was forbidden in Vienna till
1901, eight years after it was freed in Berlin. So there was the
curious result that the censorship seemed less oppressive than in
Germany, and yet all the great breakthroughs occurred in
Germany. In 1914 the Austrian parliament proposed that censorship should be exercised only where there were strong grounds for
believing that a performance might cause a breach of the peace or
render the author liable to criminal proceedings. It proposed also
that the censorship authorities should include persons 'of a
psychological and literary education' in order that the more
absurd decisions should be avoided.

On the other hand, there were steps towards a tightening up of the censorship. The great disparity in police actions in various parts of Prussia over Dreyer's *Das Tal des Lebens* led the Prussian Ministry of the Interior to unify censorship practice, and from 1908 all the censorship proposals of the Prussian police had to be reported to the Ministry in Berlin. The wartime censorship arrangements went a large step further in coordinating censorship throughout the Reich, and Ludendorff's decision in 1917 to place all authority in one central body, the Oberkommando in den Marken, though only as long-lived as the war, anticipates the later centralization of control under the Nazis.

Trends towards liberalization and towards centralization were all nullified by the military defeat. One of the first acts of the German as of the Austrian republican governments was to abolish the censorship. This was, as writers very soon found, by no means the end of the struggle for the unhampered freedom of publication and performance. In 1920 a Prussian Social Democratic minister threatened theatre directors with imprisonment if any were to produce Schnitzler's *Reigen*. The chief object of the writers' attack now switched from the censorship to the laws punishing obscenity, blasphemy, defamation of authority and institutions etc., the so-called 'Schund und Schmutz' laws which the governments of the Republic were as concerned to maintain as had been the pre-war governments.

Of course, the official censorship and the courts of law were not the only agencies preventing or obstructing publication, sales and performances of unfavoured works. Various authorities and institutions formed a powerful unofficial censorship. The Kaiser's influence was frequently successful in at least limiting the success of plays, and managed for instance to get Strauss's *Salome* removed from the repertoire of the Berlin court theatre. The Crown Prince and the Army Veterans' Association conducted a successful campaign in 1913 for the removal of Hauptmann's patriotic *Jahrhundertfestspiel* at Breslau. Less flamboyantly but much more effectively, Conservative and clerical influence kept unwanted books from public libraries and even bookshops, and school authorities kept them out of school libraries. Even the railway administration played a part. When railway bookstalls were set up about 1880, no monopoly was granted as in Britain or France, but the bookstalls were required to conform to regulations drawn up by the administration. These excluded from display and sale works that might disturb the public moral sense,

promote discord between the social classes or defame public
institutions or personalities. Thus, while in the first place socialist
publications were aimed at, later periodicals like *Zukunft* or
Simplicissimus were not on sale at railway stations nor books by
notorious writers. It almost goes without saying that this private
ban did not apply to anti-semitic papers, always freely on sale.

Freie Bühne

Throughout the period, the confiscation of periodicals and books,
the banning of plays, and the subsequent actions in the courts,
evoked the strongest indignation among many writers. They were
given prominent publicity in the liberal and sometimes the more
conservative papers, for on cultural matters the papers, especially
the liberal ones, tended to encourage radical opinions. A periodical like *Morgen* was avowedly non-political, and likely to
sympathize with conservative views, but it could support neither
the idea of a censorship nor the actual administration of it. The
newspapers made themselves the organizers as well as the medium
of protest, and in important cases would organize the expression of views by prominent writers and artists or draw up
manifestos to be signed by the eminent. Even a 'völkische' writer
like Adolf Bartels, who was most hostile to all works that smelled
of 'subversion' or 'decadence', and who claimed that the state had
a right to suppress works if they constituted a danger to society,
cannot avoid, in a leading article of *Der Kunstwart* in 1893,
supporting the right of poets to utter what they think to be the
truth. All the notable bans served to consolidate writers, artists
and intellectuals, and to make them feel a common interest, even
if they might be moved by different motives. For instance, when
at the end of the 1890s the proposed Lex Heinze was threatening
to sharpen the censorship regulations, a protesting manifesto was
signed by academics like the radical Mommsen and writers who
had suffered from the censorship like Sudermann, but also by the
rather conservative Liebermann and even the aged Menzel,
partly it was said because his feelings had been outraged by the
abomination of the Siegesallee. The declarations of support for
Harden, when he was sued for libel by Graf von Moltke in 1907,
united many writers who were by no means admirers of Harden's
politics or ethics, but simply believed that a man of good faith
should be entitled to publish his opinions on a matter of public

importance. When a discussion evening on the censorship, arranged by Wedekind, was forbidden by the Munich police, the list of notabilities that signed a protest included Heinrich and Thomas Mann, Arthur Schnitzler, Alfred Kerr, Max Reinhardt, Max Liebermann and Richard Strauss. A protest against the confiscation of *Aktion* Nos. 13 and 14, in 1914 joined Heinrich and Thomas Mann with Wedekind, Hugo Ball, Kandinsky and others.

These protests had mostly little more than a moral effect. But in the sphere of the theatre censorship, an effective counteraction was possible. The censorship regulations applied only to public theatres run for profit, and only to public performances. It did not apply to amateur societies and their private performances, nor to private performances of professional companies. At the beginning of the 'literary revolution' of the 1880s, Ibsen's *Ghosts* was first performed in Germany by Duke George of Meiningen at a 'closed' i.e. private performance at his own theatre, and then by amateur societies in Augsburg and Berlin. A group of publishers, newspaper editors, literary critics and writers in Berlin grasped the implication of these events, evident on a larger scale in Antoine's Théâtre Libre in Paris, and in 1889 founded the Freie Bühne in Berlin. The Freie Bühne was a club, and its members paid a subscription. A theatre was hired for an occasional Sunday matinee performance, when the stage was not otherwise engaged. The management committee gave Otto Brahm almost plenary powers as artistic director, and he drew up the programme and himself produced some of the plays (the following year he was also appointed editor of the newly founded weekly *Freie Bühne,* but filled this office less successfully). Actors were engaged for each performance. The audience was limited to club members, no payment being made at the door, and thus the performances ranked as private and were not subject to censorship. Membership rapidly rose to over a thousand, and included many people merely interested in the novelty and many who showed their distaste for the plays performed. Stefan George was a member for a short time. Most of the plays produced were banned on the public stage, including Ibsen's *Ghosts*, Tolstoy's *Power of Darkness,* Strindberg's *Miss Julie,* Hauptmann's *Vor Sonnenaufgang* and *Die Weber*, Sudermann's *Sodoms Ende,* Holz and Schlaf's *Die Familie Selicke* (the complete list is given in an appendix to J. Osborne's *The Naturalist Drama in Germany*). The impact of these performances was magnified a thousand times by the reviews in newspapers and periodicals. The opportunity the productions gave for the German writers to meet the critics and the public and to see their plays performed was of incalculable importance, and the Freie Bühne contributed greatly to the self-awareness and self-confidence of the new literary movement.

A petty dissatisfaction with the Freie Bühne over the allegedly excessive number of foreign plays produced led Conrad Alberti and Karl Bleibtreu to found a rival Verein Deutsche Bühne (1890); it lasted two seasons but failed to make any impact. Free Theatres on the Berlin model were formed in other cities, in Vienna (in which the young Hofmannsthal participated), Hamburg, Leipzig and Hanover, but at best they repeated what had been done in Berlin on a more modest scale and without the privilege of priority or the help of important newspapers. In Munich its place was taken by the Academic Dramatic Society and its successors till 1910, though their performances, not without artistic interest, were altogether more private and amateurish than those in Berlin. From time to time amateur societies did put on notable productions, for instance the Nürnberg society and the Litterarische Gesellschaft in Leipzig, that did for Wedekind something of what the Freie Bühne had done for Hauptmann.

The importance of the Berlin Freie Bühne waned rather fast. Franz Mehring, in a famous article of *Neue Zeit* praising *Die Weber*, wrote that for this performance (26 February 1893) the Freie Bühne had been 'raised from the dead', and if *Die Weber* was its greatest achievement, it was also its last significant production. The reasons for its decline are multiple. The very success of the Freie Bühne brought about a retreat on the part of the Berlin censorship authorities, so that many plays hitherto prohibited were released from the ban. Then, the cost of performances was considerable, subscriptions had to be high, and there was a limit on the numbers ready to pay. Also, the administrative problems demanded a lot of enthusiasm, skill, and time, and anyone with such abilities, like Brahm, would find a more satisfactory field for his gifts; in 1894 Brahm became director of the Deutsches Theater and had his hands full. Then, too, the membership was unstable. Mehring, the socialist, called it 'artistically the worst audience possible', by which he meant not simply that it was a bourgeois audience but that it was predominantly 'press and finance', the most rootless and unstable sort of bourgeoisie. This west-end public, savagely but not too inaccurately described in Heinrich Mann's *Im Schlaraffenland*, was eager for novelty and sensations, and soon needed a change. Its enthusiasm for the Freie Bühne waned as quickly as ten years later its enthusiasm for Ernst von Wolzogen's cabaret, Das Überbrettl. After *Die Weber* Brahm used it, till its end in 1901, at most once a year for some occasional production of no significance; it was dead long before the police, proving that people paid at the door, reimposed the censorship on its performances in 1896.

If some major battles had been won by the Freie Bühne, there could never be any question of a strategic victory over the censorship, even in Berlin, let alone elsewhere. Thus the decades following see numerous new schemes and efforts to circumvent the regulations and outwit the police. We often find proposals like Halbe's 'intimate theatre', with a low subscription and modest productions. Brahm, while director at the Deutsches Theater and later at the Lessing Theater, occasionally put on a 'private' performance, as for Dreyer's *Das Tal des Lebens* in 1903, issuing personal invitations to eight hundred notabilities and thereby promoting a debate on this play, that made mild fun of a branch of the Hohenzollerns, in the Prussian House of Representatives. In 1912 Pfemfert arranged a private performance of Wedekind's *Totentanz*, outwitting the police by issuing personal invitations; Karl Kraus had done something similar in 1905 in Vienna for Wedekind's *Der Büchse der Pandora*, which never could be publicly performed during Wedekind's lifetime. Such methods were too expensive to become normal. The periodical *Pan* (the second *Pan*, founded in 1910) created a society for dramatic performances, which soon ran into the same sort of financial trouble as had finished off the Freie Bühne. What they did was to charge substantial fees for the wardrobe, and the law courts upheld the claim of the police that this was a disguised charge for admission. *Aktion* has articles in its first years suggesting ways to get round the censorship, but the war put an end to such schemes, just as the Revolution ended the censorship itself.

The great success of the Freie Bühne in its first year led some of its members, foremost among them Bruno Wille, the Marxist among the young Berlin writers, to call into being a Freie Volksbühne, a Free People's Theatre, i.e. an organization to make possible the performance of uncensored plays before a working-class audience. Wille gained the support of representative leaders of the Social Democratic Party and of many young men of letters like the Hart brothers, Bölsche, Hartleben, J. H. Mackay the anarchist, and Brahm. The Freie Volksbühne was founded in July 1890 at a great meeting of about two thousand workers, where the radical avant-garde literary notabilities rubbed shoulders with leading and rank-and-file Socialists. The project was the theatrical equivalent of the workers' education courses just then being established in Berlin, was supported by the same persons, and ran into the same sort of difficulties. The men of literature, including Wille the first chairman, saw it as educational and non-political, a means of admitting the workers to a culture from which they were shut out, of opening their minds and helping them to think for themselves; some writers were also genuinely interested in the possibility of creating a new relationship between writers and a new type of readership. The Social Democratic representatives, on the other hand, saw it primarily as a means for arousing and consolidating revolutionary class-consciousness. At first the two sides worked in harmony. The programme, arranged by Wille, was less modern and advanced than that of the Freie Bühne, including plays of Schiller and Hebbel with a social theme. Discussion evenings were arranged between writers and working-class members that were enthusiastically reported in *Freie Bühne*, the weekly. The membership quickly rose to four thousand, the subscription being very low. But the socialist leadership was not content. Wille was suspect to the orthodox Marxists because of an individualistic, Nietzschean streak in his thought and because of his respect for the autonomy of writers. In 1892 a palace revolution ousted Wille from the chairmanship and put in his place Franz Mehring, who at that very time was calling the Naturalist theatre a 'Bordell- und Schnappskneipe'. Wille then set up an independent Neue Freie Volksbühne as a rival to Mehring's. The incident illustrates the cultural intolerance that often infected the Social Democratic party, and that was inherited by the Communist party. So we find that after *Die Weber* had had its first sensational success on the Freie Bühne in February 1893 (with C. Hackmann as producer), it was produced in October of that year on Wille's Neue Freie Volksbühne (producer Emil Lessing) and in December by Mehring himself on the Freie Volksbühne, where it turned into something like a political demonstration.

Throughout their existence the police maintained that these Volksbühnen were political organizations, and as such came under police surveillance and control. They several times tried to have performances and meetings prohibited on the grounds of political agitation, and lengthy lawsuits sometimes brought the cancellation, sometimes the confirmation of the police ban. In 1896 the admission of non-members led to the closure of both Volksbühnen, but both revived in the following year. Slowly their objectives came closer as the original organization came under the control of socialist revisionists like Bloch, Stampfer and Eisner, and from 1912 they worked together on a programme closer to Wille's than Mehring's, the transmission to the working class of classical and modern culture, through the production of plays, lectures, and discussions. The Neue Freie Volksbühne received the support of many intellectuals and writers, and shortly before the war reached a membership of fifty thousand. By this time Freie Volksbühne was something under twenty thousand, though it too called on the services of bourgeois intellectuals like Rudolf Steiner and Theodor Heuss.

Similar organizations were created elsewhere, for instance in Hamburg in the 1890s, where *Vor Sonnenaufgang* and *Die Weber* were performed. The most considerable was established in Vienna upon the initiative of Stefan Grossman, a socialist, journalist and writer. Between 1910 and 1912 he built a most successful organization, very much on Wille's lines, with a membership reaching thirty thousand. Grossmann as artistic director was allowed a free hand with the programme, though the board of management included representatives of the Social Democratic party and the trade unions. The repertoire he chose was not markedly modern nor political, and he too fell foul of the sectarian socialists. In his absence through illness the board claimed control over the artistic director, and Grossmann resigned; the coming of war put an end to the enterprise. Altogether, the artistic importance of the Volksbühnen was extremely slight, and their repertoires were timidly classical. The participation of workers in a cultural organization and in discussions with playwrights and intellectuals was however to have a considerable aesthetic as well as political importance after the war, in Austria as in Germany.

In the short space of its existence, the original Free Theatre too had only a limited artistic importance. Not much could be done in productions for a single performance, in a hired theatre with hired scenery and a cast collected for that performance alone. The development of Brahm's ensemble acting and his realistic settings, his fame as an interpreter of Ibsen and Schnitzler, rest on his work as director of the Deutsches Theater 1894-1904 and from then to his death at the Lessing Theater. The Freie Bühne performances were too occasional to establish a theatrical or dramatic tradition and to encourage writers to write for them and their audiences, and the audiences themselves were, as Mehring said, the worst sort of first-night votaries. Their chief artistic value was to give authors whose works were banished from the stage the chance of seeing them played, and thus to help them to develop their own style – this was evidently of the greatest importance for Hauptmann and it might be said that Wedekind's work suffered from the lack of such opportunities. The greatest achievement was their success in breaking through the censorship especially at that decisive moment round 1889, demonstrating to their audiences the dramatic quality of works known only in print and often decried on theatrical grounds, and at the same time enchancing the self-awareness and solidarity of the new generation of writing.

Writers as a Social Class

Features of the Class

The purpose of the preceding chapters has been to sketch the involvement of imaginative literature in social life, the reflection in literature of social situations, movements and ideas, and the contribution of literature to social consciousness. Reflection and contribution may be very indirect, and often take the form of an apparent rejection of social concern, but this rejection itself is a social fact and often betrays a conscious social attitude. It has not been possible to develop a particular theory of the relationship of society and literature (or art), not least for the reason that both are extremely elusive concepts. Not only do writers vary greatly in their artistic purposes and aim at very different psychic functions and responses, but also their social experience varies vastly, according to their upbringing, their region, their temperamental and rational presuppositions and the influence exerted on them of ideological valuations, and a whole host of other conscious and unconscious factors that preselect, as it were, what social experience they are to be aware of. What has, it is hoped, become clear is that the writers of this period stand very consciously in a network of social relationships, and that their work, personal as it must be, is also the product of a social experience they share with their contemporaries; their work is a battle with the specific reality of their times just as is the work of other intellectual workers. The difference between an artistic response and a practical or theoretical one has only been touched on here and there, and it cannot be systematically examined in the framework of a historical study, since the functions of the imagination clearly originate deep down in human history and serve much more than an immediate social reality.

Here we have had to be content with a more pragmatic handling of aesthetic matters. M. G. Conrad, writing in *Von Zola bis Hauptmann* about the source of French and German Naturalism, says they derived from a 'kunstethisches Prinzip' and not a 'kunsttechnisches Prinzip' (as Arno Holz argued), that is, that the modern movement in literature arose from the will to make art serve the purpose of changing the social world, or at least the ethical consciousness of men. If the Naturalists' rather naive hope of social reform faded about 1893 – *Die Weber* was its climax – the following generations were involved in different sorts of protest, social and aesthetic, until with the wartime Expressionists explicit social-revolutionary purposes once again declared themselves, in forms appropriate to a new situation. The study of the relationships between artistic forms and social reality, through the medium of social consciousness and ideologies, is endless and at all points in this book it will be evident that limits have been almost arbitrarily set. In whatever direction one chose to expand it, it would not be possible to eliminate its incompleteness, and the author himself closes his book feeling that he has been trying to drain a sea with a bucket.

However, one further group of questions has to be attacked. On many occasions the term 'writers' has been used in this book, with its implication that the attitudes of poets, dramatists and novelists belonged together in some special way. It is a loose term, and often may cover as well non-imaginative writers like critics, literary editors and publishers, cultural journalists, people engaged in theatrical productions and other cultural enterprises, comparable in this looseness to the terms 'die Geistigen' or 'die Intellektuellen' as they were used by contemporaries. Is the term legitimate, and so loose a usage appropriate? Do the writers, together with other types of artists and men and women engaged in literary and cultural productions, from a recognizable social group with distinctive characteristics? If so, what sort of group? how specific to the modern age?

There is nothing new in the formation of groups of writers in the service of some shared objective, and allegiance to the Romantic 'school' or 'Young Germany' meant a common attitude to social, political and religious as well as aesthetic questions. In our period the Naturalists, Symbolists, Impressionists, Heimatdichter, Neo-Romanticists, Expressionists and numerous subgroups form loose groupings of this character, often of a very transient nature – like the various groups of painters, the Naturalists, Symbolists, the Brücke or Blaue Reiter groups. That is, most writers who opposed an established literary habit formed groups (one would not expect writers of kitsch to do so, since they were exploiting not challenging established tastes). But we are here concerned not primarily with an ideological or artistic group, but with a larger and more permanent phenomenon, a social stratum or class engaged in culture. This did not exist in Germany before the establishment of the Reich. A writer might, before this time, exist by his pen, especially if like Heine or Freytag he was also a journalist; but these were rare cases, and most depended on a profession, a legacy, or on the good will of a princely patron or the favour of an Intendant. Now, the private patron was decisively, though not absolutely, superseded by the market, the sales in bookshop and box-office, and the unification of Germany meant that this market was, to all intents and purposes, nationwide. For the first time a large and rapidly growing number of people were able to live solely by the creation and reproduction of culture.

Not all the writers were completely dependent on the public. Some had an inherited private income, like George, Hofmannsthal, Wolfskehl, Heinrich Mann. Some entered a profession : Schnitzler, Benn, Döblin were doctors, Dehmel and Thomas Mann, like Kafka, worked for a time in insurance offices. But most writers lived on what they earned by their pen, and abandoned other professions as soon as they could. Most belonged in a very direct way to what one may call the culture-industry – an industry since, whatever the private or aesthetic principles motivating writers, publishers, and theatrical producers, in the last resort the accounts had to be balanced, the public had to be persuaded, cajoled, bullied to play their part. Authors were necessarily concerned to find an echo, a readership, quite apart from the financial results of sales; even George or the unworldly Rilke was keenly interested in sales from this point of view. For most writers success meant the freedom and leisure to write, even if this freedom often brought a new enslavement to the public favour. It meant also the accessibility of pleasures and comforts, travel, a comfortable home, commitments that often, as with the extravagant Hauptmann, imposed the obligation of almost continuous publication and that in part account for the occasional journalism of many and for the lecture tours that the Manns, Hofmannsthal, Rilke and many others engaged in.

This industry had various branches with extensive ramifications. Closely connected with the imaginative writers was the publishing business, with entreprenuers like S. Fischer, Paul and

Bruno Cassirer, Anton Kippenberg, G. Bondi, Eugen Diederichs, Kurt Wolff, and with publishers' readers like Moritz Heimann whose discrimination and intelligence were of the utmost importance. The peculiar character of this 'business' of literature is evident when one mentions such names, for these were men truly devoted to literature, to talent, who fostered new writers, sometimes supporting them over many unprofitable years with advances and sympathetic appreciation, like Kippenberg with Rilke or Paul Cassirer with Heinrich Mann or Barlach (or with the painters of the Brücke group). They might hope ultimately to make a profit, and did all they decently might towards this end, but they were ready to suffer loss for a writer or a trend they believed in, and their business was also a labour of love. Some are an integral part of literary history. Fischer fostered the experimental avant-garde from Naturalism to Expressionism, as well as becoming in this period the publisher of the new literary 'establishment' and its chief periodical *Die neue Rundschau*. Bondi is inextricably implicated in the George circle, as Kurt Wolff with the wartime and post-war Expressionists. Diederichs is as closely involved with the Heimatdichter and the new nationalism. Paul Cassirer and Paul Flechtheim performed the same service for painting.

Many of these book-publishers were also publishers of periodicals. The literary periodical had, of course, for two centuries or more been the medium for the advocacy of literary attitudes, and in this period the number runs into hundreds, short-lived and long-lived, broad in appeal and sectarian. It had the great advantage of being cheap to produce, requiring little capital, no offices, little more resources than would pay for printing and support an editor and perhaps pay fees to contributors. Many of these periodicals were published by the editors themselves, not only the ephemeral ones but also the long-lasting and substantial ones like *Die Zukunft* (Maximilian Harden), *Der Kunstwart* (F. Avenarius), *Die Fackel* (Karl Kraus), *Der Sturm* (Herwarth Walden), *Aktion* (Franz Pfemfert), so that the policy of the journal remained firmly in the hands of its editor throughout. *Blätter für die Kunst* remained similarly, through the agency of C. A. Klein, under the direct control of one man, Stefan George, as also *Jahrbuch für die geistige Bewegung*, whose nominal editors were Gundolf and Wolfskehl. *Die neue Rundschau*, on the other hand, was from its start as *Freie Bühne* the child of Samuel

Fischer the publisher, and in the early years the editors and editorial policy changed frequently until Oskar Bie began his long reign as editor (1894-1922). When Diederichs took over *Die Tat* in 1912 from its founders, the Horneffer brothers, a change of editorial policy resulted. All these journals, in so far as they had a circulation worth speaking of, had great importance not only in providing fees for contributors and an income for editors, but also in creating a more or less devoted public for writers, and a consciousness of a public in the writers: a consciousness in the writers, therefore, that they belonged to a wider group of which they were in some sense the spokesmen, oddly enough by virtue of being different, as articulate artists. The journals linked imaginative writers with a wider world in another way too. Most of them published imaginative literature, stories, sketches, poems, plays, but also regularly carried, in addition to articles on aesthetic and cultural matters, articles on political and social issues. The imaginative writers were thus, if perhaps only in a vague sense, committing themselves to the sort of concerns discussed in the other articles of a periodical in which their work was published, and finding a public among readers likely to respond to these other issues and views. In these ways the periodicals consolidated the social consciousness of the writers.

The theatres provided more dramatic opportunities for this. Here there was of course a big apparatus of cultural workers, Intendants at the court and municipal theatres, producers, dramaturgists (Reinhardt might travel with half-a-dozen in his train), stage-managers, designers, business managers, actors and actresses, not to speak of dozens of theatre critics. Theatrical productions were supremely important social and perhaps cultural events, as the space given them in newspaper feuilletons indicates, and liable to give rise to sensational fracas since rival parties could be present. Traditionally the court theatres, though often providing light entertainment, had been mindful of a somewhat paternalistic mission to elevate and educate, while the capitalistic theatrical enterprises, like the Berlin theatres of Barnays or Blumenthal, were mainly concerned with profit and amusement. In the 1880s and after, and especially in Berlin, the capitalist theatre undertook a cultural mission, and all the great artistic innovations originated with them, while the court theatres in spite of their much greater financial resources held back timidly. This liberation of the serious theatre from patronage meant the formation of a new audience and allegiance. For not only the Freie Bühne and similar organizations based on a membership, but also producers like Brahm and above all Reinhardt sought to consolidate their audience into a devoted community, a 'Gemeinde'. It had been the practice of many court theatres to issue informative sheets for theatre-lovers, but this practice acquired a new importance in Berlin. Bruno Cassirer, the publisher, founded a theatrical journal *Das Theater* (1903-5), which in its second year became the house-journal of the two Reinhardt theatres (Christian Morgenstern was its editor). In 1905 S. Jacobsohn founded and edited *Die Schaubühne*, mainly for reviews of productions, which in its last years became more political and radical and turned in 1918 into *Die Weltbühne*. From 1911–14 Reinhardt had his own *Blätter des Deutschen Theaters*, edited by Felix Holländer and A. Kahane.

It was therefore not only the glamour of the stage that gave the theatre so great a prestige in these decades. The performance of a play extended and enriched the social and personal involvement of the writer. A large and gifted body of professional workers bound the work and its literary creator closely with a larger visible and invisible audience, brilliant producers like Brahm, Reinhardt, Felix Holländer, Leopold Jessner, critics like Mauthner, Bahr, Kerr, Harden, Schlenther, Kraus, Bierbaum, Blei. Through their work the plays of the classics, Sophocles, Shakespeare, Calderon, and of the foreign moderns, Ibsen, Tolstoy, Strindberg, Shaw, Gorki and the rest, became alive and pertinent, linked with the new Germans. The success of many dramatists is closely bound up with a producer or a theatre – Ibsen and Schnitzler with Brahm, Hauptmann with the Freie Bühne and later Reinhardt, Hofmannsthal with Reinhardt. And one must not forget the contribution of the gifted actors and actresses whose talent and intelligence often got more out of a part than the writers had put in – Joseph Kainz, Friedrich Mitterwurzer, Friedrich Kayssler, Adalbert Matowski, Alexander Moissi, Albert Bassermann, Emil Jannings, Werner Krauss, Paul Wegener, and Gertrud Eysoldt, Agnes Sorma, Tilla Durieux, Helene Thimig, Lucie Höflich . . .

A more extensive, though anonymous, audience was provided through the newspapers, in particular the weekly cultural supplements, the feuilletons, carried by all the great newspapers. These contain the most direct evidence of the changing tastes of the period, and in their columns the great artistic issues were argued out. The literary editorships of the feuilletons were the plums of the profession. If such editors had to court their readership, they had also great influence, and themselves were courted by critics, publishers and often by writers. Thus Paul Lindau of the *Berliner Tageblatt* and Karl Frenzel of the *Nationalzeitung* (who would also write in periodicals like *Die deutsche Rundschau*) became symbols of the opposition to modernism round 1890. Though most newspapers were politically committed, the feuilletons were traditionally allowed considerable ideological latitude – Heinrich Mann with some justification claimed in *Im Schlaraffenland* that the once radical editors or owners of liberal papers tolerated radical views in their feuilletons as a sop to their conscience and a public demonstration of their virtue, though not to the point where serious consequences might ensue. So we find the radical company of modernist critics of *Freie Bühne* (till 1892 a weekly) writing articles for newspapers and periodicals of a much more conservative tendency. However, the extreme Conservative press remained obdurate, as indeed did the main socialist papers too, with rare exceptions.

There is a shady side to this newspaper criticism, about which many writers had cause to complain. The reception in the literary columns of a new type of writing, whether we think of Naturalism, the George circle, Expressionism, Wedekind or many others, shows a remarkable degree of obtuseness and malice. Many of these newspaper critics were hacks, doing the job cheaply, and perhaps really obtuse; but in any case they were so concerned to write what might please their readers and their employers that many almost unconsciously adopted conventional attitudes that were guaranteed safe. Even the most hostile however made the names and work of writers known, and the best, like Brahm or Kerr or Bahr, could not only make a writer more aware of his own artistic purpose but also be a medium between him and the public. The importance of this critical activity can hardly be overestimated. Already by 1890 the conservative *Die Post* was jeering at the Naturalist authors because of their journalist 'protectors' and the 'critical terrorism' the latter were exercising, and the self-assertion of all the later groups was almost without exception accompanied by critical battles in the newspapers. Even Stefan George and his friends, who so disapproved of the vulgar appeal of newspapers and theatres and journalism, none the less from about 1896 sought ways of addressing a wider public and winning adherents, and their *Jahrbuch für die geistige Bewegung* was a polemical literary-social-political journal like others, except that it was unusually fierce, arrogant, and dogmatic. It was not perhaps only the war fever that led Gundolf and Wolfskehl to contribute to newspapers.

The newspaper engendered a style very different from that appropriate to weightier periodicals, and a journalistic lightness, mobility and wit are characteristic of critics like Schlenther, Mauthner, Bahr, Bierbaum, Kerr. Many of the literary journalists learned the tricks of the trade from Börne and Heine, and overloaded their articles with unexpected sallies, personalities, puns, capricious associations that have become the stock-in-trade of popular journalism, and one can sympathize with a Kraus or a Hofmannsthal who could not abide this sort of overbearing winsomeness (Kraus however could never resist a pun). But such devices do not lessen the force, intelligence and insight that the best critics often demonstrate; they were the price a successful publicist had to pay, and certainly Kerr and Bahr and Bierbaum and Blei enjoyed displaying them, and did so to good advantage. Siegfried Jacobsohn complained in 1914 that, whereas twenty years before it was difficult to get theatres to put on new plays, now the directors, even Reinhardt, simply threw themselves at any new (Expressionist) play, however extravagant, immature or absurd. While this greed for novelty was in part simple business enterprise, it also testifies to the remarkable adaptability of German audiences, and this itself must be ascribed in large part to the skilful interpretations, intelligence, cajoling and bullying of the newspaper critics.

It would be a most difficult task to try to assess what influence the newspaper critics had on writers, for instance on those whose chief concern was popularity, or on those who needed to hear a friendly and helpful voice and gratefully accepted 'moral' support without making concessions. But the implication of a sharp difference of function between critics and imaginative writers is false. A large number of critics were also writers (should one put it the other way round?), and are remembered today chiefly for their imaginative work, like Fontane, Lindau, or Spitteler (the Swiss) of the older generation, and Bahr, Bierbaum, Morgenstern, Hiller, Sternheim, Edschmid, Döblin of the younger. There is no abrupt breach between these and Heinrich and Thomas Mann, whom one might call essayists. Hofmannsthal once expressed his admiration for the type of journalism practised by Edward Carpenter and Lowes Dickinson in England, and several of his own most famous essays appeared first in newspapers. The relationship between critics and writers and the combination of both functions in the same person is important chiefly as indicating the ever-present consciousness of a large public and of a social connexion.

The links between public and writer established by the press and the theatre were strengthened in nearly all the larger cities by literary and cultural societies which invited literary notables to speak to them or read from their works; literary agents and publishers often took a hand in arranging tours for their clients. Amongst others Thomas Mann (with enjoyment), Hofmannsthal (with readiness), Rilke (with groans) went on such cricuits. They might like Rilke be taken aback by the kind of people who formed their audience, just as even the most respected author might well be alarmed at the way he was read, but still, the social backing could be felt. When Heinrich Mann in his reminiscences, *Ein Zeitalter wird besichtigt*, spoke of the great credit that 'Geist' enjoyed before 1914, he must have meant the credit it enjoyed in such circles and meetings.

On a more practical plane, various associations came into being which showed the beginning of a professional solidarity among writers and indeed among cultural workers generally, like the Association of Theatre Employees with its practical concern for wages, contracts and pensions. The Schutzverband der deutschen Schriftsteller had some similar objects, though they remained much more nebulous since writers were not employees. One of its chief concerns was the censorship and the laws governing publications, and it was its protest that caused Thomas Mann to resign from the Advisory Council to the Bavarian censor in 1913. These consolidations were rather rudimentary in this period, and necessarily feeble in view of the individualism of writing, but they are symptomatic of a growing consciousness of common interests among writers, and hence of themselves as a distinct social grouping. They anticipate the Councils of Writers ('geistige Arbeiter') formed in 1918 to enlist the energies of writers in the revolutionary movement.

Altogether, writers had never before been so closely linked in a practical and ideological network, so supported by direct and

indirect contacts with the publicistic media and with their readership. These connexions were strengthened in many other ways,
even before the era of radio and television. It became the custom
in this period to report through the newspapers the opinions of
writers and intellectuals on the most diverse subjects, on women's
emancipation, for instance, or international cooperation and
peace, and writers were often interviewed for this purpose or
asked to fill in questionnaires. They would from time to time show
their consciousness of belonging together by drawing up joint
protests, against the censorship perhaps, or on behalf of the
freedom of the press, or against the use of aeroplanes in war. All
police actions against publications or works of art, the hostility to
the modernist movements expressed by the Kaiser and his
Ministers by word or deed, served to enhance the self-awareness
of writers as a class. In *Europe in the Age of Imperialism*, H.
Gollwitzer identifies the emergence in this period of a social
grouping of the so-called 'free professions', i.e. lawyers, doctors,
architects and such, not state or municipal employees, who played
a significant part in the radical and revolutionary movements of
the times. One can claim that the writers too form a marked and
distinctive social grouping. Though they were in some ways
comparable with the members of the free professions, being self-
employed, and though some of them shared the same political
inclinations, it will be evident from this book that their social
impact was diffused over many areas of life and in some, for
instance in politics, was very ambiguous. Yet it was real and
powerful, and gave rise to characteristic schemes like that propa-
gated by the Austrian Hueber in 1911 for an 'Organisation der
Intelligenz' to promote the cultural interests of humanity, to be
guided by an international committee of prominent intellectuals
and writers who were to be empowered to carry out their proposals with the proceeds of a tax on capital.

The Artistic Calling

Two factors profoundly influenced the self-awareness of the
writer in this period. First, he was aware that he was one of a
large social group engaged in the creation of culture; second, he
was aware that his character, occupation and social attachment
were distinctly other than those of members of other professions.
This double awareness explains why the exalted conception of the

artist or poet, that originated among the Romantics, became so common a theme and often so pretentious a claim. From the Naturalists to the Expressionists writers repeatedly claim to be seers, guides, prophets, and if Hofmannsthal and Thomas Mann do not succumb to the blatant self-exalting myth-making frequent among others, even they attribute unique insight to the poet as an interpreter of his times, as one who penetrates to the deepest levels, a 'seismograph' or 'knower'. Innumerable plays and novels take the poet or artist as their theme, and the student can sympathize with Richard Strauss's outburst, in a letter to Hofmannsthal, that he is sick of literary works about poets. One of the pleasantest jokes of the time was an imaginary interview with the retired Bismarck invented by Heinrich Hart in *Freie Bühne* 1893, a parody of the interviewing technique that Hermann Bahr had introduced from France. When asked what is his dearest wish, Bismarck replies: 'To see a German poet and then die.'

Of course, a number of writers identify the artist by quite superficial marks. A suspicion of charlatanry always creeps in when a writer asserts his class allegiance by his dress or manners, and particularly when this means that he lives as a bohemian in a café-haunting coterie. A peculiar, Wagnerian type of cap and cloak, obstreperously non-bourgeois behaviour and language, defiance of conventional proprieties, are only too easily adopted by the would-be artist. The sexual freedom in bohemian and artist colonies had a profounder meaning and appeal, and with some justification enhanced the prestige of art and the artist; Henri Murger's *Scènes de la vie de Bohème* (1851) was the source of two operas as popular in Germany as elsewhere. But there was a less suspect reason for the prestige of the name. For both Simmel, the philosopher, and Rathenau, the entrepreneur, the artist embodies the resistance of the individual personality, the 'soul', against the pressures of mass-society and mechanization, the anonymity of the market, the reduction of things to commodities. In contrast to all other workers the artist, for them, is 'zweckfrei', that is, his work is subject to no external purpose or compulsion. The world, it is true, imposes itself, certain types of experience and reality, on everyone, but in the artist these experiences are given a self-determined shape in a work that detaches itself from the laws of cause and effect and is its own purpose. In the creation and the enjoyment of art the irrational, intuitive functions of man, insight and imagination, more and more threatened by the practical intelligence that is promoted by modern organization and management, are exercised in their purest form. The supreme quality of art is that it is not assessable by an external, quantifiable, analysable properties; the artist is the human soul living for its self-realization. This was the claim. The image seems almost ludicrously idealistic when one considers the many works of the time that portray the collapse of the artist under external pressures or his self-destruction through sex, drink, vanity, or some other temperamental weakness. But it is the hidden presence of this image that gave pathos even to failures like the hero of Bierbaum's *Stilpe*.

The image of the poet-artist that we find in imaginative works is more confused and polemical than the generalized concept of Simmel and Rathenau. The early tendency among the Naturalists to see the poet as a social investigator and moralist was modified by Holz and Schlaf's formalistic conception of the craftsman and rejected by George and Hofmannsthal, the German counterparts to Mallarmé and Wilde. The aestheticism of the early George rehabilitated the unique character of the artist, and the cult of beautiful form for its own sake liberated the artist from moral and social responsibilities as it did art from society – 'Art is a rupture with society.' But this rupture, even in the early period, seems to be more a breach with a particular society and social creed – bourgeois capitalism, utilitarianism, positivism – than with social life as such. *Algabal* embodies a Nietzschean immoralism that has social implications no less than Nietzsche's own immoralism. In Hofmannsthal the love of sensuous imagery, of mystery, dream and symbol, so strong in the 1890s, is also not a simple repudiation of the claims of society, for it evokes in him at the same time a painful consciousness of the attendant loss of vitality and self-fulfilment, a feeling of role-playing, a terror of confusing dream and reality, an estrangement from others and even from words, the human link. Later, both George and Hofmannsthal retained an exalted consciousness of the peculiar dignity and mission of the artist, but both recognized that his roots and purposes lie beyond art. In a sense George remained within an ivory tower of symbolic statement, but with his *Zeitgedicht* he opened a window through which he addressed and sought to guide the world. Hofmannsthal's thoughts were occupied, long before his political commitment during the war, with a public and social message, notably in such works as *Briefe eines Zurückgekehrten* and the major essays like *Der Dichter und diese Zeit,* in which he defines the poet as a 'seismograph' of his world. His correspondence with von Andrian and von Bodenhausen testifies to his eagerness to avoid segregation with writers.

Throughout the period we find this double attraction: on the one hand, a constant harping on the distinctive uniqueness of the artist, his dissociation from normal moral and social obligations etc.; on the other the accentuation of his representativeness, his social mission, that often takes the form of a claim to be called to redeem mankind. This polarity reaches its highest tension among the Expressionists, for instance in the typical case of Sorge's *Der Bettler,* where the Poet repudiates the normal social values but also becomes the leader of the spiritual renewal of the world. The repeated image of the poet-redeemer, whose message wins the enthusiastic allegiance of the masses, is a delusory expression of this double attachment of the artist. But it occurs in a more sober form also in many of the pre-1914 stories of Thomas Mann. He repeatedly describes the artist as temperamentally so much the social outsider as to be a misfit. But this view leads him both to a sympathetic analysis of his lot and to the cruel satire of *Tristan* and *Beim Propheten,* where the narcissism and perversity of the artists put a question-mark against their genuineness altogether. *Tonio Kröger,* on the other hand, though kept within rather personal, confessional confines, seems to suggest that the artist's separateness is justified only in the dialectical context of social attachment. *Der Tod in Venedig* goes further, since it attributes to Aschenbach the qualities of discipline and devotion characteristic of his ancestors, Prussian administrators and generals. Mann does not, in this pre-war period, find a consistent formulation, and it was only after the war that he came to recognize that the poet combines separateness with representativeness.

When so many people were tempted to claim special consideration as artists, it is not surprising that many and vain attempts were made theoretically to distinguish the genuine from the false. The most influential was the distinction between 'Dichter' and 'Literat' made by Lagarde. The littérateur is concerned with publicity, ideology, money, success, prestige etc., while the poet obeys an imperious intuition that comes from regions beyond selfhood. Langbehn took up this distinction as part of his attack on modern culture, and even a modern critic like Julius Bab adopted it in his book on Bernard Shaw (1910). The distinction is however an ideological and not an aesthetic or qualitative one, for in this tradition the littérateur is simply a writer of democratic leanings and an intellectual cast of mind. Thomas Mann acknowledging his sympathy for 'intellectuals', reproved Bab in a letter of 1910 for adopting this distinction. When in the course of the war Mann himself made such play of the contrast between 'Dichter' and 'Zivilisationsliterat', he was unabashedly using socio-political criteria, and here it is only too plain that it is not a question of commitment or non-commitment to society, but rather of a choice between one form of society as against another.

All the same, if polemical crudities of this sort can be ignored, it was troubling that traditional idealistic and humane criteria no longer seemed applicable to a work of art or a poetic gift, and especially that normal moral values seemed to be irrelevant. From the very beginning of 'die Moderne' the older critics like Lindau and Spitteler constantly bewailed the disregard of the new writers for healthiness and balance of mind, for happiness, and their obsession with ugliness, the sordid sides of life, the evil in man etc. In his essay, 'The Fate of Pleasure' (in the volume *Beyond Culture*, 1966) and in his book *Sincerity and Authenticity* (1972), Lionel Trilling has pointed out how with Dostoyevsky and Nietzsche there begins a profound reversal of values, in that secular usefulness, happiness, harmony are rejected as hostile to true humanity and to man's deepest freedom. Not only society but culture also is denounced, and the new spirituality that is asserted is expressed in and through hate, violence, destruction (he is thinking of the Dostoyevsky of *Notes from the Underground* rather than *The Idiot*). Hermann Conradi was one of the first to defend what he admits are bestial and demonic propensities in Dostoyevsky, diagnosing them as the revenge taken by the sensitive artist for the suffering inflicted by society and as an indirect tribute to an ideal of full human self-realization that society has betrayed. In this essay of 1889 Conradi attributed this modern trend to the precarious social position of the writer and intellectual, caught between the hostile powers of the authority above and the 'fourth estate' below. Trilling sees it as an antagonism inherent in civilization itself, not attributable to any specific social cause. Whatever its cause, it is a powerful current in the modern period, present in the consciousness of artists as an irrational antagonism and predilection; often enough the hatred and violence, the preference for the infamous and inhuman, are so powerful as almost to obliterate any ideal purpose.

Thus there is a certain inhumanity in the German literature of this period. *Entartung*, Nordau's peevish broadside against every feature of contemporary literature, sees everywhere symptoms of 'ego-mania' or what we might call narcissism. Nordau deserves little respect as a cultural analyst, yet with our knowledge of writers yet to come on the scene, Trakl, Sorge, Hasenclever, Kaiser, Becher and many others, we cannot deny at least a superficial validity to the charge made in 1893. This excessive concern with the self is peculiar in that there is, in comparison with earlier periods, a marked decline in the literature of personal relationships and private personal feeling, just as there is a lack of imaginative and sympathetic insight into characters other than the central 'hero' of plays and novels. Generally, poetry is tending towards the function that T. S. Eliot defined as 'escape from personality'. A writer like Gerhart Hauptmann stands out as a peculiar case because of his capacity for sympathy, for that famous 'tone' that Kerr detected when his dramatic characters, even the simplest, find the words that reveal a soul. None of the significant lyric poetry of this time is personal, there is little personal love-poetry. Dehmel's once admired *Zwei Menschen*, the text of an early Schoenberg composition, is rhetorical and demonstrative, while all the important work, of George, Rilke, Trakl, Heym and others, emerges when personal values and problems are superseded by a trans-personal anguish or exaltation. This process is of course not complete or abrupt, and in George or Rilke for instance we can trace the emergence of their work out of the cult of personal feeling and the personal soul.

George's poetry is of particular interest since this transformation occurs not by his abandoning Romantic themes but by finding a new form for them; because of this his poems were an important tool in the making of Schoenberg's modern musical idiom. Schoenberg's earliest compositions embodied a highly expressive, dramatic Romanticism even when he was setting lyrics by poets closely associated with Naturalism (Dehmel, Heinrich Hart, Johannes Schlaf) and the *Gurrelieder* of J. P. Jacobsen. His definitive breakthrough from the old Romantic tonalities and expressiveness is associated with texts from George ('Litanei' and

'Entrückung' from *Der siebente Ring* in the second Quartet, op. 10, 1907, and *Fifteen Songs for voice and piano*, op. 15, 1909, from George's *Buch der hängenden Gärten*). What Schoenberg discovered in these poems, which do not belong to George's political ideology, was still the Romantic dreamworld, exotic, bewitching, but distanced, controlled and shaped into symbols through a language and a rhythmical structure that resists emotionality and personalization. In the brief period after 1907 when Schoenberg turned to painting, he exhibited and was closely associated with the Blaue Reiter group, and here again, in Kandinsky's famous manifesto of 1912, we find George explicitly connected with the artistic revolution.

The 'ego-mania' that Nordau spoke of did not arise from a naive self-interest or self-aggrandizement therefore, but rather was associated with a strange depersonalization, even distrust of the self. Positively it was associated with an intense concern with existential problems, metaphysical values, intuitions and intimations, that demonstrates and intensifies the isolation of the poet. When Romain Rolland was advising Richard Strauss to look for libretti without the 'unhealthy' neurotic features of the Wilde *Salome*, Rolland wrote to his friend (1907): 'Beware your German poets ... They lack the generous power of sympathy.' And there was truth in this warning. Most German writers were too self-directed in this complex sense, too preoccupied with the metaphysical barrenness of existence, with their loneliness, their suffering over the grotesque and repulsive distortions imposed by modern society, and with compensating ideals and ecstasies, to find room for this sympathy. Those who did, often did so at the expense of truth, and their works belong to popular sentimental literature.

Hitherto we have been concerned with the higher culture of this period, however difficult it is to define it, and with the writers, critics, publishers, producers, who contributed to it. Another culture, or other cultures, flourished at the same time, not without many connexions with the higher, nor by any means always differing in artistic or moral motivations, though in these areas no doubt concern with profit, popularity, and amusement played a larger part. To this popular art belong the relaxation theatres, the music halls and variety theatres, the cheap suburban theatres and shows in beer halls, the circus, and towards 1914 the cinema. At this time film production was almost entirely in the hands of distribution agencies, and hence governed by the search for profit. Its thrills, sentimentalities, slapstick, and actualités began to be immensely successful and to spell the doom of the suburban theatre. It is extremely seldom that one finds an appreciation of the circus, music hall, or cinema in the devotees of the higher culture. Wedekind, like the bohemian Altenberg, loved the circus and farce, and adopted some of their features in his anti-naturalistic technique; Kafka, like Hoddis and Rilke, created symbols out of the circus; and occasionally one finds perceptive comments on circus and film in essays by Brod or Döblin, the latter of whom may well owe something of his style to the film. But when in 1913 H. H. Ewers defended the artistic potentialities of the film (at the opening of a new Berlin cinema, where *Quo Vadis* was to be shown), he was greeted with a storm of disapproval from advanced as well as conservative critics. *Aktion* constantly attacked the degradation of art through the cinema, and in view of its depraving influence on the masses opposed the film art itself; it held Hauptmann and Schnitzler to have betrayed their artistic trust in signing away the film-rights of works of theirs. It was in fact only during the war that the ideological power and artistic potentiality of the film began to be more fully explored, and only after the war did writers begin at all significantly to appreciate its cultural possibilities; before then, its rejection on intellectual, social and artistic grounds (like that of the circus) indicates the deep cleft between 'higher' and 'popular' culture, and the unconscious social assumptions of the cultured altogether.

The same sort of simple satisfactions were offered by a vast book and magazine industry. Many publishers issued novels in series with titles like 'Der Roman für Alle', 'Der Roman für Sie', 'Der neue spannende Roman', 'Romane des Feierabends'; the publishers might be newspaper publishers, like the Ullstein press, but 'quality' publishers like Fischer also had their popular series. The new markets available through the growth of the population, the spread of education, and the increase of wealth and leisure, were consolidated by the extension of the public library system, numerous book societies, and lending libraries set up by trade unions and the Social Democratic party. The contemporary great development of cheap editions of the classics, the Reclam, Bongs Klassiker, Helios Klassiker, Tempel Klassiker and other more specialized series, demonstrates the growth of a large serious read-

ing public, and with this grew also a huge demand for light
literature, sentimental novels, thrillers, 'revelations' of vice etc.

We can only guess at the social composition of the readership of
serious and light literature. To some extent the distinction is one
between the educated and those with only elementary schooling,
i.e. between bourgeois and petty bourgeois or proletarian,
between men and women, old and young. But many in all classes
shared a desire to escape from real concerns into the delights of
trash, just as Christian Buddenbrook haunted the music hall, and
in the working class, as elsewhere, there were great variations in
reading tastes. The reports of the monthly *Der Bibliothekar*
(1909-14), founded to promote the work of the socialist and
trade union libraries, do not give a reliable overall picture of
reading habits, as borrowing habits were not widespread, trash
was not held by these libraries, and the basic political books might
be bought rather than borrowed. The useful but brief account of
these reports and of a number of articles on workers' reading in
Die neue Zeit and *Sozialistische Monatshefte* that Fülberth gives
in *Proletarische Partei und bürgerliche Literatur* is vitiated by the
author's distaste for anything smelling of 'revisionism'. A better
idea is gained from personal statements, like that of Bromme in
his *Lebensgeschichte*. These show that the entry of a working-
class man into socialist activity meant also his introduction to
serious imaginative literature and participation in a campaign
against the sensationalist rubbish on which his workmates fed.
The reading lists that Bromme gives are interesting in several
ways, both in showing the differences in reading tastes between
the political worker and his mates and those between the socialist
worker and the educated middle class. In the latter case the
differences are due less to literary quality than to social relevance,
e.g. Gorki not Strindberg, Zola not Thomas Mann.

Among the German authors that Bromme mentions are a
number whose work is not cheap or vulgar and was then esteemed
by the best critics, but who now would be consigned to the waste-
land of kitsch, a term difficult to define and assign a sociological
status. Among Bromme's reading of this class are Julius Wolff
and Clara Viebig, once best-sellers and now forgotten. The list of
best-sellers compiled by D. R. Richards (*The German Best Seller
in the Twentieth Century*) contains many other such names,
among them K. E. Franzos (remembered for his edition of
Büchner), Paul Keller, Rudolf Herzog, Rudolf Stratz, Gustav

Schröer, Ernst Zahn, Heinz Tovote. Others in his list, like Frenssen and Courts-Maler, may still be read, and Karl May is still immensely popular. Though all these would now be ranked as kitsch, almost all were serious writers with literary and moral pretensions. It is fairly easy to see why Rilke's *Cornet* was the only work of his to reach best-seller status in his lifetime, and why it gave him little joy. It is understandable that *Buddenbrooks* over a span of thirty years topped the sale figures, though not easy in this case to maintain that popularity betrays a fault.

The general elements of kitsch are not hard to enumerate, though some of them may be found in good literature. They are typically displayed in Frenssen's *Die Sandgräfin* (1896). Nice girls are always 'schlank' and good men are rough but honest and above all 'ernst'. The author's sympathy goes to youth that is energetic but respects age, that earns material success but despises wealth. The good and bad are sharply distinguished, and religion helps and confirms the practical success of the good. A sentimental sympathy with the aristocracy allows the bourgeoisie to inherit its status with a good conscience; the poor and oppressed deserve compassion and help unless they become socialist malcontents and agitators. The trick of kitsch is, not to obliterate social reality but to charm away the conflicts. Clara Viebig repeatedly reconciles the rebellious independence of a young woman with her devoted obedience to father or husband. These traits are often evident in writers considered in their day, by the public and themselves, to be rebels, such as Kretzer and Sudermann. *Wer ist der Stärkere?*, a novel by Conrad Alberti, one of the boldest of the young Berlin Naturalists around 1890, shows typical kitsch features: sympathy with the Prussian nobility and young officers in particular, horror at speculation and the vice that attends its success, sympathy for the working class but naive abhorrence of socialist agitators (who also turn out to be corrupt). His heroes all challenge the establishment, but their eventual success means we are to rejoice over their admission to it. Good men and women are sexually chaste, and adultery is a habit of the wicked wealthy. Good men are rough but idealistic and honest, good girls are proper; Alberti like a dressmaker's salesman allows an admired girl to have a 'full' as well as 'slender' figure. Kitsch is often the cause of the success of a best-seller, though usually it is not calculated but springs from the same sort of earnestness and conviction as good literature.

The sociological meaning of the popularity of best-sellers is very difficult to assess if one has only the sales figures. What is equally important is who read them and how they were read. For instance, the immensely popular books of Löns appealed to readers with a liking for nature and a feeling of being deprived of nature, and also readers with nationalist or 'völkische' sympathies. But many who read them must have ignored, perhaps not noticed, the politico-social aspects of (say) *Das zweite Gesicht*. The large sales of Lienhard's books must have been based partly on a desire to explore with him unknown parts of provincial Germany, and only partly on agreement with his völkische views. The huge sales of Popert's *Helmut Harringa* must mainly have gone to members of the Temperance movement. Frenssen's popularity, on the other hand, extended into higher circles; Rilke gave his *Jörn Uhl* a favourable review and Thomas Mann noticed it, even if rather condescendingly (it proves, he says, that these days even country parsons know how to write novels).

There are instances where the success of a work might be ascribed to the skilful calculation of sentimentalities, as in some of Sudermann's works, or of erotic titillation, as in Bierbaum's astonishingly successful *Irrgarten der Liebe*. On the whole, however, a large number of writers, among them the best, seem to make no concessions to popular taste and to resist the appeal of mere success and popularity, in spite of the fact that all were happy to be read and to stir an echo in their readership. This is the peculiar character of the cultural or literary 'industry', in that the importance of its products cannot be assessed by direct social measurements such as sales, and, more important still, that the productions themselves come from a different source than consideration for a market. Culture has a double meaning. In simple societies, especially in static societies, it can and must mean the whole habit, material and ideological, of the society. In a modern dynamic society like Germany, it can mean certain commonly shared habits and attitudes. But many habits and attitudes are not commonly shared, and those that are least 'common' may indeed be most decisive for the future, and may reflect realities commonly ignored. The popular, conventional literary culture is largely overlooked in this present study, not because the attitudes and habits it enshrines are to be despised, but because in the 'higher' literature a greater totality is embodied through which the conventional and customary is placed in the context of conflicting and emergent realities and values. This might be taken, indeed, as a definition of 'higher' culture. For we have been concerned not with a static reality, but a dynamic and changing one, in which values can only be assessed in the light of their spiritual productivity in the future. For the same reason, if we maintain that writers do (with other artists) form an identifiable social group, it has to be understood that this social group is a peculiar one and subject to peculiar motivations.

'Geist' and 'die Geistigen'

If any common commitment or 'interest' of the writers was present in their consciousness, it was that of 'Geist'. It is characteristic of this social group that this is not a material interest, and indeed it is applied to so many varied attitudes that it is untranslatable and difficult to define. This ambiguity was its convenience.

Originally bearing a religious-theological meaning, it denoted the spiritual, the holy, as contrasted with the flesh, the world, secular interests. Although in the eighteenth century it emerged from a predominantly religious context, it retained in its varied meanings the implication of the spiritual as the 'higher' part of man. This was so even where it was used to denote man's capacity for thought and reflection, whether intuitive or rational, but more strikingly where it indicated man's capacity for freedom, when he asserted his inner spirit in defiance of utilitarian calculation, common sense or natural causation. Thus it continued to distinguish that element in man that serves ideal and super-personal purposes. It embraced more than mind and intellect, emphatically more than science and learning, and affirmed a pledge to positive 'spiritual' values and goals. This group of meanings lurks within most usages of the term in our period.

There is another trend, deriving more particularly from Herder and Hegel. In this period of science and scepticism Hegel's conception of the universe as a process of self-realization of spirit, the butt of the ridicule of Schopenhauer and Nietzsche, was discarded both because of its speculative character and because it seemed too obvious a substitute for Providence. His dialectic too held little appeal for an empirical generation. But the comprehensive interpretation of Geist, in his and Herder's thought, the awed veneration with which they speak of it, still lived on. Its most popular form was in the combination

Volksgeist, the spirit of a people, a term that has left a long trail of nationalism and racism. But we are concerned here with a different type of implication. For Herder and Hegel, all the institutions of society – church, state, law, school, workshop etc. – are concretizations of an evolving national or local Geist, just as much as the more obviously spiritual manifestations in thought, art, or poetry. But this national spirit itself is only a manifestation of a general, universal spirit. When philosophers like Dilthey or Simmel use the terms 'objektiver Geist' for social, institutional, practical structures and 'subjektiver Geist' for mental and imaginative, they mean the human spirit itself progressively imposing meaning on life. In this usage they reject any purely spiritual interpretation of the word, not only because they reject making in this context a distinction between soul and mind, the irrational and the rational, but also because they recognize concrete realities, institutions, buildings or things, the physical aspects of culture, since they are shaped and guided by mind, as belonging to Geist. In this tradition of thought, the distinguishing feature of Geist is its creative energy, the imposition of a human pattern on the world through understanding and activity. In Nietzsche the mind that serves only knowledge serves the status quo and is abominated; the 'most spiritual' ('geistigsten') natures, he writes, serve life in the sense of dynamic change. Perhaps no line of poetry caused a more tense throb in these years than Hölderlin's 'Wer das Tiefste gedacht, liebt das Lebendigste'.

This comprehensive meaning is rare. A cursory review shows that in more popular usage Geist can have an intellectual and an anti-intellectual connotation, it can be rationalistic or irrational, active or contemplative, inwardly or socially directed, conservative or revolutionary. Yet it is on everyone's lips, as if its meaning were self-evident and agreed. Only a thorough set of investigations could uncover all its meanings and relate them; here only a few representative and suggestive usages can be mentioned, and we can ignore its enlistment, for instance, to justify the war of 1914.

The philosopher Simmel uses the term frequently in his works, and centrally in the essay 'Die Groszstädte und das Geistesleben'. Geist he understands as the principle of the mental effort of men to come to terms with the new economic and social conditions of the city. But he uses it in two contrary senses. On the one hand, men adapt themselves to the modern economy, he says, by becoming more rational, adaptable, mobile in their ideas and habits; they are no less 'geistig' than in earlier societies, but Geist changes. But when Simmel considers 'das Geistesleben' as the world of art, literature, religion, of values, he comes to somewhat contrary interpretations and conclusions. The heart of culture is, he expounds, the defence of the 'soul' against the encroachments of the social world, the defence of individuality, the consistent personality, against adaptations to external social pressures. In the same way Simmel, in *Fragment über die Liebe*, calls human love 'geistig' since it transcends the genetic function of sex and the means-end nexus governing sex, in this being comparable to art.

Even the philosopher is not clear in his use of the term, but at least he does limit its range of meaning. For examples of more usual and conventional usages we might look rather to letters than essays, since there is a better chance of finding in them an uninhibited use of the term. The letters of Christian Morgenstern are particularly valuable in this respect. Morgenstern was a poet who, as a reader for Cassirer's publishing house and editor of a theatre periodical, lived in close touch with Berlin cultural life. A modest, sincere, gentle person, undogmatic and unpretentious, he responded appreciatively to a wide variety of cultural experiences: to Reinhardt, whose brilliance and shallowness alternately attracted and repelled him; to Lagarde's individualistic Germanism, to Kierkegaard's absolute religious commitment, to Nietzsche's affirmation of life, to Goethe's and Tolstoy's humanity, to Ibsen (of whose plays he was commissioned by Reinhardt to do a new translation), to Hauptmann's *Emanuel Quint*, to Wilde, George and Hofmannsthal, to Rudolf Steiner whose Anthroposophical Society he joined. From his letters we see that this generosity of sympathy is not the result of a lack of discrimination, but is inspired by a principle, what he calls Geist or Geistigkeit; and Geist means spiritual values and freedom. It is the opposite of power and power politics, the search for wealth and the delight in ostentation. He reproves the anti-semitism of a close friend on the grounds that the Jews, Kerr in particular, represent a higher 'Geistigkeit' than the Germans. He detests 'bourgeois' culture, i.e. a culture impregnated with moralistic as well as materialistic values as opposed to 'Geist', and praises Dostoyevsky for his 'de-bourgeoisification' of culture. His *Galgenlieder*, he says, originated in an exuberant nonsense game, but are justified by their 'Geistigkeit', by which he means the free play of the mind discarding 'gloomy seriousness' which belongs to the materialistic world. He wrote religious poems of a mystical bent, and he joined the anthroposophists because he needed a philosophy that refused to see man as totally subject to natural law and emphasized the freedom of his spirit (for the same reason he detested the occultism prevalent among some Steiner adherents).

The arch-enemy of Geist is, for Morgenstern, materialism, and by materialism he means, beyond its obvious moral implications, the positivistic doctrine of natural law and man's self-adaptation to a universe encased in law. He speaks of poetry as 'redemption from matter'. As a concomitant Morgenstern tends to deny Geist to all practical men, to science and technology, and to all institutions. In this he represents a very common tendency among the cultured to equate Geist with art, poetry, religion, philosophy, to think of it as belonging to a particular 'spiritual' stratum of society, distinguished from politicians and businessmen, from all people engaged in productive life, from the universities, social institutions and social reform movements. Morgenstern's opinions, the unstrained comments of daily life, perhaps because of this are more truly representative than more coherent statements. Certainly this tendency to divide society into two parts, the 'Geistigen' and what was formerly called the philistine would, but now appears usually as the bourgeois, and to look on culture as the creation and property of the former, underlies much of the consciousness of the social group engaged in the creation and dissemination of culture, and is one of the signs of their actually being a social group.

It is true, some of the narrower literary groupings claimed 'Geist' for themselves, to mark themselves off from others, and this was an aggressive feature of the George circle. In the second *Folge* of *Blätter für die Kunst* Gérardy defines their purpose as 'eine geistige Kunst', a symbolical art directed towards mystical truths, as opposed to Naturalism. When Wolfskehl in subsequent years calls the artist 'a priest of Geist', or says 'Only the artist lives for Geist', he is contrasting their aims and work with realistic and moralistic art, that he calls bourgeois-plebeian, as well as with trivial entertainment art. The negative meanings of Geist are more clearly evident than the positive, until the crisis of the 'Cosmics' round 1900. In their hostility to social and ideological rigidities, Schuler and Klages advocated a return to a primitive chaos, and in the service of the creative 'soul' they attacked the more intellectualistic Geist. When George rejected these temptations, his renewed emphasis on Geist meant the creation in his poetry of ideal structures of authority, ideal forms of relationship the very opposite of the chaos worshipped by Schuler. Geist is here, as with Nietzsche, not spiritual alone, but emerges from the fusion of body and soul as structured energy. Indeed, in the arrogantly titled *Jahrbuch für die geistige Bewegung*, the vitalistic element of Geist is emphatically elaborated. Not only are the rational and liberal connotations of Geist, like justice, humanity, tolerance, swept away as hostile to the 'movement from the depths', the impassioned intuition, but the vitalistic conception also excludes scientific and scholarly objectivity, so that the *Jahrbuch* brought about a serious breach with some of George's closest academic friends like Simmel and Breysig. In 1916 Blüher's *Die Intellektuellen und die Geistigen* continued this trend to deny 'Geistigkeit' to the rational intellect and appropriate Geist as the organ of intuitive insight and irrational symbol-building.

This type of conception of Geist as a vital organ distinct from or even opposed to the rational intellect is the dominant one. Even a Rathenau considers it prior and superior to the intellect, which is suspect as a usurping servant. There were of course other interpretations. In Naturalist circles round 1890 Geist has usually the simpler meaning of the faculty that discovers general principles or laws, in society as in nature; though even in the more Marxist of the contributors to *Freie Bühne*, like Gustav Landauer or Bruno Wille, we find also the Nietzschean concept of Geist as a power that asserts values over against so-called laws of nature and releases energy to break through the confines of established reality and its laws. At the very time when *Jahrbuch für die geistige Bewegung* appeared, the most notable of the rationalistic interpretations appeared in Heinrich Mann's *Geist und Tat* of 1910. Geist for Mann is the source of the great liberal normative concepts like truth, justice, freedom, equality, human dignity, the critical organ that detects spurious claims to power and authority and subjects all beliefs and habits to a rational test. But Mann's conception, though of great importance to the younger intellectuals trying to resist the lure of the irrational war-fever, remained very abstract, and because of this seems dogmatic; to most contemporaries it seemed to embody only regulative principles, not a vital purpose. During the war this opposition appeared in the drastic form of peace as against war, internationalism as against nationalism, democracy as against authoritarianism, and Thomas Mann subjected his brother's notions to a far deeper, if biased, analysis than Heinrich ever did. Thomas polemicies consistently against the identification of Geist with rationality, democracy, and pacifist principles. He elaborates on the Nietzschean theme that life takes precedence over rationality, and claims that the true artist is not an intellectual, a man pledged to reason, but a man pledged to life, which means the irrational, the barbaric, the inhuman. Dissociating Geist from any active political principle, Mann seems to deny the 'Geistigen', in particular the artists, any political role. However what he actually does, like his chosen mentors Nietzsche and Dostoyevsky, is to harness Geist to certain anti-liberal political values and authorities.

Kurt Hiller, who subscribed to Heinrich Mann's concept of 'Geist' and his thesis that it must embrace political action and become realized in social institutions, preferred before the war the term 'die Intellektuellen' to 'die Geistigen', no doubt because of the reactionary and irrational connotations of the latter in the George circle. But, as the leader of the Neuer Club and the Neopathetisches Cabaret, he also advocated 'pathos', expressive feeling, rhetoric, to ensure the emotional energy required to promote action to change circumstances. This curious alliance of intellect and emotion indicates the persistent consciousness of the sterility of the analytic intellect that, as was often stated, cannot provide motivation for action and, as it analyses reality and uncovers hidden processes and laws, lays bare man's chains, not his freedom. The one thing needful, we hear from all sides, is personal and social renewal, the possibility of escaping from the laws of cause and effect, of transcending observable nature altogether, and the only agency for such transcendence is the spirit. This is the theme of Kandinsky's *Über das Geistige in der Kunst* of 1912, a most influential essay that links up the most revolutionary modern art with George and beyond him the early Romantics. Geist for Kandinsky challenges scientific laws, determinism, the rational consciousness; it means spirit, inner values known intuitively, freedom. This is normal usage, and explains for instance the sympathy he expresses for theosophy and occultism. But he takes his opposites to an extreme, and asserting that spiritual freedom means absolute freedom from nature he proclaims that reality and nature are only obstacles to the spirit, and therefore that the spiritual content of art is only obscured or destroyed by representational forms. The non-representational abstract art he is half imagining will be a communication of soul to soul without the intervention of the tyrannical external world of nature, and will hence be the pure expression of the autonomous spirit. Paul Klee was to argue similarly in *Über die moderne Kunst*, a lecture given in 1924, for the autonomy of the artist's spirit, and similarly to claim that there is no external criterion for the work of art, only an intuitive responsive vibration in the viewer. It is strange that modern non-representational art, that was ushered in with such claims, has in fact so often demonstrated the very opposite of this 'autonomy of the spirit', for instance in its dependence on subconscious automatisms, on the promptings and problems of the technical medium, and even on random composition.

Kandinsky's formulations echo throughout the writing of the Expressionist generation, with the significant modification that socio-political action, in 1912 considered by Kandinsky to be contaminated by materialism, is later subsumed under Geist. Kandinsky himself came during the early years of the Soviet Revolution to interpret it as the victory of the spirit, and for the Expressionist generation likewise the overthrow of materialistic capitalism was a work of the spirit. In the first of the *Ziel* publications Kurt Hiller now (1916) uses the term 'Geistige' instead of 'intellectuals', since he is advocating something more creative than the mental activity of philosophers or scientists or practical men. Indeed a mystical note creeps in and he speaks of 'die Geistigen' as prophets and guides, inspired interpreters of the nation. In his blueprint for the future constitution of a reformed Germany he suggests a legislative Upper Chamber formed of 'die geistigen Führer'. Rubiner, Edschmid, Pinthus and others celebrate Geist even more recklessly and ecstatically as the one human power free from the chain of necessity, a principle as superior to dialectical materialism, that only formulates the material interests of the working class, as it is to the greed and hypocrisy of the bourgeoisie. The worship of Geist as freedom leads not only to attacks on empiricism and science but also to a repudiation of reality itself in the name of a mystical self-transcendence. The counterpart of these views, which in their hyperbole reflect the mounting anguish of the war, is found in the plays of Hasenclever, Kaiser, Toller and others, where the message of the spirit compels so swift and flattering a response in the masses. It is quite consistent with this outlook that a sceptical and disillusioned Carl Sternheim, in his summing up at the end of 1918 in *Aktion* (*Gesamtwerk*, ed. Emrich, IV), attributed the disasters of war and the failure of revolution to 'contempt for Geist'.

Perhaps he could more accurately have said 'contempt for die Geistigen'. In their usage of the term Geist it has lost all the comprehensive, historic meaning it had for Hegel or Goethe, as indicating the struggle of man with his environment and himself, from the simplest operations of labour to the most complex social organization, from the most rational thought to the most imaginative self-projection in art. Instead it has become something ethereal, intangible, arbitrary, and above all divisive in its contempt for the practical, rational functions of mind. The extravagance of the claims made for Geist, and their divisive purport can be explained as the revolt of sensitive men against the application of mind to the gigantic destruction of war, but they can hardly be accounted for unless one also understands that a whole group of cultural workers were sustaining one another in these beliefs. How otherwise could it come about that numerous essays by writers already mentioned, and by others like Korrodi, Flake and Werfel, sublimely dismiss the validity of empirical knowledge and happily foresee that Geist will usher in a realm of freedom in which social organization and law will be superseded? Only a few of the young writers appreciated the contradictions involved, and perhaps the most logical position was Carl Einstein's who, rejecting such utopias, combined a social theory of 'permanent revolt' with an aesthetics based on the thesis that each work of art brings with it its own artistic criteria and thus embodies the autonomy of man's 'geistige Existenz'.

Faith in Geist never recovered its exuberance after its collapse in 1919, though it persisted in more sober forms in such organizations as the Pen Club or the League for the Rights of Man. Audiences gathered in Britain to protest against Hitlerism in 1933 were reminded of its existence when, to their bewilderment, they heard refugee German intellectuals defining Hitler's essential crime to be betrayal of 'den Geist'.

In *Ideologie und Utopie* (1929) Karl Mannheim defined the 'intelligentsia' as a 'relatively classless stratum' in between the major classes whose values are determined by great material interests. In his view, this 'Intelligenz' – which he does not precisely define, though it includes writers, artists, intellectuals and members of the so-called 'free' professions – does not form a class proper nor align itself with the major classes, and because its activity takes place largely in the intellectual area it has the capacity of mediating between the other classes, even of providing what Mannheim calls 'a dynamic synthesis' of conflicting interests. What Mannheim overlooked was a fact already demonstrated in the Expressionist movement: namely, that the relative release of the intelligentsia from material interests and the major classes entailed the temptation to conceive of social reality in the image of their own status, to attribute to itself a social power it cannot acquire or wield, and even to invent an esoteric language and idiom which is meaningful only to its own members. The vagueness, multivalency, and uplift of the term Geist made it the appropriate slogan for this group.

Literature and Society

The many interpretations of Geist, including many that defy summarization here, reveal many untested assumptions and dogmatic convictions. These however are not capricious and betray more than the eccentricities of individuals. They mirror the real dilemmas of the time and have social and cultural relevance. They contribute to our identification of artists as forming the centre of a particular social group blurred at the edges like most social groups, and differentiated into numerous functions from the directly economic to the most unworldly. The consciousness of belonging to this class usually expresses itself indirectly rather than directly, but is an important constituent in the literary work of its members. In all this the development in Germany is closely akin to that in other economically advanced European nations; and it may be suggested that the multiple modernisms in literature and art that have proliferated since that time are signs that this class has grown still larger and more self-confident in the affluent society.

Many factors contributing to this consolidation could not be examined within the framework of this book. One such is the immense development of mental communication, through newspapers, periodicals and books; the role of the feuilleton would repay detailed analysis. There is also the rapidity and ease of material communication, especially international and intercultural, enhanced by the development of mechanical techniques of art reproduction. Worldwide trade had for centuries accumulated collections of objects from remote cultures, and now these were supplemented by numerous exhibitions of Far Eastern and African art and still more thrillingly by the visits of Japanese players, dancers from Indo-China, and the Russian ballet. What was most remarkable was the ready receptivity to remote cultures and the swift assimilation of formal elements from them into European art. The many other comparable enlargements of sympathy, for instance the interest in Buddhism or Hindu religions, the new appreciation of archaic Greek art and that of ancient Egypt, contributed to some sort of conviction of the universality of the spirit, and of art as its most tangible expression, that itself reinforced the self-awareness of the European cultural strata.

It therefore seems paradoxical that one of the most common and harrowing themes of modern literature is loneliness, the feeling of alienation of man from man, individual from society, life from meaning, that seems to be specifically related to the modern artistic sensibility in spite of the fact that the writer was as never before a member of a group, buoyed up by countless intermediaries, benefiting from cultural institutions and a lively publicity. It was this alienation that Freud in 1929 called 'das Unbehagen in der Kultur', an unease within civilized life that often evokes a longing to reject it at the same time as its benefits are enjoyed. Freud sees it as the resentment of erotic and aggressive egoism against the inhibitions that culture requires, and there is evidence of this in the new cult of barbarism of Nietzsche and Worringer and others. But Freud fails to take into account the specific features of this period that exacerbated the feeling of revulsion and alienation. Already marked in the Romantic writers, exalted and haunted by the irrational, tortured by the fragility of the personality, it spread now, with the transformation of society, the displacement of social habits and ancient hierarchies, the decline of religion, the uncertainty of all perspectives, over a much wider intellectual field. It was the price of his much-vaunted freedom that the writer was acutely vulnerable to the insecurities caused by the dissolution and erosions of habitual ties, and even the group to which he belonged was subject to the market and the principle of competition, so that professional solidarity was sorely qualified by rivalries that were often bitter. This personal and professional situation of the artist may help to explain why the theme of alienation was so widespread. Its significance however is due to its being true of a whole society. The major statements of the theme belong to writers like Rilke, Hofmannsthal, Thomas Mann, Musil and Kafka, who felt themselves to be speaking representatively.

In his excellent study, *Der deutsche Dichter um die Jahrhundertwende*, Rosenhaupt distinguishes a number of forms under which this feeling of being a stranger in the world appears in literature: for instance, as a feeling of loss of purpose, or of confidence, or of will, a feeling of the unreality of the self and of the environment, of role-playing, of the fragmentation of the personality. R. H. Thomas's essay 'Das Ich und die Welt: Expressionismus und Gesellschaft' indicates the forms this consciousness took in the Expressionist generation and its relationship to the general social situation. A survey such as has been attempted in this book, limited as it is, suggests that this feeling of alienation acquired a general cultural significance because of the specific character and trend of modern industrialized society. We have seen that, while the outstanding socio-political feature of Germany in this period was a violent and impetuous progress in the political, economic and technological fields, a vast accumulation of power and wealth and an endless enrichment of scientific and historical knowledge, this was accompanied by a growing awareness of the powerlessness of the individual to control events and even to participate in the exercise of political or social authority. It was accompanied too by corrosive doubts—doubts of the ethical substance of social and political being, doubts over the spiritual quality of social life, the culture of the city, the claims of authority in state and home, the churches and religion, the meaning and worth of personal and social life. The imaginative writers made themselves the spokesmen of these doubts, sometimes in their explicit shape, often in the transferred form of psychological and existential uncertainties about, for instance, the moral status of reality or the identity of the self. The most profound psychological cause of existential loneliness seems to lie in the complex dislocation of habitual life and expectations under the stress of uncontrollable and often cruel change, so that social connexions were reduced to the flimsiest and most accidental of ties. In part it might be considered to be due to the natural conservatism of the emotive and imaginative faculties in man, that find difficulty in adapting to even beneficent change, but it was nourished too on an awareness of the advance of forces in bourgeois industrial society that threatened the foundations of a humane existence.

The writers did not reach a separate, single, unambiguous conclusion on any of the great questions of these generations. Some look backward to an obsolete solace, some forward to an unrealizable utopia, some suggest reforms and some express despair, some create ideal models while others indict the world through distortion and grotesque fantasy, some realistically reflect the social world, some create stylized forms, some project their dreams and nightmares. If their medium is specific to them, the issues that preoccupy them are those with which the more educated and reflective Germans were widely concerned, and their attitudes usually fit into already established patterns. Yet what they wrote was felt by them themselves and their readers and audiences to have some specific quality, and indeed this can still be claimed for them and justifies a study like this present one, the theme of which, if definable, is not just the testimony in literature to social realities but the peculiar contribution and debt of the literary imagination to social consciousness. In what lies its peculiarity?

It can hardly be claimed that writers felt social problems with a unique intensity. There is plenty of evidence that they were indeed intensely distressed by social evils of different and often contradictory kinds, just as they were intensely moved over other aspects of the human condition. But in a period so full of extravagant and fanatical movements, intensity of feeling is by no means the exclusive or distinguishing property of the writers. Nor is expression their exclusive property, or at any rate expression of the more general social problems, for the period is overflowingly articulate. We know that they stand, if for one cause, for that of Geist, for the freedom of the human spirit; but here again they are one group among many, and they share the contradictory interpretations of Geist common among the educated. What is peculiar to them is the imaginative mode of expression, and the central question to be asked is, what does the choice of the medium of poetry or rather 'Dichtung', imaginative literature, imply in respect to the social function of what is written?

The fundamental characteristic of poetry (in this broader sense) is that its statements are symbolical. They are not statements about a particular actuality, referable to it in respect for instance to their truth or historicity. As Sir Philip Sidney put it, they 'do not affirm'. This is less self-evident in literature than in other arts, since the stuff of literature is words, the medium normally used for practical affirmations. But even the 'I' used in the most confessional lyric is not the empirical I of the man who writes, but a different, postulated being, and the question of whether the poet really wandered in the mountains is irrelevant. In the more complex genres, novel or drama, clearly the whole exists in a mode emphatically different from that of normal practical life and thought. These elementary observations are not made in order to assert that art has nothing to do with real life. Even an artist like Paul Klee, whose art rejects all associations with nature and the normal world of human activity, recognizes in his *On Modern Art* that the 'roots' of art lie in the world of experience, even if the work of art itself, the 'crown' of the tree, the product of the artist's experience of a surrounding reality, is in no sense the 'image' of the root. In the literature of our period we have nothing, except perhaps Dada, so unrelated to the commonly experienced world as the art of Klee; but still there is nothing more important about the imaginative literature than the fact that its form does detach it from the nature of discursive non-imaginative writing.

As symbolic expression, literature enjoys a peculiar freedom, one might call it irresponsibility. Not just in the sense that it is not bound to historical, circumstantial truth. It is free also in the sense that it does not have to draw conclusions, that consequential action is not implied, and that judgements of a work's 'meaning' may be ambiguous. It can thus be extreme in its presentation of the fragment of experience with which it deals, intensifying despair or hope, horror or ecstasy, distorting and idealizing, without misleading. It can, that is, be free of compromise and practical prudence because these have no role in its sphere. For these reasons the writers were able to do more than embody in a visual and tangible form the known and recognized realities of, say, exploitation or war; they were also able to speak of suffering that is normally excluded from consciousness and expression until some countering remedy or solace makes it envisageable. This applies equally to spiritual suffering such as we become aware of in the poetic expression of existential loneliness. To this property of literature can be ascribed some of its most brilliant and significant insights, very clearly for instance in respect to the reality of sex. This freedom of art is strongly buttressed by the social situation of writers as a class. For in this respect too writers are detached from normal social functions, since the attachment of their class to the economy is of so curious a kind that they are scarcely identified with an economic interest. Writers therefore, though they may adopt any of a variety of political and social attitudes, are not deeply identified with any interest, and therefore hampered less than most classes by the blinkers of conscious or unconscious interest in their vision of the world around them.

If the social position of writers as a class offers such opportunities, it also imposes barriers. It is for instance striking how rarely the poetic imagination copes in this period with experience that lies, socially, outside that of the cultured bourgeoisie. It is rarely successful in recreating the personalities and activities of active social life, statesmen and politicians, political agitators, manufacturers and industrial workers. A prerequisite of insight is sympathy, and it is noticeable that the most successful, i.e. the fullest and richest, works concerned with these social areas are those dealing with the artisan, like Kretzer's *Meister Timpe*, or the old-fashioned merchant, like Mann's *Buddenbrooks*, or the semi-rural factory worker, like Hauptmann's *Die Weber*. The modern industrialist, like the modern industrial worker and the socialist leader, appears almost only in caricature that betrays a lack of knowledge as well as a lack of sympathy in the writer, for instance in Sternheim's *Tabula Rasa* or Döblin's *Wadzeks Kampf mit der Dampfturbine*. On the other hand, drop-outs and failures meet with abundant sympathy. It would be naive not to recognize that the valuations in imaginative literature may be the product of professional bias or narrowness.

New opportunities and limitations in the more formal aspects of poetry were also profoundly influenced by the social position of the writer. One of the most prominent trends of modern literature, in France first and then elsewhere, has been symbolism, a term which can be applied not only to groups calling themselves symbolists but also to writers such as Rilke and the Expressionists. The symbolist procedure means the wrenching of words out of their normal context, function and meaning and the attribution to them of new meanings in new contexts, a procedure that is often accompanied by violent syntactical innovation. This is, of course, a process as old as language, but it has been so intensified in the modern period as to suggest that it was possible on such a scale only because writers as a class were relatively free of the practical, utilitarian pressures of society and of normal communication, and were able to manipulate rather arbitrarily the instruments – the words – they inherit. Some of the greatest achievements of modern poetry have been due to this ability to turn the indifferent, dehumanized things and facts of everyday experience into symbols of spiritual experience. The cost of this freedom was the threat of lack of communication, a certain arrogance towards the practical world of shared reality, and a confusion of the spheres of symbol and reality that led some poets, for instance, to adopt the posture of guide and prophet.

The pervasive faith in the power of Geist to defy and alter circumstances is a further example of this profit and loss. In this respect it is illuminating to compare the German writers with their contemporaries in Britain. We find in Britain a similar social stratum, with a similar dominantly anti-bourgeois ideology. But the British writers, whether like Wells they come from the 'lower' classes, or like Shaw from the lower middle class, or like the Bloomsbury group from the upper middle class, were much firmer rooted in existing society than the Germans, and as a consequence much further from revolutionism and utopianism. There was no German parallel to the close attachment of Bloomsbury to Cambridge, the setting for G. E. Moore's ethics of personal relations that contrasts so sharply with the aggressive individualism of Nietzsche. A very widespread hostility to bourgeois culture, to uncontrolled capitalism and imperialism, found expression in the Fabian Society, itself the creation of intellectuals and writers, and membership meant integration in a loosely disciplined movement and acceptance of a slow evolutionary process. By contrast, Social Democracy in Germany rejected any such undisguised compromise, and its dogmatism and discipline offered integration to writers at a price they could not pay. Their opposition to bourgeois society therefore easily became extreme and capricious. The social and political criticism of the British writers was more concrete, less irreconcilable, less intense than that in Germany; it was more conventional in form and more modest in theme. The Germans were altogether bolder in linguistic and formal experiment as they were in their attack on conventional morals, capable of higher ecstasies and deeper despairs; they were also more pretentious, rhetorical, egotistic. They were more subject to self-delusion, particularly to a delusory faith in the power of an idea or a conviction to change the world – a faith that Marx and Engels had castigated in *Die deutsche Ideologie* as the typical delusion of a class that lives on ideas. The message of E. M. Forster, 'Only connect', is limited and modest; but the idea of mutuality is strikingly absent from the German literature, that mostly balances a strong individualism only with some great generality like man, Germany, or destiny.

The relationship of German literature to the Wilhelmine 'age' has proved very difficult to define. Hans Schwerte in his essay 'Deutsche Literatur im Wilhelminischen Zeitalter' considers the decisive principle of good writing to have been opposition to the 'age', to capitalism, positivism, materialism etc. In a similar way Jost Hermand sees Expressionism as a protest against industrial society, militarism, imperialism, 'bourgeois-capitalistic forms of life' generally ('Expressionismus als Revolution' in *Von Mainz nach Weimar*). Both writers recognize exceptions. Schwerte notes for instance that Stefan George created something that might be called a 'Wilhelmine cult-style', while Hermand detects certain bourgeois features in the Expressionists, for instance the concept of work. The evidence accumulated in the four volumes of Hamann and Hermand's *Deutsche Kunst und Kultur von der Gründerzeit bis zum Expressionismus* shows indeed the persistence of all sorts of 'bourgeois' preconceptions and forms in the 'anti-bourgeois' literature of this period, and the investigations embodied in the present study strengthen the conclusion that if the majority of writers almost ostentatiously proclaimed their opposition to bourgeois capitalism, bourgeois ethics, and the bourgeois style of life, at the same time this opposition itself was inspired by principles that can only be called bourgeois, for instance the worship of Geist, the devotion to personal freedom and belief in the autonomy of the will, the sacral conception of art and the artist, the élitist conception of culture.

The uncertain use of the term 'bourgeois' itself indicates the complexity of actuality. Contemporary bourgeois society was neither economically nor socially uniform, but made up of units of varying structure, all in rapid process of change; the political and administrative structures likewise varied greatly, from the authoritarian to the democratic. In a dynamic situation like this, bourgeois morality and self-consciousness were also in flux and full of contradictions. It is therefore no accident that it is very difficult to find a precise sociological definition of the culture of this period. It is much too simplistic to say, as the Marxist Georg Lukács repeatedly does in his pre-1945 writings, that the quality of art is commensurate with the criticism of bourgeois presuppositions. Even in his much more generous analysis in *Wider den miszverstandenen Realismus* of 1958, Lukács will admit that the bourgeois writer of the modernist period (e.g. Kafka) can produce work of high artistic quality only if his work expresses the repulsive hollowness of bourgeois society in the framework of some sort of faith in the liberating force of the socialist movement. Wilhelm Emrich more persuasively argues, in *Protest und Verheissung*, that one of the basic principles and themes of this literature – the revolt against the reduction of the individual to a mere social function – arises in any large-scale industrialized society, whether capitalist or socialist, and therefore cannot be exclusively identified with a particular social class. It would seem justified to conclude that while the anti-bourgeois revolt of the writers was of bourgeois origin and due to a social situation largely created by the bourgeoisie, it acquired a wider, more universal validity and in part released itself, under the stress of the totality of modern experience, from its attachment to a social class. Yet the conclusion towards which this study of the interconnexions of literature and society would point does not confirm the cultural diagnosis that Lionel Trilling makes in *Sincerity and Authenticity*. Trilling sympathetically expounds Freud's conclusion that the natural state of man in civilized society is a neurotic one, and argues that the anarchical self-laceration and self-degradation of man expressed in modern literature is bound up with civilization as such, not with a particular condition or organization of society. The alienation, the bitterness, the conflicts expressed in the literature we have here reviewed would seem, however, to belong, in their challenge and despair, their positive as well as negative images, to the specifically modern form of Western civilization, to the nation state, to large-scale economic and administrative structures, and to a class-structure and a variety of religious and ethical beliefs and ideologies that accord with these. Though the 'self-estrangement of spirit' in the Hegelian sense is a necessary and permanent condition of all creative culture, we necessarily must infer that any far-reaching social change must result in a change in the actual and ideological forms of this self-estrangement, and these as we know from history do not inevitably take the negative, sordid, and inhuman forms that Trilling with good reason singles out as characteristic of the imaginative self-projection of the modern consciousness.

Before 1914 Thomas Mann, adopting the cliché that artist and burgher are incompatible, considered his own inclination to reconcile the two to be exceptional. After the war, when in *Lübeck als geistige Lebensform* (1926) he was reviewing his achievement, he came to the conclusion that he had all along been far more of a representative German than he had thought, and that in general the artist, although 'emancipating himself' from the habitual social environment and although speaking 'in a different, freer, more spiritualized form' than his burgher fellows, yet does speak from a general, shared experience. In the *Tischrede* of 1925 Mann puts the same thought: 'You [the writer] think you only give yourself, you speak only about yourself, and lo and behold, you have given something super-personal arising from profound connexions and an unconscious community with others'. The present study has shown that concepts like 'community' and 'others' are more complex than Mann could suggest in an after-dinner speech, but the conviction he expresses might well have served as the hypothesis from which these investigations set out.

Bibliography

The bibliography extends to those social and ideological fields that impinge on literature. It excludes, for reasons of size, imaginative works and purely literary studies; many of the books listed here contain substantial bibliographies of the work of imaginative writers and critical studies of them, for instance B. von Wiese's *Deutsche Dichter der Moderne*, 2nd ed. 1969, and H. Kunisch's *Handbuch der Gegenwartsliteratur*, 1965. For the same reason, though a number of autobiographies are listed, the published correspondence of writers has not been included. It will, however, be readily understood that the well-known editions of the letters of Rilke, Stefan George, Hugo von Hofmannsthal, Thomas Mann, and many other writers are of the greatest importance in a study like the present one. Also, though extensive use has been made of periodicals, it has been possible to refer to specific articles only rarely.

A few abbreviations have been used, e.g. 'dt' for all forms of 'deutsch', 'lit' for all forms of 'Literatur', 'Gesch' for 'Geschichte' etc.

The following major bibliographical aids have been used:

C. G. Kaysers vollständiges Bücherlexikon, Leipzig, from 1911 entitled *Deutsches-Bücherverzeichnis* (an annual register of all publications in Germany).

Kosch, W., *Deutsches Literatur-Lexikon*, revised ed. 4 vols (Bern 1949).

P. Merker and W. Stammler, *Reallexikon der deutschen Literaturgeschichte*, 4 vols (Berlin 1925–41), revised W. Kohlschmidt and W. Mohr (in progress).

Allgemeine deutsche Biographie, 56 vols (Leipzig, 1875–1912) (dead-line 1899), and its sequel *Neue dt. Biographie*, 9 vols (1953–72, unfinished).

Literary and Cultural Periodicals

These are the richest source for the study of cultural trends in this period, particularly those periodicals that carry in addition to articles on literature and art others on social and ideological topics, so that they give an image of the general context of literary culture. Many of these periodicals have been reprinted recently, as indicated below. Most helpful accounts of many of them are given in the following:

Pross, H., *Literatur und Politik* (1963).

Raabe, P., *Die Zeitschriften und Sammlungen des literarischen Expressionismus 1910–21* (1964).

Schlawe, F., *Literarische Zeitschriften*. Teil I, 1885–1910, Teil II, 1910–1933 (2nd revised edition 1965).

In view of the full information given in these books the following list (reaching to about 1918) can be selective and brief. The closing date of a periodical is not given if it survived beyond 1918. Since editors frequently changed, it was necessary in some cases to indicate only the more important names.

Aktion weekly Berlin 1911– , ed. F. Pfemfert (reprint of years 1911–14, ed. Raabe, 1961).

Argonauten, Die monthly Heidelberg 1914–21, ed. E. Blass (Kraus reprint 1969).

Blätter für die Kunst, irregular 'Folgen' Berlin 1892–1919, ed. C. A. Klein (reprint Stefan-George-Stiftung 1968).

Blätter, Die weissen monthly Leipzig 1913–16, Zürich and Berne 1916–18, Berlin 1919–20, ed. R. Schickele (Kraus reprint 1969).

Brenner, Der fortnightly Innsbruck 1910–15, then irregular, ed. L. v. Ficker (Kraus reprint 1969).

Fackel, Die three issues monthly Vienna 1899– , ed. K. Kraus.

Freie Bühne für modernes Leben weekly Berlin 1890, monthly from 1892, ed. O. Brahm, W. Bölsche. Became 1894 *Die neue deutsche Rundschau*, ed. O. Bie; from 1904 *Die neue Rundschau*, ed. O. Bie (Kraus reprint 1890–1903, 1970).

Gegenwart, Die weekly Berlin 1872– , ed. T. Zolling and others.

Gesellschaft, Die monthly Munich 1885–1902, ed. M. G. Conrad (Kraus reprint 1970).

Hilfe, Die weekly Frankfurt 1895, from 1897 Berlin, ed. F. Naumann.

Hochland monthly Munich 1903– , ed. K. Muth.

Hyperion bi-monthly Munich 1908–10, ed. F. Blei and others (Kraus reprint 1970).

Insel, Die monthly Leipzig 1899–1902, ed. O. J. Bierbaum (Kraus reprint 1970).

Jahrbuch für die geistige Bewegung annual Berlin 1910–12, ed. F. Gundolf and F. Wolters.

Jugend illustrated weekly Munich 1896– , ed. G. Hirth.

Kunstwart, Der fortnightly Dresden 1887, from 1894 Munich, ed. F. Avenarius.

März fortnightly Munich 1907–17, from 1911 weekly, ed. L. Thoma, H. Hesse and others, 1913 T. Heuss (Kraus reprint 1970).

Morgen weekly Berlin 1907–9, ed. W. Sombart, G. Brandes, Richard Strauss, H. v. Hofmannsthal and others (Kraus reprint 1970).

Pan (i) illustrated quarterly Berlin 1895–9, ed. O. J. Bierbaum, J. Meier Graefe, from 1897 C. Flaischlen and others.
Pan (ii) fortnightly Berlin 1910–14, from 1912 weekly, ed. P. Cassirer and others, then A. Kerr.
Revolution fortnightly Munich 1913–14, ed. H. Leybold, then F. Jung (Kraus reprint 1969).
Rundschau, Die deutsche monthly Berlin 1874– , ed. J. Rodenberg.
Rundschau, Die neue monthly Berlin 1904– , ed. O. Bie (see *Freie Bühne* above).
Rundschau, Oesterreichische fortnightly Vienna 1904– , various editors.
Rundschau, Wiener fortnightly Vienna 1896–1901, ed. Rudolf Strauss, then C. Christomanos and F. Rappaport (Kraus reprint 1970).
Schaubühne, Die weekly Berlin 1905–18, ed. S. Jacobsohn (became *Die Weltbühne*).
Simplicissimus satirical illustrated weekly Munich 1896– , ed. A. Langen and others.
Sozialistische Monatshefte monthly Berlin 1895– , ed. J. Bloch.
Sturm, Der weekly Berlin 1910– , fortnightly 1914– , monthly 1916– , ed. H. Walden (Kraus reprint 1970).
Süddeutsche Monatshefte monthly Munich 1904– , ed. W. Weigand, K. Hofmiller, F. Naumann and others.
Tat, Die monthly Jena 1909, ed. E. Horneffer, from 1912– E. Diederichs.
Türmer, Der monthly Stuttgart 1898– , ed. J. E. v. Grotthuss.
Ver Sacrum illustrated monthly Vienna 1898–1903, ed. various.
Zeit, Die weekly Vienna 1894–1904, ed. I. Singer, H. Bahr and others.
Zeit, Die neue weekly Stuttgart 1883– , ed. K. Kautsky and others.
Ziel, Das annual Munich 1916, 1918, and later, ed. K. Hiller.
Zukunft, Die weekly Berlin 1892–1922, ed. M. Harden.
Zwanzigste Jahrhundert, Das monthly Berlin 1890–96, ed. E. Bauer, F. Lienhard, H. Mann, T. Schröter in succession.

Selections

Raabe P. (ed.), *Ich schneide die Zeit aus; Expressionismus und Politik in Pfemferts Aktion 1911–18* (1964).
Schütze, C. (ed.), *Simplicissimus. Facsimile Querschnitt* (1963).
Zahn, Eva (ed.), *Jugend. Facsimile Querschnitt* (1966).
Zimmermann, Magdalene (ed.), *Die Gartenlaube als Dokument ihrer Zeit* (1963).

General Political and Social History

Balfour, M., *The Kaiser and his Times* (1964).
Bergsträsser, L., *Gesch. der politischen Parteien in Dtland* (1965).

Clapham, J. H., *Economic Development of France and Germany 1815–1914* (1921).

Crankshaw, E., *The Fall of the House of Habsburg* (1963).

Dahrendorf, R., *Gesellschaft und Demokratie in Dtland* (1965), (*Society and Democracy in Germany*, 1968).

Demeter, K., *Das dt. Offizierkorps in seinen historisch-soziologischen Grundlagen* (1930).

Eyck, E., *Bismarck*, 3 vols (1941–4). *Das persönliche Regiment Wilhelms II*, 1948.

Feldman, G. D., *Army, Industry and Labor in Germany, 1914–18* (1966).

Fischer, F., *Griff nach der Weltmacht. Die Kriegszielpolitik des kaiserlichen Dtlands, 1914–18* (1962).

Gollwitzer, H., *Europe in the Age of Imperialism 1880–1914* (1969).

Henderson, W. O., *The Industrialisation of Europe 1780–1914* (1969).

Kehr, E., *Der Primat der Innenpolitik*, ed. Wehler (1965).

Mann, G., *Dt. Geschichte des 19 und 20 Jahrh.* (1958), (*The History of Germany since 1789*, 1968).

Mayhew, H., *German Life and Manners in Saxony* (1865).

Mehring, F., *Deutsch Geschichte* (1910).

Mommsen, W., *Politische Gesch. von Bismarck bis zur Gegenwart, 1850–1933* (1935). *Deutsche Parteiprogramme*, 3 Teile (texts) (1951).

Naumann, F., *Die politischen Parteien* (1910).

Rassow, H., *Dt. Geschichte im Uberlick*, with classified bibliographies (1953).

Ritter, G., *Die Arbeiterbewegung im wilhelminischen Reich* (1959).

Rosenberg, A., *Die Entstehung der dt. Republik 1871–1918* (1928), (*The Birth of the German Republic*, 1931).

Ryder, J., *The Independent Social Democratic Party and the German Revolution 1917–20* (1958).

Schnabel, F., *Dt. Geschichte im 19 Jahrh.*, 4 vols. (1929).

Schorske, C. E., *German Social Democracy 1905–17* (1965).

Sombart, W., *Die dt. Volkswirtschaft im 19 Jahrh.* (1901). *Der moderne Kapitalismus* (1902). *Sozialismus und soziale Bewegung im 19 Jahrh.* (1908).

Taylor, A. J. P., *The Habsburg Monarchy 1815–1918* (1941). *Bismarck: the man and the statesman* (1955).

Intellectuals and the War 1914–18 (see also *Autobiographies* and *Periodicals*)

Bernhardi, F. v., *Dtland und der nächste Krieg* (1911).

Binding, R., *Aus dem Kriege*, diaries (1925).

Blei, F., *Menschliche Betrachtungen zum Krieg* (1916).

Carossa, H., *Rumänisches Tagebuch* (1924).

Dehmel, R., *Zwischen Volk und Menschheit* (1919).

Eucken, R., *Die weltgeschichtliche Bedeutung des dt. Geistes* (1914).

Förster, F. W., *Mein Kampf gegen das militaristische und nationalistische Dtland* (1920).

Förster, F. W., Otto, R. and others, *Geistige und sittliche Wirkungen des Kriegs in Dtland* (1927).

Harnack, A. v., Troeltsch, E., Meinecke, F. and others, *Die deutsche Freiheit* (1917).

Hiller, K. (ed.), *Das Ziel. Jahrbücher* (1916, 1918, 1919, 1920).

Hofmannsthal, H. v., 'Die Idee Europa' (1916) 'Die österreichische Idee' (1917), (*Gesam. Werke*, ed. H. Steiner, *Prosa* iii, 1952).

Kraus, K., *Die letzten Tage der Menschheit* (1922). *Werke*, ed. H. Fischer, xiii, 'Weltgericht'.

Krieck, E., *Die dt. Staatsidee* (1917).

Lienhard, F., *Dtlands europäische Sendung* (1914).

Mann, H., 'Zola' (*Die weissen Blätter*, 1915).

Mann, T., *Betrachtungen eines Unpolitischen* (1918).

Marwitz, B. v. der, *Stirb und Werde*, ed. H. v. Königswald (1931).

Meinecke, F., *Die dt. Erhebung von 1914*, essays and addresses (1914).

Meinecke, F., Oncken, H. and others, *Deutschland und der Weltkrieg* (1915).

Natorp, P., *Von der Gerechtigkeit der dt. Sache* (1915). *Der Tag des Deutschen* (1915). *Deutscher Weltberuf*, 2 vols (1918).

Naumann, F., *Mitteleuropa* (1915).

Preuss, H., *Das dt Volk und die Politik* (1915).

Rohrbach, P., *Der dt. Gedanke in der Welt* (1914). *Zum Weltvolk hindurch* (1914).

W. Rothe (ed.) *Der Aktivismus 1915–20*, texts (1969).

Scheler, M., *Der Genius des Kriegs und der dt. Krieg* (1915).

Simmel, G., *Der Krieg und die geistigen Entscheidungen*, essays and addresses (1917).

Sombart, W., *Händler und Helden* (1915).

Sternheim, C., *Berlin oder Juste milieu* (1920).

Troeltsch, E., *Dt. Glaube und dt. Sitte in unserem grossen Kriege* (1915).

Witkop, P. (ed.), *Kriegsbriefe gefallener Studenten* (1928).

Ziegler, L., *Der dt. Mensch* (1915).

Ziegler, T., *Der Krieg als Erzieher* (1914).

The Jewish Question

Contemporary Texts

Ahlwardt, H., *Der Verzweiflungskampf der arischen Völker mit dem Judentum* (1887).

Alberti, C., 'Judentum und Antisemitismus', *Die Gesellschaft* v and vi (1889–90).

Bartels, A., *Die dt. Dichtung der Gegenwart*, 8th ed. (1910). *Judentum und Literatur* (1912). *Rasse und Volkstum*, collected essays (1920).

Blüher, H., *Secessio judaica* (1922).

Braunthal, J., *In search of the millenium* (1945).

Brod, M., *Streitbares Leben* (1960).

Brod, M., Buber, M., Wolfskehl, K., Wassermann, J., and others, *Vom Judentum* (1913).

Buber, M., *Ereignisse und Begegnungen* (1917). *Reden über das Judentum* (1923).

Chamberlain, H. S., *Die Grundlagen des 19 Jahrh.* (1899).

Dühring, E., *Die Judenfrage als Racen-, Sitten-, und Kulturfrage* (1881),

Freud, S., *Autobiographische Studie* (*Werke*, 1928, II; *Complete Works*. XX, 1959).

Goldstein, M., 'Deutsch-jüdischer Parnass', *Der Kunstwart* (1912), reprinted with further material *Year-book of the Leo Baeck Institute*, ii (1957).

Grossmann, S., *Ich war begeistert* (1931).

Harden, M., 'Stoecker' and 'Karl Lueger', *Köpfe* i and ii, 44th ed. (1921).

Holitscher, A., *Lebensgesch. eines Rebellen* (1915).

Krojanker, G. (ed.), *Juden in der dt. Literatur* (1922).

Lagarde, P. de, *Deutsche Schriften* (1886).

Langbehn, J., *Rembrandt als Erzieher* (anon. 1890) (enlarged from the 37th ed., 1891).

Lessing, T., *Europa und Asien* (1914). *Der jüdische Selbsthass* (1930). *Einmal und nie wieder* (1935).

Marcuse, L., *Mein zwanzigstes Jahrhundert* (1960).

Marr, W., *Der Sieg des Judentums* (1873).

Rathenau, W., 'Höre Israel', *Die Zukunft* v (1897). *Zur Kritik der Zeit* (1912).

Schnitzler, A., *Jugend in Wien* (1968).

Sombart, W., *Die Juden und das Wirtschaftsleben* (1911). *Die Zukunft der Juden* (1912).

Sombart, W., Naumann, F., Nordau, M., Weber, M., Wedekind, F., Dehmel, R., Bahr, H., and others, *Judentaufen*, ed. A. Landsberger (1912).

Toller, E., *Eine Jugend in Dtland* (1933).

Treitschke, H. v., 'Unsere Aussichten', *Preussische Jahrb.* (1879).

Treitschke, H., Bresslau, H., Graetz, H., Cohen, H., Mommsen, T., and others, *Der Berliner Antisemitismusstreit*, ed. W. Boehlich, texts (1965).

Wassermann, J., *Mein Weg als Deutscher und Jude* (1933).

Weininger, O., *Geschlecht und Charakter* (1903).

Werfel, F., *Zwischen Oben und Unten* (1946).

Zweig, S., *Die Welt von Gestern* (1947).

Studies

Brod, M., *Der Prager Kreis* (1966).

Finkelstein, L., *The Jews*, 2 vols (1949).

Kohn, H., *Karl Kraus, Arthur Schnitzler, Otto Weininger. Aus dem jüdischen Wien der Jahrhundertwende* (1962).

Liebeschütz, H., *Von Georg Simmel zu Franz Rosenzweig* (1970).

Parkes, J., *The Emergence of the Jewish Problem, 1878–1939* (1946).

Pulzer, J. G., *The Rise of Political Anti-Semitism in Germany and Austria* (1964).

Silbergleit, H., *Die Bevölkerungs- und Berufsverhältnisse der Juden im dt. Reich* (1930).

Weltsch, R. (ed.) and others, *Yearbooks of the Leo Baeck Institute* (these contain much valuable information).

The City

Arendt, M., Gandert, O. F. and Faden E., *Geschichte der Stadt Berlin* (1937).

Bab, J., *Die Berliner Bohème* (1905).

Brod, M., *Der Prager Kreis* (1966).

Bücher, K., Ratzel, F., Simmel, G. and others, *Die Groszstadt. Vorträge und Aufsätze zur Städteausstellung*, (1903), (*Jahrb. der Gehe-Stiftung, IX*).

Demetz, P., *René Rilkes Prager Jahre* (1953).

Endel, A., *Die Schönheit der grossen Stadt* (1908).

Hellpach, W., *Nervosität und Kultur* (1902).

Janik, A. and Toulmin, S., *Wittgenstein's Vienna* (1973),

Kralik, R., *Gesch. der Stadt Wien* (1926).

Leixner, O. v., *Soziale Briefe aus Berlin 1888–91* (1891).

Lienhard, F., *Die Vorherrschaft Berlins* (1900).

Mumford, Lewis, *The City in History* (1961).

Pascal, R., 'Georg Simmels "Die Groszstädte und das Geistesleben"', (1969). *Gestaltungsgeschichte und Gesellschaftsgeschichte*, ed. H. Kreuzer (1969).

Rölleke, A., *Die Stadt bei Stadler, Heym, und Trakl* (1966).

Rothfels, H. (ed.), *Berlin in Vergangenheit und Gegenwart* (1961).

Scheffler, K., *Berlin: Wandlung einer Stadt* (1931).

Schuster, R., *Das Berlinertum in Literatur, Musik, und Kunst* (anon.), (1895).

Simmel, G., *Philosophie des Geldes* (1900). *Die Groszstädte und das Geistesleben* (1903), (See above, Bücher, K.) reprinted in *Brücke und Tor*, essays by Simmel selected by M. Landmann (1957) and trans. in *Georg Simmel*, ed. K. H. Wolff (1959).

Tietze, H., *Wien* (1923).

Tönnies, F., *Gemeinschaft und Gesellschaft* (1887).

Tramer, H., 'Prague, City of Three Peoples', *Yearbook of Leo Baeck Institute*, IX (1964).

Wagenbach, K., *Franz Kafka, Eine Biographie seiner Jugend, 1883–1912* (1958).

Weber, M., *The City*, ed. and trans. D. Martindale and G. Neuwirth (1958).

Ziegler, K., *Die Berliner Gesellschaft und die Literatur* (see above, Rothfels).

The Emancipation of Women

Bachofen, J., *Das Mutterrecht* (1861).

Bäumer, Gertrud, *Die Frau in Volkswirtschaft und Staatsleben der Gegenwart* (1914). *Lebensweg durch eine Zeitenwende* (1933).

Bebel, A., *Die Frau und der Sozialismus* (1883).

Braun, Lily, *Frauenbewegung und Sexualethik* (1909). *Memoiren einer Sozialistin*, 2 vols (1909–11).

Büchner, Louise, *Die Frau* (1878).

Engels, F., *Ursprung der Familie* (1884).

Erler, J., *Ehescheidungsrecht und Ehescheidungsprozess* (1893). *Der aussereheliche Geschlechtsverkehr. Seine straf- und zivilrechtlichen Folgen* (1898).

Hirschfeld, M., *Der Konträrsexualismus in bezug auf Ehe und Frauenfrage* (1895).

Key, Ellen, *Das Jahrhundert des Kindes*, trans. from the Swedish (1902). *Die Frauenbewegung* (1909).

Lange, Helene, *Frauenbildung* (1889). *Die Frauenbewegung in ihren modernen Problemen* (1907). *Fünfzig Jahre Frauenbewegung* (1915). *Lebenserinnerungen* (1920).

Lange, H. and Bäumer, G. (eds), *Handbuch der Frauenbewegung*, 4 parts (1901–2).

Mill, J. S., *The Subjection of Women* (1869).

Pataky, Sophie, *Lexikon deutscher Frauen der Feder*, 2 vols (1898).

Riehl, W. H., *Die Familie*, 9th enlarged ed. (1882).

Zahn-Harnack, Agnes, *Die Frauenbewegung* (1928).

Zetkin, Clara, *Die Arbeiterinnen- und Frauenfrage der Gegenwart* (*Berliner Arbeiterbibliothek* I, Serie 3).

Sexuality and Morality

Andreas-Salomé, Lou, *Die Erotik* (1910).

Belmore, H., 'Sexual Elements in Rilke's Poetry', *German Life and Letters* XI (1966).

Berg, L., *Das sexuelle Problem in Leben und Kunst* (1891).

Bierbaum, O. J. 'Die pornographische Hochflut', *Morgen* (1907).

Blüher, H., *Die deutsche Wandervögelbewegung als erotisches Phänomen* (1912). *Die Rolle der Erotik in der männlichen Gesellschaft*, 2 vols (1917-19).

Bölsche, W., *Das Liebesleben in der Natur*, 3 vols (1898-1902).

Freud, S., *Die Traumdeutung* (*The Interpretation of Dreams*), (1900). *Das Unbehagen in der Kultur* (*Civilisation and its Discontents*),(1929). *Gesam. Werke*, ed, Anna Freud and others (1940-68); *Complete Works*, ed. J Strachey and others (1953-65).

Hirschfeld, M., *Paragraph 175. Die homosexuelle Frage im Urteil der Zeitgenossen* (1898).

Krafft-Ebing, R. v., *Psychopathia sexualis* (1886). *Der Conträrsexuale vor dem Strafrichter* (1894).

Kraus, K., *Werke*, ed. H. Fischer, 13 vols (1952-65), especially, XI, 'Sittlichkeit und Kriminalität' and XII, 'Die chinesische Mauer'. (Selections in K.K., *Die chinesische Mauer* (1967), Fischer Bücherei 779).

Meisel-Hess, Grete, *Die sexuelle Krise* (1909).

Michels, R., *Grenzen der Geschlechtsmoral* (1914).

Moll, A., *Die konträre Sexualempfindung* (1891).

Moll, A. (ed.), *Handbuch der Sexualwissenschaften mit besonderer Berücksichtigung der kulturgeschichtlichen Beziehung* (1912).

Petersen, W., *Die Prostitution in Berlin* (*Zeitfragen des christlichen Lebens*), (1887).

Przybyszewsky, S., 'Erotomanie', *Aktion* (1913).

Starkenburg, H., *Das sexuelle Elend der obern Stände* (1898).

Weininger, O., *Geschlecht und Charakter* (1903).

Youth and Culture

Becker, H., *German Youth: Bond or Free* (1946).

Blüher, H., *Wandervögel. Gesch. einer Jugendbewegung* (1912).

Bondy, C., *Die proletarische Jugendbewegung in Dtland* (1922).

Foerster, F. W., *Jugendlehre* (1906).

Frobenius, Else, *Mit uns zieht die neue Zeit* (1927).

Gurlitt, L., *Die Schule* (1907).

Krong, W., *Sein zum Tode* (1955).

Pannwitz, R., *Die Erziehung* (1909).

Paulsen, F., *Die dt. Universitäten und das Universitätsstudium* (1902). *Die höheren Schulen Dtlands und ihr Lehrerstand in ihrem Verhältnis zum Staat und zur geistigen Kultur* (1904).

Paulsen, F., *Geschichte des gelehrten Unterrichts ... vom Ausgang des Mittelalters bis zur Gegenwart*, 2 vols (1919-21).

Pross, H., *Jugend, Eros, Politik* (1964).

Samuel, R. H. and Thomas, R. H., *Education and Society in Modern Germany* (1949).

Wyneken, G., *Was ist Jugendkultur?* (1914). *Die neue Jugend* (1914).
Ziemer, B. and Wolf, H., *Wandervogel und Freideutsche Jugend* (1961).

Religion and the Churches

The encyclopedia *Die Religion in Geschichte und Gegenwart*, 6 vols. 3rd ed. by Kurt Galling (1957–62) is very helpful. Apart from the specialist theological and church periodicals, the following are addressed to a wider public and concerned also with social and literary matters: *Die Christliche Welt* (Protestant), 1886– , *Die Hilfe* (Protestant), 1895– , *Der Türmer* (Protestant), 1898– , *Hochland* (Catholic) 1903– , and *Der Gral* (Catholic) 1906– . Account has also to be taken of periodicals like *Die Sphinx* (occultist), *Der Monist* (T. Haeckel), and *Der Atheist* (Social Democratic party).

Blavatsky, H. P., *The Secret Doctrine*, trans. as *Die Geheimlehre* (1897–8).
Bonus, A., *Dt. Glaube* (1897). *Zur religiösen Krisis*, 4 vols (1911–12). *Zur Germanisierung des Christentums* (1911).
Boventer, H., *Rilkes Zyklus 'Aus dem Nachlass des Grafen C.W.'* (1969).
Buber, M., *Ekstatische Konfessionen* (1909).
Drews, A., *Die Christusmythe* (1909).
Drews, P., 'Die freien religiösen Gemeinden der Gegenwart', *Ztschr. für Theologie und Kirche* XI (1901).
Egidy, M., *Ernste Gedanken*, (anon.), (1890).
Eucken, R., *Die Einheit des Geisteslebens* (1888).
Foerster, F. W., *Christentum und Klassenkampf* (1909).
Frank W., *Hofprediger Adolf Stoecker* (1928).
Göhre, P., *Drei Monate Fabrikarbeiter und Handwerksbursche* (1891).
Haeckel, T., *Die Welträtsel* (1899).
Harnack, A. v., *Lehrbuch der Dogmengesch.*, 3 vols (1886–90). *Das Wesen des Christentums* (1900). *Reden und Aufsätze*, 2 vols (1904). *Aus Wissenschaft und Leben*, 2 vols (1911).
James, W., *The Varieties of Religious Experience* (1902).
Kaftan, I., *Glaube und Dogma* (1889).
Kalthoff, A., *Die Religion der Modernen* (1905).
Kautsky, K., *Der Ursprung des Christentums* (1908).
Kupisch, K., *Zwischen Idealismus und Massendemokratie. Eine Geschichte der evangelischen Kirche in Deutschland, 1815–1945* (1955). *Quellen zur Gesch. des dt. Protestantismus 1871–1945* (1965).
Lagarde, P. de, *Die Religion der Zukunft* (1878). *Deutsche Schriften* (1886).
Mann, T., 'Okkulte Erlebnisse', *Die neue Rundschau* (1924).
Mohme, E. T., *Die freireligiösen Anschauungen im Drama und Roman der neuren dt. Literatur 1885–1914* (1927).
Naumann, F., *Briefe über Religion* (1903).

Otto, R., *Das Heilige* (1917).

Prel, C. du, *Entdeckung der Seele durch die Geheimwissenschaften*, 2 vols (1894).

Ritschl, A., *Die Christliche Lehre der Rechtfertigung*, 3 vols, 4th ed. (1895).

Robinson, J. M. *The Beginnings of Dialectic Theology*, 2 vols (1968).

Schrenck-Notzing, A. v., *Materialisationsphänomene* (1914).

Schweitzer, A., *Die Geschichte der Leben-Jesu-Forschung* (1906),(trans. as *The Quest of the historic Jesus*). *Denken und Tat*, ed. R. Grabs (selections), (1950).

Simmel, G., *Die Religion* (1906).

Spiero, H., *Die Heilandsgestalt in der neueren dt. Dichtung* (1926).

Steiner, R., *Goethes Weltanschauung* (1897). *Theosophie* (1904). *Die Geheimwissenschaft* (1910).

Tillich, P., *Perspectives in 19th and 20th century Protestant Theology*, ed. C. Braaten (1967).

Troeltsch, E., *Die Soziallehren der christlichen Kirchen und Gruppen*, 2 vols (1908–12), (*Gesam. Schriften* I, 1912). *Gesam. Schriften*, vols 2 and 4 (1913 and 1925), contain many essays on religious, ethical, and social matters.

Weber, Max, *Die protestantische Ethik und der Geist des Kapitalismus* (1905), *Gesam. Aufsätze zur Religionssoziologie*, 3 vols (1920–21), (trans. E. Fischoff as *The Sociology of Religion*, 1963).

Positivism and its critics, Lebensphilosophie, Nietzsche

Andreas-Salomé, Lou, *Friedrich Nietzsche* (1894).

Antoni, C., *From History to Sociology* (1959). (Dilthey, Troeltsch, Meinecke, Max Weber, Wölfflin.)

Bertram, E., *Nietzsche* (1918).

Bollnow, O. F., *Wilhelm Dilthey*, 2nd ed. (1955). *Die Lebensphilosophie*, 1958.

Brandes, G., *Nietzsche* (1889).

Buber, M., *The Philosophy*, ed. Schilpp and Friedman (1969).

Büchner, L., *Kraft und Stoff* (1855).

Cohen, H., *Ethik des reinen Willens* (1904).

Dilthey, W., *Einleitung in die Geisteswissenschaften* (1883); *Einleitung in die Philosophie des Lebens; Der Aufbau der geschichtlichen Welt in den Geisteswissenschaften. Gesam. Schriften* (1922–36), vols. 1, 5–6, 7.

Engels, F., *Herrn E. Dührings Umwälzung der Wissenschaft*, 3rd ed. (1894), (trans. as *Anti-Dühring*).

Eucken, R., *Die Einheit des Geisteslebens* (1888).

Gundolf, F., *Goethe* (1916).

Habermas, J., *Erkenntnis und Interesse* (1968).

Haeckel, T., *Natürliche Schöpfungsgeschichte* (1868). *Die Welträtsel* (1899).

Hodges, H. A., *Wilhelm Dilthey* (1944), (introduction and selections).

Husserl, E., *Logische Untersuchungen*, 2 parts (1900–1).

Klages, L., *Vom Wesen des Bewusstseins* (1921). *Der Geist als Widersacher der Seele*, 3 vols (1929–32).

Lange, F. A., *Gesch. des Materialismus und Kritik seiner Bedeutung in der Gegenwart*, 2 vols (1873).

Lukács, G., *Die Zerstörung der Vernunft* (1954).

Mach, E., *Die Analyse der Empfindungen und das Verhältnis des Physischen zum Psychischen* (1886).

Mauthner, F., *Beiträge zu einer Kritik der Sprache* (1901–2). *Die Sprache* (1907).

Meyer, R. M., *Die dt. Literatur des 19 Jahr.*, 3rd ed. (1906). *Grundriss der neueren dt. Literaturgesch.* (1902, 2nd ed. 1907). *Nietzsche, Leben und Werke* (1913).

Misch, G., *Lebensphilosophie und Phänomenologie* (1930).

Nietzsche, F., especially *Menschliches, Allzumenschliches* (1878); *Also Sprach Zarathustra* (1883–91); *Jenseits von Gut und Böse* (1886); and *Der Wille zur Macht*, first published 1901 in the first collected edition, *Werke* (1895–1904). The most convenient and reliable modern edition is *Werke* 3 vols, ed. K. Schlechta (1954).

Oehler, M., *Die deutsche Nietzsche-Literatur seit 1890* (1938).

Rée, P., *Der Ursprung der moralischen Empfindungen* (1877). *Die Entstehung des Gewissens* (1885).

Richter, R., *Nietzsche* (1903).

Rickert, H., *Die Grenzen der naturwissenschaftlichen Begriffsbildung*, 2 parts (1896, 1902). *Die Philosophie des Lebens* (1920).

Riehl, A., *F. Nietzsche, der Künstler und der Denker* (1895).

Scherer, W., *Gesch. der dt. Literatur* (1880–2).

Schlaf, J., *Der 'Fall' Nietzsche* (1907).

Simmel, G., *Die Probleme der Geschichtsphilosophie* (1892). *Einleitung in die Moralphilosophie*, 2 vols (1892–3). *Schopenhauer und Nietzsche* (1907).

Steiner, R., *Nietzsche. Ein Kämpfer gegen seine Zeit* (1895).

Strauss, D. F., *Der alte und der neue Glaube* (1872).

Troeltsch, E., *Der Historismus und seine Probleme* (*Gesam. Schriften*, III, 1922).

Vaihinger, H., *Nietzsche als Philosoph* (1902). *Die Philosophie des Als Ob* (1911).

Weber, M., *Gesam. Aufsätze zur Wissenschaftslehre*, ed. J. Winckelmann (1951).

Wolff, K. H. (ed.), *Georg Simmel*, essays by various authors on G.S. (1959).

Wundt, W., *Essays* (1885).

Political and Cultural Ideology

Contemporary Texts:

Bloch, E., *Der Geist der Utopie* (1918).

Burckhardt, J., *Die Kultur der Renaissance in Italien* (1860). *Weltgeschichtliche Betrachtungen* (1905).

Chamberlain, H. S., *Die Grundlagen des 19 Jahrh.* (1899).

Conradi, H., *Wilhelm II und die junge Generation* (1889), (*Gesam, Schriften* ed. Ssymank and Peters, 3 vols, 1911).

Delbrück, H., *Regierung und Volkswille* (1914).

Dessauer, F., *Technische Kultur?* (1908).

Fuchs, G., *Der Kaiser, die Kultur, und die Kunst* (1902).

Harden, M., *Köpfe* 2 vols (44th ed. 1921). *Prozesse* (17th ed. 1921).

Heimann, M., *Prosaische Schriften*, 3 vols (1918). *M. Heimann* (selections), ed. W. Lehmann (1960).

Hellpach, W., *Nervosität und Kultur* (1902).

Kessler, H. Graf, *Walter Rathenau* (1928).

Kotowski, G. (ed.), *Das Wilhelminische Reich. Stimmen der Zeitgenossen* (1965).

Lagarde, P. de, *Deutsche Schriften* (1886).

Lamprecht, K., *Dt. Geschichte*, 19 vols (1892–1913). *Dt. Geschichte der jüngsten Vergangenheit*, 2 vols (1912–13).

Langbehn, J., *Rembrandt als Erzieher* (anon.), (1890).

Lange, F., *Reines Deutschtum* (1893).

Lassalle, F., *Reden und Schriften*, ed. E. Bernstein, 3 vols (1892–3).

Mann, H., 'Geist und Tat', *Pan* (1910). 'Zola', *Die weissen Blätter* (1915).

Mann, T., *Betrachtungen eines Unpolitischen* (1918). *Adel des Geistes*, selected essays (1945).

Marx, K., *Das Kapital* (1867).

Marx, K. and Engels, F., *Gesam. Schriften 1841–50*, ed. F. Mehring, 4 vols (1902).

Mehring, F., *Karl Marx. Geschichte seines Lebens* (1918).

Meinecke, F., *Weltbürgertum und Nationalstaat* (1908).

Moeller van den Bruck, A., *Der preussische Stil* (1916). *Das Recht der jungen Völker* (1919).

Naumann, F., *Mitteleuropa* (1915).

Nietzsche, F., *Unzeitgemässe Betrachtungen* (1873–6). *Menschliches, Allzumenschliches* (1878). *Also sprach Zarathustra* (1883–91). *Jenseits von Gut und Böse* (1886). *Der Wille zur Macht* (1901).

Nordau, M., *Die conventionellen Lügen der Kulturmenschheit* (1883). *Entartung* (1893).

Paulsen, F., *Philosophia militans. Gegen Klerikalismus und Naturalismus* (1901). *Zur Ethik und Politik* (1905).

Rathenau, W., *Zur Kritik der Zeit* (1912). *Zur Mechanik des Geistes* (1913). *Von kommenden Dingen* (1917).
Ratzel, F., *Politische Geographie* (1897).
Schoeps, H. J. (ed.), *Zeitgeist im Wandel. I. Das Wilhelminische Zeitalter*, texts (1966).
Simmel, G., *Philosophie des Geldes* (1900).
Sombart, W., *Der Bourgeois* (1913).
Spengler, O., *Untergang des Abendlandes* (I, 1918; II, 1922).
Tönnies, F., *Gemeinschaft und Gesellschaft* (1887).
Treitschke, H. v., *Zehn Jahre dt. Kämpfe*, (1879); *Neue Folge* (1896). *Politik*, ed. Cornicelius, 2 vols (1897–8).
Troeltsch, E., *Deutscher Geist und Westeuropa*, ed. H. Baron (1925), (essays and addresses).
Weber, M., *Gesam. Aufsätze zur Soziologie und Sozialpolitik*, ed. Marianne Weber (1924), (*Essays in Sociology*, trans. Gerth and Mills, 1948). *Gesam. politische Schriften* (1921).
Wolters, F., *Herrschaft und Dienst* (1909).
Ziegler, T., *Die geistigen und sozialen Strömungen des 19 Jahrh.* (1901).

Studies

Antoni, C., *From History to Sociology*, trans. H. White (1959).
Boehn, M. v., *Die Mode im 19 Jahrh.*, iv. *1871–1914* (1925).
Dronberger, I., *The political thought of Max Weber* (1971).
Farquharson, A. (ed.), *The German Mind and Outlook* (1945).
Gebauer, K., *Dt. Kulturgeschichte der Neuzeit* (1932).
Freud, S., *Das Unbehagen in der Kultur* (*Civilisation and its Discontents*), (1929).
Gooch, G. P., *History and Historians in the 19th century* (1920).
Habermas, J., *Erkenntnis und Interesse* (1968).
Hamann, R., and Hermand, J., *Dt. Kunst und Kultur von der Gründerzeit bis zum Expressionismus*, 4 vols (1959–67). i. *Gründerzeit* (1965). ii. *Naturalismus* (1959). iii. *Impressionismus* (1960). iv. *Stilkunst* (1967).
Heuss, T., *Friedrich Naumann* (1937).
Jackson, H., *The eighteen-nineties* (1913).
Korsch, K., *Karl Marx* (1938).
Lübbe, H., *Politische Philosophie in Dtland* (1963).
Lukács, G., *Die Zerstörung der Vernunft* (1954).
Mannheim, K., *Ideologie und Utopie* (1929), (*Ideology and Utopia*, 1936). 'Ideologische und soziologische Interpretation der geistigen Gebilde', *Jahrbuch für Soziologie* II (1926).
Mayer, G., *Friedrich Engels*, 2 vols (1934).
Mayer, J. P., *Max Weber and German Politics* (1944).
Mohler, A., *Die konservative Revolution in Dtland* (1950).

Mommsen, W. J., *Max Weber und die dt. Politik, 1890–1920* (1959).
Pascal, R., 'Nationalism and the German Intellectuals' (see Farquharson above). *The Growth of Modern Germany* (1946).
'Moeller van den Bruck', *The Third Reich*, ed. E. Vermeil (1955).
Pflaum, M., 'Kultur und Civilisation', *Wirkendes Wort* XV (1965).
Pfeiler, W. K., *War and the German Mind* (1941).
Pross, H., *Die Zerstörung der dt. Politik* (1959).
Steinhausen, G., *Dt. Geistes- und Kulturgeschichte von 1870 bis zur Gegenwart* (1931).
Stern, F., *The Politics of Cultural Despair* (1961), (Lagarde, Langbehn, Moeller v.d. Bruck.)

Literature and its Context

Contemporary Texts

Alberti, C., 'Die Bourgeoisie und die Kunst', *Die Gesellschaft* IV (1888).
Bab, J., *Die Berliner Bohème* (1905).
Bahr, H., *Die Überwindung des Naturalismus* (1891).
Bartels, A., *Die dt. Dichtung der Gegenwart* (1898, 8th enlarged ed. 1910).
Berg, L., *Der Naturalismus. Zur Psychologie der modernen Kunst* (1892). *Der Übermensch in der modernen Literatur* (1897).
Bölsche, W., *Die naturwissenschaftlichen Grundlagen der Poesie* (1887).
Bücher, K., *Arbeit und Rhythmus* (1896).
Conrad, M. G., *Von Zola bis Gerhart Hauptmann* (1902).
Dilthey, W., *Das Erlebnis und die Dichtung* (1905).
Edschmid, C., *Frühe Manifeste: Epochen des Expressionismus* (1957).
Einstein, C., *Gesam. Werke*, ed. E. Nef (1962).
Ellman, R. and Fiedelson, C. (eds.), *The Modern Tradition. Backgrounds*, critical documents (1965).
Ernst, P., *Der Weg zur Form* (1906, enlarged ed. 1928).
Francke, K., *A History of German Literature as determined by social forces* (1901). *German Ideals of Today* (1907).
Freud, S., *Psychoanalytische Studien an Werken der Dichtung und der Kunst* (1924), (*Complete Works*, IX).
Friedmann, H. and Mann, O., *Expressionismus*, documents, (1956).
George, S., *Der George-Kreis*, ed. G. P. Landmann (selections), (1965).
Gottschall, R. v., 'Die Lektüre des heutigen Lesepublikums', *Deutsche Revue* XXXIII (1908).
Hart, H., *Literarische Erinnerungen 1880–1905* (*Gesam. Werke* III, 1907).
Heym, G., *Dokumente zu seinem Leben und Werk*, ed. Schneider and Burckhardt (1968).
Hofmannsthal, H. v., 'Der Dichter und diese Zeit' (1907), (*Gesam. Werke*, ed. H. Steiner, *Prosa* II, 1951).

Holz, A., *Die Kunst. Ihr Wesen und ihre Gesetze* (1891). *Das Werke*, X, (1925).

Huelsenbeck, R., *Dada. Eine literarische Dokumentation* (1964).

Landsberg, H., *Nietzsche und die dt. Literatur* (1902).

Lublinski, S., *Die Bilanz der Moderne* (1901). *Der Ausgang der Moderne* (1909).

Mann, T., *Rede und Antwort*, collected essays (1922).

Mayer, Hans (ed.), *Dt. Literaturkritik im 20 Jahrh.*, (1965).

Mehring, F., *Die Lessinglegende* (1892). *Gesam. Schriften zur Literaturgesch.*, 2 vols, ed. Fuchs (1929).

Moeller van den Bruck, A., *Die moderne Literatur in Gruppen- und Einzeldarstellungen*, (1899–1902). *Die Zeitgenossen* (1906).

Pörtner, P. (ed.), *Literatur-Revolution 1910–25. Dokumente* (1961).

Raabe, P. (ed.), *Expressionismus. Der Kampf um eine literarische Bewegung*, texts (1965). *Ich schneide die Zeit aus. Expressionismus und Politik in Pfemferts Aktion*, texts (1964).

Rank, B. O., *Der Künstler. Ansätze zu einer Sexualpathologie* (1907). *Das Inzestmotiv in Dichtung und Sage* (1912).

Rothe, W. (ed.), *Der Aktivismus 1915–20*, texts (1969).

Ruprecht, E. (ed.), *Lit. Manifeste des Naturalismus 1880–92* (1962). *Lit. Manifeste der Jahrhundertwende 1890-1910* (1970).

Schröder, O., *Vom papiernen Stil* (1889).

Soergel, A., *Dichtung und Dichter der Zeit* (1911).

Wustmann, G., *Allerhand Sprachdummheiten* (1891).

Studies

Adorno, T. W., *Noten zur Literatur*, 3 vols (1958–61–65).

Bergsträsser, A., 'Die Dichtung und der Mensch des technologischen Zeitalters', *Merkur* VII (1953).

Böckmann, P., 'Die Bedeutung Nietzsches für die Situation der modernen Literatur', *DVLG* 27 (1953).

Boonstra, P. E., *H. Mann als politischer Schriftsteller* (1945).

Bradbury, M., *The social context of modern English literature* (1971).

Brentano, B., *Kapitalismus und schöne Literatur* (1930).

Brinkmann, R., 'Expressionismus-Probleme. Forschungsbericht', *DVLG* 33–4 (1959–60).

Broch, H., 'Hofmannsthal und seine Zeit', *Dichtung und Erkennen* I (1955).

Brombacher, K., *Der dt. Bürger im Literaturspiegel von Lessing bis Sternheim* (1920).

Coghlan, B. L. D., *Hofmannsthal's Festival Dramas* (1964).

Demetz, P., *Marx, Engels, und die Dichter* (1959).

Dietze, K., *Diederichs und seine Zeitschriften* (1940).

Dörffel, M., *Kurt Tucholsky als Politiker*, diss (Berlin 1965).

Dosenheimer, E., *Das dt. soziale Drama von Lessing bis Sternheim* (1949).

Drahn, E., *Gesch. des dt. Buch- und Zeitschriftenhandels* (1916).

Emrich, W., *Protest und Verheissung* (1960).

Fischer, S., *S. F. Verlag. Vollständiges Verzeichnis der Werke . . . mit Anmerkungen zur Verlagsgesch, 1886–1956* (1956).

Fülberth, G., *Proletarische Partei und bürgerliche Literatur* (1972).

Greiner, M., *Die Entstehung der modernen Unterhaltungsliteratur* (1964).

Haake, W. (ed.), *Handbuch des Feuilletons*, 3 vols (1951–3).

Hamburger, M., *From Prophecy to Exorcism* (1965).

Hauser, A., *Sozialgesch. der Kunst und Literatur* (1953).

Heller, E., *The Disinherited Mind* (1952).

Hermand, J., 'Zur Literatur der Gründerzeit' and 'Expressionismus als Revolution', *Von Mainz nach Weimar* (1969).

Hohendahl, P. Y., *Das Bild der bürgerlichen Welt im expressionistischen Drama* (1967).

Holl, K., 'Der Wandel des dt. Lebensgefühls im Spiegel der Kunst seit der Reichsgründung', *DVLG* 4 (1926).

Jackson, H., *The eighteen nineties* (1913).

Jenny, E., *Die Heimatkunstbewegung* (1934).

Johann, E., *Die dt. Buchverlage des Naturalismus und der Neuromantik* (1935).

Jullian, P., *Oscar Wilde*, trans. Wyndham (1967).

Killy, W. (ed.), *Das 20 Jahrh., 1880–1933* (*Die dt. Literatur*, VII).

Koch, H., *F. Mehrings Beitrag zur marxistischen Literaturtheorie* (1959).

Kolinsky, E., *Engagierter Expressionismus* (1970).

Kreutzer, K., *Die Bohème* (1968).

Kuczynski, J., *Gestalten und Werke. Soziologische Studien zur dt. Lit.* (1969).

Kunisch, H. (ed.), *Handbuch der Gegenwartsliteratur* (1965).

Kutscher, A., *Frank Wedekind*, 3 vols (1922–27–31).

Loffler, K., *Gesch. der katholischen Presse* (1924).

Lukács, G., *Die Seele und die Formen* (1911). *Theorie des Romans* (1920). *Studies in European Realism*, trans. Bone (1950). *Wider den missverstandenen Realismus* (1958) (*The Meaning of Contemporary Realism*, trans. Mander, 1963). *Schriften zur Literatursoziologie*, ed. Ludz (1961). *Essays on Thomas Mann*, trans. Mitchell (1964).

Mandelkow, K., 'Orpheus und Maschine', *Euphorion* LXI (1967).

Martini, F., *Dt. Literatur im bürgerlichen Realismus 1848–98* (1962).

Mayer, H., *Von Lessing zu Thomas Mann* (1959).

Meiner, A., *Reclam. Geschichte der Universal Bibliothek* (1942).

Merker, P. and Stammler, W., *Reallexikon der dt. Lit.gesch.*, 4 vols (1925–41); new ed., W. Kohlschmidt and W. Mohr (1948, in progress).

Naef, K. J., *H. v. Hofmannsthal* (1938).

Nutz, W., *Der Trivialroman* (1962).

Osborne, J., *The Naturalist Drama in Germany* (1971).

Pascal, R., *The German Novel* (1956).

Paulsen, W., *Expressionismus und Aktivismus* (1935).

Pross, H., *Literatur und Politik* (1963).

Richards, D. R., *The German Best-Seller in the 20th Century* (1968).

Riha, K., *Moritat, Song, Bänkelsang* (1965).

Roberts, D., *Artistic consciousness and political conscience. The novels of Heinrich Mann* (1971).

Rose, W., *Men, Myths, and Movements* (1931).

Rosenhaupt, H. W., *Der dt. Dichter um die Jahrhundertwende und seine Abgelöstheit von der Gesellschaft* (1939).

Roth, E., *Simplicissimus. Ein Rückblick* (1959).

Rothe, W., 'Der Mensch vor Gott. Expressionismus und Theologie' (in the following item).

Rothe, W. (ed.), *Expressionismus als Literatur* (1969).

Ruttkowski, W. V., *Das literarische Chanson in Dtland* (1966).

Samuel, R. H. and Thomas, R. H., *Expressionism in German Life, Literature, and the Theatre* (1939).

Schmidt, A., *Sitara und der Weg dahin* (1963), (on Karl May).

Schulze, F., *Der dt. Buchhandel und die geistigen Strömungen der letzten 100 Jahre* (1925).

Schwerte, H., 'Dt. Lit. im Wilhelminischen Zeitalter', *Wirkendes Wort* XIV (1964).

Sichelschmidt, G., *Hedwig Courts-Maler* (1967).

Szondi, P., *Theorie des modernen Dramas* (1956).

Thomas, R. H., 'Das Ich und die Welt. Expressionismus und Gesellschaft', *Expressionismus als Literatur*, ed. Rothe (1969). 'Carl Einstein and Expressionism', *Essays in German Language, Culture, and Society*, ed. Prawer, Thomas and Forster (1969).

Trilling, L., *Beyond Culture* (1966). *Sincerity and Authenticity* (1972).

Wellek, R., *Concepts of Criticism* (1963). *A History of Modern Criticism*, IV (1966).

Wiener, P. B., 'Bertha von Suttner and the Political Novel', *Essays in German Language* etc., ed. Prawer and others (1969).

Wiese, B. v. (ed.), *Dt. Dichter der Moderne* (1965, enlarged 1969).

Ziegler, K., 'Dichtung und Gesellschaft im dt. Expressionismus', *Imprimatur* N.F. 3 (1961–2). 'Das Drama des Expressionismus', *Der Deutschunterricht* (1953).

The Theatre

For legal and social aspects see *Handwörterbuch der Staatswissenschaften*, ed. J. Conrad, L. Elster, W. Lexis, and E. Loening, 3rd ed. (1908–11); and *Handbuch des dt. Theater-, Film-, Musik- und Artistenrechts*, ed. P. Dienstag and A. Elster (1932).

Bab, J., *Das Theater im Lichte der Soziologie* (1931).

Bächlin, P., *Der Film als Ware* (1945).
Bahr, H., *Wiener Theater 1892–8* (1889). *Glossen zum Wiener Theater* (1907).
Blei, F., *Über Wedekind, Sternheim und das Theater* (1915).
Brahm, O., *Kritische Schriften über Drama und Literatur*, ed. P. Schlenther (1913). *Kritiken und Essays*, ed. F. Martini (1964).
Brod, M., Hasenclever, W., Lasker-Schuler, E. and others, *Das Kino-Buch* (1913).
Budzinki, K., *Die Muse mit der scharfen Zunge* (cabaret), (1966).
Fuchs, G., *Revolution des Theaters* (1909).
Grohmann, W., *Das Müncher Künstlertheater* (1935).
Harden, M., *Literatur und Theater* (1896).
Henze, H., *Otto Brahm und das Deutsche Theater Berlin* (1930).
Hoffmannsthal, H. v., 'Das Reinhardtsche Theater' (1918–9), (*Gesam. Werke*, ed. H. Steiner, *Prosa* III, 1952).
Houben, H. H., *Verbotene Literatur von der klassischen Zeit bis zur Gegenwart*, 2 vols (1924, 1928).
Ihering, H., *Von Reinhardt bis Brecht*, ed. Badenhausen (selected reviews), (1967).
Jacobsohn, S., *Jahre der Bühne*, ed. Karsch (selected reviews), (1965).
Kerr, A., *Die Welt im Drama*, 5 vols (1917), (*Gesam. Schriften*, erste Reihe).
Kullmann, M., *Die Entwicklung des dt. Lichtspieltheaters*, diss. Nürnberg (1935).
Nestriepke, S., *Gesch. der Volksbühne Berlin*, 1, 1890–1914 (1930).
Osborne, J., *The Naturalist Drama in Germany* (1971).
Rotha, P., *The Film till Now* (1930).
Saylor, Olive, *M. Reinhardt and his Theatre* (1924).
Schley, G., *Die Freie Bühne in Berlin* (1967).
Stern, E. and Herald, H. (eds.), *Reinhardt und seine Bühne* (1919).

Art and Architecture

Buchheim, L-G., *Die Künstlergemeinschaft Brücke* (1956).
Conrad, U., *Programmes and Manifestos on 20th century Architecture* (1970).
Giedion, S., *Space, Time, and Architecture* (1949).
Gombrich, E. H., *Art and Illusion*, new ed. 1962.
Gropius, W., *The New Architecture of the Bauhaus* (1935).
Gross, G., *Das Gesicht der herrschenden Klasse* (1921).
Hamann, R., *Kunst und Kultur der Gegenwart* (1922). *Der Impressionismus in Leben und Kunst* (1923). *Die dt. Malerei vom Rokoko bis zum Expressionismus* (1925).
Hamilton, G. H., *Painting and Sculpture in Europe, 1880–1940* (1967).
Hausenstein, W., *Die Kunst und die Gessellschaft* (1916).

334 From Naturalism to Expressionism

Hauser, A., *Sozialgesch. der Kunst und Literatur* (1953), (*Social History of Art*, 2 vols, 1951).

Hermand, J., 'Jugendstil. Ein Forschungebericht', *DVLG* 38 (1964).

Hildebrand, A. v., *Das Problem der Form in der bildenden Kunst* (1839).

Jugend, Die, Facsimile Querschnitt, ed. Zahn (1966). *3000 Kunstblätter der Münchner Jugend*, ed. G. Hirth, 1909.

Jullian, P., *Esthètes et Magiciens* (1969), (*Dreamers of Decadence*, 1971).

Justi, L., *Von Corinth bis Klee* (1931).

Kandinsky, W., *Über das Geistige in der Kunst* (1912).

Klee, P., *Über die moderne Kunst* (1924). *Dokumente und Bilder aus den Jahren 1896-1930* (1949). *Tagebücher 1898-1918*, ed. Felix Klee (1957). *Das bildnerische Denken*, ed. J. Spiller (1964).

Kollwitz, Käthe, *K.K.*, ed. O. Nagel (1963), (trans. for Studio Vista, 1971).

Liebermann, M., *Das Liebermann-Buch*, ed. H. Ostwald (1930). *Gesam. Schriften* (1922).

Loos, A., *Samtliche Schriften* (1962).

Marc, F., *Briefe, Aufzeichnungen und Aphorismen*, 2 vols (1920).

Myers, B. S., *Expressionism. A generation in revolt* (1963).

Neumann, C., *Der Kampf um die neue Kunst* (1896).

Pevsner, N. B. L., *Pioneers of Modern Design from William Morris to Walter Gropius* (1936). *An Outline of European Architecture* (1942).

Read, H., *A Concise History of Modern Painting* (1959). *A Concise History of Modern Sculpture* (1964).

Scheffler, K., *Gesch. der europäischen Malerei vom Impressionismus bis zur Gegenwart* (1927).

Schmutzler, R., *Art nouveau – Jugendstil* (1962).

Schwartz, P., *The Cubists* (1971).

Seling, H., *Jugendstil. Der Weg ins 20 Jahrh.* (1959).

Simplicissimus, Facsimile Querschnitt, ed. C. Schütze (1963).

Van de Velde, H., *Vom neuen Stil* (1907).

Waldman, G., *Die Kunst des Realismus und des Impressionismus* (1927).

Wölfflin, H., *Kunstgeschichtliche Grundbegriffe* (1915).

Worringer, W., *Abstraktion und Einfühlung* (1908).

Zille, H., *Kinder der Strasse* (1908). *Mein Milljöh* (1914).

Music

Erhardt, O., *Richard Strauss. Leben, Wirken, Schaffen* (1953).

Goehr, W., *European Music in the 20th Century* (1957).

Gutman, R. W., *Richard Wagner* (1968).

Mitchell, D., *The Language of Modern Music* (1963).

Newmann, E., *The Life of Richard Wagner*, 4 vols (1933–47).

Reich, W., *Schoenberg oder der konservative Revolutionär* (1968), (trans. 1971).

Stuckenschmidt, H. H., *Arnold Schoenberg* (1951), (trans. 1959).

Wagner, Richard, *Gesam. Schriften und Dichtungen*, 10 vols (1883).

Autobiographies and Reminiscences

(See Bode, I., *Die Autobiographien zur dt. Literatur, Kunst, und Musik 1900–65*, 1966.)

Altenberg, P., *Vita ipsa* (1918). *Mein Lebensabend* (1919).

Andreas-Salomé, Lou, *Lebensrückblick*, ed. E. Pfeiffer (1968).

Bahr, H., *Selbstbildnis* (1923).

Barlach, E., *Ein selbsterzähltes Leben* (1928).

Bäumer, Gertrud, *Lebensweg durch eine Zeitenwende* (1933).

Bebel, A., *Aus meinem Leben*, 3 vols (1910–11).

Binding, R. G., *Erlebtes Leben* (1935).

Blei, F., *Erzählung eines Lebens* (1930).

Braun, Lily, *Memoiren einer Sozialistin*, 2 vols (1909–11).

Braunthal, J., *In Search of the Millenium* (1945).

Brentano, L., *Mein Kampf um die soziale Entwicklung Dtlands* (1931).

Breysig, K., *Aus meinen Tagen und Träumen*, ed. G. Breysig and M. Landmann (1962).

Brod, M., *Streitbares Leben* (1960).

Bromme, M. T. W., *Lebensgeschichte eines modernen Fabrikarbeiters*, ed. P. Göhre, (1905), (reprint 1971 with Nachwort by B. Neumann).

Buber, M., *Ereignisse und Begegnungen* (1917).

Carossa, H., *Ungleiche Welten* (1951).

Conrad, M. G., *Von Emile Zola bis Gerhart Hauptmann* (1902).

Corinth, L., *Selbstbiographie* (1926).

Dessoir, M., *Buch der Erinnerung* (1946).

Diederichs, E., *Selbstzeugnisse und Briefe von Zeitgenossen* (1967).

Duncan, Isadora, *My Life* (1928).

Durieux, Tilla, *Eine Tür steht offen* (1954).

Ernst, P., *Jünglingsjahre* (1931).

Eyth, M., *Hinter Pflug und Schraubstock* (1898).

Fechter, P., *Menschen und Zeiten* (1948).

Foerster, F. W., *Erlebte Weltgeschichte* (1953).

Foerster, W, *Lebenserinnerungen und Lebenshoffnungen* (1911).

Freud, S., *Autobiographische Studie* (1928), (*Gesam. Werke*, XIV and Complete Works, XX, 1959).

Grossmann, S., *Ich war begeistert* (1931).

Halbe, M., *Scholle und Schicksal* (1933). *Jahrhundertwende. Gesch. meines Lebens 1893–1914* (1935).

Hart, H., *Literarische Erinnerungen 1880–1905* (*Gesam. Werke*, III, 1907).

Hauptmann, G., *Das Abenteuer meiner Jugend*, 2 vols (1937), (with *Das zweite Vierteljahrhundert* and other material in *Die grossen Beichten*, 1966).

Hausenstein, W., *Lux perpetua* (pseudonym J. Armbruster), (1947).

Hillard, G., *Herren und Narren der Welt* (1955).

Hoffmann, Marguerite, *Mein Weg mit Melchior Lechter* (1966).

Holitscher, A., *Lebensgeschichte eines Rebellen* (1915).

Honigsheim, P., *On Max Weber* (memoirs etc) (1968).

Kassner, R., *Buch der Erinnerung* (1938).

Kessler, H. Graf, *Gesichter und Zeiten* (1935).

Kollwitz, Käthe, *Aus meinem Leben* (1957).

Lange, Helene, *Lebenserinnerungen* (1920).

Lepsius, Sabine, *Stefan George: Geschichte einer Freundschaft* (1935).

Lessing, T., *Einmal und nie wieder* (1935).

Mahler, Alma, *Gustav Mahler. Erinnerungen und Briefe* (1940).

Mann, H., *Ein Zeitalter wird besichtigt* (1947).

Mann, T., *Autobiographisches*, ed. Erika Mann (1968).

Mann, V., *Wir waren fünf* (1949).

Marcuse, L., *Mein zwanzigstes Jahrhundert* (1960).

Martens, K., *Schonungslose Lebenschronik* (1921).

Mauthner, F., *Erinnerungen* (1928).

Meinecke, F., *Erlebtes 1862–1919* (1901 and 1919).

Morgenstern, C., *Alles um des Menschen willen*, ed. Margareta Morgenstern (1962).

Mühsam, E., *Namen und Menschen* (1949).

Salin, E., *Um Stefan George* (1948).

Schnitzler, A., *Jugend in Wien* (1968).

Schweitzer, A., *Aus meinem Leben und Denken* (1950).

Simmel, G., *Buch des Dankes an G. Simmel*, ed. K. Gassen and M. Landmann (1958).

Sternheim, C., *Vorkriegseuropa im Gleichnis meines Lebens* (1936).

Thoma, L., *Erinnerungen* (1919).

Toller, E., *Eine Jugend in Deutschland* (1933).

Vallentin, B., *Gespräche mit Stefan George* (1961).

Walden, Nell, *H. Walden; ein Lebensbild* (1963).

Walter, B., *Reminiscences* (1947).

Wassermann, J., *Mein Weg als Deutscher und Jude* (1933).

Weber, Marianne, *Lebenserinnerungen* (1948). *Max Weber: ein Lebensbild* (1926).

Weisbach, W., *Und alles ist zerstoben* (1937).

Werfel, F., *Zwischen Oben und Unten* (1946).

Wolfskehl, K., *Wolfskehl-Verwey. Dokumente ihrer Freundschaft 1897–1946*, ed. M. Nyland-Verwey (1968).

Zweig, S., *Die Welt von Gestern* (1947).

Index